How the Web was Born

James Gillies is a science writer/editor at CERN, the European Organization for Nuclear Research. After graduating in theoretical physics from Bedford College, London, he received an Oxford doctorate for experimental work done at CERN. He went on to work as a physicist at the Rutherford Appleton Laboratory for five years, and then was Head of Science at the British Council in Paris from 1993 to 1995. He returned to CERN in 1995.

Robert Cailliau has worked at CERN since 1974. He graduated from the University of Ghent and went on to receive an MSc in computing at the University of Michigan. After a spell leading CERN's Office Computing Systems group, he joined Tim Berners-Lee in the Web project in 1990. He started the International WWW Conference series in December 1993, helped transfer Web development from CERN to the global Web consortium during 1995, set up CERN's Web office, and launched the European Commission's Web for Schools initiative.

How the Web was Born

The Story of the World Wide Web

James Gillies & Robert Cailliau

OXFORD
UNIVERSITY PRESS

OXFORD
UNIVERSITY PRESS
Great Clarendon Street, Oxford OX2 6DP

Oxford University Press is a department of the University of Oxford.
It furthers the University's objective of excellence in research, scholarship,
and education by publishing worldwide in

Oxford New York

Athens Auckland Bangkok Bogotá Buenos Aires Calcutta
Cape Town Chennai Dar es Salaam Delhi Florence Hong Kong Istanbul
Karachi Kuala Lumpur Madrid Melbourne Mexico City Mumbai
Nairobi Paris São Paulo Singapore Taipei Tokyo Toronto Warsaw

with associated companies in Berlin Ibadan

Published in the United States
by Oxford University Press Inc., New York

First published 2000

British Library Cataloguing in Publication Data
Data available

Library of Congress Cataloging in Publication Data
Data available

ISBN 0-19-286207-3

1 3 5 7 9 10 8 6 4 2

Typeset in Severin
by Invisible Ink
Printed in Great Britain
on acid-free paper by
Cox & Wyman Ltd,
Reading Berkshire

To the Memory of Mike Sendall
and Donald Davies

Acknowledgements

'The process of technological development is like building a cathedral. Over the course of several hundred years, new people come along and each lays down a block on top of the old foundations, each saying, "I built a cathedral." Next month another block is placed atop the previous one. Then comes along an historian who asks, "Well, who built the cathedral?" Peter added some stones here and Paul added a few more. If you are not careful you can con yourself into believing that you did the most important part. But the reality is that each contribution has to follow on to previous work. Everything is tied to everything else.

'Too often history tends to be lazy and give credit to the planner and to the funder of the cathedral. Maybe we should take the care to avoid the simplifications and say, "Okay, this person did this or did that, and that person did so and so." No single person can do it all, or ever does it all. But we are lazy and tend to give all the credit to a single person most closely identified with an activity and forget all the others who really made it all possible.'

—*Paul Baran, 5 March 1990*

'It is always important to bear in mind that anything as important as packet switching and the Internet cannot be created by a single individual or indeed by any small group of individuals. Thus, many folks will have well-founded views of the importance of their own contributions vis-à-vis others. In all of this it is unlikely there will be consensus on everything. This is both natural and healthy.' —*Bob Kahn, 19 March 1998*

'You can't have a project like this and expect everybody to see it from a common point of view.' —*Bob Kahn at Act One*

The development of the Internet and the World Wide Web involved scores of people over several decades. There are probably as many histories of the Internet as there are people involved. This is just one of those stories, but the authors believe that it is a fair one. If it reflects an accurate account of the development of computer networking, that is due largely to the help of many patient people who have agreed to be interviewed and who have carefully read the drafts. Any opinions expressed here are those of the authors, and if any errors remain they are the authors' sole responsibility. The planners and the funders get their share of the limelight, certainly, but we have tried not to forget the many others who made it all possible.

Those who have given up their time to be interviewed or find things out for us are far too numerous for us to mention them all by name. However, we would particularly like to thank those who have read and commented on all or parts of the draft: Norm Abramson, Derek Barber, Tim Berners-Lee, Keith Clarke, Dan Connolly, Bob Cooper, Andy van Dam, Donald Davies, Doug Engelbart, Jean-François Groff, Wendy Hall, Joseph Hardin, Jean-Marie Hullot, Tony Johnson, Frank Kappe, Paul Kunz, Daniel Karrenberg, Mark McCahill, Hermann Maurer, George Metakides, Lou Montulli, Clifford Neuman, Dave Raggett, Peggie Rimmer, Ben Segal, Christian Serre, Dave Thompson, Al Vezza, Pei Wei and Nicole Yankelovich. A special word of thanks is also due to Patricia Hemmis at the Charles Babbage Institute at the University of Minnesota for being our guide through the institute's wonderful archives, which yielded up no end of valuable resources about the early days of computer networks.

One of us, James Gillies, reserves particular thanks for his wife Catriona Charlesworth, not only for putting her life on hold for over a year while the book was in the making, but also for helping in more tangible ways. What began as moral support, proof-reading and help with research eventually turned into the first draft of chapter 3, which survives largely unchanged.

One name that does not appear above is that of Mike Sendall. In 1989 Mike did not say no to Tim Berners-Lee and consequently the Web got off the ground. At the same time Mike was diagnosed with an incurable form of cancer. We didn't know this until many years later. Throughout his later years, Mike continued to be the foremost supporter of the Web, the driver, conciliator, and moderator. He maintained a level of optimism and good spirits that we have no words for. His dry British sense of humour kept the team going. When he died in July 1999, a very important Web resource went with him: his detailed memory of its history. But above all we lost a truly great person and a dear friend.

We learned just before this book went to press that cancer had claimed the life of another of its major characters. Donald Davies was a man who never sought the limelight, but who deserves as much as anyone to be thought of as the father of computer communication. An unassuming computer scientist working at the UK National Physical Laboratory, Donald's invention of packet switching is what made the Internet, and ultimately the World Wide Web, possible.

The information revolution is far from complete and decades from now what seems important today may be forgotten. It may seem a little early, therefore, to be writing a history of the World Wide Web. But presenting an accurate historical record was just one of our goals. We also wanted to tell a story of human endeavour, and to provide a good read in the process. We hope we have succeeded.

Geneva, January 2000 JG and RC

Contents

List of Plates

We would like to thank the following individuals and institutions who have kindly given permission to reproduce the photographs listed below:

Pl. 1: Nobel Prizewinning French physicist Louis de Broglie. © AIP Emilio Segre Visual Archives.

Pl. 2: British networking pioneer Donald Davies with Derek Barber and Roger Scantlebury. Photo © UK Crown Copyright 1977. Reproduced by permission of the Controller of HMSO.

Pl. 3: Louis Pouzin with members of the Cyclades team. Courtesy Louis Pouzin.

Pl. 4: Vannevar Bush. © The MIT Museum, Cambridge, Massachusetts.

Pl. 5: The first computer mouse. Courtesy the Bootstrap Institute.

Pl. 6: Screen shot from Doug Engelbart's 1968 demonstration of NLS. Courtesy the Bootstrap Institute.

Pl. 7: A networking tour de force at the International Conference on Computer Communication '76. Photo © UK Crown Copyright 1976. Reproduced by permission of the Controller of HMSO.

Pl. 8: The control room for CERN's PS accelerator. © CERN.

Pl. 9: Mike Sendall at the Prix Ars-Electronica 1995 award ceremony. © ORF Linz (Austrian Broadcasting Corporation).

Pl. 10: Tim Berners-Lee at the Hypertext '91 conference. Robert Cailliau.

Pl. 11: Tim Berners-Lee and Nicola Pellow. © CERN.

Pl. 12: A gathering of WWW Wizards. Courtesy Stanford Linear Accelerator Center.

Pl. 13: Robert Cailliau and Bebo White. Robert Cailliau.

Pl. 14: The Norwegian team that put up the Lillehammer Winter Olympics Web site. Courtesy Steinar Kjærnsrød.

Pl. 15: Tim Berners-Lee at the 'Internet, Web, What's Next' event in 1998. © CERN.

Pl. 16: Tim Berners-Lee, Ted Nelson, and Robert Cailliau. Courtesy Håkon Lie.

List of Figures

1 The Foundations

What is the World Wide Web?

The World Wide Web is like an encyclopaedia, a telephone directory, a record collection, a video shop, and Speakers' Corner all rolled into one and accessible through any computer. It has become so successful that to many it is synonymous with the Internet; but in reality the two are quite different. The Internet is like a network of electronic roads criss-crossing the planet—the much-hyped information superhighway. The Web is just one of many services using that network, just as many different kinds of vehicle use the roads. On the Internet, the Web just happens to be by far the most popular. The arrival of the Web in 1990 was to the Internet like the arrival of the internal combustion engine to the country lane. Internet transport would never be the same again.

Until the arrival of computer networking, the telephone system was the only medium for electronic mass communication. Although the two are intimately linked, there are important differences between the way people talk to each other and the way computers converse. In a telephone conversation, people tend to talk continuously, or even both at once. For that reason, the electronic link between them is reserved exclusively for them and remains open for as long as they wish to speak. Computer conversation, on the other hand, is a rather more staccato affair. It comes in fits and starts so keeping a link open continuously would be extremely wasteful.

Communicating by telex or telegram is a bit closer to computer communication. Information is bundled up into discrete packages and a line is held open just long enough for the package to be sent. Once the message has been received, the connection is closed and the message can be digested 'off-line'.

The telephone network

When you pick up the telephone and dial a number, the telephone system finds you a line to the person you want to talk to. In a small community, you could imagine every telephone being connected to every other, with each one knowing what number corresponded to every phone. The problem with such a system is scalability: it is hard to make the system grow larger. For each new subscriber, every telephone would have to be modified to accommodate the new number and a new cable would have to be laid to each existing subscriber. Such a system would not scale up easily to more than a handful of subscribers.

The solution is circuit switching. Instead of every subscriber having a line to every other, each one just has a single line to a central switch. It works because most people are off the phone most of the time and only a fraction of all possible pairs of phones are connected to each other at any given moment. In the old days there would be an army of switchboard operators connecting calls. Now it is all done automatically; but the basic principle is the same.

A circuit-switched system makes the scalability problem more tractable. Each community has its own local switch and different communities are linked by long-distance connections between switches. It still happens from time to time that your call doesn't get through because the long-distance lines are all busy. But as cables give way to optical fibres, which can carry much more traffic, and as telecommunications operators get better at judging expected demand and install sufficient capacity, this happens less and less often.

Circuit switching links you to the person you are calling by establishing a circuit between the two of you. That circuit may be made from several pieces of wire and lengths of optical fibre, but as long as you want it, it is exclusively yours. You are also paying for it even when you are not saying a word, and no one else can use it as long as you are on the line.

The capacity of a circuit is called its bandwidth: it is the amount of information the circuit can carry per second. Simple information, like a human voice, doesn't take up much bandwidth, and for even greater compactness telephone networks don't always transmit the full frequency range of the human voice. If you have ever wondered why people sometimes sound different on the phone, that is the reason. High-fidelity stereo takes up nearly thirteen times as much bandwidth, and television-quality pictures need nearly 30 000 times the bandwidth of speech.

The quality and length of a cable determines the bandwidth it can

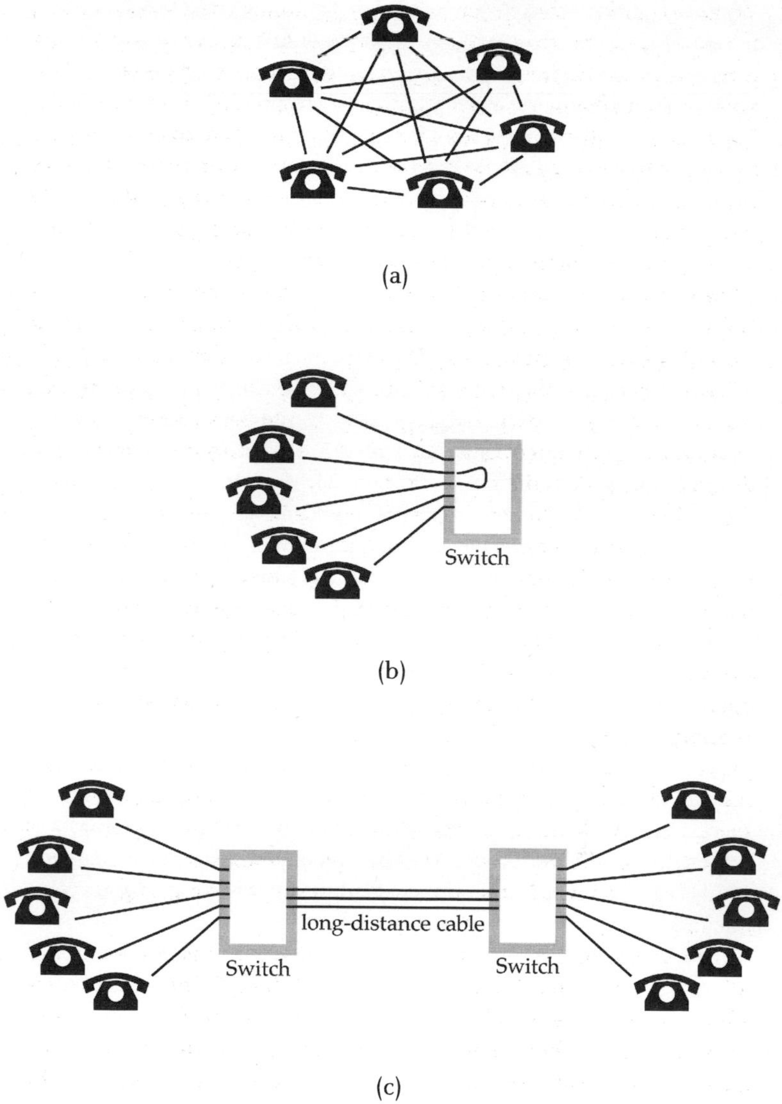

Figure 1: Circuit switching makes telephone networks scalable. Without it, every telephone would have to be connected to every other (a). Adding a switch means that in a local community, each telephone only needs to be connected to the switch (b). Long-distance calls may be routed through several switches (c).

carry, but the bandwidth of a circuit is no better than that of its weakest link. Optical fibres can carry a massive three million conversations at once, but if the wire connecting your house to the local switch can only carry one, that is as good as your circuit will ever be. For things like browsing text on the Web or making a telephone call, that's fine, but if you wanted to use the Web to look at high-quality video, you would need a higher-quality cable. Most telephone companies have replaced their long-distance copper wires with optical fibres, but it will still be some time before optical links connect us all to our local switches. This means that at the moment it is more accurate to say that when you make a phone call you get exclusive use of the wire connecting you to the local switch, but after that it is your share of the fibre that is exclusively yours for as long as you want it.

The Internet

Every time we make a phone call or meet someone in the street, we use a set of protocols to conduct our communication. When we bump into someone we know, we say, 'Hello.' We might shake hands, enquire about our acquaintance's state of health, or comment on the weather as a preliminary to our conversation. And when it is time to go, there is another protocol at work. We could say, 'My word, is that the time? I must rush!' There are many variations on this theme, but in general they follow a clear set of rules that both we and our interlocutors recognize.

Computer communication also relies on protocols, and the similarities with human protocols are so great that part of the procedure is even called handshaking. One computer might call another, ask 'Are you there?', and wait for a reply, or handshake, from the other computer before going on. Even if there were only two identical computers on the Internet, a simple protocol such as handshaking would still be needed. But because the Internet is far more complex than that, protocols come in 'stacks', with the 'Are you there?'-type protocols near the bottom of the stacks, hidden from most computer users, and more specialized protocols governing specific services such as e-mail, file transfer, or the World Wide Web closer to the top. The familiar 'http', Hypertext Transfer Protocol, is the name of the protocol governing Web traffic on the Internet.

The Internet works more like the postal service than the telephone network. All post offices are indeed connected, but by a system of roads, not wires. Special trucks move letters and packages between them. Suppose you send a letter to your bank. You will have to provide at least three things: the bank's address, your own address so the bank can reply, and a message. You drop the letter into a postbox and the postal system takes care of it. Your letter will be taken to the nearest post office where it will be sorted to be sent further, according to the destination address you gave. This may happen again in several intermediate offices and routing places before your letter arrives on your bank manager's desk.

One big difference between this kind of system and the circuit-switched telephone system is that it would be very unusual for your letter to be carried all alone in a single truck to its destination: it will share a truck, or even several trucks, with other packages. You do not monopolize a link between you and your bank manager; others will be making use of the same link, or at least they will share parts of the journey with your letter. Another important difference is that if the postal service is working as it should, you are guaranteed that your message will arrive though you do not know when it will get there. With a telephone call, the person you want to talk to may be out so unless they have an answering machine your message may not always get through.

Now suppose that you have a rather long message to send and the postal service allows you to use only postcards. You will have to split up your long letter into several short bits, each fitting onto one card. When you drop them all into the postbox they will get separated and mixed up with other cards. So you need to provide another piece of information. As well as the bank's address, your address, and the message, you will have to put a sequence number on each card. Your bank manager will then be able to put the cards back into order and reconstitute your message. Your cards share the communication lines between the post offices and routing centres with everyone else's and all cards eventually reach their destinations, although they don't all necessarily take the same route or arrive in the same sequence as they left.

Cutting up messages into chunks of the same size may not be very practical for a postal service, but it is the way the Internet works. The idea came about in two places in the mid-1960s, motivated by entirely different reasons. At the height of the cold war, nuclear paranoia gripped the United States where Paul Baran, the son of Polish immigrants, conceived a bombproof network such that if one 'road' were taken out by military action, packets of information would simply take an alternative route. Meanwhile in England at the National Physical Laboratory in Teddington, Donald Davies, a 41-year-old mathematician pondering the inefficiency of circuit-switched systems for computer communications, hit upon the same idea and called it packet switching. His reasoning had nothing to do with bombproofing; he just wanted to let computers to talk to each other. Donald Davies's packets correspond to the postcards sent to the bank.

The Internet is a collection of computer networks talking to each other using packet switching. All communication between computers on the Internet happens by cutting things up into small packets and sending them through a system of electronic routing stations to their destinations. Imagine a computer network made up of computers A to F connected through routers 1 to 5, then a message from A to E might pass through routers 1, 4, and 3, but if 4 broke down the message could still pass through 2 or 5. Even if the first packet of a message went via 4 before it broke down, the remaining packets could take different routes and F would still be able to reassemble them into a coherent message. Each router would contain a routing table telling it which way to pass on the message, with a back-up pass-on address in case the first didn't work.

If all computer networks had been developed to a single standard, there would be no Internet, just one big, ever-expanding network. But

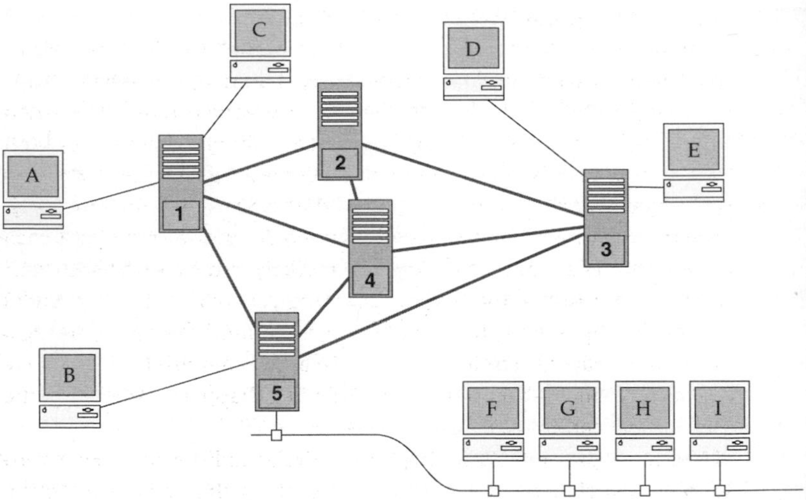

Figure 2: Computers communicate through a sub-network of routing computers that forward messages to their destinations.

that is not what happened. Many different packet-switching networks using many different protocols have been developed, and the Internet is the result of connecting them all together.

The basic set of protocols at work on the Internet is called TCP/IP. IP, the Internet Protocol, is the lingua franca of computer communication: it is the protocol that routers use to pass packets on. Individual networks may use protocols other than TCP/IP, but the router connecting them to the Internet, known as a gateway, must hand packets over using IP. TCP, Transfer Control Protocol, is the protocol at work in the sending and receiving computers. Its job is to break information up into packets, each one properly labelled with the sender's and receiver's address, to ensure that they all arrive, and to reassemble them when they do. If IP loses a packet, it is TCP's job to ask that it be resent.

The system just described is fine for connecting via routing computers. But in office buildings a different approach is used to connect numbers of similar machines without having to pass through intermediate routers. Such a dense, localized network is called a Local Area Network (LAN). Computers F to I in Figure 2 are connected to a LAN. IP controls the LAN's communication with the larger network, but on the LAN itself the protocol at work can be completely different. The most common kind of LANs today use something called the Ethernet, where computers are connected to a single cable, as dinner-party guests might sit around a single table. Around the table everyone is free to talk when they wish, but if two guests start off at once, as often happens, they both stop and agree who goes first. On an Ethernet cable, computers do something very similar. If two of them start at the same time they both back off, each waits for a randomly chosen amount of time, and each starts again. The randomness makes it unlikely that they will both start up at the same time. Other LANs, called rings, connect all the computers to a single loop of wire. Information travels around the loop carrying a little banner saying, 'I'm for computer G,' and if computer G is not busy it pulls the information out of the cable. If G happens to be busy, the information continues for another lap.

In terms of protocol stacks, the actual wire of an Ethernet is level zero of the protocol stack: it is the most basic thing that is specific to the Ethernet, and the Ethernet standard even determines what colour it should be. The protocols governing how information is put onto the wire and pulled off again would start with level 1, and protocols like http would run over the top of these. Http is an example of a 'host-to-host protocol' running over as many networks as necessary to carry information from one 'host' computer to another.

Similarities and differences

Packet-switching systems have several properties that make them well suited to communication between computers and are essential to how the Web works. Packet-switching systems are 'asynchronous': you know when a packet leaves your computer but you don't know when it will arrive. A circuit-switched system like the telephone network, on the other hand, is synchronous: communication must happen when the line is reserved for it. Packet-switching systems share network resources more efficiently than the telephone system. This means that a computer can stay connected to the Internet indefinitely; it only puts information onto the lines when it sends packets. In the telephone system, all telephones are usually on the hook, which means that they are disconnected from the network. As soon as you lift the receiver, you occupy a line and no one else can use that line for as long as you are talking. With a circuit-switched system there is no guarantee that the connection you ask for will be created. The person you want to talk to might be busy, all lines could be engaged, or the respondent may simply not pick up the phone. Charging is relatively easy: the initiating party pays for the communication and payment depends on the length of the communication and the distance between the parties.

On the Internet, your packets mingle with others on the same lines just as letters share a ride in post office vans. This is an important difference between the telephone system and the Internet. In packet-switching systems, service quality goes down gradually as traffic increases, just as it does on the road network. Everyone suffers equally when the traffic gets dense. In contrast, when there is a burst of traffic on the telephone system, as might happen in an emergency, the first callers get through, and once all the lines are taken, nobody else does. On the Internet, things might slow down but everything normally gets through eventually. Another important difference concerns errors: the telephone network is synchronous but not error-free. Everyone has experienced crackle or other sound degradation during a phone call, but we generally manage to make sense of what is being said because the information reaches our ears in the same sequence as it leaves the lips of the person we are talking to. On the Internet, however, it is the other way round. Since all packets normally reach their destinations eventually, the communication can be made error-free. That is not to say that it would be better for voice, however, since there is no guarantee that information will arrive in the same order as it leaves. Packets taking different routes can easily get out of sequence, perhaps turning 'hello' into 'o hell'. The Internet phone application then has to make a choice: either

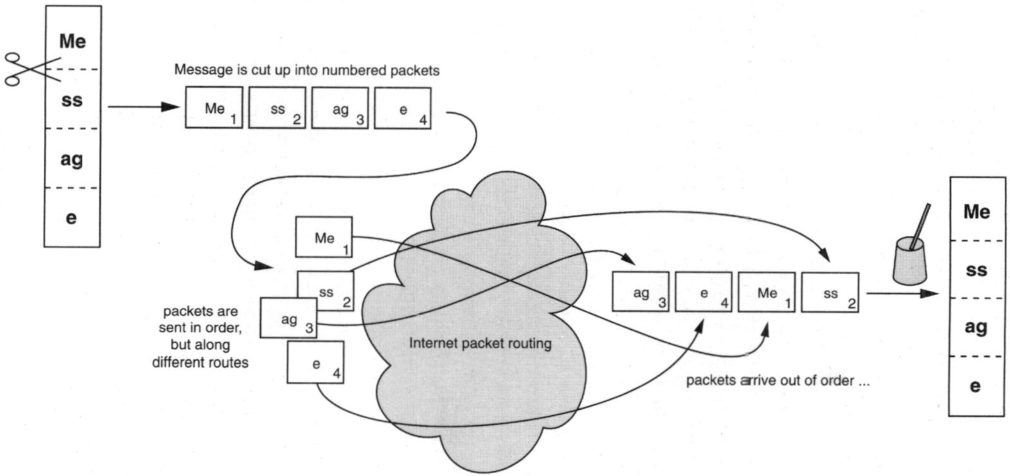

Figure 3: Packet switching works by splitting messages up into a series of numbered packets that are sent over the network individually and reassembled in the right order at their destination.

packets have to be reassembled before being delivered, creating an irritating delay, or packets that are not there yet have to be skipped, leaving gaps.

When you are connecting your computer to the Internet, it is better to be on a line with a large capacity (bandwidth), capable of carrying many packets per second, than on a slow one. But since charging for Internet use is usually done by bandwidth rather than by time, you pay more for the privilege of having an Internet 'motorway' into your computer rather than a 'B'-class road. This is not a choice available to many private users today. Most people have to call up a local Internet Service Provider (ISP) through ... the telephone! This method relies on modems to make the last little link from the real Internet at the ISP into the computer at home. Your 'Internet' subscription pays for the ISP's real Internet connection and, depending on where you live, you might also have to pay a telephone company for the call.

So much for differences between the two systems. What about similarities? Both systems have a global name space as a fundamental element. This is a standard way of identifying any telephone or any computer anywhere in the world. For telephones, international agreements moderated by the International Telecommunications Union (ITU) have led to the distribution of country codes and standards for international dialling. Similarly for the Internet, a system of naming is used that assigns a unique name to each computer. Names are grouped into 'domains'. There is one domain for each country: .uk for the United Kingdom, .ca for Canada, .us for the United States, .fr for France, .de for Germany, .ch for Switzerland, and so on. Inside each domain there are sub-domains; .cern is a sub-domain of .ch, so all computers at CERN have names ending in .cern.ch. CERN's main Web server, for example, has the name www.cern.ch. There are also domains classified by activity: .com for commercial sites, .edu for educational sites, and .gov for governmental sites (though the last two of these only apply to the USA).

	Telephone	Internet
synchronism	yes	no
connection/delivery	not guaranteed	guaranteed
bandwidth	guaranteed	not guaranteed
standard domain names	yes	yes
can be made error-free	no	yes

Higher levels

Many different protocols are built upon the basic TCP/IP. Apart from those carrying information around LANs like Ethernet, there are protocols for transferring files between computers, protocols for logging in to computers remotely, and protocols for carrying electronic mail. Most of these were developed with the academic community in mind, since for two decades the Internet remained the reserve of academia. Specialized knowledge was needed to tap the Internet's vast reserves of information and complex computer commands had to be typed in to pull a file across the network. With the explosion of personal computing in the 1980s, however, it was only a matter of time before Internet access became easier. As the '80s gave way to the '90s, systems with names like archie, gopher, WAIS, and the World Wide Web sprang up. The Web with its point and click simplicity turned out to be the most successful, bringing Internet access to anyone with a computer and a phone line. The Web is the ultimate expression of an asynchronous packet-switching system; over a circuit-switched network it just wouldn't have worked.

The birth of the Internet

On 31 January 1958, the United States launched Explorer I, its first satellite, although few now remember that. The event that caught the world's attention had come a few months earlier, when the Soviet Union put Sputnik I into orbit on 4 October 1957. It was an event that changed the course of American research thinking. President Eisenhower declared that never again would the USA be caught off guard by the USSR and he tuned his defence research and development strategy to making sure that America stayed one step ahead. Eisenhower was a soldier, but he had more faith in scientists than the military to manage long-term R&D. He appointed a presidential scientific adviser and surrounded himself with the nation's top scientific talent. Even his Secretary of Defense, Neil McElroy, had no military background. He had worked his way up the ranks of Proctor and Gamble from salesman to company president, pioneering the soap opera along the way as a means of selling his company's products. One thing McElroy strongly believed was that the free rein Proctor and Gamble gave to its R&D department was essential to the company's success. He wanted to transfer this approach to the Department of Defense, and he proposed creating a single centralized agency with a mandate for long-term thinking in the conduct of all military-related R&D. It was an idea that didn't go down well with America's military chiefs, but Eisenhower liked it. On

7 January 1958, the President went to Congress to request funding for the new agency, and Congress liked it too. Two days later, in a State of the Union Message focused firmly on the problems of the cold war, Eisenhower informed the nation that 'in recognition of the need for single control in some of our most advanced development projects, the Secretary of Defense has already decided to concentrate into one organization all the anti-missile and satellite technology undertaken within the Department of Defense'. He went on to underline his belief in science by recommending a 'five-fold increase in sums available to the National Science Foundation for its special activities in stimulating and improving science education'.

The new Advanced Research Projects Agency (ARPA) opened its doors soon after with responsibility for anti-missile weapons and satellites. It was a bold start but short lived, since hardly had ARPA's first director, Roy Johnson, hung up his coat than Eisenhower transferred the space programme to the newly created NASA. Civilian space programmes, he believed, should not be under military control, even in a semi-detached agency like ARPA. To make matters worse for ARPA, Eisenhower also created a new position, a Director of Defense Research and Engineering, to oversee all military R&D including that which had just been assigned to ARPA. The new agency was in danger of being left without a mission. It might all have ended then, but ARPA's staff saw the change as an opportunity. With the inevitably short-term goals of missile research off their hands, ARPA could live up to its name and become an agency for really advanced blue-sky research with a nod in the direction of military applications. University research teams would be brought on board, with ARPA acting as the central coordinating body. This was an ARPA the powerful military establishment could live with, and the young agency lived to see another day.

By 1962, ARPA's reinvention was complete. The agency had identified suitable areas of long-range research and divided itself up into a number of separate offices to handle each one. The major programmes handled ballistic missile defence and nuclear test detection, but there was also a small office, taking up less than 10 per cent of ARPA's budget, called the Information Processing Techniques Office (IPTO), with J. C. R. Licklider as its leader. Licklider, 'Lick' to those who knew him, had been headhunted from Bolt, Beranek and Newman (BBN), a small R&D company in Cambridge, Massachusetts, where he had been a vice-president. Licklider was a psychologist by training whose career at Harvard and the Massachusetts Institute of Technology (MIT) had seen his interest move steadily towards human–computer interactions. Back in the sixties, that meant something very different from what it does today. Some computers were so big they had internal corridors for service technicians. To communicate with them, you didn't sit down to type at a keyboad and screen: you had to prepare all your instructions using a desk-size machine to punch holes into cards in a code the computer could understand. You would then hand your cards to an operator who would feed them to the computer, and you would come back later to pick up the results.

Before leaving BBN, Licklider had presented a landmark paper with his colleague Welden Clark at the 1962 Spring Joint Computer Conference of the American Federation of Information Processing Societies in San Francisco. In it, they pinpointed the central problem with human–computer interactions at the time. 'The conventional computer-center mode of operation, patterned after that of the neighborhood dry cleaner—in by ten, out by five—is inadequate for creative man–computer thinking,' they said, going on to describe research in progress at BBN that would do something about it. At the root of the problem was the high cost of large-scale computers, which meant that there was a lot of pressure to take full advantage of their speed. 'Since men think slowly,' explained Licklider and Clark, 'that pressure has tended to preclude extensive on-line interaction between men and large-scale computers.' They went on to identify the principal talents of humans and computers—decision-making and analysis on the one hand, rapid and accurate computation, data storage, and data retrieval on the other. In other words, people would do the thinking; computers would do the donkey work. Their answer to the cost problem was time-sharing, so that several people could use the same computer at the same time. Whilst one human was plodding through some slow thought process, the computer would not be idle. It would be applying its formidable computing power to someone else's problem. Licklider had first heard about time-sharing from 'a young Britisher' at a UNESCO-sponsored International Conference on Information Processing in Paris in 1959. The 'young Britisher' would probably have been Christopher Strachey, who went on to become Oxford University's first Professor of Computation. It is difficult to say, however, whether Strachey really invented the idea. Like packet switching later, it was an idea whose time had come.

Licklider and Clark showed remarkable foresight in their conference paper, which went on to describe various human-computer interaction projects under way at BBN. One was computer-based learning, where direct interaction with the teaching computer was vital because 'effective teacher–student relations involve nearly continuous interchange of information, and anything that interferes with the communication is likely to impair effectiveness'. Under a US Air Force contract, BBN had developed programs for interactive language learning. Planning and design was the subject of another BBN project that predicted the modern widespread use of Computer Aided Design (CAD) techniques.

A third aspect of BBN's work concerned visualization of the operation of computer programs. 'The covertness of the operation of the programs of electronic computers makes it difficult for us to develop of them the same direct, perceptual kind of comprehension that most of us have of familiar mechanisms, the moving parts of which we can see and touch,' explained Licklider and Clark. This project betrayed Licklider's origins in psychology, where introspection—looking inwards to find the solution to a problem—was an early diagnostic technique. For humans, introspection has its shortcomings. Not all the processes of the brain are accessible, nor can they be described. A subject's reports are not always reliable and the very process of examining can interfere with the processes being studied. With computers, however, Licklider and Clark realized that these shortcomings could be turned to advantage. Whilst it was certainly true that asking a computer to display its own internal processes would interfere with its operation, the way it would interfere would be by using up memory and time—commodities in plentiful supply. They concluded that 'it might be interesting to experiment with programs that display the various aspects of the internal operation of a computer', anticipating modern debugging techniques.

Over time, everything in Licklider and Clark's paper would come to pass, but perhaps the most acute of their predictions was that 'twenty years from now, some form of keyboard operation will doubtless be taught in kindergarten, and forty years from now keyboards may be as universal as pencils'. And they spelled out the way to achieve their vision: 'to begin is everything, even if it is necessary at first to build research systems along lines that would be uneconomic for widespread application.' Happily for computers and networks, ARPA was an organization that shared this belief, and by hiring Licklider, it put itself firmly on the road to networking.

When Licklider arrived in Washington he took over ARPA's Command and Control division with the task of applying computing power to fast-moving battlefield situations. The military recognized the power of computers, but the 'neighbourhood dry cleaner' approach to using them clearly wouldn't be fast enough. After all, thought Licklider, 'who can direct a battle when he's got to write the program in the middle of the battle?' Computing power would be no good to military commanders if they had to wait hours for the results. For command and control applications, direct access to the computer was vital.

Time-sharing seemed to be the answer. It meant that several people could have terminals on their desks connected to the same central computer. They wouldn't actually have their own personal computers, but that is what it would feel like, and most importantly for command and control, they would interact directly with the machine rather than handing a batch of punched cards to an operator. At BBN, Licklider had been at the heart of the time-sharing world. Boston was where it was all happening, and BBN was where everyone in the Boston area got together. 'BBN was a kind of hybrid version of Harvard and MIT in the sense that most of the people there were either faculty or former faculty at either Harvard or MIT. A lot of the students at those places spent time at BBN. It was kind of like a super hyped-up version of the union of the two,' remembers Bob Kahn, an MIT mathematician who later played an important role in building the Internet. 'It was sort of the cognac of the research business, very distilled.'

One of the first things Licklider did when he sat down behind his new desk at ARPA was assemble a team of computer scientists capable of putting the time-sharing idea into practice. But time-sharing was just the start. To Licklider, computers were capable of being much more than just glorified calculating machines, no matter how many people could work on them at the same time. The series of projects he had worked on at BBN bore witness to that. When he called his team the Intergalactic Computer Network, it was clear where his thinking was leading. In a 1963 memo to the Network, he described the problem of computer communication as being 'essentially the one discussed by science fiction writers—how do you get communication started among totally uncorrelated "sapient" beings?' He went on to conclude, 'nebulously', that computer networking was something that should be done. Later on in his memo he predicted the kind of network applications that would take another thirty years to be developed, with the network, or computers on it, deciding which computer would be best to do a particular job.

Few people spent long at ARPA and Licklider was no exception. He left in 1964, but in the short time he was there, he had shifted the emphasis away from military-oriented command and control to basic research in advanced computing techniques. The new label, IPTO (for Information Processing Techniques Office), on the door of the office he handed over to his successor Ivan Sutherland reflected this change. The creation of IPTO was an important shift for ARPA, creating a haven of pure research at the heart of the Pentagon. Licklider had initiated a number of big contracts to put IPTO on the map. He hadn't set up a computer network but he had got things moving in that direction. He had created a community spirit between ARPA and its contractors and he had shared his vision with those who followed him. Sutherland 'was a brilliant person, and he was a true believer in the things I was a believer in, and in my view, better at it', explained Licklider, with the modesty that was his hallmark.

Another believer was Bob Taylor who was hired by Sutherland in 1965 and later succeeded him to become IPTO's third director. Taylor's association with ARPA went back further than 1965. Like Licklider, he began his career as a psychologist and only made the switch to computing after graduate studies. So when Licklider invited him to join an informal committee of government programme managers funding computing research, the two found they had a lot in common. They would discuss the way computing was going and together they formed the germ of an idea. When Sutherland left IPTO in 1966 and Taylor took over, he saw the opportunity to put that idea into practice.

Taylor's new office had three computer terminals in it, each connected to a different computer because there was no such thing as a single terminal that could talk to all three. On top of this, Taylor inherited an office that was receiving more and more demands for funding, as every computer science department wanted to buy or build the latest, most powerful computer. With so much duplication, it seemed clear that there must be a cheaper way of doing things. Taylor's idea was that every department would have its computer, but they would have to share their computing resources. The way to do that was by building a computer network across the country. Taylor lost no time in convincing ARPA's director, and by February he had an extra million dollars in his budget.

Money, however, wasn't all Taylor needed; he also needed a manager, and he knew exactly who he wanted. Larry Roberts was a young computer scientist from MIT's Lincoln Labs who had come to IPTO's attention earlier in 1966. IPTO had funded a project to link MIT's TX-2 computer with another machine at the System Development Corporation (SDC) in California using a telephone line. The TX-2 was the successor to the world's first transistorized digital computer, the TX-0 ('TX' being derived from 'transistorized experimental'), which had been built at MIT by Ken Olsen, who later founded the Digital Equipment Corporation (DEC). The experiment to link it to SDC's Q-32 computer had been proposed by an entrepreneur who ran a small computer company in California. ARPA liked the idea but preferred to entrust the project to one of its more familiar partners, Lincoln Labs, and wanted Roberts to be put in charge.

Unfortunately for Taylor, Roberts was perfectly happy working on computers and didn't want to go off and become a manager in Washington. But Taylor was tenacious and when he realized that over half of Lincoln Labs' funding was provided by ARPA, he had found the lever he needed to prise Roberts away from Boston. 'I blackmailed Larry Roberts into fame,' he was later to claim. By the end of the year, Roberts had a desk at the Pentagon and was drawing up plans for the ARPA Computer Network, later shortened to ARPANET.

One day early in 1967 Bob Taylor organized a meeting of ARPA's principal investigators where the main topic for discussion was the network project, and Larry Roberts was the main speaker. What he presented was an extension of the experiment he had already carried out. He proposed linking several computers around the country by getting them to make a phone call to each other and communicating across the existing telephone network. There would be problems, of course, since each computer had a different operating system, so for every different computer you wanted to call, your computer would have to learn a new language.

An ex-colleague of Roberts' from Lincoln Labs, Wesley Clark, was at the meeting. Networking wasn't really his thing, so he just sat quietly and listened, but just as the meeting began to break up he realized there was a better way to build a network. It had been a long day and Clark wanted to go home, so rather than prolong the meeting he just handed Roberts a note. 'I see how to solve the problem,' it said. Clark had helped build the TX-2 that Roberts had used in his original networking experiment, and a year or so earlier he had used the same machine to demonstrate digital computer programming to J. C. R. Licklider, so he was well qualified to comment. Roberts was intrigued, and in a taxi ride on the way back to the airport Clark explained how he thought the network should be built. By using small computers to route data around, each of the big computers on the network would only have to learn one new language: the one needed to speak to the small routing computers. Wesley Clark had come up with the idea of the sub-net, and Roberts quickly worked it into the plans he was drawing up for the ARPANET.

By the time of one of the year's big computer meetings in October, organized by the world's oldest computing society, the Association for Computing Machinery (ACM), in Gatlinburg, Tennessee, Roberts had turned Clark's idea into a paper. The small routing computers had become IMPs, Interface Message Processors, and the architecture of the ARPANET was almost complete. There was one important ingredient missing, however, and Roberts would learn what it was at the conference from Roger Scantlebury, a computer scientist from England who had been working with Donald Davies on a networking project himself.

The invention of packet switching

One day in the summer of 1941, Donald Davies was walking to school when he met all his classmates heading in the opposite direction. 'We've got a half-day holiday,' they said, 'because of you!' Davies had just been awarded no fewer than four university scholarships, an event so rare at his Portsmouth school, evacuated to Brockenhurst in the New Forest for the war, that it warranted celebration. Davies took his scholarship to Imperial College in London, where he got a first in physics after two years before being assigned to work for Rudolf Pierls in Birmingham on the 'Tube Alloys' project, a cover for atomic bomb research. 'I spent most of my time supervising groups of computers,' he remembers, who at that time were people, not machines. 'So obviously the need for more rapid and efficient calculation was ground into me during that time.'

After the war, with one year's scholarship money still in hand, he returned to Imperial to take another degree, this time in mathematics, and was awarded the University of London's Lubbock Memorial Prize as the best maths student in his year. 'It was very much an applied maths degree, and because there was so much overlap between that and the physics course, which was very much a mathematical physics course, I was able to rush through in the year,' he recounts with typical modesty.

During this final year at Imperial, two things happened to steer Davies in the direction of computing. The first was an inspirational lecture by American cybernetics pioneer Norbert Wiener, and the second was a talk by John Reginald Womersley, who was setting up a mathematics division at the National Physical Laboratory (NPL). Womersley had just recruited Alan Turing, fresh from his wartime code-breaking exploits, and his talk was about the digital computer Turing was building at the NPL. 'I rushed down to the front at the end of the lecture and said, "Look, how can I join?"' Davies was handed an application form, and towards the end of 1947 he found himself working on Turing's Automatic Calculating Engine (ACE) project. A scaled-down prototype, the Pilot ACE, was working by 1950 and it was 'much the fastest machine, probably anywhere, because of the way in which Turing had designed access to the rotating mercury delay line memory so that, provided you were clever enough in your programming, you could manage to get the data you needed out at just the right time'. But the full ACE was a long time in coming and by the time it arrived in 1958 it was almost obsolete. The invention of a new kind of memory based on magnetic ferrite had turned the ACE's mercury delay line memory system into an industrial dinosaur. Programming a computer in those days involved more than just writing down a logical sequence of commands; you also had to think of when the information your program needed would be available from memory. If you got the timing wrong your program would run more slowly whilst it waited for the relevant piece of information to come round again. By providing effectively instant access, magnetic ferrite memory made programming much easier.

Davies used the pilot ACE to study traffic flow, modelling the movement of cars through traffic-light-regulated intersections. Later he designed warning systems for coal mines to alert miners in a sequence that would ensure no bottlenecks formed as they made their way to the escape shaft. Davies soon earned a reputation as a high-flier, working on projects that were way ahead of their time, such as computer translation and handwriting recognition. He made regular trips to the USA, spending a year there in 1954–5 on a Commonwealth Fellowship, so he was always in touch with developments on the other side of the Atlantic. By this time Licklider was back at MIT in charge of Project MAC, an ARPA-funded project he had started up the month after he joined ARPA in 1962. Depending what floor of MIT's 545 Tech Square you happened to be standing on, MAC stood for 'Multiple Access Computers' or 'Man and Computer'. Whichever way you looked at it, however, Licklider's stamp was on it. Project MAC was where the best work in time-sharing was happening, and a time-sharing system called Multiplexed Information and Computing Service (Multics) was being developed there.

In 1965, on returning from a US study tour, Davies organized a meeting at the NPL to spread the new time-sharing doctrine in the UK. Davies's meeting took place on 2 and 3 November, with Project MAC members forming the majority of invited Americans. Larry Roberts was among them. 'We talked about many things,' says Davies, 'particularly about problems of programming very large systems.' Computer communication was among the things discussed, but it was way down the agenda. Nevertheless, recalls Davies, 'I began to feel that there was something wrong about the way we were talking about getting computers to communicate with each other.'

All the talk of networking up to this time had been based on the telephone network simply because it was already there. But it seemed to Davies that circuit switching was not the answer for computer communication where short periods of rapid information exchange were interspersed with long silences. He started to think along the lines of message switching, the method that was used for sending telegrams. This seemed to offer a better solution because no direct connection was established. A message was simply sent out and the recipient replied when and if they felt like it. The drawback with message switching as it stood in the early 1960s, however, was that it was anything but rapid. It was a direct descendent of beacons on hills, indian smoke signals, and semaphore towers. Messages were relayed from one place to the next until they reached their destination using a store-and-forward approach. The trouble was that the 'store' part often took much longer than the 'forward'. 'When you dumped a message in to a message switch you expected it to take hours before it came out again,' explains Davies. 'You had a paper tape with your message on it, you put it through a reader, and it got sent over a telephone line to a punch at the other end.' Operators would tear off the arriving tapes, hang them on hooks, and sort them according to destination before feeding them into another reader to send them on to the next relay station until they reached wherever they were going.

By the time Donald Davies was thinking about applying message switching to computer communication, the torn tapes and operators had been replaced by automatic systems, but these had been designed to do exactly the same as the operators had done before. All the shortcomings of human systems had been built into the new automatic message switches. Messages were always sent whole, which meant that if you dropped a message saying 'Meet me at the George and Dragon at six' just after someone else had dropped off their magnum opus, your message would have to wait for the whole of the magnum opus to be sent and your friend would probably turn up at six the next day. Another drawback was that once a switch received a message, it was its responsibility not to lose it; and if a message did get lost, there was no way of knowing. In the language of computer communication, there was no end-to-end, or host-to-host, protocol; the receiving end didn't know what it was supposed to be receiving and so couldn't complain if it didn't arrive.

'I knew that message switching literally took hours and could probably be brought down to minutes, but I didn't believe it could be done faster,' says Davies. But then he did a simple calculation to see how long it would take to send a short message over the fastest lines then available and he got a surprising answer. For messages equivalent to a line of type, the average time spent by any message at a switch was just two milliseconds. 'It's a simple idea: you don't send the whole message, you send it in short pieces so that you beat the delay problem,' Davies explains. Moreover, he calculated that if the network were running at up to 80 per cent saturation there would be no more than two packets waiting in a queue at any switch at any time. 'So you could imagine that a modest-sized network could deliver a message in 10 milliseconds, which was quite beyond what we thought was even necessary,' he says. Davies had calculated that 100 milliseconds would be quite fast enough for people not to notice the delay. Above 80 per cent saturation, however, Davies foresaw problems because the queue lengths he calculated became infinite. Several years later, when NPL was demonstrating a new Europe-wide network, these infinite queues would briefly come back to haunt him.

What Davies had done was to merge the ideas of message switching with those of computer time-sharing. Time-sharing works by allocating processing time equally on a round-robin basis to all the tasks that a computer is handling, so that a long program doesn't unduly delay the execution of a short one. Packet switching does just the same thing. If the 'George and Dragon' message arrived at a switch at the same time as the magnum opus, packets from each would alternate, and the short message would not be unduly hampered by the long one. On 10 November, Davies circulated a note at NPL describing his 'short message' data service and predicting that if implemented it would soon take over the telegraph service.

As the months went by, Davies refined his ideas. After consultation with NPL linguists, his 'short messages' became packets, because that was a word that could easily be translated into many languages. The concept of packet switching was born. He had also worked out a way around the end-to-end protocol problem, since each packet would contain information about sender, destination, and how many packets made up the whole message. By March 1966, Davies felt that his new

Figure 4: Packet switching means that a short message is not unduly delayed by a longer one.

idea was ready to be presented to a wider audience, and he gave a lecture at the NPL. Over 100 people came, including several from the Post Office and one Arthur Llewellyn from the Ministry of Defence.

After the lecture, Llewellyn took Davies to one side and told him the news that someone else had had the idea before him. Paul Baran had published a paper in 1964 covering much the same ground Davies had just discussed. Baran was an electrical engineer who, in 1959, had taken a job at the Research and Development (RAND) Corporation, a policy think-tank based in Santa Monica, California. RAND had the reputation of being a pure ideas place, so much so that a common joke had the 'N' standing for 'no', to make 'Research And No Development'.

It was no accident that the MoD man knew about Baran's work when Davies himself did not. Baran's concern was how to defuse the unstable position of two neurotic nuclear powers trying to stare each other down. With a vulnerable communications system, he believed that there was a dangerous temptation for either party to misunderstand the actions of the other and fire first. 'If the strategic weapons command and control systems could be more survivable,' he explains, 'then the country's retaliatory capability could better allow it to withstand attack and still function; a more stable position.' Baran's work may have been prompted by a military goal, but its motivation was a safer world for everyone. 'We chose not to classify this work and also chose not to patent the work,' he pointed out years later. 'Not only would the US be safer with a survivable command and control system; the US would be even safer if the USSR had a survivable command and control system as well!'

The telephone network, with its centralized switches, was clearly vulnerable. What was needed was a network where even if large pieces were destroyed, messages, especially voice messages, could still find their way around, allowing military commanders to stay in control. Baran envisaged a network in which each node would be connected to several of its neighbours, and he sat down to calculate just how many connections a node would need to give it a reasonable chance of staying in touch after an attack. He found that the number was surprisingly low. 'The first interesting thing I found out very early in the game in early 1960 was that it would only take about three or four times as many links as the minimum needed to connect all the nodes to produce an extremely robust structure,' he explains. 'That is, any node that survived the physical attack would almost always be able to communicate with the largest group of surviving nodes.'

Having worked out that a survivable network could be built relative-

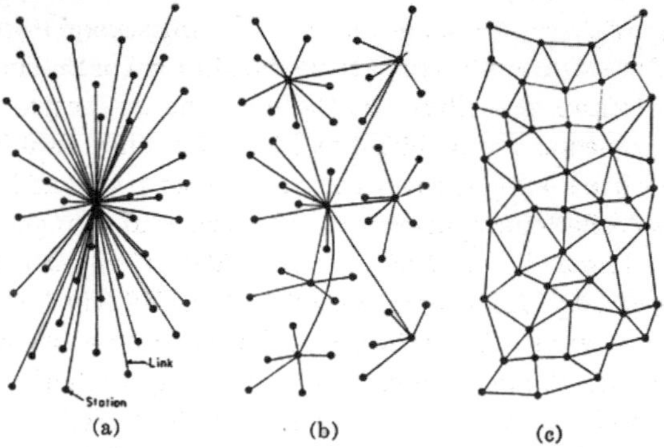

Figure 5: The simplest kind of network has a star configuration (a) and is clearly very vulnerable to attack. At the other extreme is the kind of completely distributed network Paul Baran considered (c) where each node is connected to several others. In practice, networks are a combination of the two (b). (From Paul Baran, 'On Distributed Communications Networks', IEEE Transactions on Communications Systems, March 1964.)

ly easily, Baran turned to the task of deciding how messages should be sent around it. He reached the same conclusion as Donald Davies, that messages should be broken down into 'standardized format message blocks', and he even chose the same size for his blocks. Baran also invented what he called the 'hot potato' method of routing packets. Each router would have a sort of look-up table telling it the best routes to any destination on the network. If the first-choice route were busy or destroyed, the router would send the packet off along the second best, but it would get rid of it as quickly as it could, like someone being tossed a hot potato at a party.

Davies had been shocked to find that someone else had invented packet switching before him but took comfort in the fact that Baran had reached such similar conclusions. All subsequent NPL papers on the subject referenced Baran, and later on when the two men met, Davies congratulated Baran on his work, adding, 'Well, you may have got there first, but I got the name.' Paul Baran had to agree: 'It's a much better word—the English are very good at that sort of thing.'

Denied the honour of being the first to come up with the concept of packet switching, even if he did get the name, Davies was nevertheless soon able to ensure his place in computing history. Five months after presenting his paper on packet switching, he was promoted to head of

NPL's Division of Computer Science, which meant that he had the resources at his disposal to build a packet-switching network. The reception his talk had received had been mixed, so he decided that the best way to convince people of the value of his idea was to build a network and show them how good it was. One of the first things he did in his new job was to appoint Derek Barber, who had been working on a standard interface for devices like terminals and printers to computers, to head up a data communications research group. Barber's team was made up of himself, Roger Scantlebury, Keith Bartlett, and Peter Wilkinson, and it got to work straight away. Davies had had the same insight

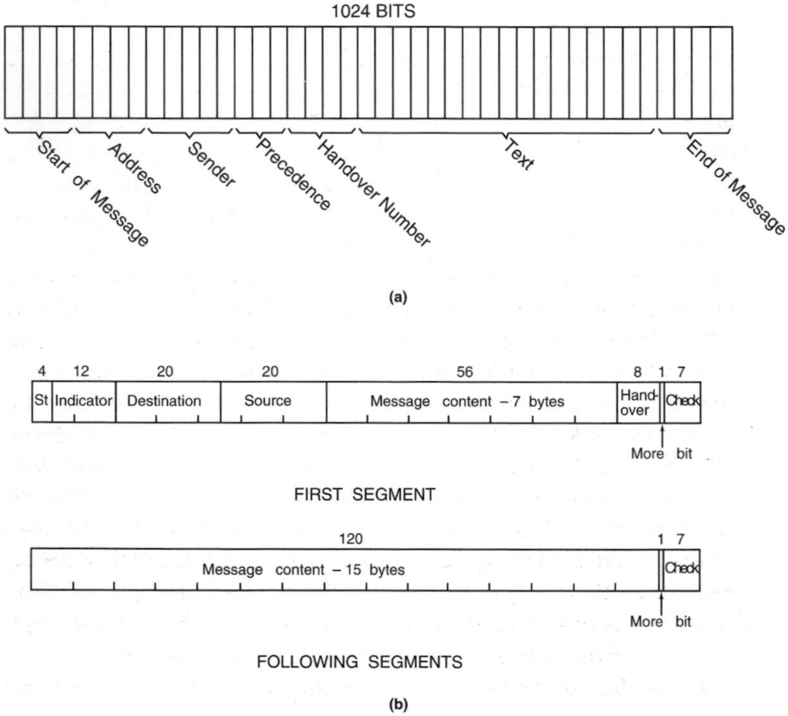

Figure 6: Although invented independently, Paul Baran's message blocks (a) and Donald Davies's packets (b) look remarkably similar. They are the same length and were made up of similar components. (From Paul Baran, 'On Distributed Communications Networks', IEEE Transactions on Communications Systems, March 1964 (a), and D. W. Davies et al., 'A Digital Communication Network for Computers Giving Rapid Response at Remote Terminals', ACM Symposium on Operating System Principles, October 1967 (b).)

as Wesley Clark, that computer communication should be carried out using a small, dedicated packet-switching computer. Working out the requirements for this computer was the group's first task. They worked up their ideas into a detailed design for a network spanning the NPL site, and by the end of the year they had roughed out the requirements for the packet-switching computer. In 1967, Scantlebury went to the ACM meeting in Gatlinburg to report.

Gatlinburg

Back at ARPA, Bob Taylor and Larry Roberts knew nothing of the work of either Baran or Davies, and Gatlinburg proved to be a more important meeting than either of them could have imagined. There were three presentations in the Computer Networks and Communications session. The first was Larry Roberts's report on the ARPA project, in which he described the plan to link the nation's most powerful computers. This was followed by a talk from Jack Dennis of MIT that discussed the merits of a more general-purpose data communication network, leading, Scantlebury reported with satisfaction on return to England, 'nicely into the technical solutions proposed in the NPL paper which followed.'

After the presentations were over, Scantlebury was surprised to learn that the ARPA people were not aware of Paul Baran's work and that his talk had been the first they had heard of packet switching. 'It would appear that the ideas in the NPL paper at the moment are more advanced than any proposed in the USA', Scantlebury concluded, but Roberts was quick to latch onto a good idea. 'Suddenly I learned how to route packets,' he later said of the Gatlinburg conference. Soon Paul Baran was hired as a consultant to ARPA and packet switching became the ARPANET's chosen means of communication. Some time later, when Donald Davies visited Larry Roberts to check on progress at ARPA, he noticed a copy of his 1965 NPL note. 'It was lying on his desk in tatters,' he observed. 'It had obviously been very heavily thumbed and turned over and he grilled me on a number of aspects of it.'

In 1967, the world's computer networking community couldn't quite be counted on the fingers of one hand, but it was still pretty small. Almost everyone involved in the emerging field had been at Gatlinburg, and from then on it was teamwork that would build the global packet-switching computer network. One of the first things to do was to convince the world of the necessity for such a network. Donald Davies and his team got their first chance to present the NPL network to the world at the 1968 International Federation of Information Processing (IFIP) meeting in Edinburgh. A whole session was devoted to packet switching and two-thirds of the papers came from the NPL. But the reaction they got from the telecommunications industry was sceptical to say the least. Message switches, the telecoms experts said, were extremely complex beasts best left to the experts. 'What they hadn't twigged is that we were not doing that,' said Davies. 'One of the main reasons why their message switches were complex was that they'd taken it on themselves to simulate every single property of torn-tape systems which had grown up around human actions and they'd tied themselves up in knots doing it.'

During this time, Donald Davies became firm friends with another networking pioneer on the conference circuit. Leonard Kleinrock was a professor at the University of California at Los Angeles (UCLA), who as early as 1959 had turned his attention to the question of computer networking whilst working for his Ph.D. at MIT. 'His work was highly theoretical, very, very clever, and concerned with solving every kind of network delay problem,' explains Davies. 'He did that in a brilliant way but it didn't seem motivated by the real applications of neworking.' Nevertheless, while it was Baran and Davies who independently came up with the practical solution of packet switching, Kleinrock's painstaking study of message flow and delay was later to prove invaluable in facing up to the resistance of the telecommunications establishment. 'Packet switching was new and radical in the 1960s,' explains Larry Roberts. 'In order to plan to spend millions of dollars and stake my reputation, I needed to understand that it would work. Without Kleinrock's work on networks and queuing theory, I could never have taken such a radical step. All the communications community argued that it couldn't work.'

So despite a lukewarm reception from the telecommunications establishment, the ARPANET and the NPL network were going ahead. In 1967, ARPA awarded a contract to Elmer Shapiro at the Stanford Research Institute (SRI) to come up with a design for the IMP network. His study fed into the request for proposals issued by ARPA the following year to supply the first four IMPs, with more to follow if the experiment were a success. The first four host establishments had been chosen because they were already members of the ARPA community: leading computer R&D sites that could be relied upon to put in the effort required to make the network a success. ARPA was an important source of funding for them after all, so they had good reason to cooperate even if they were worried that all networking would bring was more demand on their computers.

One hundred and forty potential bidders asked for the request for proposals, and twelve submitted bids. The big guns of the computer and telecommunications industries declined to bid, and the contract went to BBN, the firm that Licklider had left to join ARPA. The winning team was headed by Frank Heart, who had moved to BBN from Lincoln Labs and had just eight months to deliver under Larry Roberts' tight schedule. Shortly after being awarded the contract, BBN received a message from Massachusetts Senator Edward Kennedy, who was in the habit of congratulating local companies on important contracts. 'Our particular telegram was an interesting one,' remembers Heart. 'It was maybe more prophetic than it knew.' Kennedy congratulated the firm on winning the contract for the 'interfaith' message processor. History doesn't record whether Heart was inspired or simply amused by the implied spiritual dimension to the work he was about to begin.

Heart had assembled a handpicked team of experts, many of whom had worked with him before at Lincoln Labs. Severo Ornstein was responsible for the hardware and was joined by Ben Barker. Bob Kahn had been interested in networking for some time, and had even sent Larry Roberts a letter about it before the ARPA network project was announced. When BBN was awarded the IMP contract, Kahn was working on phone line error problems, and he brought this expertise to the team. Once the ARPANET was up and running, this turned out to be an important part of the work and BBN became very good at it. 'We would call from Cambridge to the phone company in California,' recounts Frank Heart, 'and say, "Sir, your phone line from UCLA to Utah is going to break soon." And they would say, "Where are you calling from?" And we'd say, "We're calling from Cambridge, Massachusetts." They would either laugh uproariously or think we were complete liars.' But Heart and his team at BBN always got the last laugh, since the telephone line would invariably break, just as they had predicted. Telephone lines have become a lot more reliable since computers started to talk to each other using them.

Potholer Will Crowther, better known for writing the world's first computer game, Adventure, based on his caving experiences, joined Dave Walden on the software team with Bernie Cosell. Hawley Rising, Jim Geisman, Bill Bertell, Marty Thrope, and Truett Thach in Los Angeles made up the team. It was a small and unusually talented group. 'All the software people knew something about hardware, and all the hardware people programmed,' says Heart. 'It was a set of people who all knew a lot about the whole project. I consider that pretty important in anything very big.'

Heart based his design around the compact and robust Honeywell

DDP-516, the same computer that had coincidentally been chosen by the NPL team when their first choice, the British Plessey XL12, was cancelled. When Honeywell delivered IMP number zero, the first prototype, to BBN in spring 1969, it didn't work. Circuits were unpicked and rewired, new software was written, and within a few months Heart's team had a working specification ready for Honeywell to produce the first production IMP. After a couple of weeks' debugging at BBN, IMP number one was flown out to Leonard Kleinrock's lab at UCLA in August, where it was met by Truett Thach. He was horrified to see that it was upside down, 'which meant that it had been turned over an odd number of times,' he was later able to joke after IMP number one had worked as soon as it was plugged in and switched on.

UCLA was the obvious choice for the first node on the ARPANET. When Ivan Sutherland was in charge of IPTO, ARPA had funded a networking experiment to link IBM computers in three of the University's departments. UCLA had also played an important role in specifying the measurement software that BBN implemented in each IMP. That, coupled with Kleinrock's work on communications networks, which was so important for Larry Roberts's plans, clinched it for UCLA. After all, who better than Kleinrock to understand what was going on when the packets started to flow? UCLA became the Network Measurement Centre, responsible for compiling statistics and analysing the network.

Whilst BBN was debugging IMP number zero, the race was on at UCLA to build an interface between the IMP they were expecting in August and the university's Sigma 7 computer. The Sigma 7's manufacturers wanted too much time and too much money, so the task fell to enterprising graduate student Mike Wingfield, who built the interface in six weeks flat. Meanwhile, two other UCLA graduate students, Steve Crocker and Vint Cerf, wrote the code that ensured both software and hardware were ready on time. Crocker and Cerf knew exactly what they were doing. Earlier they had helped a local California company called Jacobi Systems prepare a bid to build the IMPs. Jacobi may have lost out to BBN, but for Crocker and Cerf that was just the beginning.

Two months later, SRI took delivery of IMP number two, and the world's first packet-switching network was in business. On 29 October, when SRI had hooked up its host computer to the IMP, it was time to send the first ever packet-switched message. 'I had one of my programmers sit down at our host and SRI had one of theirs at SRI,' remembers Kleinrock. 'Each had a headphone with a voice line connecting them.

All we wanted to do was log on from UCLA to SRI.' At UCLA they typed in an 'L', and SRI acknowledged that they had received it. They typed in an 'O', and that was received as well, but when they typed in a 'G', the system crashed. 'So the first message was "LO", or, if you will, "Hello",' says Kleinrock with a smile. Later the same day, they found out what had gone wrong, and on the second attempt the network worked.

The University of California at Santa Barbara took delivery of IMP number three in November, and the fourth IMP was installed in Utah in December, completing the original four-host network. BBN itself had to wait for IMP number five, delivered in March 1970, before it became attached to the network. By the end of 1970, the ARPANET was growing at the rate of about one host per month, as fast as Honeywell could turn out IMPs.

BBN had the job of building the IMP network, but there was no contract for working out how host computers would be attached to it, or how they would use the network to talk to each other. This became the job of the Network Working Group (NWG) set up unwittingly by Elmer Shapiro when he called a meeting for programmers from each of the first four sites in summer 1968 to start thinking about protocols for the network. 'That first meeting was seminal,' remembers Steve Crocker. 'Most of us were graduate students and we expected that a professional crew would show up eventually to take over the problems we were dealing with.' A month later, that crew still hadn't arrived, and the group decided to start documenting its discussions. On 7 April 1969, four months before his lab got its IMP, Crocker made a little bit of history when he sent out a memo to the NWG with the title 'Request for Comments' (RFC). 'I remember having great fear that we would offend whomever the official protocol designers were, and I spent a sleepless night composing humble words for our notes. The basic ground rules were that anyone could say anything and that nothing was official.' RFCs quickly became the modus operandi for the ARPANET crowd. It suited their way of doing things, as there was no authority decreeing what should and shouldn't be done. If you had a good idea, you simply put out an RFC and let the community decide. By 1987, there had been 999 RFCs, and two people, Joyce Reynolds and Jon Postel, decided that it was time to establish some kind of order. Their RFC 1000 was entitled 'The Request for Comments Reference Guide'. Some RFCs have become the official standards of the Internet and were marked as such in RFC 1000. Some have been memorable for their names. RFC 602, for example, 'The Stockings Were Hung by the Chimney with Care,' was written by Bob Metcalfe in 1973 in response to the risk of hackers breaking in to the network. It advised the NWG 'not to sit in hope that Saint Nicholas would soon be there'. Other RFCs simply became obsolete. Postel went on to become the unofficial archivist of the Internet, preserving its history for posterity.

RFC number one concerned protocols. It was all very well having IMPs and hosts, but without protocols all that hardware would be useless. The first protocols on the ARPANET, telnet and FTP, were hastily assembled by the NWG. Telnet allowed someone sitting at a terminal attached to a computer at one site to login to a computer at another, thus solving the problem that had led Bob Taylor to propose the network in the first place. FTP, file transfer protocol, allowed files to be transferred between computers. This was a start, but it wasn't enough. What Larry Roberts wanted was a more general protocol whose job was simply to carry information from host to host. Protocols like telnet and FTP would then run on top of this base-level protocol. The NWG went back to the drawing board and the result was the Network Control Protocol (NCP) whose implementation began in 1970. NCP's job was simply to get packets to their destination, without a care for what sort of information they contained. Going back to the roads analogy of networking, if the ARPANET were a network of roads, the roads themselves would be the bottom level of the protocol stack. Instructions like 'Keep left, stop for red traffic lights' would equate to NCP. There might be a higher-level 'car' protocol whose job was to deliver people to different places on the network, or a 'truck' protocol for delivering goods. These would be analogous to telnet and FTP.

While all this was going on in the USA, Donald Davies's network was also taking shape. With just one node and a single campus to cover, the NPL network was much more modest than the ARPANET, but Davies saw it as a 'working prototype for a national network'. He had a champion in the form of Stanley Gill, outspoken Professor of Automatic Data Processing at Imperial College. Davies was in a delicate position; the government-owned Post Office had a monopoly on telecommunications provision and Davies himself was a government employee, so he couldn't afford to be seen to be treading on their patch. Gill resolved this problem for him. He founded a group known as the Real Time Club to lobby the Post Office to build a national packet-switching network. In July 1968, the Real Time Club organized a major event, 'Conversational Computing on the South Bank' at London's Royal Festival Hall. The *Financial Times* reported that 'Professor Gill wants design of a pilot network to start this year. Both he and industry agree that the system designed by Mr D. W. Davies of the National Physical Laboratory is the best solution.' The article went on to conclude that 'What Professor Gill and users fear is the "too little too late" syndrome which has kept British industry behind world competitors for years.' Gill outlined two scenarios for networking in Britain. His optimistic forecast had Britain exporting network hardware by 1972. The pessimistic one detailed a catalogue of official dithering resulting in 'massive and expensive imports of American equipment beginning in 1980.' He was just one year out. Britain's first full-scale commercial packet-switching service started up in 1981 using hardware licensed from the USA.

The NPL took delivery of its Honeywell DDP-516 node computer in 1969 and the network was up and running by January 1970. In its initial configuration, hosts could be either computers, as with the ARPANET, or simpler devices like terminals. Unlike the ARPANET, there was just one packet-switching node with several hosts and terminals connected to it in a star shape. Experience showed that treating terminals separately would make life easier, so in the NPL network the DDP-516 was asked to behave as if it were two computers, one corresponding to the ARPANET's IMPs, the other connected to the first and behaving as if it were a separate host computer. This terminal processor, as it was called, handled traffic between terminals without a host computer of their own. At around the same time, Heart and his team had reached a similar conclusion, and in 1971, the ARPANET had its

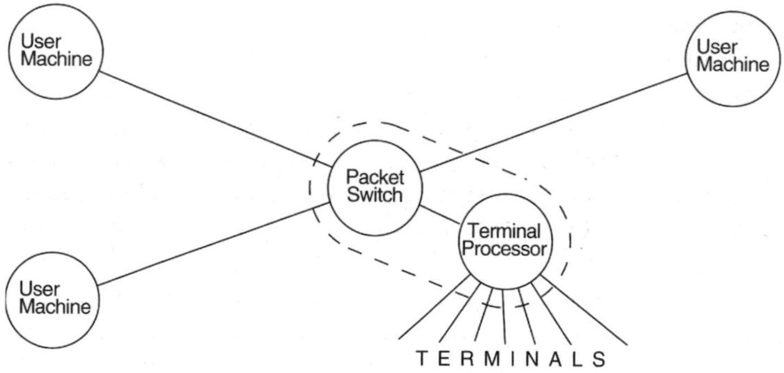

Figure 7: The NPL network's Honeywell DDP-516 node computer performed two tasks. It acted as the packet-switching computer, like the ARPANET's IMPs, and it handled traffic between terminals without a host computer of their own. (From David M. Yates, *Turing's Legacy: A History of Computing at the National Physical Laboratory 1945–1995*, London: Science Museum, 1997.)

first Terminal IMP, or TIP for short, connecting terminals directly to the network.

In 1972, ARPA became DARPA. The 'D' stands for Defense and was added as a consequence of a Department of Defense directive that aimed to tie ARPA research more closely to the military. As far as IPTO was concerned, the immediate changes were small. 'You didn't really have a prayer of starting something up unless you could show that it was good for the military,' explains Steve Crocker, by now at DARPA himself; but 'On the other hand, technology is good for the military in very broad ways, and so it wasn't very hard to do that. But you had to have a reason.'

So despite the political shuffling, IPTO's work carried on as before, and 1972 turned out to be a landmark year for the ARPANET. At BBN, Ray Tomlinson had written a protocol for transferring files between the company's DEC PDP-10 computers, and another program for sending and reading mail on a single PDP-10. He decided to try them together to see if he could send mail from one computer to another. It worked, but Tomlinson lacked the sense of history shared by other communications pioneers. Whereas Samuel Morse's 1844 telegraph message read 'What Hath God Wrought', Tomlinson's first e-mail probably read something like 'QWERTYUIOP'. The first message of substance, however, came shortly after when Tomlinson sent an e-mail to his colleagues explaining how to send messages from one computer to another. Thus the first use of network mail announced its own existence, and it wasn't long before Tomlinson's programs had been grafted onto other file transfer protocols so that users of different computers could use them. Tomlinson's trick was to use the @ character with the user's name before and their host computer's name after. 'My reasoning at the time was that "@" did not appear in the name of any person nor in the name of any computer host. It had the additional advantage of indicating that the person was "at" the computer.' The choice was almost perfect, unless you happened to be working on Multics, where, as Tomlinson explains, 'typing @ would delete whatever had been typed on the current input line.' This proved to be only a minor setback and within just a couple of years e-mail accounted for the bulk of ARPANET traffic.

The other major event of 1972 was the ARPANET's first public demonstration. The ARPANET was already running so reliably that DARPA was beginning to think that its enabling role was over and someone else should take over day-to-day network management. The problem was that the network was empty. It was 'like having a highway system that was perfectly capable of handling automobile traffic except there were no cars around, or no on-ramps or off-ramps', explains Bob Kahn. The network was working fine, but many of the computers that were connected to it simply couldn't use it yet; their host sites hadn't had the incentive. Kahn had the idea that by organizing a demonstration, those host sites would be galvanized into action to 'put cars on the highway', as he expresses it, and once the cars were there, the world would be able to see how useful the network really was.

The first International Conference on Computer Communication (ICCC) at the Washington Hilton in October 1972 gave DARPA the ideal opportunity to show off. Bob Kahn was about to move to Washington to join Larry Roberts at DARPA, but before he did they agreed he should organize a network extravaganza to convince the world that packet switching was the communications technology of the future. The demonstrations were spectacular. There was a simulation of a distributed air traffic control system: when a plane left one computer's region, it would be picked up by another. In another demonstration, put on by MIT, a computer-controlled robotic turtle ran around the room. With yet another, you would sit down in Washington, login to a computer at BBN, pick up some code, ship it to UCLA to run, and have the output printed back in Washington. Leonard Kleinrock remembers this one well: 'Jon Postel sat down to demonstrate this thing: logon to BBN, shift it over to UCLA, compile and execute and then send it back to print. Nothing happened! He couldn't figure out what was wrong! He kept looking around. Then he found turtle on the floor, and turtle was jumping around.' It turned out that Postel's output was going to the turtle, and the poor robot's gyrations were its dutiful attempt to do what it was being told. Despite this little hiccup, by the end of the day the demonstration had paid off. Thousands of people had seen it and had gone away impressed. 'This was the watershed event that made people suddenly realize that packet switching was a real technology' remembers Kahn with satisfaction.

Enter the Menehune

In 1968, Norm Abramson was toying with the idea of radio access to computers. He was on the faculty at the University of Hawaii, a university with seven separate colleges on four islands and a number of remote research stations thrown in. Keeping them all in touch with the university's central IBM computer using dial-up telephone lines was consuming the lion's share of the University's computing budget and Abramson was looking for an alternative. He had been following the developments in computer networking with interest and, like Donald

Davies, had concluded that the telephone network wasn't the ideal medium to handle computer communication. 'Indeed,' he explains, 'It would have been surprising had such a network architecture, shaped by the requirements of voice communications at the end of the nineteenth century, been compatible with the emerging requirements of data communication networks at the end of the twentieth century.'

Unlike Donald Davies or ARPA, however, Abramson took the bold step of dispensing with cables altogether. In a project supported initially by the US Air Force Office of Aerospace Research and then by Larry Roberts at ARPA, Abramson's team put together the world's first packet radio network, the ALOHANET. It was a project that fitted in perfectly with ARPA's brief. Driven by a civilian need to provide distributed access to a university's central computing facility, it had obvious potential military applications. Without cables, network nodes could perhaps be mobile, on battlefield tanks for example, and ARPA was later to take a lead from Abramson and support a range of packet radio and satellite projects.

Having decided to use radio as the means of transmitting information, there remained the question of how. Simply letting each computer use a different frequency channel wasn't an option, at least not in the late 1960s, so at an ALOHA project meeting in 1969 the idea of transmitting information in short high-speed packet bursts on a shared channel was chosen. The ALOHANET mechanism wasn't packet switching, but packet broadcasting. Once that decision had been made, the rest of the design quickly fell into place. Two frequency bands were chosen for the ALOHA channels, one for transmission from the central campus near Honolulu to the other ALOHA sites, the other for return traffic.

Inspired by the ARPANET's IMPs, the Hawaii group built their 'Menehune' to handle packets in and out of the central computer. It was based on a small computer built by Hewlett Packard, and it took its name from a legendary Hawaiian elf.

The ALOHANET was asymmetric by nature, a collection of remote terminals connected to a central computing facility. That meant traffic on the outgoing ALOHA channel from the central facility to the terminals was handled in a very different way from incoming traffic. The Menehune organized broadcast of packets to the terminals in an orderly fashion, but in the other direction the terminals were free to transmit whenever they wanted. This approach was chosen in order to allow each terminal to have access to the full speed of the ALOHA channel, rather than dividing the channel up into small, slow segments for each terminal. The way the ALOHA protocol worked was that a terminal would transmit a burst of packets and wait for an acknowledgement from the Menehune. If a packet got through correctly, the Menehune would send the OK along the outgoing channel. If a packet didn't arrive, or arrived garbled, there would be no acknowledgement and the terminal would wait for a random amount of time before resending.

This randomness was the key feature of the ALOHANET because the main reason for packet loss was too many terminals talking all at once. If two or more terminals transmitted at the same time, their packets would interfere with each other and there would be no acknowledgement. If they waited a fixed amount of time, they would again all transmit at once, and packets would never get through. Abramson's solution borrowed from the familiar dinner-table phenomenon of everyone starting to talk at once. When this happens, everyone tends to stop and then, after a brief pause, someone starts up again. It is unlikely that everyone will start talking again at the same time, so conversation smoothly resumes its course. The ALOHANET's random restart was designed to ensure that terminals have good table manners, but just in case a third terminal butted in on a retry, terminals could retransmit several times if necessary.

The ALOHANET started up in June 1971 with the Menehune installed at the university's central Manoa Valley campus near Honolulu and its first remote terminal in Abramson's home about a mile from the university. By the end of the year there were four terminals, and the network soon grew to support several hundred active users. Since it was funded by ARPA, it seemed a natural step to connect the ALOHANET to the ARPANET, and in 1972 Norm Abramson was sitting in Larry Roberts' office in Washington with just this on his mind. Like many of its beneficiaries, Abramson found ARPA to be a funding agency like no other. 'Roberts contributed to the success of the project in a way not ordinarily obtained from funding agencies,' he explains. 'In a real sense, Roberts acted as another member of the research staff of the project.' But in 1972, Larry Roberts's mind was elsewhere. The ARPANET was in full expansion, and he was busy organizing the installation of IMPs around the country. At one point during the meeting, Roberts was called away from his office and Abramson noticed a blackboard listing sites awaiting IMPs along with delivery dates. He picked up a piece of chalk and added 'the ALOHA system' to the list with the date 17 December. He had planned to discuss this with Roberts when he returned, but the conversation turned to other things and Hawaii's IMP was never raised. Abramson had forgotten all about it when 'about two weeks before the December 17 date, we received a phone call from the group charged with the responsibility of installing the IMPs asking us to prepare a place for the equipment'. The IMP arrived right on schedule, and Hawaii's IBM machine became the first ARPANET node to be connected to the network by satellite. Soon after, Abramson's group turned its attention to using ALOHA channels on a satellite network, and in 1973, PACNET started up as the first packet-broadcasting satellite network linking Hawaii to sites in Alaska, Japan, Australia, and California. Abramson's pioneering efforts had put the wheels in motion that would eventually lead to the portable Internet terminals that are now beginning to appear built in to mobile telephones.

The French Connection

The year before Bob Kahn had his triumph in Washington, the French Délégation à l'Informatique hired Louis Pouzin to build a network *à la française*. French individuality is legendary, and as Pouzin explains, 'At the time, the French government was very much involved with developing French computer science. They had heard of the ARPANET and they were a little anxious to do something similar, not to get left too far behind.' Unlike Britain, there was no way the French were simply going to buy into American technology without at least trying to do it their own way. Gallic pride demanded nothing less. When French computer company Bull passed into American hands in the early 1960s, the government launched the 'Plan Calcul', setting up the Institut de Recherche en Informatique et en Automatique (IRIA) and a state-owned computer company called Compagnie Internationale pour l'Informatique (CII). The Délégation à l'Informatique was itself a product of the Plan Calcul.

The task Pouzin was handed was to link the databases in each department of the French administration. 'Databases were fashionable at the time,' he explains. 'All the French administrations created databases in a very technocratic spirit—that is to say, "We'll make databases but we don't really know how we are going to use them."' Each department guarded its information jealously and the idea of a network was regarded with horror, but the Délégation à l'Informatique, which answered directly to the Prime Minister, had the clout to enforce its will. 'There was a second political goal behind the plan,' explains Pouzin: 'to create a tool that would allow our administrations to exchange data.' And Pouzin was the enforcer.

Pouzin had worked for the French meteorological service developing communications systems. He had been at the Edinburgh conference in 1968, so he knew the major players in the emerging networking field and what they were doing. His approach was ambitious: 'We were only second so we wanted to be best,' he explains with disarming Gallic charm, and his starting point was to visit a number of ARPANET sites as a sort of self-declared spy. He wanted to learn what the ARPANET's weak points were so that his network, which he called 'Cyclades' after the Greek archipelago, could go one better. 'One weak point was the hardware: they had used special cards. A second weak point was the packet switching, which was too tied to the hardware; the addresses were physical addresses, for example. The third weak point was the inefficiency of the host-to-host protocol.' Although he had identified three weaknesses, they all boiled down to much the same thing. Pouzin thought that the ARPANET designers had placed too much faith in their hardware.

The basic difference between hardware and software approaches is speed versus ease of operation. Having something like an address hard-wired in is quicker than having to look it up in the computer's memory, but on the other hand having it in memory means that if you ever want to change it, it is easier to do. Imagine the problems British Telecom would have had if they had had to go round and rewire everyone's telephone to add a '1' to the front of every dialling code. Pouzin was convinced that the greater flexibility of a software-oriented approach would more than compensate for any slight reduction in speed that might result.

The fact that the ARPANET was hardware based was as much due to an accident of history as to design. ARPA had started by designing the sub-net, the network that would allow the IMPs to talk to each other, and only later worried about how the host computers would actually use the network. Pouzin, with the benefit of ARPA's experience, could do things the other way round. He thought about how he would like his hosts to talk to each other, and then designed the sub-net to fit in.

The result was that Cyclades put far less reliance on hardware. Addresses were 'virtual' rather than 'physical', which meant that instead of rewiring a routing computer every time you wanted to change its address, all you would have to do would be to type a few lines at the keyboard. Pouzin also used software to correct what he considered the weakness of the ARPANET's host-to-host protocol. The ARPANET was a bit like the old message-switching systems in that once a packet was injected into the sub-net, it was assumed that it would reach its destination in sequence. Complete faith was put in the IMPs to achieve that. Pouzin's team, on the other hand, designed protocols that transferred that responsibility to the host computers, leaving them to check whether all packets reached their destination and resend them if they didn't. In Pouzin's approach, the network was considered to be fallible and the host software kept an eye on it.

The Cyclades sub-net was based on Mitra 15 computers made by CII, so Pouzin originally called it 'Mitranet'. 'But there were politicians in France who found that "net" was not French,' explains Pouzin, 'so we changed the name to Cigale', French for cicada. For demonstration purposes, the Cyclades team had wired up a speaker to each Mitra 15 so that, as Pouzin explains, 'each time a packet passed it went to a loudspeaker, so you heard the packets pass, it went "chirp chirp chirp" like cicadas'. What could be more obvious?

Like the ARPA people, Pouzin realized that it would be impossible to build a network without the help of the academic community. So, like the ARPANET, Cyclades' first nodes were in universities. At its height, the network grew to some twenty hosts including the government departments it was designed to connect, academic institutions, industry, and even the computer centre of the European Space Agency in Rome.

But in France as elsewhere political winds change, and in 1974 Gaullism gave way to Giscardism. 'When Pompidou died, Giscard [d'Estaing] became President and most of the people who had administrative power were changed,' explains Pouzin. The hands-on approach of Gaullism gave way to the politics of laissez-faire with disastrous consequences for Cyclades. It became the political fashion to treat computing as an industry like any other, with the government's role limited to working towards standardization through the appropriate international organizations. It had always been the government's intention that French industry should pick up the reins as soon as the technology was ripe, but when government support was cut, industry wasn't interested, and Cyclades gradually crumbled as voluntary maintenance efforts ran out. By 1979, the network was defunct, but its legacy lives on in the Internet.

The Internauts

Despite its international dimension, the networking community was still small in the 1970s. Everybody knew what everybody else was up to. They all attended each other's meetings and it was a time of great cross-fertilization of ideas. After leading the ARPANET demonstration in 1972, Bob Kahn moved to DARPA and initiated projects in packet radio and packet satellite networks: the ARPANET without wires. The ALOHANET was up and running but packet broadcasting wasn't exactly what Kahn had in mind. 'ALOHA was a centralized system,' he

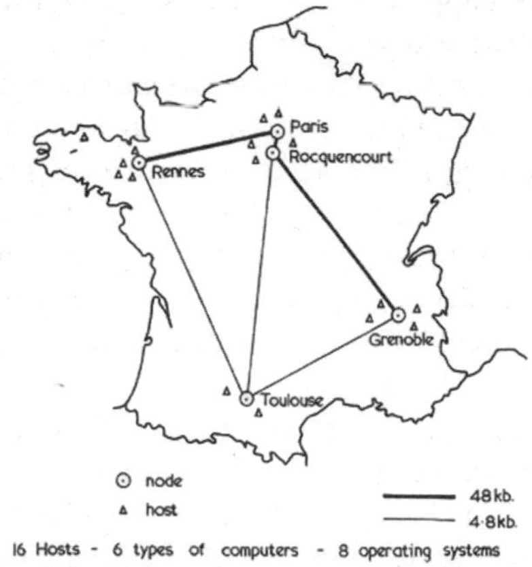

Figure 8: In 1973 the Cyclades network linked sixteen host computers across France. (From Proceedings of the NATO Advanced Study Institute on Computer Communication Networks, September 1973.)

explains. 'That is, packets were sent from a user's location to the central computer location on one frequency and answers were sent back on another. So ALOHA was a one-hop system. Packet radio turned the ALOHA idea into a network concept by essentially finding ways to route packets from node to node, to allow nodes to be in motion relative to each other, to deal with the vagaries of an environment where you didn't have a tall central antenna that everybody could see, where people could be in tunnels part of the time, and all the vagaries of trying to build a net like that.'

Kahn realized that such a wireless computer network wouldn't work using NCP as a host-to-host protocol because that assumed the underlying network would take care of keeping packets in sequence. This was not necessarily the case for radio transmission, where packets might easily get lost and have to be retransmitted. Kahn gave a contract to Vint Cerf at Stanford to work out how to send data on packet radio networks and how to get those networks to talk to the ARPANET. The concept of internetworking was born.

Around this time, the idea of Local Area Networks began to take off. The NPL network, although built along the lines of a Wide Area Network like the ARPANET, had become an indispensable part of the NPL landscape, proving the worth of networking on a small scale. Then in 1975, Cambridge computer pioneer Maurice Wilkes, who had ushered in the modern computer age in 1949 when he built the EDSAC, the world's first practical stored-program computer, came up with a LAN design called the Cambridge Ring that rapidly took off in European academic institutions. Cambridge Rings dominated the LAN market in Europe for several years, but the LAN that finally came to dominate was made in the USA.

In 1970, Bob Taylor moved to Xerox's new Palo Alto Research Center (PARC) taking with him the same approach to research he had used to great effect at ARPA. 'His job was to create an environment at Xerox PARC, particularly the computer science lab, where you could do great work, and he was really great at that,' remembers Bob Metcalfe, an early recruit. The result was an ideal environment for research in which Metcalfe invented a LAN technology called Ethernet. Metcalfe had come from Boston where he had put MIT on the ARPANET and been turned down for a Ph.D. by Harvard who found his ARPANET work to be insufficiently theoretical. Although Taylor had offered Metcalfe a job as a Ph.D. graduate, he told him to come anyway, and promptly sent him off to Hawaii to work with Norm Abramson for a month. That experience gave Metcalfe the input he needed to turn his dissertation into one that Harvard would accept, as well as being the inspiration for Ethernet. He took the idea of random access and retransmission from ALOHANET and decided to improve on it. Before he hit on the name Ethernet, his new network even went under the label of the Alto Aloha Network. Its job was to link some new small computers called Altos that Xerox was developing. Altos were small enough to fit on a desk and they were in the vanguard of the personal computer explosion. Linking them with a scaled-down ARPANET would be prohibitively expensive for a small local network, but Metcalfe recognized that the ALOHA approach provided an affordable alternative. Ethernet was like packet broadcasting, but it differed in two important ways from the ALOHANET. It ran along cables and it wasn't asymmetric; each Alto computer was treated equally by the network. Ethernet was a great success and eventually became the ubiquitous local networking standard. The spread of LANs that it helped to spark was another reason that internetworking was needed.

In June 1973, Cerf, Kahn, and Metcalfe started to work on the design of a host-to-host protocol for internetworking. They called it Transfer Control Protocol (TCP), and they were helped by a fourth person: Gérard Le Lann, who had worked with Louis Pouzin on Cyclades and was taking a sabbatical at Stanford. Le Lann's experience with Cyclades proved decisive. 'Gérard came to Stanford for a sabbatical during the period of critical design of the TCP protocol,' says Cerf, going on to recall that 'some of Pouzin's datagram ideas and sliding window ideas ended up in TCP'. 'Datagrams' extended the notion of the packet. Instead of leaving the underlying network, IMPs in the case of the ARPANET, to arrange packets into a sequential stream like carriages on a train, each datagram would be delivered independently, with the host-to-host protocol being responsible for assembling them when they arrived. 'Sliding windows' speeded things up. Instead of waiting for each packet to be acknowledged before sending the next, a protocol using sliding windows does not pause until several packets are pending acknowledgement. The number of packets sent before pausing for acknowledgement is called the window. The adoption of these Cyclades features into TCP meant that, just as Cyclades had taken inspiration from the original ARPANET, so the fledgling Internet built on the success of Cyclades. A robust host-to-host protocol, TCP, was one ingredient of the new networking ideas; gateways would be the other. Gateways are the Internet's interpreters. They are routing computers like IMPs whose job is to link networks together, translating packet formats from one network's protocol language to another.

In September 1973, the NATO Advanced Study Institute on Computer

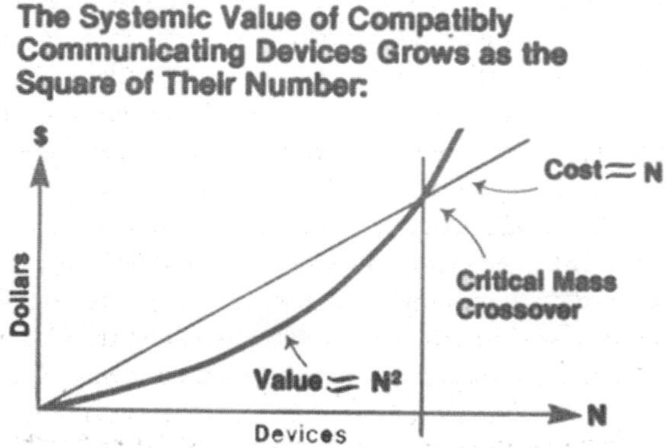

Figure 9: One reason that Ethernet became so successful is that Bob Metcalfe insisted on having it recognized as a standard before allowing companies to produce their own implementations. Xerox PARC took out patents, and once the Ethernet standard was established, licensed it for a nominal sum. This graph, which has since become known as 'Metcalfe's law', helped to convince Xerox that such an approach was in their interest. It shows that after a certain point, the value you get from connecting computers and devices outstrips the cost. Since Xerox was in the business of selling printers, they needed a way to connect those printers to computers. Metcalfe convinced them that standardizing and then freeing up Ethernet was the way to go. (Courtesy of Bob Metcalfe.)

Communication Networks was held at Sussex University in Brighton, England. It was a notable event because Vint Cerf and Bob Kahn had chosen the occasion to introduce TCP to the world. The first version of TCP seriously underestimated the way networks were going to take off. At its core was an Internet address using thirty-two bits, eight of which specified the network. This meant that TCP could handle a maximum of just 256 networks. At that time, no one had foreseen the switch from a world with a small number of big computers to one with a big number of small ones all grouped together in local area networks. By the late nineties, the number of individual networks connected to the Internet exceeded 100 000.

One IX instead of many

After Brighton, Cerf and Kahn set about getting the new protocol adopted. With Cerf still at Stanford, Kahn at DARPA, and Bob Taylor at Xerox PARC, they were well placed to do so. From Pouzin's French perspective, it seemed that Kahn 'massively financed all the local network companies to put TCP in their routers'. TCP versions soon appeared for a wide range of computers, but it wasn't only through TCP that DARPA planned to put its vision of future computing into practice. It had already been realized that standardizing every ARPANET host on a single kind of computer wasn't practical or even desirable; but perhaps developing a standard operating system that would run on all kinds of computers would help to streamline the ARPANET. Similar reasoning had already led to the internetworking project itself.

In the late 1960s, a new operating system that was soon to take the academic world by storm had come out of AT&T's Bell Labs. Called Unix, its name was a weak pun on the Multics system that had inspired it: where Multics was designed for many users, Unix was designed for just one, a single 'IX' instead of multiple ones. Unix became legendary for its quirkily named commands. To notify someone of incoming e-mail, for example, you typed 'biff' because, as the folklore would have it, that was the name of Berkeley graduate student Heidi Stetner's dog and Biff had a reputation for barking at postmen: logical enough, but you had to know. There was more to Unix, however, than a geeky sense of humour. It was part of an important shift in computer thinking. Hardware had become so compact and affordable that time-sharing was no longer such a pressing need. It was becoming possible for everyone really to have a personal computer all to themselves. AT&T had a fairly open policy towards Unix, so when in 1974 Bob Fabry from the University of California at Berkeley asked if he could have a copy to work on, they were only too happy to oblige.

The following year, a new graduate student, Bill Joy, arrived at Berkeley and was soon taking an interest in Unix. In 1977, Joy responded to requests for copies of some of the code Berkeley had been working on by putting together the Berkeley Software Distribution (BSD). Little did he know that he was setting the scene for much of the recent furore about shared software. BSD was absolutely free to anyone who asked for it, and as a consequence it rapidly spread. Feedback from users was quickly incorporated and the system went from strength to strength. The first BSD was followed in 1978 by a second release, 2BSD. By this time, Unix had come to the attention of DARPA as the most likely candidate for their standard operating system and they were looking for someone to develop it the way they wanted. Bob Fabry put in a proposal to DARPA in autumn 1979, and when Bill Joy organized the successful release of 3BSD in December, Berkeley clinched the deal.

Fabry quickly negotiated terms with AT&T for use of their system, and Joy was put in charge of the DARPA project. In October 1980, 4BSD was released and further upgraded to 4.1BSD the following June. DARPA was sufficiently happy with the results to renew Berkeley's contract, and this time they had a request that was to change the face of networking. In 1978, TCP had become TCP/IP, two protocols instead of one. IP stood for Internet Protocol and it had the job of routing packets around. TCP handled things like reassembling them and checking that they had all arrived. DARPA's request was to build TCP/IP into BSD Unix. Working with his colleague Sam Leffler, Bill Joy started the job, but soon after announced that he was leaving Berkeley. Leffler was left to see the release of 4.2BSD through to a successful conclusion in August 1983, complete with TCP/IP built in. Joy meanwhile had teamed up with an entrepreneurial group from the Stanford Business School to set up a company called Sun Microsystems, 'Sun' being derived from Stanford University Network. Soon they were shipping out computers running the 4.2BSD Unix operating system complete with TCP/IP and ready to join the Internet.

The end of the ARPANET

As the seventies passed their halfway point, the network snowball really picked up momentum. In 1975, DARPA declared that the ARPANET could no longer be considered a research project and handed over responsibility to the Defense Communications Agency. The Xerox Internet started the same year using the home-grown XNS protocols;

Bob Metcalfe had left Vint Cerf to his own devices and managed to be the first to have an Internet up and running. The DARPA-sponsored experimental Internet started in 1977, when the number of hosts passed the 100 mark, and right from the start TCP was made freely available. Xerox, on the other hand, kept XNS under wraps, leaving Vint Cerf to wonder, 'If they hadn't kept it secret, we might all be using XNS instead of TCP.'

By the end of 1982, the experimental Internet had done its job, and the Internet bandwagon was ready to roll. The ARPANET prepared for a 'Big Bang' change to TCP/IP on 1 January 1983, and although the ARPNET wasn't officially decommissioned for another seven years, that was the day the Internet as we now know it came into existence. Along with the change to TCP/IP, the ARPANET was split in two. The civilian half took the name ARPA Internet, and the military part went under the name MILNET.

It was already clear that Vint Cerf's and Bob Kahn's initial estimate for the number of hosts and networks was not going to be enough. In 1983, Paul Mockapetris issued RFCs 882 and 883 setting out a detailed proposal for a hierarchical Domain Name System (DNS). Instead of each host on the network having a single name, like Smith, they would have a full address along the lines of Smith.Acacia-Drive.Canterbury.Kent.UK. That way there could be as many Smiths in Canterbury as there were roads, as many Acacia Drives in Kent as there were towns,

```
                              |
       +----------------------+----------------------+
       |                      |                      |
     COLORS                FLAVORS                 TRUTH
       |                      |
 +-----+-----+                |
 |     |     |             NATURAL
RED  BLUE  GREEN              |
                              |
          +-------------------+-------------------+
          |                   |                   |
      CHOCOLATE            VANILLA           STRAWBERRY
```

Figure 10: Paul Mockapetris's illustration of the hierarchical domain name system he proposed in 1983. (From P. Mockapetris, RFC 882.)

and so on. Mockapetris described his domains as a tree structure, giving the example set out in Figure 10 in RFC 882.

As Mockapetris explains, this system came with its own built-in administrative structure. 'If we wished to add a new domain of ARTIFICIAL under FLAVORS, FLAVORS would typically be the administrative entity that would decide; if we wished to create CHIP and MOCHA names under CHOCOLATE, CHOCOLATE.NATURAL.FLAVORS would typically be the appropriate administrative entity.' DNS made the amount of information that any one router had to know about more manageable. The idea was just like the way the postal service works. If Smith's friend Jones dropped a postcard into a letterbox in California, the only part of the address the US Postal Service would care about is the top domain, UK. Once the card arrived in the UK, the first sorting office would then just care about the next domain down, and send it to Kent, and so on until the final router, a Canterbury postman, would pop the card through the letterbox in Acacia Drive. He would know the roads of Canterbury like the back of his hand, but there would be no reason for him to know anything about the higher domains in the address, or even where they were.

Along with Craig Partridge of BBN and Jon Postel, Mockapetris worked out the details of the Domain Name System, and in 1985, as the number of hosts approached the 2 000 mark, DARPA persuaded the Internet community to adopt it. Postel added DNS administration to his role as Internet archivist, roles that he continued to play selflessly until his death in 1998. His meticulous archiving of RFCs and administration of domain names played a vital role in bringing the Internet to maturity. The logical, straightforward, DNS way of addressing was one of the things that later fed into the World Wide Web. 'Jon has been our North Star for decades, burning brightly and constantly, providing comfort and a sense of security while all else changed,' says Vint Cerf. At the time of his death, Postel was in the process of setting up a not-for-profit international body to take over the jobs he had done voluntarily from the earliest days of the Internet.

By 1990, the year the ARPA Internet was decommissioned, the Internet had some 2 000 networks. Six years later, that number had grown to 94 000. Over the same time scale, the number of hosts rose from three million to nearly thirteen million. By the time the ARPANET was switched off on 28 February 1990, it wasn't just a network; it had become a part of those who had made it happen. On the ARPANET's twentieth anniversary, when the end was already in sight, Leonard Kleinrock organized a symposium, which he called 'Act One', at UCLA to look back over the project. 'There was a lot of poetry at Act One,' he remembers. There was also a lot to follow. One lyric contribution came from Vint Cerf who was moved to write an epic twenty-seven verse 'Requiem for the ARPANET' that closed with the words:

> And so, at last, we knew its course had run,
> Our faithful servant, ARPANET, was done.
> It was the first, and being first, was best,
> But now we lay it down to ever rest.
>
> Now pause with me a moment, shed some tears.
> For auld lang syne, for love, for years and years
> Of faithful service, duty done, I weep.
> Lay down thy packet, now, O friend, and sleep.

The story of the Internet's pioneers had been one of incredible creativity, international collaboration, and above all a shared vision and conviction that they were building something that would change the world. It might have happened in England: 'They had the ideas, but they did not have the money,' explains Larry Roberts. It might have happened in France, but the political winds of change cut Louis Pouzin's Cyclades down before it had a chance to flourish. So it was left to ARPA, with its unique free and open system of funding, finding the best people and letting them get on with it, to bring computer networking to the world. And to one man's vision in particular. 'I think the most significant advances in computer technology, especially in the systems part of computer science over the years—including the work that my group did at Xerox PARC where we built the first distributed personal computer system—were simply extrapolations of Licklider's vision. They were not really new visions of their own. So he's really the father of it all', says Bob Taylor. The World Wide Web would simply be the icing on the cake.

Setting the Scene at CERN 2

In a Europe still licking its wounds in the aftermath of the Second World War, one man had a vision to create a world-leading scientific research laboratory. His name was Louis de Broglie, a French aristocrat and one of the last of a dying breed of gentleman scientists. De Broglie belonged to a golden era of scientific discovery that straddled the late nineteenth and early twentieth centuries. He was awarded the Nobel Prize in 1929 for his contribution to the revolution that threw out the comfortable mechanistic world ushered in by Newton two centuries before and replaced it with an unpredictable and ghostly quantum wonderland where an ability to believe seven impossible things before breakfast was an essential prerequisite for success. As one of de Broglie's contemporaries, the Danish physicist Niels Bohr, once famously quipped, 'Anyone who is not shocked by quantum theory has not understood it.' Nevertheless, despite its improbability, the physics of quantum mechanics has survived the test of time and lies behind a whole host of modern devices. Without quantum mechanics, there would be no transistors. Without transistors, radio sets would be the size of sewing machines and computers the size of houses. Personal computing as we know it simply wouldn't exist, and nor would the World Wide Web. Without de Broglie and his contemporaries,Tim Berners-Lee's ideas for the World Wide Web would have had nowhere to grow.

By 1949, Louis de Broglie was 57 years old. His scientific achievements had established him at the forefront of European science and his opinions carried considerable weight. The war had started an exodus of young scientific talent from Europe to the United States and de Broglie wanted to stem the tide. At the European Cultural Conference in Lausanne he pinned his colours to the mast. Unable to attend the conference himself, it was Raoul Dautry, former government minister and Administrator-General of the French Commissariat à l'Énergie Atomique who delivered de Broglie's message. 'At the very time when the talk is of uniting the peoples of Europe, our attention has turned to the question of developing this new international unit, a laboratory or institution where it would be possible to carry out scientific work above and beyond the framework of the various nations taking part,' Dautry read out. He underlined de Broglie's ideal with words of his own, concluding that 'what each European nation is unable to do alone, a united Europe can do and, I have no doubt, would do brilliantly'.

Science brings nations together

Energetic scientists from all over Europe took up the call and they were joined by the American Nobel Prizewinner Isidor Rabi. Rabi had recently helped to establish the Brookhaven Laboratory on Long Island, New York and he saw a link between de Broglie's idea and the new American laboratory. Brookhaven was set up as a sort of club whose members were universities; they paid a subscription and in exchange their scientists had access to the laboratory's facilities. Rabi's suggestion was that the new European laboratory should be run in the same way but instead of universities, its members would be countries.

By 1952, the Conseil Européen pour la Recherche Nucléaire, CERN, had been established. Two years later, representatives of twelve European nations signed the treaty that formally brought the organization into existence. Geneva, a city at the heart of Europe with a cosmopolitan heritage, was chosen to be the new laboratory's home, and a precedent for Europe-wide cooperation was set.

Louis de Broglie went on to live to 95 and so had the pleasure of watching his idea mature into a very successful reality. By 1999, CERN's membership had swelled to twenty countries. Scientists from all over the world participate in the laboratory's programmes and as well as the European full members of the CERN club, a kind of associate membership has been created for countries beyond the European region. Israel, Japan, the Russian federation, Turkey and the United States enjoy this status and their researchers play a full role in the CERN scientific programme. Although retaining the acronym CERN, in 1991 the laboratory adopted the subtitle 'European Laboratory for Particle Physics', to reflect the changing nature of its research.

CERN's mission is and always has been research for the sake of curiosity. The scientists who work there are motivated by the same questions that led Leucippus of Miletus to postulate the existence of atoms in fifth-century BC Athens, and Copernicus to propose the heretical notion that the Earth wasn't the centre of all things. Scientists working at CERN want to know what the universe is made of, what holds it together, and why it behaves as it does. The basic technique of particle physics is to take tiny sub-atomic particles, the building blocks of matter, and smash them together at very high energy. By analysing such collisions, physicists painstakingly piece together the laws of nature. Curiosity is the reason for CERN's existence and knowledge is its principle product. Nevertheless, the technologies that the laboratory's physicists demand have generated many spin-offs of which the World Wide Web is just one. Modern medical imaging owes much to CERN; computer chip manufacture, contraband detection, and even the techniques used to paint soft-drink cans have their origins in particle physics research.

As the 1970s drew to a close, CERN was in bullish mood. The end of the century was approaching, scientists dreamed of another golden era, and CERN was the place they planned to make it happen. The laboratory was already one of the world's leading fundamental physics research laboratories and ambitious plans were on the table to make it even better. Thanks to the genius of retiring Dutch physicist Simon van der Meer and the powerful leadership of the fiery Italian Carlo Rubbia, CERN took the decision in 1978 to build an antimatter factory. This would allow physicists to collide matter and antimatter, in the form of protons and antiprotons, head-on, creating tiny fireballs of pure energy. The stakes were high. An idea expounded by the Americans Sheldon Glashow and Stephen Weinberg along with Pakistan's most prominent physicist Abdus Salam had just brought physicists a step closer to their Holy Grail: the unification of all the forces of nature in a single theory. According to their idea, electromagnetism, the force that carries light and energy to us from the sun, and the weak force responsible for radioactivity were one and the same. The goal of CERN's antimatter project was to put this notion to the test.

Modification of CERN's particle accelerators began straight away and the laboratory's flagship Super Proton Synchrotron (SPS) accelerator became the machine in which protons and antiprotons would collide. Meanwhile two collaborations of physicists, larger in number than the world had ever seen, came together to build the massive particle detectors that would record the results of these proton-antiproton collisions. The largest, called UA1 and headed by Rubbia, involved at its peak 224 scientists from twenty-three institutes. UA2 was not much smaller. Although particle physics has always been a global venture, and the pursuit of knowledge for its own sake does not recognize geographical boundaries, the sheer scale of these experiments had never before been seen. It was a foretaste of things to come.

At about the same time as the antimatter project got the go-ahead, the European physics community began to think about the long-term future of research at CERN. The laboratory's Director-General at the time was the brilliant self-taught British engineer, John Adams. Under his leadership, a new particle accelerator was proposed. Like the SPS, this new machine would collide matter and antimatter, but instead of protons and antiprotons, it would collide the much lighter electrons and their antimatter equivalents, positrons. The new machine was named LEP, the Large Electron–Positron collider. The small size of electrons and positrons was to be LEP's big advantage over the SPS. Electrons and positrons are as far as we know fundamental particles: there is nothing smaller inside them. As a consequence, when they collide their entire mass (m) is converted to energy (E) according to Einstein's famous prescription, $E = mc^2$, and new particles are created from the energy they release. Studying these particles allows physicists to probe the forces that hold matter together.

Because of the fundamental nature of electrons and positrons, the collisions are clean: there is no other debris to confuse the picture. Protons and antiprotons, on the other hand, are made up of smaller particles called quarks. When a proton and an antiproton collide, a quark from the proton collides with an antiquark from the antiproton producing the new particles that physicists want to study. But the picture is muddied by myriad other particles that also emerge from the debris of the proton and antiproton. With the SPS collider project scheduled to take CERN research into the mid-1980s, colliding electrons and positrons presented the obvious way forward for CERN's long-term future.

Although the advantage of electrons and positrons was clear, there was also a major hurdle to be overcome. LEP was designed as a circular machine, so that bunches of electrons and positrons could be made to circulate in opposite directions and meet at well-defined places around the ring. These bunches would be a few centimetres long and fractions of a millimetre broad and high. They would contain millions of particles, but electrons and positrons are so small that if they were blown up to the size of grains of wheat, nearest neighbours in LEP's bunches would be as far apart as London and Paris. That meant that bunches would be able to stay in the machine for hours since, despite the vast number of particles in the bunches, collisions would still be quite rare. The hurdle with LEP arose because when fast-moving electrons and positrons are bent around corners they lose energy by throwing out x-rays. So LEP had to be built as big as possible to make the corners as gentle as possible. Its circumference was set at 27 kilometres, making it the biggest machine of any kind ever built.

Along with LEP's size came more complexity, more cooperation between CERN and industry, and collaborations that would dwarf even those of UA1 and UA2. Several proposals for experiments at LEP were made and four were finally chosen. The smallest involved some 300 scientists, the largest over 700, from places as far flung as Oxford and Tokyo.

For such large collaborations to work effectively together in building their detectors, writing computer simulations, and eventually analysing the data they would collect, new ways of communicating were needed. The plan was for LEP to begin operation in the second half of the 1980s, so solutions were needed fast. Several groups started working straight away to examine the possibilities for computer networking at CERN and its collaborating institutions around the world.

The Internet comes to Europe

NORSAR

Whilst Larry Roberts was laying the foundations for the ARPANET, another division of the Advanced Research Projects Agency was setting wheels in motion that would eventually see the ARPANET jump the Atlantic to sites in London and Oslo. The Nuclear Monitoring Research Office had the job of setting up a series of seismic monitoring stations that would circle the Soviet Union, allowing the USA to detect any underground nuclear tests on Soviet soil. This was another strand in ARPA's remit never again to allow America to be caught off guard. Three seismic monitoring stations were established: one in Alaska, one in Montana, and a third, the Norwegian Seismic Array (NORSAR) based at Kjeller near Oslo. NORSAR was established in 1968 when a government-to-government agreement was signed between the USA and Norway. In those days, international communications were primitive by today's standards, and a direct satellite link between NORSAR and the USA was not possible. Peter Kirstein, a young computer scientist recently arrived at London's University College (UCL) with an impressive track record including a degree from Cambridge, a Ph.D. from Stanford, and a stint at CERN, remembers, 'the only satellite earth stations were in Britain and one or two others, but there were certainly none in Scandinavia. So it was going to Britain by satellite and then by undersea cable to Norway.'

The fact that the NORSAR link passed within a few miles of Donald Davies and his pioneering packet-switching network at the NPL was not lost on Larry Roberts, who proposed that the link be broken in the UK, and ARPANET nodes be established at the NPL and Kjeller. Politics, however, came close to scuppering the project. In Britain at the beginning of the 1970s, Euroscepticism was a long way off, and a highly Europhilic Heath administration was preparing to lead the country into the Common Market. Any hint of a special relationship between the UK and the USA was to be avoided, and a UK national laboratory putting transatlantic links first was simply out of the question. Luckily, however, Peter Kirstein was ideally placed to step in and save the day. As a university academic, government policy didn't weigh as heavily on him as it did on Donald Davies. 'Donald and Larry agreed that it should be UCL instead. So that's why an ARPANET node came to UCL and an ARPANET node came to Kjeller,' he explains.

But getting the UK node installed wasn't easy. Agreement was one thing; actually paying for the project turned out to be quite another. Larry Roberts agreed to provide a Terminal IMP (TIP) and cover the cost of the transatlantic link if Kirstein could provide the resources to break the NORSAR link in London and also connect the UK's biggest computer, an IBM 360/195 housed at the Rutherford Laboratory in rural Oxfordshire, to the ARPANET. To Kirstein this looked like an offer too good to refuse, and by 1971 he had presented a technical proposal to British universities, the Department of Industry (DoI), and the Science Research Council (SRC). The TIP alone was worth some £50 000, and the Americans had also agreed to cover the cost of the transatlantic link. 'Looking back,' says Kirstein, 'we would expect that all the British authorities must have welcomed this unique opportunity.' But that turned out not to be the case. The SRC turned down the proposal as being too speculative and uncertain. The DoI wanted statements of interest from industry but the UK computer industry lacked the vision to back the project even to that extent. Kirstein remembers one representative of the UK's principal computer manufacturer announcing that 'one would gain more from a two-week visit to the US than from a physical link.' Universities were no more forthcoming. They didn't want to support a project that in their eyes would be entirely UCL's baby and hold nothing for them. So by 1972 things were looking bleak for a British extension of the ARPANET. To compound Kirstein's difficulties, a new Scandinavian satellite earth station at Tanum in Sweden had come on stream and there was no longer any need to bring the NORSAR link down to earth in Britain.

But then the Post Office stepped in to save the day. Two senior directors, Murray Laver and Alec Merriman, agreed to fund an ARPANET link from the UK to Norway for one year. On top of this, Donald Davies agreed to put up as much money as he had authority to sign for, £5 000, to support the project. With this scant support, Kirstein remembers, 'I told Larry Roberts that we would proceed.'

NORSAR became the first ARPANET site outside the USA in June 1973 and was due to be followed soon after by UCL, but Kirstein's worries were not yet over. Although Larry Roberts had covered the cost of the TIP, HM Customs and Excise still wanted their share. Peter Kirstein argued that since the TIP was an instrument on loan it should be duty-exempt. Import duty was duly waived, but the customs authorities at Heathrow still refused to release the TIP until value-added tax (VAT) payment had been guaranteed. So Kirstein signed over all he had in his budget as a guarantee subject to appeal, and the TIP was finally delivered. The UCL ARPANET node passed its first packets on schedule on 25 July 1973. The ARPANET had arrived in Europe, but Kirstein's battles with the customs authorities had only just begun.

It took a definite commitment from Hermann Bondi at the Ministry of Defence (MoD) to coax the reluctant British academic community on board the networking project. Born in Vienna, Bondi had come to England at an early age and after a Cambridge education gone on to a distinguished scientific career. One of his best-known hypotheses was the controversial steady-state theory of the universe developed with fellow-mavericks Fred Hoyle and Tommy Gold. According to this, the universe has always been there and always will be, in stark contrast to the more widely accepted Big Bang theory that has the universe appearing in a cataclysmic explosion some 15 billion years ago.

In 1974, Bondi was in the middle of his term as chief scientific advisor to the MoD and he strongly urged the ministry to support a project linking unclassified MoD sites to the ARPANET. In a move that would secure the development of the ARPANET in Britain, the MoD agreed to fund the project from 1974 to 1976. Soon after, the Science Research Council subscribed to the project, agreeing to support research into network protocols and satellite access. The British Library was also on board because it could access the US National Library of Medicine's MEDLINE service through the ARPANET. Even the once-sceptical DoI had connected its Cambridge Computer Aided Design Centre to the ARPANET through Kirstein's UCL node.

The Post Office was still a keen participant in the project, concentrating in particular on satellite access to the network. Two MoD sites were connected, Aldermaston, whose interest was seismic monitoring, and the Royal Signals and Radar Establishment in Malvern. The Queen officially inaugurated the latter in March 1976 when she sent an e-mail to all ARPANET users announcing 'the availability on ARPANET of the Coral 66 compiler provided by the GEC 4080 computer at the Royal Signals and Radar Establishment, Malvern, England'. The significance of Coral 66 or GEC's 4080 computer may not have been as great as Her Majesty might have wished, but hers, nevertheless, was the first official involvement of any head of state with computer networking, showing perhaps that in the mid-1970s, Buckingham Palace had more foresight than much of the UK's government and computer industry.

Despite the ARPANET's royal seal of approval, Peter Kirstein's appeal to HM Government for VAT exemption continued to drag on. Things came to a head in 1976, when the appeal was finally refused. Matters were further complicated by the fact that an IMP had been supplied to the Post Office's Goonhilly Downs earth station for satellite access to the network, and the equipment at UCL had been upgraded. Kirstein's guarantee would not be enough to pay the bill if push came to shove, and his only remaining option was an appeal to the highest levels of the Treasury. He chose to exploit the military angle. 'At this point,' he explains, 'I stated that I would export all this equipment, which belonged technically to the US Department of Defense, and re-import it under the Exchange of Forces Agreement Act.' The result was a landmark agreement that was to make UCL the focus of UK networking for many years to come. The Treasury said to Kirstein, 'the equipment that you have imported, and any future equipment brought in under the same agreement, would be free of duty and VAT.'

Over the next few years, the importance of computer networking became more and more apparent along with the success of the UCL ARPANET node. 'As usual, a successful activity had no shortage of parents,' says Kirstein ruefully. The DoI made considerable capital out of the connection of its CAD centre, and even the SRC, which by this time was funding the project, pointed to the link as evidence of its far-sighted funding policy. But Kirstein remained in control. 'Many times,' he recalls, 'different government bodies considered trying to take over the UCL operation but they were immediately discouraged by the magnitude of the VAT and duty bill that they would incur.' So, thanks to the Treasury's concession, the development of network protocols at UCL remained free from officialdom until well into the 1980s, when the ruling fell foul of European regulations and UCL's exemption had to be cancelled. 'But by that time,' Kirstein happily recalls, 'we no longer needed fresh imports; the concession had served its purpose.' In the end, Peter Kirstein had reason to be grateful for HM Customs and Excise's early intransigence.

The NPL reaches out

Although UCL played a vital role in bringing the ARPANET to Europe, Peter Kirstein was not the only one working on wide area networks in Britain. The Post Office had been slow to respond to Stanley Gill's rallying call, but in 1973 it announced its intention to build a nationwide Experimental Packet-Switched Service (EPSS). The starting date Gill's optimistic forecast had suggested for British exports of network hardware had already passed, and by the time EPSS came into service in 1977, his pessimistic date for US imports to begin was looming dangerously close. Nevertheless, EPSS was built around home-grown hardware and it gave Donald Davies his first opportunity to connect the NPL network to the outside world. He needed a gateway computer to do so because the Post Office was too firmly rooted in circuit-switching methodology to adopt the kind of protocols in use at the NPL. It insisted on setting up 'virtual circuits' rather than using the 'each-packet-to-itself' datagram approach incorporated in the NPL network. The first step on the way to the EPSS was a testbed link set up in 1974 between the NPL and the same Computer Aided Design Centre that Peter Kirstein had already connected to the ARPANET, so despite the fact that the political winds were blowing towards Europe, the NPL had its route to the ARPANET after all.

With the Post Office finally declaring an active interest in networking, the government deemed the emerging technology worthy of a new committee. Secretary of State for Industry Eric Varley set up the National Committee on Computer Networks, whose members were representatives of industry, academia, the Post Office, and the Post Office Engineering Union. Donald Davies was on the committee, which was chaired by Jack Howlett, who had been director of the Atlas Computer Laboratory since 1961. At the time, the Post Office still enjoyed the powers granted by the Post Office Act of 1969, which gave it a monopoly for communication 'between persons and persons, things and things, or persons and things.' Since computers were clearly things, the Act covered any kind of networking activity, and Post Office cooperation with the committee's conclusions would be important. The committee nevertheless proposed sweeping changes to the Post Office's monopoly and concluded that 'the need for a Public Switched Data-transmission Service in the UK, with international connections, is seen as important and urgent'. It admired overseas efforts, particularly Transpac, a new national network that the French PTT (Post, Telephone, and Telegraph) was happy to run at a loss to encourage use.

When the Committee's report was published in October 1978, complete with its free-market recommendations, its main dissenter was surprisingly not the Post Office but the Post Office Engineering Union. The union's representative, B. Stanley, did not agree with proposals to create a free market in supply of telecommunications equipment, such as modems, attached to the Post Office's lines. Nor did he agree that it should be possible to link private networks to the public Post Office network, or that such private networks should be able to carry information in competition with the Post Office's own services. In line with the times, however, Stanley's opinion was brushed aside by the government when British Telecom was privatized three years later and the telecommunications market was opened up to competition.

The reason for the Post Office's complicity with the report may simply be that at the time they just didn't believe that data communication would ever be more than a marginal telecommunications activity. The Post Office representative's only disagreement with the Committee's findings concerned the rate of growth foreseen for the Post Office's planned Packet-Switched Service announced to take over from the EPSS. The committee thought that the Post Office's estimate was too low. The Committee welcomed the announcement of the PSS, but in an echo of Stanley Gill's pessimistic scenario for networking in the UK, 'regretted that, as yet, there has been no formal commitment to the provision of this service'.

When EPSS was wound up a few years later, it hadn't been a great success. 'They set the tariffs wrongly', explains Donald Davies. 'Their object was to make it pay right from the start.' Nevertheless, the Post Office deserves some credit just for trying. Back then, data communication was just a tiny fraction of telecommunications traffic and few had foreseen the huge explosion in network use that was to come. The Post Office had been one of the first established telecommunications operators to offer packet switching as a service. Soon after, however, Stanley Gill's pessimistic prophecy was fulfilled when the Post Office launched a full-scale Packet-Switched Service in 1981 using technology licensed from American telecommunications giant GTE.

The European Informatics Network

The NPL's second chance to link to the outside world came from the European Economic Community, which in 1968 had set up a framework for international collaboration called COST (Coopération Européenne dans le Domaine de la Recherche Scientifique et Technique). This was before Britain was a member of the Community, but happily for the NPL, COST membership was open to other European countries. Just before Christmas in 1970, Donald Davies popped in to Derek Barber's office and said, 'Derek, there's a meeting in Brussels and they want a technical advisor for the UK delegation. Could you get to it?' A few days later Barber walked through the doors of a meeting room in Brussels, looked around, and said 'Where's the UK delegation?' It turned out that he was it. The upshot of the meeting was that COST Project 11, to build a European Informatics Network (EIN), was established with Derek Barber as its chairman.

The following year, an agreement was reached to set up the EIN, and in June 1972 Barber held a preliminary meeting at the NPL to hammer out the technical details. Delegates came from all over Europe, and Barber arranged a gala evening including a military band concert with fireworks. 'Much to my horror,' he recalls, 'they played the 1812 overture, but the French delegate took it very well.' Ratification of the EIN agreement was to take another year as rubber stamps from participating nations were collected, but everyone knew it was only a matter of time and they could get on with the business of building the network.

The EIN was never intended to be permanent. Barber's brief was to build a network as a model for future networks, commercial or not, and this turned out to be the root of a number of early problems. Barber's meetings were attended by champions of the datagram school of thought as well as by representatives of the national telephone companies, or PTTs, who preferred the virtual circuit way of doing things. This made it pretty hard to agree on anything. For example, if the datagram camp said, 'Let's have dual connectivity from the host machine to the network for reliability,' that was immediately incompatible with the virtual circuit approach because you might not know which of the two available paths a given packet had taken. 'In the end the only way I could actually get agreement,' explains Barber, 'was to have two network designs in the one switch.' That meant that people could choose which one they wanted to use and it allowed Barber's group to get on with the serious business of drawing up a specification for the network. As work progressed, Barber remembers another diplomatic near-miss to equal the gala evening affair. Kurt Müller from Zurich was one of the Swiss delegates in Barber's team. 'At one of the first meetings he was late—didn't turn up for about an hour or more,' recalls Barber. 'I'd sent an NPL car to pick him up and eventually the phone rang and there he was still at the airport. It turned out that the NPL driver met the right flight, held up the sign saying Dr. Müller for the NPL. A chap came forward and said, "I'm Dr Müller." They got in the car and they drove off.' After a while the chap said to the NPL driver, 'This isn't the right way.' It turned out that he was on his way to Nestlé's Processing Laboratory.

Both Drs Müller eventually reached their respective NPLs and before long the EIN specification was ready. Calls to tender for the sub-net attracted over fifty replies from European companies and was won by a joint venture between Britain's Logica and the French company SESA. The node computers were the same as had been used in Cyclades, Mitra 15s made by CII, their choice seemingly bearing out Stanley Gill's notion that short-term investment would lead to long-term export opportunities. CII's ultimate fate, however, revealed that it takes more than just state investment to succeed in the computer world. In 1975, CII joined forces with Honeywell-Bull, bringing the company back into majority French ownership. This apparent success is tempered by the fact that CII had been selling its products at a loss, despite billions of francs of state investment, and the resulting company, again called Bull, is but a small player on the world stage. American success stories like DEC and Apple were launched for the equivalent of less than a single day's funding of the French Plan Calcul and that from private funds. The lesson to be learned is that state investment alone isn't the answer. France's Délégation à l'Informatique included not a single computer scientist, and was motivated by national pride rather than economic viability, noted a 1997 French government report. Partly because of this, 'the failure of CII was written in its genes,' one former director of Bull was moved to say. The American approach, on the other hand, most strongly expressed through ARPA, had been to support good ideas coming from the ground up rather than trying to impose something from the top down.

The EIN's participating institutes were the Politecnico di Milano in Italy, the Eidgenössische Technische Hochschule (ETH) in Zurich, the French Institut de Recherche en Informatique et en Automatique (IRIA), which was still funding Louis Pouzin's Cyclades network, the European Communities Joint Research Centre at Ispra in Italy, and the NPL. It was fitting that the first link be established between the two pioneers of European networking and so it was that in 1974 Cyclades was linked to the NPL network. The full EIN network followed on schedule the following year and was demonstrated shortly after. It was at this demonstration that Donald Davies's infinite queues came back to haunt him. 'We had great fun on the opening day,' he remembers. All the participating institutes had invited VIPs to a grand opening, but then something seemed to be going wrong. 'Just before it started we found masses of packets were being generated from somewhere, we didn't know where—they were trying to conceal the origin. We discovered it was somebody trying to saturate the whole network and sabotage the demonstration.' But all was not lost. As well as providing Derek Barber to head the project, the NPL also hosted the Network Control Centre that monitored network traffic. 'It was very fortunate that we had this control centre. Admittedly our first guess as to where the packets were coming from was wrong, but the second time we hit the spot and we could actually turn them off,' says Davies. After that, the demonstration went well, though with one fewer participant than foreseen. It turned out later that the offending institute, ETH, had been trying to make a point. Despite the fact that they had caused him some jitters, Davies had some sympathy with the would-be saboteurs: 'They had decided that there was something wrong with a network in which you could put in packets in an uncontrolled way and that eventually it could become saturated, which is true, of course.'

By the time the EIN shut down in 1980 it had more than fulfilled its role of setting a model for European networking. It had pulled together the fledgling data communications communities around the continent and it had been Europe's first successful internetworking project. The

Figure 11: The European Informatics Network. (From NATO Advanced Study Institute proceedings, 1973.)

EIN had even briefly stretched across the Atlantic to Toronto where it was used to display pages from the BBC's Ceefax service at the 1976 ICCC conference. 'Most of the time people were coming and trying to see the latest cricket results,' remembers Barber. But another piece of NPL software demonstrated in Toronto had a more profound influence. David Yates's 'Scrapbook' program allowed text and diagrams from a central file store at the NPL to be viewed and edited anywhere on the network; in practical terms that meant databases, word processing, and e-mail, things we now take for granted but were still startling in 1976. 'Scrapbook,' says Derek Barber, 'was way ahead of its time.' The EIN had done its bit to show the world what could be achieved by linking computers together.

Commercial interest

By the mid-1980s, just as the particle physics community at CERN was preparing for fundamental change, so was the world of computer networking. Industry had started to take the field seriously and networking products were available off the shelf. Not surprisingly, BBN had been among the first to exploit the new technology commercially, spinning off a subsidiary networking company, Telenet, as early as 1973. But even BBN took some cajoling. When Bob Kahn left the company to join DARPA in 1972, it was partly in frustration that BBN was holding back. 'One of my reasons for accepting the DARPA job was because it just didn't look like BBN was interested in capitalizing on any of the technology we had developed,' he explains. Soon after, BBN lost another employee, Lee Talbert, who left taking a handful of colleagues with him to found his own company, Packet Communications Incorporated. This proved to be the incentive BBN vice-president, Steve Levy, needed to act. 'Right after they left BBN, I recall Steve Levy coming into my office and basically saying that BBN had just revisited the whole networking situation and they thought my idea was now timely, and they were all ready to go make something happen,' says Kahn. 'Steve and I worked together to set up Telenet,' he continues, and they hired Larry Roberts from DARPA to run it. Telenet was taken over by GTE in 1979, marking the first tentative steps of a US telecom operator into the unfamiliar territory of packet switching. GTE turned out to be so happy with its purchase it later went on to buy BBN itself for $616 million in 1997.

Telenet was based on a set of protocols called Open Systems Interconnection (OSI), being defined by the Comité Consultatif International de Télégraphie et Téléphonie (CCITT) of the International Telecommunication Union (ITU), a body representing the world's telecommunications companies. CCITT has the task of setting the international standards that ensure that when you pick up a telephone in England and dial a number in Germany, a phone does indeed ring at the other end. It is not CCITT's responsibility, however, to ensure that the person who picks up the phone speaks the same language as you. Making sure you can actually communicate is up to you. For person-to-person communication, it is clear that no international standards body is ever going to decree that everyone speak English, or Esperanto, or whatever. With computer communication, however, it is possible to set standards for the language different computers speak, although doing so was beyond the remit of the CCITT. As time wore on, the International Standards Organization (ISO) took on responsibility for this role, and along with the CCITT set about defining a set of international data communications standards tailored to suit existing telecommunications operators. A protocol called X.25 eventually formed the backbone of the ISO standards. This was the protocol that dealt with the nitty-gritty of moving bits of information from one place to another, regardless of whether they were e-mails, file transfers, remote logins, or anything else.

The ISO standards were one of three options if you wanted to do networking in the mid-1980s. The open standards approach that the ISO wanted everyone to adopt was heavily steered by the interests of the telecommunications operators for whom making a profit was the overriding concern. Moreover, actual working ISO protocols were slow in coming. The second option came from computer manufacturers who often wrote their own proprietary protocols. But proprietary protocols were by definition not open: they only worked on a particular manufacturer's computers. Finally, there was the Internet, the only truly open standard available. But the Internet was still young and seen by many as lacking the authority conferred by a well-established standards body or a major company's backing. The result in the mid-1980s was that manufacturers' proprietary systems ruled the networking roost. This was a situation that flew in the face of everything the network's pioneers had been striving for. But it couldn't last. The demand for open systems was rising to a clamour and soon computer manufacturers would be forced to build computers that could talk to those of other manufacturers.

Open Systems Interconnection

The strongest European effort to establish internationally accepted protocols for computer networking grew out of the work done by Donald

Davies's and Louis Pouzin's teams. In 1967, Davies visited the ITU in Geneva and introduced the CCITT to the concept of packet switching. The CCITT operated on a four-yearly cycle of study periods punctuated by plenary meetings. Each plenary would hear reports from the past four years and determine a course of action for the next. In 1967 the CCITT was getting ready for the 1968 plenary and Davies was attending a briefing meeting on computer communications. He was there as part of a Post Office delegation and wasn't scheduled to speak, but listening to a talk from Fred Warden of IBM prompted him to do so. As Davies recalls, what Warden said boiled down to the message: 'We know all about computers, you know all about communications. We don't want you to get into our business and we're not going to tell you how to do communications. You provide us with leased lines of high bandwidth at low cost and we will organize computer communications.' This view was complete anathema to Davies, who believed that telecommunications operators should provide packet-switching services, so at the coffee break he collared the meeting's organizer and got his name on the agenda. Later on, after giving a one-hour lecture on packet switching, he delivered his bottom line. 'Look,' he said, 'you'd better set up some study on packet switching.' The motion was carried and the CCITT set up a joint study group on new data networks for its 1968 to 1972 session. Not much happened in that first study period. 'CCITT worked extremely slowly,' Davies explains, and it was only during the next study period that the CCITT actually started to produce detailed standards and the ISO started to take an interest.

Both the ITU and the ISO are global organizations and the USA is a full member, but historically these organizations have tended to be more important in Europe than in the United States. Whereas the USA is a single country using the same electric plugs and measurement systems from New York to Los Angeles, Europe's many independent nations have each at some time in the past made their own decisions on what standards to use. International standardization bodies have therefore found Europe more fertile ground for their efforts and have met with considerable success. A kilogram in France weighs the same as a kilogram in Italy, for example, and even in Britain it is now more common to buy petrol by the litre than by the gallon. Not every standardization effort has been so successful, however, as the plethora of adapter plugs on sale in airport departure lounges testifies.

For weights and measures, it is very annoying if some parts of the world use different scales than others; it sometimes even leads to accidents, like the loss of NASA's Mars Climate Orbiter in 1999, attributed to a confusion of scales. In telecommunications, having no standards is simply impossible: imagine the problems you would have making international calls if all countries had different numbering standards. Necessity has therefore driven the global adoption of ITU standards for telegraphy and telephony, so when the CCITT and the ISO decided it was time to pronounce on computer communication, the entire world was bound to take notice. Larry Roberts was among the first Americans to take part in the CCITT discussions and, fresh from his ARPANET experience, he couldn't understand the ponderous way the organization chose to work. The incomprehension was mutual, as Donald Davies remembers: 'Larry Roberts, being a rather forthright individual, could never get to understand the peculiar ways of CCITT in Geneva. You had to be very very polite there. When you got up to speak, first of all you'd complement the chairman on doing a good job and then you'd thank the previous speaker for his comments and say how valuable they are and then you'd proceed to tear them to pieces.' Larry Roberts was more used to simply getting things done than standing on ceremony, so his relationship with the CCITT was an uneasy one. Nevertheless, he played an important role in defining the nascent ISO standards. By this time, Donald Davies, having introduced the CCITT to packet switching, had melted into the background and the development of the basic ISO Open Systems Interconnection (OSI) packet-switching protocol, X.25, was left largely to the Americans and the French.

The first X.25 standard was published in 1976 at the end of the second study period in which the CCITT had looked at networking. Instead of the ARPANET's eight months, the CCITT had taken eight years. X.25 was designed to be easy to charge for in terms of packets sent, distance, and connection time. In 1976, when the CCITT set up a network architecture working group, the French were officially represented by the state-owned PTT. Louis Pouzin had to get in by the side door. His group took part in discussions not as part of the French delegation, but as members of the International Federation for Information Processing. The PTT's animosity to Pouzin and his datagrams was later to prove fatal for Cyclades. Whilst the French government was subsidizing the new Transpac network, which used X.25, Cyclades was being allowed to languish. Nevertheless, Cyclades' legacy to the networking world was ensured. Hubert Zimmermann from Pouzin's group went on to become president of the CCITT network architecture working group. From then on, no matter whether it was TCP/IP or OSI that became the dominant data communications protocol, Cyclades would have played its part in moulding it.

A clash of cultures

With governments and the established telecommunications operators beginning to get involved in networking, two distinct camps were beginning to emerge. The Internet camp consisted of the network's pioneers and their followers, whose overriding concern was to facilitate the human–computer interaction envisaged by Licklider over a decade before. The official camp consisted of organizations who wanted to regulate the network and make it pay.

One of the most important characteristics of the Internet has nothing to do with its working mechanisms but rather with the way it developed. From the very beginning, ideas were conceived by individual scientists working together in a 'society' that was not contained within a single company or even a single country, but was dispersed around the world. This may be one of the reasons why large companies and telecom operators have traditionally taken a negative attitude towards Internet technologies: they did not fit in to an identifiable corporate culture. When Steve Crocker sent out RFC 1, he established the bottom-up approach that survives to this day in the Internet mentality.

With time, however, organization inevitably crept into the system. At first there was the Network Working Group (NWG), and then at the ICCC conference in Washington in 1972, the International NWG was formed with Vint Cerf as its chair. In 1983, an Internet Activities Board (IAB) was created. An Internet Engineering Task Force (IETF), whose job is to ensure standardization of TCP/IP implementations, and an Internet Research Task Force (IRTF) to coordinate advanced networking research, followed soon after. If anything, organization served to enshrine the Internetters' anarchistic way of doing things. The Internet Engineering Task Force was founded on a credo that the established telecommunications industry must have found quite shocking. It runs as follows: 'We reject kings, presidents, and voting. We believe in rough consensus and running code.' In other words, anyone could bring a new idea to the great melting pot of packet-switching Internet technologies. Their idea would never be judged on academic background, corporate affiliation, or rank. Instead, the idea itself would have to prove its worth. Peers did not refrain from sharp and immediate criticism of faults and sloppy thinking. And so the Internet grew in a way that would not have been unfamiliar to Charles Darwin or Alfred Wallace. It evolved as if it had a life of its own, and when it came to programs and applications the rule was simply survival of the fittest. The fledgling Internet did not follow any hard and fast rules laid down by man.

In 1992, the two Internet task forces were incorporated into the Internet Society which was created, with CERN as a founder member, to provide 'a forum for government, industry and individuals to debate and formulate network policies and procedures'. But even now, these bodies are reactive, ruling by consensus rather than decree. The same contrast between bottom up and top down had led to CII's relative failure compared to US computer manufacturers, but the lesson had not been learned. People still ask, 'Who governs the Internet?' 'Where is the headquarters?' 'Who is responsible?' And the answer is simply, 'rough consensus and running code'—especially running code, and that is what the ISO failed to grasp when it tried to impose its own set of networking standards.

By the time the ISO took an interest in networking, the ARPANET was already up and running in its own anarchistic but effective way. There was plenty of consensus among its users, and the code in place ran. With hindsight, it is clear that the ISO's efforts to impose a new standard were doomed from the start. By contrast with Internet society, the ISO and CCITT were firmly embedded in a conventional regimented top-down culture peopled by chiefs and indians. The chiefs were those who managed the well-established telephone systems, who got together believing that technical issues should take a back seat to their own political agendas. Their interest was in maintaining the status quo rather than forging something new. Consequently, they concentrated their efforts on designing a system that would be easy to charge for rather than one that would be easy to use. Such financial questions did not concern the Internet pioneers, who were largely academics whose salaries did not depend on the commercial performance of what they did. While this produced a working network, it also left all the commercial questions dangling, resulting in a confusion about who pays that we still experience today.

But the ISO approach was not entirely commercially motivated; it also carried its own brand of idealism. The plan was first to define the ultimate set of protocols for computer networking and then go off and build them. In contrast, the opposite camp was characterized by pragmatism. It was peopled by the pioneering community that had built the ARPANET. Four-yearly meetings were not an option for these people, as they had a much quicker way of doing things: they could keep in touch using e-mail over the network they had built. And as for charging, nothing could have been further from their minds. The ARPANET had not been built for commercial purposes. These were crucial differences that were to play a major role in the Internet's eventual supremacy.

The Queen's network

Despite the handicap of four-yearly meetings, the ISO and the CCITT had considerable political clout behind them and there was a lot of pressure for their protocols to be adopted. It seemed at the time as if ISO protocols were just over the horizon and that soon world standards for networking would be decreed from Geneva, just as they are for any other form of telecommunication. Even in the USA, home of TCP/IP, there was political pressure to toe the ISO line. In the UK the pressure to adopt OSI was so strong that in 1976, Peter Kirstein was ordered stop what he was doing with TCP/IP and the new Internet project and concentrate instead on getting the OSI protocols established. He refused, but one important UK group to accept the concept of ISO standards was the universities and research councils, which set up the Joint Network Team in 1979. The JNT's role was to develop a networking programme based on the use of open-access non-proprietary networking standards. Bob Cooper, a founding member of the JNT, remembers a highly fragmented networking situation in the UK at the time. 'The research councils were doing their own thing, you had national centres with their own networks, you had early regional networks where a few universities were getting together, and all of this was incompatible.' The JNT's task was to pull it all together. Its approach had a lot in common with that of the ARPANET's pioneers but the JNT's starting point was different. The ARPANET people had no existing networks to worry about, while the JNT had several. Internetworking was therefore essential from the start. 'We saw networking as an enabler, not as a solution for a particular requirement,' says Cooper. The JNT's vision was of a unified network formed by interconnecting Local Area Networks through a single Wide Area Network so that as many people as possible could benefit. Many different network technologies would be connected together, but to users it would all look like one big network.

The possibility of adopting ARPANET as the basis for a UK network had been considered by the academic community in the mid-70s, but it was not pursued because the JNT did not believe that the technology was mature enough. Moreover, developments in the UK were tending towards the ISO approach, with the Post Office's announced national Packet-Switched Service (PSS) being an X.25 network. 'I think the feeling was that we should align our networking program with UK developments rather than something from across the Atlantic which at the time didn't look like the basis for a large-scale service network but more like a research activity,' Cooper explains. The JNT had been set up with a specific remit to develop a networking programme based on open, non-proprietary networking standards. To them it seemed natural to adopt international standards where possible, so X.25 was the obvious choice.

By the end of 1980, however, the JNT had concluded that running an academic network serving some two hundred sites across the UK over PSS was not an option. PSS was designed for people who could predict how much network traffic they were going to use and budget for it in advance. The Post Office effectively charged by the byte. What the JNT wanted was a network with leased communications lines where the price would be the same no matter how much the network was used. 'We were pioneering new applications for networks,' says Cooper. That meant that the amount of traffic was unpredictable, and with the Post Office's method of charging there would be a risk that the network might have to be shut down for lack of money halfway through the financial year. 'We went to the Post Office and said "Can we have a better way of doing this?" and the answer was no.' That left the JNT with a bit of a problem. Before PSS, a few private networks, such as the one used by the research councils, were tolerated, but once the Post Office had its own network to sell that was no longer the case. The Post Office still enjoyed a complete monopoly and the alternative to PSS was heresy. The JNT proposed it anyway. 'We then took the radical step of saying we ought to have a private network,' explains Cooper. 'That was an illegal suggestion at the time—they could have put us in prison!' But having a private network would mean that once it was in place, there would be no charges to use it and the academic community could generate as much traffic as the network could handle all year round.

In the end nobody went behind bars. It turned out that the Post Office didn't mind the academic community having its own network and even saw the chance of profiting from the experience, as long as the JNT's network didn't challenge their monopoly in voice communication. And so with the Post Office's blessing the Joint Academic Network, JANET, was launched in 1984. There was still, however, the problem of making it legal. Somebody had the bright idea that since the Queen did not need a license to operate services for the Crown, the Crown could perhaps be the nominal owner of JANET. 'For about five years,' explains Cooper, 'it was the Queen's network!'

Having decided to adopt X.25 and run it on a private network, the next hurdle the JNT faced was one that proved to be a recurring problem for network builders over the coming years. Although X.25 existed, higher-level OSI protocols were still not available. The ISO had got as far as describing its ideal network but hadn't actually produced working protocols for things like file transfer and e-mail. The delegates in Geneva would worry about how many levels of protocol were needed, and they eventually hit upon the magic number of seven. This was 'like some sort of Holy Grail', remembers Cooper. 'Every time you were developing protocols you had to fit them into this seven layer model.' No one argued with the common sense behind layering protocols. Keith Bartlett had been the first to hit upon the idea back in 1968 and he presented it at the Edinburgh IFIP meeting, arguing that 'if interfaces between adjacent levels can be defined, improvements in technology at any one level do not involve redesign or change at any other level.' In other words if you had an e-mail protocol, for example, which is just a particular kind of file transfer, running over a file transfer protocol (FTP), you could tweak the e-mail protocol as much as you liked as long as you didn't change the way it interacted with the FTP. This suited the CCITT's way of doing things to a tee. It meant that they could define a set of layers and then assign work on each layer to a group of people who wouldn't need to talk to each other for the next four years. It was somehow natural, then, for the CCITT to define its layers first and then go off to produce the protocols. But that was no consolation for the JNT, whose only option was to adopt interim protocols while they were waiting for the ISO to deliver. These were called the 'Coloured Books', since each protocol was described in a book with a different coloured cover. Blue was for file transfer, for example, and grey for the e-mail protocol that had been copied from the ARPANET and modified to run over Blue Book FTP.

At the same time as JANET was being developed, local area networks started to appear. The first were the domestically produced Cambridge Rings, which were easily attached to the wider network using a new Orange Book protocol. But soon Bob Metcalfe's Ethernet started to make inroads. 'Ethernet, of course, was coming with TCP/IP ready to use,' says Bob Cooper, so the Pink Book protocol that connected Ethernets to JANET faced an uphill struggle against TCP/IP from the start.

As soon as JANET was up and running, the JNT demonstrated its faith in ISO by implementing a transition strategy from the interim Coloured Book standards to the definitive ISO standards. This strategy was published in 1987 in the last of the Coloured Books, 'fittingly a White Book,' grins Cooper, but it was never fully implemented. The TCP/IP bandwagon was rapidly picking up speed, and in 1991 JANET started to run TCP/IP alongside X.25. It wasn't long before the community made its choice between the two protocols. Ethernets had become the local area networks of choice, and they came with TCP/IP built in.

Unix, particularly the version that came with the Berkeley Software Distribution, was becoming the preferred operating system in the academic community and it also came with TCP/IP built in. The use of X.25 slipped away while TCP/IP flourished.

By 1989, Bob Cooper had risen to be the UK academic community's Director of Networking and he made a proposal to develop SuperJANET, a high-performance network running over high-capacity optical fibres. This would make all manner of new applications possible using high-resolution graphics, video, and sound. The Government was won over by 1991 and approved funding of £5 million a year for four years. There was just one string attached. With the first instalment, the JNT had to prove that SuperJANET would be worth the investment. 'They gave us six months to build this network from scratch and we really needed all the help we could get,' remembers Cooper. Telecommunications monopolies in the UK were long gone by this time and British Telecom, the privatized telecommunications wing of the Post Office, was more than happy to provide that help. A contract was signed in November 1992 and the six-month countdown began. Eight sites were selected for the pilot network, each chosen because it had some application that could be used to provide a spectacular demonstration over the network.

Right from the start, the SuperJANET pilot network carried data around seventy times faster than JANET had ever reached. Put another way, that meant that five and a half thousand pages of text could be transmitted in under a second if that was what you wanted to do. But text was not the reason for building SuperJANET. There was no longer any objection to a private network carrying voice or even video and these were the kinds of things that the pilot SuperJANET demonstrated in London right on schedule in May 1993. 'One minute they were switching up to Manchester to see rare medieval Persian illuminated manuscripts from the university library. Then they were switching down to the Royal Postgraduate Medical School in London to study 3-D brain scans. It was incredible—moving images, high-quality colour images—they'd never seen anything like that on a network before,' explains Cooper. Another application demonstrated on SuperJANET was a newcomer called the World Wide Web. 'That's going to be a winner,' thought Cooper, admiring its ease of use and open protocols that could easily be adapted to run on any operating system. Needless to add, the demonstration was a success and SuperJANET's next three instalments were secure. By 1994, the new network was a nationwide reality.

The pilot SuperJANET used TCP/IP from the start. 'It was obvious TCP/IP was going to become the open standard,' says Cooper. 'X.25 died out with JANET.' The Internet was by now well established, the old arguments that it looked like a bit of research no longer applied, and ISO had still failed to deliver reliable high-level protocols. The result was that when the full-scale SuperJANET was launched in 1994 using TCP/IP and the higher-level protocols that ran on top of it, it spelled the end for the interim Coloured Book standards. By this time you could literally buy Internet protocols off the shelf at your local computer store, if they did not already come free with your computer.

JANET was not the first major X.25 network. BBN's Telenet, the French PTT's Transpac, and the Post Office's PSS all ran on X.25. Like JANET, all these networks had adopted the only international standard there was. And like JANET, they were all to switch to TCP/IP. But JANET had been a pioneering network in its own right. It was the first national network anywhere in the world to offer access to the entire academic community right from the start based on open non-proprietary networking standards. Although managed by the JNT, JANET was user driven. Whatever applications its users wanted to run were supported and when the user community voted with their keyboards to use TCP/IP rather than X.25, the JNT responded.

CERN goes it alone

In 1976, Peter Kirstein received an official request from CERN for a connection to the ARPANET, but the Post Office obliged him to turn it down. The reason was that involving another country's communications authorities was deemed to be too complex. Exclusion from the ARPANET, however, didn't turn CERN into a networking backwater. Far from it. At a laboratory covering two large sites separated by several kilometres, computer networking was a must, and in the mid-1970s two important CERN networks came into operation. One, CERNET, was developed entirely in house to carry data from experiments to the laboratory's central computing facilities. The second, which was known as the TITN network, had the job of controlling one of CERN's big particle accelerators.

In the late 1960s, desktop computing was still a thing of the future, and CERN had developed a computing strategy based around powerful number-crunching computers called mainframes housed at a central computer centre. This made CERN a natural place for networking to develop. Two distinct systems of point-to-point connections linking remote computers to the computer centre were quickly established.

One, OMNET, was based around one of CERN's biggest experimental facilities called OMEGA. Its job was to transfer data from OMEGA experiments to a dedicated computer whose task was to analyse them in real time—as the experiment was actually taking place. This allowed the physicists to visualize what was going on inside their particle detectors as it was happening. The other, FOCUS, linked a number of experiments to the laboratory's computer centre. Its job was slightly different from OMNET's, allowing experiments to send small data samples to the central computers for analysis. Neither system was designed for large quantities of experimental data, most of which would be carried to the computer centre on magnetic tapes. Mike Gerard, a member of the CERNET team who had learned about packet switching whilst working as a summer student at the NPL in the 1960s, remembers that CERN's main data network was 'the famous bicycle on-line technology that was developed for data transport'. Physicists would take the tapes off their data acquisition computers and rush them over to the computer centre on their bikes, where they would load them on one of the big number-crunchers for analysis. 'It's a hell of a bandwidth, that, when you work it out,' laughs Gerard. The central computers would process jobs at different priorities, and the bicycle online priority came top of the stack. By 1975, however, both OMNET and FOCUS were becoming over-stretched, so the laboratory decided it was time to build a general-purpose data communications network and put an end to the on-line bicycle, leaving physicists to get their exercise elsewhere.

The resulting network, CERNET, had all the features of the modern Internet despite being developed completely independently. Without an ARPANET link, the CERNET team was on its own, but the solutions it came up with looked pretty much like those Vint Cerf was developing in the USA for the DARPA experimental Internet. CERNET used packet switching in Louis Pouzin's datagram mode, and its robustness against node failures would have pleased Paul Baran. The motivation was a little different from Baran's, however. CERN's particle physicists are known for working in shifts round the clock for weeks on end, whereas the laboratory's computer scientists prefer to go home at night. Rather than match the physicists' shifts, they preferred to build a robust network so that physicists' packets would still be delivered even if a node failed at two in the morning. Their approach paid off, with CERNET rapidly achieving reliability of around 99 per cent, the bulk of the missing per cent being due to host computers failing rather than to failures in the network itself.

The first phase of CERNET was completed in 1978 with links connecting the laboratory's remote site, called the North Area, to the computer centre. A new experiment, the European Muon Collaboration (EMC), began using the network straight away for sending fast-track data to the computer centre for analysis, just the kind of task the online bicycle would have performed in the past. The EMC was a huge collaboration for its time, with some fifty physicists putting their names to its results. The experiment was designed to look inside protons and neutrons, the particles that make up atomic nuclei, with the aim of understanding the behaviour of the smaller particles, called quarks, inside them. The collaboration's technique was a bit like using a very high-power electron microscope, except the electrons were replaced by their heavier relatives, muons. CERN's accelerator complex would fire a beam of muons at a target every few seconds and some of these muons would bounce off the quarks. By analysing millions of scattered muons, the EMC's physicists were able to learn a lot about quark behaviour. Each pulse of muons would contain millions of muons, but only around one hundred would scatter from the EMC's target, leaving most to pass right through the apparatus unscathed. This allowed a second experiment to be installed behind the EMC. The brainchild of CERN's future Nobel Laureate, Carlo Rubbia, this experiment too was an early user of CERNET. For over a decade these two experiments enjoyed a friendly rivalry, and it is perhaps symptomatic of this that the EMC chose to analyse its data on the computer centre's IBM computer while Rubbia's experiment chose the alternative CDC.

By 1980, the second phase of CERNET was complete, extending the service to over fifty computers distributed all over CERN's two main sites. The sub-net used American computers made by Modular Computer Services Inc., Modcomp for short, but these node computers were the only components that were bought in. CERN itself had been involved in designing a modular computer interfacing system called Computer Automated Measurement and Control (CAMAC) specifically designed for experimental data acquisition, and it seemed logical to make the CERNET interfaces out of CAMAC modules so that all an experiment would have to do to connect to the network would be plug an extra CAMAC module in to their system. The protocols were also home grown. X.25 had yet to make an impression at CERN, and without an Internet, the laboratory's computer scientists were out of day-to-day touch with the ARPANET and NPL work although they had heard about them from conferences and journals. Even the operating system of the Modcomp machines was partially rewritten in house. 'After attempting a dialogue with Modcomp, it became clear that the best course for CERN was to abandon all hopes of the necessary changes being done by Modcomp,' claims a 1980 progress report on CERNET. In those days, it was commonplace to buy computers with bug-ridden operating systems, incomplete operating systems, or no operating systems at all. The days of computers that can be taken from the box and simply plugged in are surprisingly recent.

The end of CERNET was a familiar story. In the mid-1980s, Mike Gerard remembers, 'local area networks based on Ethernet started springing up around CERN and we created a way of using CERNET to interconnect Ethernets.' CERNET became an internetworking project in its own right. Ethernet packets were small enough to fit inside CERNET packets, so the technique consisted of using CERNET to link Ethernets, and putting CERNET 'envelopes' on the Ethernet packets whilst they were being routed from one Ethernet to another. 'It looked like CERN

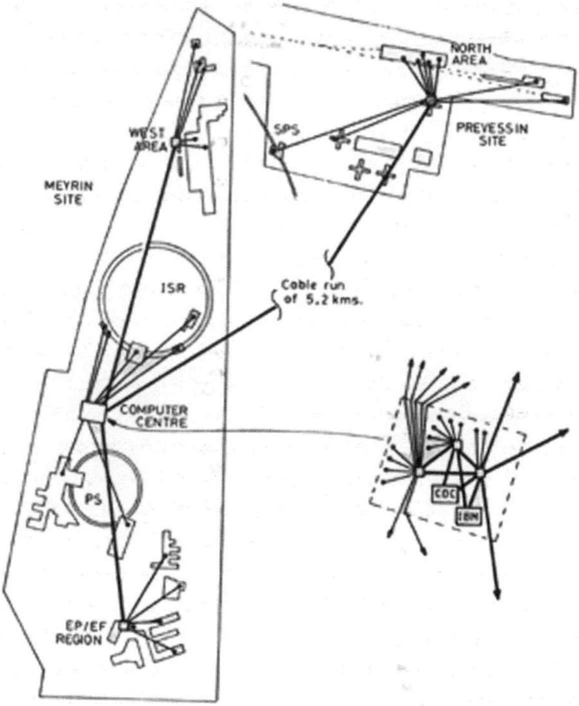

Figure 12: The CERNET network linked the laboratory's computers to the central computing centre using Internet-like protocols developed in house. (From CERN report 81-12.)

had one big Ethernet for the whole of CERN', explained Gerard. 'Later on that literally did become one big Ethernet because CERNET was taken away and a genuine Ethernet structure put in its place.' CERNET was like the Internet in miniature. Its development had mirrored that of the ARPA Internet, taking its inspiration from Donald Davies and Louis Pouzin and evolving into an internetworking project under pressure from the growing influence of Ethernet.

CERNET began as an experiment in networking and ended up as a reliable service for experiments to use. But when drawing up CERN's other important network of the 1970s, Jacques Altaber couldn't afford the luxury of an experimental phase. His job was to build a network that would link together all the computers controlling the laboratory's biggest atom-smasher, the 7-kilometre-circumference SPS. Altaber didn't have the time or manpower to build a network from scratch, but nor could he just buy a network off the shelf: at the time there was nothing available. His solution was to define the specifications for the network he wanted and to put out a competitive call to tender. The resulting contract was awarded to the French company Traitement de l'Information et Techniques Nouvelles (TITN). Altaber's specification covered both hardware and software and included an application layer called NODAL that allowed commands to be written in one place and executed somewhere else. This was a particularly far-sighted feature of the specification, being rather like an early form of the modern 'Java' programming language. Another innovative feature of the TITN network was that it was designed to be run at a distance, so each host computer was connected by two wires. One carried packets of information, the other was there for control purposes, allowing SPS operators to reboot remote computers on the network from a central control room. The TITN network came on stream in 1977 along with the SPS itself. Soon after, it was extended to cover other CERN accelerators, and it remained in service until 1995.

Although CERN had never had an ARPANET connection, CERNET and the TITN network kept the laboratory very much at the forefront of network infrastructure design in the late 1970s. As a consequence, when the Internet started to spread CERN was ideally placed to make the most of it.

Because it's there

The 1980s saw a network explosion as all the big computer manufacturers, as well as the ISO and the fledgling Internet community, tried to get their protocols accepted. Networks sprang up all over the place, and among the most important was BITNET, the 'Because It's There Network' established by Ira Fuchs at the City University of New York (CUNY). Back then, the big players in the computing market were not the same as they are today. As Brian Carpenter, then head of networking at CERN, explains, 'You have to remember that was not a world dominated by Microsoft, so what was available on the PC was not the issue. The key issue turned out to be what was available on mainframe computers.' These were the big centralized computing facilities like the ones in CERN's computer centre, and IBM was the world's biggest supplier. IBM supplied networking software, called the Remote Spooling Communications Subsystem (RSCS), on all its machines. This prompted Ira Fuchs to send a letter in March 1981 to some fifty computer departments on the east coast of North America inviting them to set up an inter-university network of computers running RSCS. The response was overwhelmingly positive, and in May 1981 BITNET came into being when a first link was established between CUNY and Yale. At first the network didn't have a name, but it acquired one at the end of 1981 when Ira Fuchs published a promotional article with the title 'BITNET Makes Splash'. The article invited more universities to join BITNET, explaining how cheap it was at $5 000 for the necessary hardware and a few hundred dollars a month for a leased telecommunication line, and it closed with the words, 'P.S. The BIT in BITNET is not an eighth of a byte; it stands for "Because It's There".' Later on, this evolved into 'Because It's Time', but the result was the same. RSCS was there, and in 1981 Fuchs deemed the time right to put it to work. Right from the start, BITNET's main use was not what the ARPANET's pioneers had envisaged for a computer network, remote access to computers, but what Ray Tomlinson had tacked on by sending himself an electronic mail message. BITNET's users readily exchanged information in the form of electronic mail, text files, computer programmes, and—a BITNET innovation—instant messages. John Smith at CUNY could simply type 'msg jones@bostonu Hi Jerry!', and seconds later the message 'FROM CUNYVM(SMITH) HI, JERRY!' would appear on Jerry's screen in Boston.

BITNET spread rapidly and was soon connecting universities across the United States and Canada. Like Britain's JANET, it was open to anyone in the academic community without regard to academic discipline, and its use for commercial purposes was prohibited. Unlike JANET, however, BITNET had no central management and no paid staff; it was a cooperative network that was kept going by the people who used it. All the initial computers on BITNET were IBMs, but before long people began to write software to emulate RSCS on other manufacturers' computers, and BITNET evolved into the kind of open network the Internet pioneers were trying to create with TCP/IP. By 1983, BITNET had sixty-five nodes and a list of fifteen more universities waiting to join.

In 1984, BITNET crossed the Atlantic when IBM agreed to fund a European branch, the European Academic and Research Network (EARN), for three years. EARN took some time to get going because of resistance from Europe's state-owned telecommunications companies, but once established it proved to be a boon for the international particle physics research community.

An early fan of BITNET was Paul Kunz, a physicist at the Stanford Linear Accelerator Center (SLAC) in California. In the early 1980s, he was working on Carlo Rubbia's Nobel-Prizewinning experiment at CERN. Before EARN, keeping in touch with his European colleagues was an arduous business. 'I had to use X.25 to login to a computer at Saclay. From there I could login to a computer at CERN,' he recalls. 'It was painful even to read the e-mail because connections would drop. If you tried to write some e-mail, before you'd get it written there would probably be a disconnection. It was extremely painful.'

Italy was the first European country to have a BITNET/EARN link to the USA. 'Apparently because the Italian PTT, if they got some money for a leased line, couldn't care less what you did with it,' says Kunz. The German PTT put up more resistance, and Paul Kunz remembers what happened when IBM heard that Germany was going to allow a link. 'They scrambled to get a line in real quick before they changed their minds,' he explains. The result was a line connecting Germany to Washington, whereas Italy's line went to New York. 'So for a few months, if you wanted to send e-mail from Italy to Germany it went all the way to New York, down through Washington, and back to Germany, which of course is rather silly,' says Kunz. Eventually the PTTs relented and allowed the EARN network to be established. 'That,' in Paul Kunz opinion, 'was the beginning of the end for the monopoly of the PTTs.'

IBM's apparent generosity was seen by many as the opening salvo in a battle to corner the protocol market, but if that was the case things didn't go exactly to plan. EARN was a big success and was soon self-supporting. This should have been good news for IBM, but it wasn't. The problem was that the European PTTs had exacted a price for their acquiescence to EARN. Unlike BITNET, EARN had to have some kind of organizational structure, and its first coordinator was CERN's David Lord, a colleague of Paul Kunz's on the Rubbia experiment. More ominously, however, EARN had to give a commitment to migrate to ISO protocols as they became available. The PTTs were relying on the ISO and they had considerable support from the network's European users. 'They felt that you cannot fight the PTTs, they have infinite power,' is Paul Kunz's explanation for his European colleagues' acquiescence. In an era of state monopolies it might well have seemed that way.

Whatever the reason, EARN adopted the stance that ISO protocols would one day rule and everything else was interim, including IBM's RSCS. No sooner had a governing body for EARN been established than it was discussing plans for migrating to OSI, but IBM was not giving up so easily. The company's response was to sponsor another European network based around IBM computers. This was the European Academic Supercomputing Initiative network (EASInet). Significantly for CERN, IBM's sponsorship included a high bandwidth line from CERN to a network called the NSFNET in the USA, and in networking circles the laboratory's name acquired a new twist. CERN became to some the Centre for European Research Networking.

BITNET's most lasting legacy to the modern Internet was a thing called LISTSERV. This is a service whereby anyone can set up a discussion forum on any subject they want and like-minded people can subscribe. Subscribers send e-mails to the listserver, which then forwards them on to all subscribers. Discussion lists quickly sprang up covering topics as diverse as clinical epidemiology and juggling, and they are still around today on the Internet.

Nascent networks

Whilst all this was going on, there was another player in the protocol wars. Ken Olson's Digital Equipment Corporation, the company he had set up on the back of the TX-0 in the late 1950s, had its own proprietary network called DECNET. DEC's computers were a big hit in the particle physics world because they offered good performance for the money, and when it became possible to link them together, DECNET networks spread like wildfire. By 1987, Brian Carpenter, speaking at the Computing in High Energy Physics conference at Asilomar, California, estimated that 'In total more than 1 000 nodes are probably interconnected through this amorphous world wide network.' DEC also played the ISO card, becoming the first big computer manufacturer to announce a migration of its proprietary network to OSI. Much was expected of DECNET's conversion, with Carpenter calling it 'the next essential milestone in the transition process towards the OSI world'. Even so, in the same talk, Carpenter noted the ground-up spread of TCP/IP protocols, saying that 'their great advantage is that they exist for computers ranging from the PC to the mainframe, and that they generally work with the minimum of problems.' The ISO's X.25, on the other hand, he described as inadequate for applications more demanding than remote login or electronic mail.

At around the same time, another important US network was established. The ARPANET had divided the US research computing community into haves and have-nots. Computer departments not connected to the ARPANET found themselves at a clear disadvantage when it came to attracting good staff and students. In 1980, they decided to do something about it. The following year, CSNET was up and running with support from the National Science Foundation (NSF). CSNET was a network of networks with the ARPANET being one of its components. Departments that wanted it had to pay a membership fee, and soon CSNET was self-financing. Networking had come a long way since Larry Roberts sold the idea to a sceptical group of computer science departments in the 1960s, each of which preferred to jealously guard its own computing facilities. But what convinced them that networking was a good thing had turned out to be not the resource sharing that the ARPANET pioneers had envisaged, but information sharing in the form of e-mail, LISTSERV, and instant messaging.

In the mid-1980s, BITNET started to run TCP/IP, with RSCS protocols for things like file transfer running on top. In 1987, BITNET and CSNET merged to form the Corporation for Research and Educational Networking. Together, these two networks had proved that networking was not just an academic curiosity, but that people were willing to pay for it.

BITNET was a network driven by its users, but it wasn't the only one. At Bell Labs, a protocol for Unix machines, Unix to Unix copy (UUCP), was invented. UUCP was so easy to use that it was rapidly deployed to carry e-mail, creating for a while what was probably the biggest network in the world. In 1979, Tom Truscott, Jim Ellis, and Steve Bellovin invented another way of using UUCP to carry 'network news' over a network they named Usenet. This was a bit like BITNET's LISTSERV except that instead of sending e-mails to every subscriber, subscribers read and posted messages on a kind of electronic bulletin board. The protocol would post messages to any computer subscribing to a particular newsgroup. At first, Usenet had two hosts, the universities of its inventors, Duke in Durham and the neighbouring University of North Carolina at Chapel Hill, but it rapidly rose to fame as the carrier of the network newsgroups. By the early 1980s, newsgroups had made their way to Europe and Australia and in 1986 earned their own dedicated protocol, Network News Transfer Protocol (NNTP), which ran over TCP/IP. The European arm was called EUnet and its focal point was the Centrum voor Wiskunde en Informatica (CWI), the Dutch national institute for mathematics and computer science. Like its US counterpart, EUnet was a cooperative venture. 'You knew somebody from another site running Unix and basically you made arrangements that you called each other and so forth,' remembers Daniel Karrenberg, who as a student had set up the German part of the network. But unlike the USA, EUnet had national boundaries to worry about, and since calling across boundaries was expensive, some kind of organization was needed to limit international traffic. This job fell largely to Piet Beertema who ran the computer at CWI that handled the transatlantic link. By the end of the 1980s when Karrenberg had finished his studies, Beertema was getting pretty busy, so Karrenberg went to Amsterdam to help out. He has been there ever since.

While all this was going on, networking was quietly taking its first steps outside the academic world. In Cleveland, Ohio, Tom Grundner, an assistant professor in medicine, did something that was to change his life. He set up a bulletin board as a way of delivering community health information to the public. By 1986, this had become the Cleveland Free-Net, which found a home as a project in the computer group of the Case Western Reserve University. The free-net provided bulletin boards and e-mail without charge as a community service. Grundner went on to establish the National Public Telecomputing Network to spread the free-net concept, and as a result, community-oriented free-nets blossomed around the world.

Although it was information sharing rather than remote access to computing facilities that was the main driving force behind the network explosion, powerful small computers were still in their infancy and remote access to big computers was still important. In the early 1980s, the NSF was supporting a small number of supercomputing centres and they wanted to make these facilities available to the entire academic community. Inspired by the success of CSNET, in 1984 the NSF established the NSFNET project. This was to be a network of networks, and it came on stream in 1986 using TCP/IP as interim protocols. The NSF's intention was to migrate to ISO standards as they became available. Like JANET, the NSFNET was intended from the start to offer access to all areas of the academic community, so it was natural that in 1987 the two networks were connected. The NSFNET was a crucial step from academic networking, where all the hardware was cobbled together in university labs or built to special order, to the commercial networking world of today, where routers can easily be bought off the shelf. 'The explosion of the Internet started when commercial routers became available,' explains Bob Cooper. 'My perception is that the major stimulus in this direction came from the NSF.'

By the end of the decade, whether or not IBM had been pump-priming in a bid to force its own products on the world had become irrelevant. The IBM-sponsored line connecting CERN to the NSFNET was running TCP/IP, as was BITNET itself. DECNET had made the transition to OSI, but in a way that could handle TCP/IP as well. In any case, the popularity of DEC computers was beginning to wane as even smaller, cheaper computers, like Macintoshes and PCs, became available. Most of the other networks that had sprung up were also moving over to TCP/IP. But nevertheless, the networking world had a lot to be grateful to BITNET for. 'It was an important precursor of the Internet,' explains Brian Carpenter, 'in the sense that it set a lot of the expectations about openness and free access.' It is hard to understate how much this revolutionized the world of particle physics research and ultimately the global development of the Internet. 'BITNET,' says Paul Kunz, 'was the one that broke the political barriers.' In doing so, it put paid to the PTTs' goal of charging for data communication by the byte. The charging model BITNET helped to establish was based on rented lines whose price is determined by their bandwidth. Once you have paid the rental for a line, how much you use it is up to you.

DECNET had also played a part in breaking down the barriers. CERN had DECNET connections to both Italy and the USA allowing people to send e-mail from Rome to Reno, something the European PTTs didn't want to allow. But the only way CERN could stop it was by unplugging the networks, because there was no way to stop the DECNET protocol forwarding messages on. 'So the PTT gave in and that was the second major blow to their barriers,' says Kunz. When EARN was established, Paul Kunz had been the first to send an e-mail from CERN to the USA. The breakdown of barriers EARN had precipitated would soon allow him to build the first Web site outside Europe.

Waiting for OSI

One of the first demonstrations of the experimental Internet came in 1977. 'Jim Mathis was driving a van on the San Francisco Bayshore Freeway with a packet radio system running on an LSI-11,' recounts Vint Cerf. Mathis was taking part in an ambitious experiment to send packets on a 94 000-mile round trip across several networks using the new TCP protocol suite. The first link was packet radio to the ARPANET followed by a point-to-point link to Norway and a land line to Peter Kirstein's UCL ARPANET node. From there the packets travelled back across the Atlantic through the satellite network SATNET, and finally back through the ARPANET to a waiting computer at the University of Southern California. It was a demonstration designed to convince the US Department of Defense that internetworking could be useful to them. 'What we were simulating,' explains Cerf, 'was someone in a mobile battlefield environment going across a continental network, then across an intercontinental satellite network, and then back into a wireline network to a major computing resource in national headquarters.' The experiment was an unqualified success: 'We didn't lose a bit,' says Cerf. For Peter Kirstein, the most impressive thing was not just that no data was lost, but that none was lost even though at one point the van had crossed the Golden Gate Bridge, whose steel structure had temporarily interrupted the packet radio link. TCP took this interruption in its stride, automatically resuming packet transmission as the van reached the other end of the bridge. 'The ruggedness of the protocol suite to this type of stress ensured its later success,' says Kirstein.

CERN, having been refused an ARPANET connection in 1976, was not involved in this exciting internetworking project. Nevertheless, it seemed that whatever step the Internet community took, CERN was taking a similar one of is own. The laboratory was a partner in the Italian STELLA project, designed to link terrestrial networks by satellite. Working independently from SATNET, the STELLA team developed its own set of internetworking protocols. During the second phase of the project, which ran from 1981 to 1983, CERNET was connected via satellite to Pisa and to the Rutherford Laboratory in Oxfordshire. STELLA had a profound influence on Ben Segal, who was later to introduce the Internet to CERN. 'As the senior technical member of the CERN STELLA team, this development opened my eyes to the potential of an Internet network protocol,' he explains.

But CERN couldn't go on mirroring the rest of the networking world forever. By this time, the ISO was promising standards for data communication, and in the absence of working ISO protocols the Internet crowd was happily spreading the word about TCP/IP. It was clear that one way or another there would soon be a set of international standards for networking: if the ISO didn't deliver, then TCP/IP would become a de facto standard, like it or not. It made sense for CERN to adopt international standards rather than keep on developing its own protocols. Choosing which camp to follow, however, was not so easy. CERN, being a government-funded international organization, was under official pressure to follow the ISO line, but on the other hand the laboratory had an obligation to its users to provide them with working network services wherever they might be.

At the same time as Ben Segal was connecting CERN to the outside world through STELLA, his old CERNET colleague Dietrich Wiegandt was setting in motion a chain of events that would lead the laboratory to a position of eminence in European networking. CERN had decided that Unix might be the operating system to settle on for high energy physics applications. Thanks to Bill Joy's Berkeley Software Distribution and the company he helped to found, small computers running Unix were providing an affordable route to powerful computing. The days of mainframe dominance for number-crunching looked to be over as people began to realize that networked Unix machines could do the job for less. Wiegandt had worked on CERN's first network project, OMNET, and had written the software connecting the laboratory's big IBM computer to CERNET. When CERN decided to evaluate Unix, it entrusted the task to him. In 1982, CERN took delivery of its first Unix system from Bell Labs. This proved to be a less than ideal solution because, as Wiegandt explains, 'Bell Labs were not inclined to give us an educational license'. It is common practice for software suppliers to give big discounts to educational establishments, and CERN usually qualifies as such, but under AT&T's definition only degree-awarding institutions count, 'meaning,' says Wiegandt, 'that we had to pay a lot of money for their Unix'.

A solution came the following year when CERN bought a VAX 11/780 computer, the latest product from DEC. This was the computer on which 4.2BSD had been developed and the license for that was much cheaper. Moreover, not only did it have the UUCP protocol, it also came with TCP/IP, unlike the Bell Labs version of Unix. Since the ARPANET switched to TCP/IP in 1983, people buying BSD Unix machines were opening up their new computers to find them ready to plug into the Internet. With OSI protocols incomplete, expensive, or unavailable, TCP/IP was gaining the upper hand.

Despite the early successes of TCP/IP, however, the final outcome was not a foregone conclusion. In 1985, a CERN strategy document pinpointed OSI as the laboratory's official choice, but it left a niche open. It allowed other technologies to be used while waiting for OSI, although it stressed that everything else would have to be interim. Even as late as 1986, the European Committee for Future Accelerators (ECFA), a body that studies the long-term prospects of particle physics in Europe, produced a document recommending the adoption of the X.25 protocol already enjoying considerable success in the UK with JANET. Members of ECFA's working group on data processing standards had heard from their American colleagues about a new network, called HEPNET, being set up to serve the particle physics community in the USA. HEPNET was to be based on X.25, showing that even in the US not everyone was convinced that TCP/IP was the way to go. The people who built HEPNET took the same stance as their ECFA counterparts: standardization was the ISO's job and sooner or later they would deliver.

The problem was that they weren't delivering, and with working OSI protocols taking so long to emerge, the interim solution of TCP/IP began to look increasingly attractive. The fact that TCP/IP was free also made it more popular with people on the ground. Ben Segal was one of the people to favour the interim and he lost no time in exploiting the niche left by CERN's strategy document. In 1984, he had CERN's first Internet project approved: he was to evaluate TCP/IP protocols for possible use at the laboratory.

Bringing TCP/IP to CERN

When Ben Segal had joined CERN in the 1970s, the idea of sharing data between computers was still in its infancy. CERNET was still several years in the future and manufacturers' proprietary networks were still dominant. There was no such thing as an open standard that would allow data to be shared between different kinds of computers; in fact, quite the opposite was true. In Ben's words, there was 'open warfare between many manufacturers' proprietary systems, various home-made systems and the then rudimentary efforts at defining open or international standards'. Across the Atlantic, the ARPANET was up and running, but it had yet to make much impression on Europe. And in the UK, Donald Davies's network was routinely switching packets of data between computers at the National Physical Laboratory.

With CERN following the political tide and putting its weight behind the ISO standards, it seemed that TCP/IP would make little impression at the laboratory. But Dietrich Wiegandt didn't ignore the free protocols he got with his Unix system. 'One thing that was more or less for free when you had Unix in your house,' he explains, 'was the Usenet news service.' He started to tinker with electronic mail and news over UUCP, and CERN soon became a European leader in these fields. Until 1990, CERN was the gateway through which all Swiss e-mail passed, and a focus for the now familiar newsgroups to which anyone may subscribe and air their opinion on countless specialized subjects from art to zoology. Since it was in precisely the areas of news and e-mail that Internet protocols first emerged triumphant in Europe, CERN's official support for OSI, despite the fact that working protocols were simply not being delivered, became increasingly awkward for the laboratory's network managers.

The wind began to change in August 1984 with Ben Segal's pilot project to install and evaluate Internet protocols on certain key CERN computers. Segal got the go-ahead on condition that he would also evaluate a number of rival protocols. It soon became clear that TCP/IP was the most promising, and in 1985 Segal became CERN's first TCP/IP coordinator. His job was to oversee the use of Internet protocols at CERN, but his remit was still restricted by the political clout of the ISO lobby. Internet was fine for communication between computers within CERN, but in no way was it to be used for external communication where it might threaten the emergence of OSI.

This situation went unchanged until 1989. But nevertheless, once the doors had been open to the Internet, there was no stopping it. Despite the small number of people working with the Internet, the original ideals of the Internet pioneers—working code, no compromise—meant that within CERN the Internet slowly but surely gained the upper hand. It was simple to use and code was cheap, if not free, and easy to get hold of.

A major battle was won in November 1985 when the group responsible for the control systems of the laboratory's new flagship accelerator, LEP, adopted Unix computers and used TCP/IP to network them. Once again, responsibility for the decision fell to Jacques Altaber. With TCP/IP readily available on Unix computers, 'the decision to adopt Unix plus TCP/IP for the LEP control system was uneasy but obvious for me,' he explains. Altaber's uneasiness stemmed not from the protocol, but from the choice of Unix. It was not clear that Unix would be fast enough for the split-second response times needed for a particle accelerator, so Altaber's team hardwired time-critical functions directly into microprocessors controlling accelerator components. TCP/IP was his choice. Unix presented the practical way to have it.

Meanwhile, back in London, Peter Kirstein had not been paying much attention to who had been using the network via UCL. But in 1985 the research councils and British Telecom wanted to know since, after all, they were paying for it. There was also pressure to put password-controlled access restrictions on the UCL Internet node. So Kirstein decided to send out an automatic message to everyone who had accessed the network during the last six months to find out who they were and warn them of what might be coming. 'When I recovered from the e-mail responses,' Kirstein recalls, 'I found I'd been sending this to some two or three thousand people when I thought there were only forty to a hundred users.' The Internet was beginning to behave as it had been planned: invisibly. These two or three thousand users were Usenet/EUnet or BITNET/EARN users posting and reading messages on newsgroups or sending each other e-mail. Most of them didn't even know that Peter Kirstein existed; the network just happened to be routing their messages through UCL. 'Suddenly they got this strange note from me saying that I was going to block all traffic. This was going to torpedo European–US traffic in unknown ways. It was only then that we started finding out what was really happening about routing. It was purely accidental.'

Soon after, Peter Kirstein's enabling role at UCL came to an end as management of UK Internet services was formally transferred to the larger University of London Computing Centre. The tax and duty exemption Peter had negotiated had done its job, ensuring that the networking project had remained in academic hands. For thirteen years, UCL had handled ARPANET traffic, and when domestic 'Coloured Book' networking came along had made sure that the two systems could talk to each other. Some of the protocol differences were apparently trivial, but even trivial differences required protocol conversions at UCL. 'The mail ones,' remembers Kirstein, 'stayed the same but opposite,' which meant that in Coloured Book parlance, UCL's address was uk.ac.ucl, but to TCP/IP, it was ucl.ac.uk. Britain's ambiguous political position, somewhat further west than geography would suggest, also meant that in the UK the perceived threat of transatlantic dominance was not as great as it was elsewhere in Europe, where a link to the ARPANET would have been unthinkable early on.

By 1986, those who looked closely enough could begin to see the writing on the wall for OSI. ECFA published another report reiterating its 1982 endorsement of X.25 and also recommending that ISO protocols be adopted in the USA. The report noted, however, the 'poor availability and high costs of X.25 services in the US'. Political pressure was still there, in the USA as in Europe, for OSI to be adopted, and had the ISO delivered, the Internet crowd might well have complied. 'There was some pressure by the late 1970s or early 1980s to have us use the ISO protocols, except that they weren't really well defined, and there were few compatible implementations,' explains Bob Kahn. Nevertheless, the ISO's efforts were not unappreciated across the Atlantic. 'They came up with a reference architecture in the mid-1970s,' says Kahn, 'which was actually a very important contribution because it gave people a way to think about protocol layers.' The concept of layers was nothing new, but the ISO's seven-layer model, love it or loathe it, was the first attempt to formally codify the idea. 'That was a real contribution,' says Kahn.

The ECFA report also recommended the adoption of another OSI standard, X.400, for e-mail, but pointed potential users to 'the EAN package which constitutes a presently available approximation of the X.400 recommendations'. It was clear even to the ISO's supporters that OSI was simply not delivering the goods. In an effort to stimulate international collaboration in networking, a Joint Association for European Research Networks, which took the name RARE from its French title, was established with the support of ECFA and the Commission for the European Communities among others. RARE's initial policy was strictly OSI.

One year later, CERN took delivery of a Cray XMP supercomputer and decided to run UNICOS, Cray's version of Unix, on it. That meant that it came with TCP/IP built in, so that was how it was networked. The decision to run the Cray this way proved to be important to the Internet's further expansion in Europe. The Cray was a supercomputer under strategic export restrictions. CERN had been obliged to restrict access to trusted physicists, and was even forced to build separating walls under the false floor customary in computing centres. Most Internet routers, the machines that serve as sorting offices on the Internet, just blindly forwarded packets towards their destinations without any concern for security. But Ben Segal knew where to get a router with security built in. A year before, he had met Len Bosack, co-founder of an up-and-coming young computer company called Cisco, at an exhibition in the USA. Bosack told him that Cisco's routers could monitor and filter traffic. This was just what was needed to connect the Cray to the network without laying it open for anyone to see. Segal bought two Cisco routers to act as filters between the Cray and CERN's public network.

The Trojan Horses from Amsterdam

In 1987, soon after he had installed the Cisco routers at CERN, Ben Segal received a visit from Daniel Karrenberg, by this time a system manager of the Amsterdam computer that acted as an e-mail gateway between Europe and the USA. At the time, European e-mail and network news were carried across the Atlantic to Usenet through EUnet, the European arm of the network that had grown from AT&T's UUCP protocol. This included some of the mail and news that Dietrich Wiegandt was routing between Switzerland and the USA. In the USA, Usenet was gradually switching over to TCP/IP and Karrenberg wanted to do the same to EUnet. The transatlantic line had already switched over but Karrenberg didn't know of any routers that could run TCP/IP over EUnet's X.25 lines. With his experience in networking the Cray fresh in his mind, Segal knew where to find the answer. 'I reached for my Cisco catalogue,' he exclaims, 'and showed him the model number he needed.' Within a few months the key EUnet sites around Europe were equipped with Cisco routers running TCP/IP packets over X.25 connections and the ISO lobby was none the wiser. Ben Segal, as well as introducing the Internet to CERN, had also played a small but vital role in bringing the Internet to Europe. The Cisco routers installed by Daniel Karrenberg were the Trojan horses of the protocol wars. Through them, the Internet arrived quietly and without ceremony, but the important thing was that it arrived. For Dietrich Wiegandt, converting e-mail and news services to TCP/IP couldn't have been easier: the protocols were already there built in to his BSD Unix operating system, and all he had to do was flip the switch. That done, CERN was on the Internet.

Internet victorious

From then on it was just a matter of time before the Internet became the world standard we know today. By the end of the 1980s, ISO stalwart Brian Carpenter's pragmatism forced him to switch camps. Carpenter had been one of the principal authors of the CERN strategy document that had earlier put its weight behind OSI protocols. According to him, that decision 'continued to make sense for three or four years, but by 1989 or 1990 it didn't make sense any more'. OSI had not delivered working products and TCP/IP was the only protocol suite to work on all the major computers in use at the laboratory. 'It wasn't until the mid-80s that the pragmatism of the TCP/IP community began to emerge and it became obvious, I think, to most people by '88 or '89 that TCP/IP was going to win,' explains Carpenter. 'It became obvious to the politicians by about 1995,' he adds, 'but that's another story.'

In 1989, CERN's network managers decided to switch to TCP/IP, and the laboratory opened its first external Internet connections. Carpenter put his name to a report for RARE recommending the adoption of TCP/IP. Big computer companies also began to embrace TCP/IP, and IBM even funded the principal Internet link between Europe and the USA, which went through CERN. By 1990, CERN had become the biggest Internet site in Europe in terms of traffic, and the laboratory's expertise was widely called upon by other organizations wishing to jump on the Internet bandwagon, including, perhaps as a final act of capitulation, the ISO itself. 'Even before the Web allowed Internet penetration in the most unexpected places,' explains Ben Segal, 'the presence of the Internet protocols at CERN had already encouraged their adoption in such influential organisations as the ITU and ISO.'

With EUnet successfully running TCP/IP, and other European networks preparing to make the switch, the European TCP/IP community took its ambitions a step further. On 29 November 1989 it founded the Réseaux IP Européens (RIPE) under the chairmanship of Rob Blokzijl to ensure the technical and administrative coordination necessary for a pan-European IP network. True to the spirit of the Internet, RIPE began as a voluntary organization with no formal membership, but its services rapidly became overstretched. In 1992, RIPE established the RIPE Network Coordination Centre (NCC), complete with offices and a paid staff headed by Daniel Karrenberg. It was a clear sign of the times that the RIPE NCC's initial funding came from ISO champions RARE along with EARN and EUnet. By this time, although officially OSI was still being pushed, it was clear to people on the ground that TCP/IP was the only realistic option. With the RIPE NCC, 'people were sort of buying insurance, if you wish,' explains Karrenberg. 'The main success was that Rob and others, including myself, were able to convince those research network guys that they should spend just a little bit of their money to help us start this.' It proved to be money well spent. By the end of the 1990s, RIPE associated networks provided access to some 6 million host computers around the world. RIPE remains as lightweight as possible, but the extent to which the Internet has spread has made its general manager Daniel Karrenberg a very busy man.

The clash between OSI and TCP/IP had polarized the networking community and everyone has their own idea about why it ended as it did. For Peter Kirstein, 'there are a number of reasons, but probably the most important was the whole policy in the US of encouraging software development in academia and making the software freely available to industry'. Kirstein also believes that the basic idea behind ARPA, decoupling military R&D from the military establishment while keeping defence firmly in mind, had a big part to play. 'Whether defence should play this forcing function is another question,' he concedes, 'but at least it exists, we don't quite have any forcing function!' And as in any war, propaganda was important. 'I remember being told by the Americans that it was impossible for X.25 to work at above 64 kilobits per second at the same time that JANET was operating at 4 megabits a second,' he says.

For Leonard Kleinrock, it was not so much the ARPA concept as

IPTO's way of doing things. 'IPTO was a prime mover for the United States in the development of computer technology through advanced thinking,' he explains. In ARPA's early days there was no room for democratic niceties like peer review; 'they just bet on people that they had confidence in.' The Internet is probably ARPA's greatest success story, and IPTO backed it to the hilt, shielding researchers like Kleinrock from the usual rigours of grant proposals and review processes. 'We never had any hassle,' remembers Kleinrock; 'no senators, no congressmen, no military, no nothing in our way.' Cynics might argue that IPTO just happened to hit lucky with the people it funded on the ARPANET and Internet projects, but for those who had been involved, DARPA's adoption of conventional funding methods marked the end of a golden era for advanced long-range research.

Bob Cooper blamed the ISO way of doing things. 'What they proved in the end was that the ISO approach to standards was just too cumbersome. What the Internet did was develop a new way of developing standards that was far more compatible with the rate at which things were going.' The ISO was too politicized, in Cooper's opinion. At the four-yearly meetings, people who had had nothing to do with developing the standards would turn up and vote. Often they would be voting to curry political favour rather than to choose the best way of sharing data over a network. 'It's not the right way to do these sort of standards,' says Cooper. 'It might work for gas fittings and things like that but it wouldn't work for this kind of thing because it's moving too fast.' Ben Segal underlined this opinion. 'I always say that the time constant of the ISO committees was longer than the time constant of the technology,' he explains. In other words, by the time the ISO got round to discussing protocols suitable for one generation of technology, the next generation had already arrived.

Derek Barber puts another angle on the ISO's failure, pointing the finger of blame at the big computer manufacturers rather than the PTTs, who in his mind were valiantly trying to merge the new data communications ideas with their own familiar circuit-switching way of doing things. 'We had a protocols group trying to work along the lines of the ISO seven-layer model,' he explains. 'The bottom three layers were done very quickly by the PTTs because they couldn't provide services unless they had a standard. But the upper layers were to do with the way computers communicate, and the big manufacturers of computers had their own ways of doing it. They didn't want success and that's why we never ever got agreement on the upper four layers.' Even X.25, the third layer in the ISO model, was compromised in Barber's opinion by the computer manufacturers' attempts to hang on to their proprietary protocols. He remembers asking an AT&T engineer who was building an X.25 interface why it had so many wires coming out of it. 'Well, we don't really know what these computer people want,' came the reply, 'so we're giving them plenty of wires so they can make their minds up.'

In 1990, the number of Internet sites in Europe was 30 000. One year later, that had grown to 100 000, as people tired of waiting for OSI protocols and turned to TCP/IP instead. Governments were still officially supporting OSI but the Internet was so widespread that few people took notice. By 1992, the number of European Internet sites had risen to half a million. 'By this time,' says Brian Carpenter, 'we knew there would be a killer application but we didn't know what it would be.' The stage had been set for Tim Berners-Lee's invention of the World Wide Web.

Bits and PCs

3

The Internet isn't the only essential ingredient of the World Wide Web. Another vital component is the personal computer. If the Internet had just connected supercomputers, it is unlikely that anything like the Web would have emerged. Hypertext is equally important: if Berners-Lee had been stuck with hierarchical ways of organizing himself, his invention might have gone world wide, but it wouldn't have been much of a Web. And even with hypertext and personal computers sweeping the globe, Berners-Lee still needed something to click with. How easy would the Web be if we didn't have the mouse?

As we may think

Today it is hard to imagine life without personal computers. Their use is widespread not only in academic institutions but also in businesses, schools, and homes. We use them to keep track of personal accounts, write letters, book plane tickets, play games, and of course surf the Web. But fifty years ago computers were thought of strictly as calculating machines, complex tools for use by engineers, mathematicians, and physicists. Nobody thought they had any place outside a scientific laboratory, let alone in a home or office.

Well, almost nobody. As early as 1945 one man, Vannevar Bush, director of the US Office of Scientific Research and Development under President Roosevelt, envisaged a lot of the things we now take for granted in computers and published his thoughts in an *Atlantic Monthly* article called 'As We May Think'. It is largely to him that the men who gave the computer a more human face owe their inspiration.

Bush was an electrical engineer who had worked in academia since 1916. On the faculty of MIT from 1919, he was made both Vice-President of the Institute and Dean of the School of Engineering in 1932. But administration was not his only forte; he was also a formidable engineer. He patented a great number of devices, from tools for measuring distances and elevations to his 'differential analyzer', an early mechanical computer, which he patented 1935. His experience with the American patent system led him to propose changes to it, to make it easier to use and less easy to abuse. During the Second World War he was chairman of the National Defense Research Committee, as well as director of the Office of Scientific Research and Development, making him a key player in, among other things, the Allied atomic bomb project.

Towards the end of the war, Bush was asked by Roosevelt to suggest what lessons of the war could best be applied to civilian, peacetime activities. Bush replied that science, which had served the war effort, should now turn its hand to work that would lead to an improvement in the human condition. He wrote to the President, 'Science offers a largely unexplored hinterland for the pioneer who has the tools for his task. The rewards of such exploration both for the Nation and the individual are great. Scientific progress is one essential key to our security as a nation, to our better health, to more jobs, to a higher standard of living and to our cultural progress.' At the same time he also proposed the creation of a national research foundation—a request that was granted when the National Science Foundation (NSF) was established in 1950 with Bush as its director. It was also in response to Roosevelt's request that Bush wrote 'As We May Think'.

In this prophetic article, Bush describes many of the problems facing mankind, among them the information explosion. So much research was being done that it was impossible to find what was relevant, let alone keep up with it. 'The summation of human experience is being expanded at a prodigious rate,' he pointed out, 'and the means we use for threading through the consequent maze to the momentarily important item is the same as was used in the days of square-rigged ships.' His solution to the problem was the 'Memex', a device that would be used for simple and rapid information storage, retrieval, and editing. Although he envisaged it as a mechanical device based on microfilm instead of microchips, since even Bush couldn't foresee the digital revolution, his Memex had much in common with a modern personal computer.

In describing the Memex, Bush also described hypertext, though no one would call it that for another twenty years. He had been thinking about the problems with hierarchical and indexed information storage systems. 'The human mind does not work that way,' he concluded. 'It operates by association. With one item in its grasp, it snaps instantly to the next that is suggested by the association of thoughts, in accordance with some intricate web of trails carried by the cells of the brain.' He didn't think that mankind could duplicate this mental process artificially, but he believed that we ought to be able to learn from it. 'Selection by association, rather than indexing,' he suggested, 'may yet be mechanized.' By building a machine that worked more like the human mind than any existing tools, he hoped to help people think. Vannevar Bush died in 1974, too early for the World Wide Web, but not too early to have seen his idea of a personal computer capable of associative rather than hierarchical links realized. The man behind that realization was Doug Engelbart.

This is ridiculous, no goals!

As a shy and unassuming young man of 20, Doug Engelbart had read Vannevar Bush's article while serving in the US navy in the autumn of 1945. He hadn't had a burning desire to enlist. 'My eyes weren't good enough so I could enlist in anything dramatic,' he remembers, but he was drafted in 1944 anyway and trained as a radar technician. Radar work had started to appeal to him back in high school. 'I'd hear these rumours among the kids,' he says, 'about this thing called radar, and that the navy had this program where they would train you by having you study, and you'd go behind closed fences and they'd take the books out of vaults and teach you and then search you when you left and put the books back in the vaults. It all sounded so dramatic!' Seduced by the mystery, he set his sights on radar.

Radar technicians were in high demand during the war, and when in 1945, having finished his training, he was sailing out of San Francisco, Engelbart was a little nervous. 'My stomach [was] doing flip-flops because all the stories were of Kamikaze planes hitting the ships right in the communications center,' he remembers with a smile. 'So, yes, we need lots of radar technicians!' But as the ship sailed past San Francisco's Chinatown his nerves were calmed somewhat. 'We were standing up there gulping, and waving good-bye to—nobody was waving at us,' he laughs. 'Then we heard lots of whistles and fire-crackers and everything else, and finally the P.A. system on the ship says "The Japanese have just surrendered." It was VJ day.' Although the crew pleaded for the ship to turn around so they could join the celebrations on the mainland, the ship kept going. Thirty-eight days later they were dropped off on the island of Samar in the Philippines and a few weeks after that they were transferred to Leyte. It was on Leyte, while waiting for his next transfer in a Red Cross library built in a native hut up on stilts with a thatched roof, that Engelbart stumbled across the Vannever Bush article that was to determine his future. 'As We May Think' had a profound effect on him. 'I remember being thrilled,' he says. 'Just the whole concept of helping people work and think that way just excited me. I can remember telling people about it. I never have forgotten that.'

Although the article influenced him at the time, Engelbart didn't realize then that it was going to shape his future. His term in the navy ended a year later and he went on to finish the degree in electrical engineering that he had started before being drafted. After graduating in 1948, he worked as an electrical engineer at Ames Research Laboratory, which later became NASA, near San Francisco. It was two years later, in December 1950, just after he got engaged to be married, that he realized with dismay that he had fulfilled his life's ambitions: to get married, to get an education, to get a job. He remembered Bush's idea of the Memex and that helped Engelbart to formulate a new goal for the future.

'This is ridiculous, no goals,' he remembers thinking when he came home from work on that December day. And so for the next few months he set about trying to find some. 'For some reason I just picked that as an explicit, conscious thing to do,' he recalls. 'I had to figure out a good set of professional goals.' Not motivated by money, Engelbart decided his new goal would involve helping humankind. But the question was how. 'I remember reading about the people who would go in and lick malaria in an area. And then the population would grow so fast and the people didn't take care of the ecology and so pretty soon they were starving again, because not only couldn't they feed themselves but the soil was eroding so fast that the productivity of the land was going to go down. So it's a case that the side effects didn't produce what you thought the direct benefits would. I began to realize it's a very complex world.' Thinking about this complexity, he saw that the probability of achieving any given goal was pretty low. And then it dawned on him that finding a way to increase this probability could be his goal.

Along with the growth in information Vannevar Bush had identified, Engelbart saw that the problems facing mankind were getting more and more complex and the time there was to solve them was getting shorter and shorter. 'It suddenly flashed,' recalls Engelbart, 'that if you could do something to improve human capability to deal with that, then you'd really contribute something basic.' At the same time he saw computers as an integral part of a tool that would help people cope with their rapidly changing environment. 'Just to complete the vision,' he recalls, 'I also really got a clear picture that one's colleagues could be sitting in other rooms with similar work stations, tied to the same computer complex, and could be sharing and working and collaborating very closely. And also the assumption that there'd be a lot of new skills, new ways of thinking that would evolve.' Engelbart decided that he would build this tool.

This was in early 1951, before computer workstations even existed, before Sputnik, and nearly two decades before the first computer networks. Computers themselves at the time were the gargantuan calculating engines like the NPL's Pilot ACE, known only to a chosen few. To have had such a vision then is truly remarkable. It would be like imagining the road transport of the 1990s just after the invention of the wheel. But Engelbart's work as a radar technician fuelled his imagination, since he knew that cathode ray tubes (CRTs) could display anything you asked them to. He didn't know too much about computers, though. 'I'll tell you what a computer was in those days,' he says. 'It was an underpaid woman sitting there with a hand calculator, and they'd have rooms full of them, that's how they got their computing done. So you'd say "What's your job?" "I'm a computer."' He did know enough about computers, the machines not the women, to know that they could control CRTs, but he didn't know much more. So he left his job and spent years at graduate school finding out. He had the choice of Stanford or Berkeley, but chose the latter because it had an actual computer project, although it didn't yet have a computer. At the time, the closest one was in Maryland.

Although his goal was clear to him, few others shared Engelbart's enthusiasm. In a way this was not surprising. His vision made him so far ahead of his time that to most people his ideas didn't seem far-sighted, they just seemed crazy. While he was at Berkeley, he explored unconventional uses for the computer. 'I was interested all the time in how, instead of just doing numeric computations, it could manipulate symbols,' he recalls. 'I was even conjecturing how I could connect it up to make a teaching machine.' Some people in the psychology department were interested, but no one in computing was. 'I don't know whether they were insulted to think of using it for such a mundane thing or what,' he says. The upshot of this lack of interest was that he had to pursue a more conventional doctorate. 'It really became clear in a disappointing way that I couldn't do what I wanted to do,' he recalls, speculating that 'the kind of things I was thinking about didn't turn them on, because the pressure behind building computers in those days was to support numeric calculations.' So Engelbart's doctorate wasn't in human–computer interactions, the subject that excited him, but in the rather more mundane field of 'bi-stable gaseous plasma digital devices'. After graduating, he stayed on at Berkeley to teach. He didn't stay long however, leaving after one of his colleagues advised him that if he kept on about his 'wild ideas' he would stay low man on the totem pole forever. In 1957, after two years sizing up the options, Engelbart ended up at the Stanford Research Institute (SRI), the institute that was to become the second node on the ARPANET, in no small part because of Engelbart's presence. There his dream would start to become reality.

Because of the lack of enthusiasm and plain misunderstanding that his wild ideas had met with since 1950, Engelbart knew that when he arrived at SRI he wouldn't be able to start working towards his goal immediately. 'I realized that what I'd really have to do is find a way to earn my room and board there,' he says, so he set out to gain a reputation as a reliable engineer. He spent several years working in conventional areas, generating a dozen patents in the process. His efforts paid off in 1959 when, with funding from the Air Force Office of Scientific Research (AFOSR), he was finally able to start his own project. In 1960, funding from SRI followed, and in 1962 he was ready to publish a report describing his dream. The report was entitled 'Augmenting Human Intellect: A Conceptual Framework'.

Shortly before its release, Engelbart wrote to Vannevar Bush. He had realized that the goal he had defined for himself twelve years earlier had been largely inspired by reading 'As We May Think' one quiet afternoon in a Red Cross library in the middle of the South Pacific. In the letter he acknowledges his debt to Bush, writing, 'I re-discovered your article about three years ago, and was rather startled to realize how much I had aligned my sights along the vector you had described. I wouldn't be surprised at all if the reading of this article sixteen and a half years ago hadn't had a real influence upon the course of my thoughts and actions.'

Augmenting human intelligence

In his report, Engelbart asks what abilities people draw on, apart from those they are born with, to increase their effectiveness. By developing language, for example, humans became better communicators, by developing spears, better hunters, and by developing these tools the human brain also evolved. This process of co-evolution between humans and their tools occurred slowly over several millennia until the twentieth century. Nowadays, with the ever-accelerating pace of progress and the arrival of new technologies, the tools are developing faster than man's ability to use them to their full extent. What Engelbart wanted to do was find a way to accelerate man's intellectual development so that he could keep up with his tools, continuing the process of co-evolution. Engelbart saw computers as the engines that could give the human intellect the same kind of boost that it got when people first learned to turn grunts into words. His report finished with a strong plea to researchers and funding agencies to pursue this line of enquiry. 'After all,' he concluded, 'we spend great sums for disciplines aimed at understanding and harnessing nuclear power. Why not consider developing a discipline aimed at understanding and harnessing "neural power?" In the long run, the power of the human intellect is really much the more important of the two.'

To a casual observer, Englelbart's ideas might have looked a bit like the notions of Artificial Intelligence (AI) that were just beginning to appear. But Engelbart thought that AI researchers were barking up the wrong tree. He didn't believe that computers would ever be able to think for mankind, nor did he believe it would be a good idea if they could. He worried that if computers could be taught to think, then man and machine would exchange places, and this was just what he wanted to avoid. Instead, his idea was to use computers to help people make the best of their abilities and work in teams, pooling their resources for maximum benefit. His was an all-encompassing vision, covering every aspect of the working environment from the seat you sat on to the device you used to input data to a computer. The goal was to find the most productive working environment.

Computers were an essential part of this environment. 'We see the quickest gains emerging from (1) giving the human the minute-by-minute services of a digital computer equipped with computer-driven cathode-ray-tube display,' he writes in his report, 'and (2) developing the new methods of thinking and working that allow the human to capitalize upon the computer's help.' Luckily for Engelbart, J. C. R. Licklider started running IPTO in 1962 and recognized what he was talking about, his own research in human–computer interactions being along similar lines. 'I was standing at the door with this 1962 report and a proposal,' recalls Engelbart. 'I had met Licklider before and heard about him setting up a program, and I thought, "Oh boy, with all the things he's saying he wants to do, how can he refuse me?"' Licklider came through with funding, and in 1963, Engelbart was able to start work.

Engelbart's system, which he called NLS, for 'oN Line System', focused on structured documentation that could be easily and immediately manipulated by a computer and displayed on a computer screen. People using the system could share documents. It was set up so that many people could view a text at the same time and take turns adding their ideas to it. Engelbart had set up a form of teleconferencing so two people working in different places could see each other on the computer screen next to the text in question. The texts themselves had named hyperlinks in them so that it was easy to jump from place to place within and between files. Engelbart also came up with 'tiled' windows, windows containing text that didn't overlap like windows on a Macintosh or a PC but that sat side by side like bathroom tiles. And in those windows you could edit text just as you can on a modern word processor by moving a cursor around the screen.

The speed of interaction with the computer was an important factor to the NLS team, but this was something that the funding agencies didn't always understand. So Engelbart came up with a graphic analogy to demonstrate why speed mattered. He asked them to imagine that the only tools we had to write with were pencils strapped to bricks. How would this have affected our ability to write and to share and store information, he asked? The team's quest for speed of interaction led them to look beyond the keyboard as a way of interacting with the computer, and they came up with two other devices that, although not so intuitive to use, were much quicker once they had been mastered. One of these was something called a chord key set, consisting of five keys that would sit comfortably under your left hand. Different combinations of keys corresponded to different letters of the alphabet. Another was a pointing device that could be manipulated by your right hand and would allow you to move a cursor around the screen. Someone called it a mouse. 'None of us would have thought that the name would have stayed with it out into the world,' said Engelbart many years later, 'but the thing that none of us would have believed either was how long it would take for it to find its way out there.' The group tried other kinds of pointing devices, ones that could be operated by your head or your knee, but they all gave rise to muscle cramps. For speed and ease of use the mouse won hands down.

Today the mouse is ubiquitous. The key set didn't fare quite so well, although the odd one can still be seen if you look hard enough. And in many ways that is a shame. Having both a mouse and a key set meant that each hand could be performing a separate task, with the mouse hand determining the position on the screen and the key set hand doing what you would normally need both hands to do on a keyboard. It might have taken a bit longer to master, but if you made the effort you could work much faster.

By the end of 1968, Engelbart was confident enough of his system to demonstrate it at the Fall Joint Computer Conference in San Francisco. It was to be a demonstration like none before. 'I was beginning to feel we could show a lot of dramatic things,' he explains, but he knew he was taking a risk. Engelbart sat on the stage with a screen and a keyboard in front of him, a key set in his left hand and a mouse in his right. The CRT display in front of him was projected on a huge screen so that everyone in the 3 000-seat hall could see what was going on. Engelbart had a headset with a microphone to talk to the audience and headphones for his team to tell him what was going on behind the scenes. It was an extremely stressful hour and a half. 'We had a lot of research money going into it,' says Engelbart. 'And I knew that if it really crashed or if somebody really complained, there could be enough trouble that it could blow the whole program; they would have to cut me off and blackball us because we had misused government research money.'

Luckily for everyone, Engelbart's demonstration worked perfectly. He had people rushing up onto the stage to congratulate him on it, but even so it didn't have the desired effect. 'I was really hoping that it would get other people seriously started in things like this too,' he explains, 'but it just didn't.' Engelbart didn't get accused of wasting government money, but nor did he get floods of offers of help to develop his system further.

Over the years his funding slowly dried up, and the world had to wait another decade and a half for the vision that Engelbart had working in 1968 to become an everyday reality. One of the people present at the 1968 demo, and who would create that reality, was Alan Kay, a graduate student from Utah who was working on a thesis about the possibility of making not only a personal computer but a portable one. 'This was the visit that changed my life,' said Kay of his early encounter with Engelbart. 'What Doug Engelbart offered was not just a vision of interacting with the [computer] system, but also a philosophical underpinning that is even more important today than it was then.'

Today it can be hard to appreciate just how innovative Engelbart's NLS system was. But compared to what was available at the time it was mind-boggling. Back then, most people still communicated with the computer using punched cards; real-time interactivity was the stuff of science fiction. The state of the art in text editing was line editors, but here was a system where you not only had full text editing, but also many of the sophisticated features of a modern word-processing program. NLS could mix text and graphics on a single screen, with hyperlinks between them, and it allowed collaborative work at a distance. It was a radical paradigm shift in how people thought about documents, connections between documents, and the whole idea of human–computer interaction.

More than fifty years after defining his goals, Engelbart has lost none of his zeal. The vision encapsulated in his 1962 report and demonstrated in 1968 has not deserted him. He still believes that computers are being underused and their potential to help people think neglected. He worries that we are being bullied by the technology, with the emphasis being on making smarter computers, not on making them tools for making humans smarter. Today the vehicle for his ideas about augmenting the human intellect is the Bootstrap Institute, which he founded with his daughter in the late 1980s. Mainstream computing has taken a different path than Engelbart would have liked. Instead of teaching ourselves new ways of working with the new technology, we have simply grafted familiar metaphors like the desktop on to it, rather like the telecom engineers did when they automated torn-tape message-switching systems. But Engelbart hasn't given up hope that we will get there eventually. In the meantime, it is to him that we owe the mouse, the concept of windows, and the first working hypertext system, without which modern computing would be very different and the World Wide Web would not exist.

The road to Xanadu

Vannevar Bush may have been the first to come up with the idea and Doug Engelbart the first to build a working system, but the name 'hypertext' belongs to Ted Nelson. With no background in computing, Nelson claims to understand software without needing to get buried in the nitty-gritty of actual programming. He sees himself as the computer world's Alfred Hitchcock, able to see the finished program or system without actually having to deal with a keyboard, just as Hitchcock, according to popular legend, was able to produce his masterpieces without having to look through the lens of a camera.

In the early 1960s, Nelson envisaged a role for computers similar to Engelbart's but with starkly different motivation. 'The fundamental difference between my wonderful and very great stepfather Douglas Engelbart and myself,' he said at the Vannevar Bush symposium in 1995, 'is that he wanted to empower working groups and I just wanted to be left alone and given the equipment and basically to empower smart individuals and keep them from being dragged down by group stupidity.' Nelson coined the term hypertext in a presentation at the 1965 Association for Computing Machinery conference in Pittsburgh. The ideas leading up to this paper, entitled 'A File Structure for the Complex, the Changing, and the Indeterminate', had been forming in Nelson's mind since he started graduate school at Harvard in 1960. But the roots that led him to hypertext, and the computerized publishing system that accompanied it, go back much further.

The son of Academy-award-winning actress Celeste Holm and Emmy-winning director Ralph Nelson, Theodore Holm Nelson was raised by his grandparents in New York City. A literary child, he had always disliked the limitations of paper. Then in the 1950s he discovered a magazine called *Flair*, in which the publisher had got around paper's linearity by using cutouts. 'Little doors and windows throughout the magazine you could pop through. You could open the door and you could see something on the next page,' he remembers with enthusiasm, adding 'I loved that! And so it was obvious that you could get around linearity in these ways but you were always limited physically. The mind could imagine much richer spaces.' He found a source of such spaces in science fiction, and was thrilled by Robert Heinlein's 'And He Built a Crooked House', where doors didn't take you quite where you expected.

But paper wasn't all bad, especially if you had a pair of scissors and a pot of glue to hand, as he discovered when he took a job at the *New York Times* in 1956. One of his responsibilities there was filling up the paste pots journalists used to cut and paste their articles together. It was nothing like what we think of today as cut and paste on a computer, where you cut out a single piece of text from one place and paste it in somewhere else. They would cut up whole stories, arrange the pieces on the table in front of them, and draw links between the pieces in their mind before pasting the story together the way they wanted it. It was a far more powerful tool than any modern word processor's version of cut and paste and it added an extra dimension to the normally two-dimensional nature of paper documentation. 'That's what William Burroughs called cut-up,' explains Nelson. 'The words cut and paste, for writers, always meant taking your material, cutting it up, and putting it all around in front of you. In parallel. So you could see it side by side. Now you create the new structure. Now you paste it together.' It is a common technique for making sense of lots of complex ideas and the links that exist between them. For Nelson, when software engineers got hold of the idea of cut and paste it all went horribly wrong. 'This is one of those wonderful examples where an engineer or a technical guy tries to wrongfully oversimplify your problem,' he says. And he is not at all impressed with the result. 'They created this god-damned thing they called the clip-board,' he fumes, 'and then the words ... the words for the revolting operations of this abomination they call cut and paste which is taking two holy words about human creativity and making them mean hide and plug.' After all, the clipboard could only hold one item at a time, so all it let you do was move a chunk of text from one place to another. And according to Nelson it didn't have to be that way. Clearly irritated, he says, 'it would have taken two more bytes to make it a stack'.

But this irritation was all still in the future when in 1955 Nelson enrolled at Swarthmore College. 'I majored in philosophy and extra-curriculars,' he remembers. He enjoyed his years at Swarthmore, although he doesn't specify which major he enjoyed most, and he found the environment inspiring. 'It was an Olympus of intellect,' he says. 'I felt free to talk to everyone, it was a world of wonderful conversation and great discussions.'

Nelson graduated in 1959 and went on to graduate school at Harvard, where he majored in sociology. 'I thought like a sociologist,' he remembers, 'I was always a cynic.' However Deborah Stone, his girlfriend at the time, was less cynical. 'She was a senior at Radcliffe and we spent a lot of time together,' recalls Nelson. 'She would stay at my place at night but that was illegal. The girls in colleges in those days, and we called them girls in those days, not women, they were not allowed to stay out overnight.' Stone, fed up with this, wanted to change the rules, but Nelson was sceptical. 'I had been a fighter for the sexual revolution for some time already before this,' he says, 'and I was by now very cynical and I said you can't change the rules, it's not going to change, you just have to work around the system.' But she was determined, as was her roommate, so they took their ideas to the president of Radcliffe, who agreed. The rules could be changed as long as the students were all in favour of it. So there was a vote, and in the end, Nelson's girlfriend and her roommate succeeded. 'I was amazed,' says Nelson, still sounding it. Nelson remained cynical, but the experience perhaps infused him with the will to create Xanadu, the computer program that he thought would change the way we write, work, and think.

Nelson didn't know much about computers when he arrived at Harvard. 'I submitted a poem to the *New Yorker* about computers when I was 15, so I had as good an idea as anyone else who was not in the field,' he recalls, adding, 'they didn't accept the poem, of course.' But he was keen to learn. In his second year at Harvard, he remembers, 'I took a computer course because I was desperate to know what computers were.' His problem was that no one would give him the answer he wanted. But he didn't give up. 'I already had a pattern,' he says, 'that I didn't trust teachers and I didn't trust people who answered my questions, I would keep asking the question of some other person until I got the answer I knew was right!' And to the question, 'What is a computer?' 'the answer is', he says, 'it was not a mechanical, a numerical device, it was not a mathematical device, it was not an engineering device, it was an all-purpose machine!' Like Engelbart, Nelson wasn't fooled by the name 'computer', which to most people's minds brings images of hard sums. 'Computer was a bad name for it,' says Nelson. 'It might just as well have been called an oogabooga box. That way, at least, we could get the fear out in the open and laugh at it.' If you consider how many people still react to computers, maybe because of all those hard sums, you can see his point.

When he enrolled in that computer course, Nelson didn't realize that he was starting a project that would last until the present day. He knew about Vannevar Bush's article and he liked the idea of having a computerized Memex for looking after his own copious notes. His project for that early course in computing was to create one. But he was after more than just an electronic filing cabinet; he wanted a tool that would not only catalogue his writings but that would also keep track of the changes he made, and allow him to compare all the different versions of any document. He wanted to be able to view different versions in parallel, just as he could with paper. Not only that, but because computer memory does not have to be linear, documents didn't have to be linear any more either. It was an ambitious project, so it is no wonder he didn't finish it. 'It seemed so simple and clear to me then,' he recalled some twenty years later. 'It still does. But like so many beginning computerists I mistook a clear view for a short distance.'

Nelson's computerized writing and storage system continued to evolve and as the 1960s were drawing to a close he began to call it Xanadu. With the arrival of computer networks, Xanadu's possibilities expanded. Instead of being a system for use on a single computer, it would be a system where people could access and publish information over the network. And this would not just be true for a specific group of people; Nelson's battle cry was 'computer liberation'. He had in mind computers for everyone: scientists and artists alike. He came to represent the dreams of the computer hobbyists who would go on to create or work at the high-tech companies of Silicon Valley. Although Xanadu has still not been finished, it has inspired others in the world of hypertext and still sets the R&D agenda today. And according to Nelson, it holds the answers to the problems that are present in the World Wide Web. With Xanadu there would be no 'dead links'—those mysterious '404 Not Found' pages you get when you try to look at a page and find that it isn't there—because nothing gets deleted. In Xanadu everyone would get credit for their own work, because if you included something from another document in one of your own, the system would keep track of who was the original author of what. Copyright, royalties, and micropayments are all still in the Web's future, but Nelson believes they have already been solved in Xanadu. In over thirty years, Xanadu may not have been completed, but that doesn't mean it has failed. Nelson's ideas have influenced a generation of computer scientists, many of whose systems were inspired by him, and his ideas on royalties and copyright may end up being incorporated into today's Web.

First steps into hyperspace

Ted Nelson's dream of a world linked by hypertext took its first step towards reality at Brown University in Providence, Rhode Island, in the late 1960s. Nelson teamed up with another former Swarthmore student, computer scientist Andy van Dam, and a bunch of van Dam's students, to produce the world's second computer-based hypertext system in 1967. They called the system HES, for Hypertext Editing System. Unknown to either van Dam or Nelson, IBM—who technically owned HES since it was paid for out of an IBM research grant—sold it to the Apollo mission team. HES was used to produce documentation that went up with the Apollo rockets. Did it really stand for Hypertext Enters Space?

Nelson stopped collaborating with Brown in 1968, but for van Dam and his students HES was only a start. They began work on a new system, FRESS, the File Retrieval and Editing System. FRESS was a step forward from its predecessors, but the technology of the time meant that it was still very different from today's World Wide Web. It ran on Brown University's IBM mainframe and it only allowed links among documents on that system. There was no video, no sound, and of course no linking between computers—networking was still science fiction at the time and the first ARPANET node didn't come online until the following year. Doug Engelbart's mouse hadn't caught on at IBM and instead a light pen was used to point at hyperlinks on the screen. It was more like point-and-kick than point-and-click: you would point with the light pen and then click with a foot pedal. Links inside a document might point to footnotes, definitions, annotations, or even a single character, and 'light clicking' on them would display the information at the end of the link in a new window. Links pointing to different documents would open up those documents in a new window.

Like several of the World Wide Web's forerunners, FRESS was in many ways more sophisticated than the Web. Links were not simply one-way arrows pointing to somewhere else; they were bi-directional. That meant that if someone linked to your page, you would know about it—links were not simply embedded in documents as they are with the

World Wide Web. And links could be labelled with keywords so that customized paths through documents could be defined. If FRESS was to be used as a teaching tool, for example, a whole class of students could annotate a set of documents, adding their own links and thoughts. But if they didn't want to know what their classmates thought, students could choose to see only those links put in by the professor, ignoring their classmates' efforts.

FRESS was used to experiment with hypertext and it was put to the test in the classroom. Two courses were designed, one on energy and one on poetry, and in the latter students did all their reading, interpretive writing, and post-class discussion on the system. Discussions were threaded, following a particular theme like those on Internet newsgroups, and they were attached to the material they referred to. The students took to it like ducks to water, writing three times as much as and getting better grades than their classmates in a control group. Normally quiet students took on seemingly new personalities online, contributing fully to the electronic discussion. Nowadays that phenomenon is well known, with some people even reserving fully developed alter egos for online communication in multi-user games and chat rooms, but then it was all new.

The teaching experiment was deemed a success, but not an unqualified one. Students may have written copiously, but they didn't use hypertext linking to full effect. One reason was simply that although there were plenty of terminals at the students' disposal, there was only one graphical one that allowed links to be created with ease. And despite the bi-directionality of links, it was easy to get lost in a complex web of documentation. People, it seems, are too used to linear media, like a book where you start at the beginning and finish at the end, to be able to make full use of a hypertext system which makes it possible to jump anywhere at will. Greater simplicity and more guidance to navigation were needed. Nevertheless, FRESS scored an important first. 'We created the first scholarly online community already in the 70s,' explains van Dam, 'with threaded discussions embedded in the hypertext web.'

Viewdata

The information revolution that never was

The arrival of the World Wide Web is accompanied by cries of 'information age', 'cashless society', and 'free speech'. Social commentators worry about the underclass of people who live without Internet access, while others shout about the wonders of the new forms of direct democracy that the Web makes possible. But what they probably don't realize is that all of this has happened before. 'Plus ça change, plus c'est la même chose,' goes the French saying: 'The more things change, the more they stay the same.' The changes being brought about by the Web, including the problems, were all envisaged more than twenty years ago on the eve of the information revolution than never was. The technology that was to make it possible went by the name of Viewdata.

In a book published in 1979, Sam Fedida, the inventor of Viewdata, and science writer Rex Malik wrote, 'We believe that Viewdata is a major new medium ... one comparable with print, radio, and television, and which could have as significant effects on society and our lives as those did and still do. Like them it may well lead to major changes in social habits and styles of life, and have long-lasting as well as complex economic effect ... Viewdata is the first of the systems to enable the mass market to be offered the wide range of services inherent in the mix of computing and telecommunications ... This has been a major aim—a dream if you will—implicit in computing since the beginning.' For a while their great claim would become reality. There was a series of Viewdata conferences. Countries in Europe, North America, and the Far East all started experimenting with Viewdata systems. But almost all of them, with the notable exception of the French Minitel system, failed. The problem was, it seemed, the mass market didn't want it.

What is Viewdata?

When Sam Fedida joined the Post Office Research Station staff in 1970, the hot topic was Viewphone. The idea was to expand the telephone and transmit a television image along with voice so that people talking on the phone could also see each other. Fedida's first job was to look into using the image technology behind Viewphone, which was very high bandwidth, to transmit data. What he realized was that transmitting data would be most easily done by using ordinary telephone lines, provided there was somewhere to store it when it arrived. The storage device that Fedida had in mind was a slightly modified television set, and he called his idea Viewdata. It was officially released by the Post Office under that name in 1973, but it is also known under the generic name Videotex.

At about the same time that Fedida was working on Viewdata, researchers at the British Broadcasting Corporation (BBC) and the Independent Broadcast Authority (IBA) were trying to think of ways to transmit more than just pictures to television sets. They had realized that there was still some space left, after they had sent all the pictures and sound, for extra information. Their idea was to transmit 'text' to the television screen. Both groups tested their systems in 1973 and released them as Ceefax, whose name was simply a phonetic version of 'see facts', and the rather more long-winded Optical Reception of Announcements by Coded Line Electronics, Oracle for short. With a decision on standards, both systems became known generically as Teletext, or sometimes Broadcast Videotex. In 1976, Ceefax pages broadcast in the UK were transported over the European Informatics Network to conferences in Paris and Toronto, another example of internetworking.

So what, you might say. What's the big deal? The big deal is that Viewdata created the possibility for an information revolution. Given that most British households had both televisions and telephones, Fedida and others saw the possibility for people, ordinary people, to have instant access to information from their homes. They foresaw a world where 'Information Providers' (IPs) would store their data on a central computer and users would download it into small decoders, which would then display it on their TV sets. And information wasn't the only item on offer. Viewdata would give people access to e-mail, electronic banking, games, and bulletin boards. There would also be services for the disabled, allowing deaf people to engage in a form of telephone conversation where one person typed while the other spoke, and services which 'read' pages to the blind.

The Post Office certainly thought it was a big deal, and they were able to convince television manufacturers and potential IPs that Viewdata was a worthy cause. TV manufacturers were to build TV sets with built-in Teletext and Viewdata decoders. Convincing potential IPs proved a harder sell. In 1977 Roy Bright, the head of Viewdata International Operations, saw it as 'the most significant and exciting challenge of Viewdata. The marshalling of tens of thousands of "pages" of information into an attractive and comprehensible "mix" appealing to the widest interests of a community prepared to pay a modest fee to access from the comfort of their home is a daunting prospect.' At the back of his mind was a paper Vint Cerf and Alex Curran had presented a few years earlier in which they concluded that creating and maintaining large databases was much harder than anyone realized.

The Post Office went ahead with it anyhow. As they saw it, the costs to the consumer weren't all that high and the potential for profit for themselves, the TV manufacturers, and the Information Providers was large. A market trial, in which 1 000 users took part, started in 1978. Of the 1 000 participants, 70 per cent were householders and 30 per cent business, and each was expected to buy or rent a specially modified TV set. The experiment was soon deemed a success, with the result that in 1979 the Post Office launched Prestel, its commercial version of Viewdata.

Despite the early promise, Prestel was a resounding flop. By the end of March 1982, there were still only 14 400 users, of which the majority, 85 per cent, were businesses. The forecast had been for 700 000 users with the home-to-business ratio reversed. While there were some 900 information providers and over 200 000 pages of information covering news, weather, and sports, some information providers were beginning to drop out. They were getting the right 'usage per customer'; there just weren't enough customers. The average use was six minutes a day, although usage surged during the Falklands crisis when people used the service to get the latest updates and also, somewhat surprisingly, on budget day. Six minutes a day was all the market researchers had expected people to use Prestel. Its downfall was simply that not enough people were using it.

One of the reasons Prestel didn't take off in the home market was cost. At around the same price as the video cassette recorders that were beginning to appear on the market, Prestel decoders were luxury items. And with personal computers just arriving in the shops, consumers were being presented with an array of new gadgets to choose from. Of those three, Prestel decoders came a poor third. Moreover, Prestel was expensive to use because, just as with EPSS, the Post Office wanted to make it pay from the start. Ceefax and Oracle, on the other hand, offered much the same information for free.

Teletext was launched in the UK earlier than Prestel but it didn't share its fate. By 1982, Teletext use had exploded. Where there were only a little over 1 200 home users of Viewdata, there were 450 000 Teletext sets in use across the country and the number was growing at a rate of 40 000 a month. Low cost was probably a factor in Teletext's popularity. A Teletext decoder cost about a third of the price of a Prestel decoder, and you only had to pay once because Teletext didn't cost anything to use. Both the BBC and IBA provided pages, the former funded by the license fee and the latter carrying advertising. The most popular pages were news, weather, travel, TV guide, and sport. Teletext was used to provide subtitling for the deaf and instant subtitling allowed the Royal Wedding and Ronald Reagan's inauguration to be subtitled even though they were live broadcasts. The same technique was soon being applied to regular news broadcasts.

Unlike Prestel, Teletext has been a resounding success. Because of its lower cost it presented a smaller risk for consumers and television manufacturers alike. In 1982, when it was clear that Prestel wasn't going to take off in the home market, the Post Office focused on Prestel for the business market. The service limped along until finally, and somewhat ironically, in 1994, Clive Fedida, the inventor's son, pulled the plug.

Liberté, égalité, fraternité, and Minitel

Across the Channel, however, it was a different story. Back in the 1970s, France's telecommunications industry was the laggard of Europe, and Gérard Théry, in charge of the French Direction Générale des Télécommunications (DGT), was determined to do something about it. 'He had pharaonic ideas,' recalls Louis Pouzin; and not only that, he also had the full support of President Giscard d'Estaing. The result is that today, France has one of the most up-to-date telecommunications networks to be found anywhere in the world. Huge investments were made in telecommunications, and part of the vision was to put a terminal that would allow people to do their banking, shopping, and myriad other things in every home in France. As well as making the phone network digital, Théry wanted to create a French version of Prestel, preliminarily dubbed Télétel.

The Télétel project received official approval in 1978. One of the reasons it found support was that it would foster the growth of Transpac, the X.25 network that led to the shut down of Pouzin's Cyclades. Prestel also had a high-tech image, like Concorde and the high-speed TGV train, and so it was deemed a project that would lead France out of its telecommunications backwater.

The first Télétel trial, known as T3V for Télétel and the initials of the three Île-de-France towns where it ran, Vélizy, Versailles, and Val de Bièvre, began in 1981. On offer were services provided by the French railways as well as a variety of retailers and banks. The trial ran from July to December, and just as the British Post Office concluded after the Prestel trial, the French PTT declared that T3V had been a success.

There were some significant differences between the French and British approaches. Where the British expected their guinea pigs to pay for their Prestel converters or Prestel-enabled television sets, the French got theirs for free. And they weren't just modified television sets, but actual dedicated terminals, leaving the television set free for people to watch. It was these terminals, known as Minitels, that were eventually to give the French Videotex system its name.

What really ensured that Minitel succeeded where its British predecessor had failed was that the policy of giving the terminal away free continued through from trial to nationwide deployment. The French PTT didn't aim to make Minitel pay for itself from the start. The plan was that by creating a demand for Minitel services, they would recoup their investment by charging for Minitel use, and allow French industry to steal a march on the rest of the world into the bargain. The project was subsidized by massive public spending, with the goal being to put a Minitel in every household in France. Mass production would reduce the cost of terminals to about 500 French francs each, much less than the cheapest Prestel converter, but still a lot of money considering the many millions of households involved. Telephone subscribers would be offered the choice between a Minitel terminal and a paper copy of the telephone directory, the former having the advantage that it is never out of date. Back in the early 1980s, hundreds of thousands chose Minitel, so that by 1989, when Tim Berners-Lee was thinking about how to keep track of information at CERN, there were five million Minitels in use, making France the most 'wired' country in the world.

State intervention was the main reason for Minitel's success, but not the only one. Just as the Internet spawned newsgroups and bulletin boards, so did Minitel. And just as the Web has developed erotic content, so did Minitel. Minitel bulletin boards carry names like 3615 EROS; they are known as 'Le Minitel Rose' and are backed up by enormous advertisements on billboards across the country and in the French press. People realized that Minitel offered a new way of making money out of sex, just as with the Web when it came along. The same sort of thing had happened on Prestel, of course, but the 'No sex please, we're British' mentality soon put a stop to it. The censors scrupulously surveyed all postings for erotic content and removed it before it had the chance to corrupt the nation. The French had no such fears, and one French PTT researcher was overheard ascribing the failure of Prestel to the 'prudishness of the British'. Whatever the case, the Minitel Rose generated enormous revenues for the French PTT. By 1994, sex services made up a substantial fraction of Minitel's estimated turnover of 500 billion francs.

The sex industry wasn't the only one to jump aboard the Minitel; respectable businesses signed up as well. It is only recently that advertisers in the rest of the world have started to include Web addresses on their Web sites, but in France, adverts that include '3615', the Minitel equivalent of 'http://', have been around for well over a decade. Just as no self-respecting company today is without a Web site, in France a Minitel presence rapidly became *de rigueur*. Instead of ringing an infor-

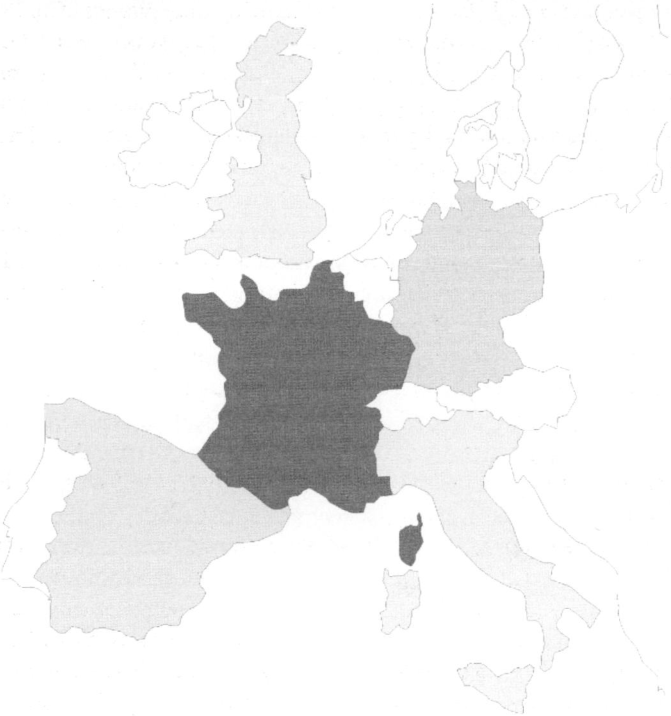

Figure 13: The darkness of shading shows the density of computer networks with white corresponding to no networks at all. In 1989, Minitel made France the world's most 'wired' country.

mation number, all a customer had to do was dial '3615' and then type the name of the company into their Minitel terminal to access the same information more quickly.

By 1989, France Telecom considered Minitel to be a resounding success. It had virtually replaced the white pages, there were five million terminals in France, French industry had had a shot in the arm, and most importantly, French pride had been restored. In a presentation to the President of the Republic, the grandly titled Minister of Post, Telecommunications, and Space stated, 'now, for the first time in this field, without a doubt France is in the lead. Without displaying misplaced jingoism, it is comforting to see engineers from the greatest foreign nations coming here to study the phenomenon, at the same time as the press reproaches ministers for what it considers to be their failure in this domain.' From being a telecommunications laggard, France was now leading the world.

But the story was not so simple. The reason why the Minister was strutting so proudly before the President was that Minitel was under attack by the National Audit, which had noticed a 5.3 billion franc hole in the PTT's accounts. This, as far as they were concerned, was a breach of promise, since the PTT had said that by providing people with Minitels it would be saving money. The auditors questioned the wisdom of investing so much public money in a single technology, given the risk of obsolescence in such a rapidly changing field. They worried about new laws that could be imposed on France by the European Union, foreseeing the liberalization of the market. They also pointed out a problem that still exists with the Web today. The law courts, they said, were nervous, because this area was developing before there were laws to cover it. The Minister brushed aside these charges, pointing out that the auditors had conveniently overlooked a number of entries on the plus side of the balance sheet. The revenues from Transpac, for example, the network that carried Minitel traffic, amounted to 650 million francs. He also pointed out the benefits to French industry, which he estimated at 6 billion francs in 1988 alone, comfortably enough to recoup the investment.

Despite the court case, Minitel went on to enjoy many more years of success. Even now its days are far from over. There are still some things that Minitel does better than the Web. Because Minitel is based on the telephone network, people feel more confident about typing their credit card numbers into a Minitel terminal than a Web browser. The information never leaves France Telecom's network, so the chances of anyone other than the intended recipient getting hold of it are much smaller than on the Internet. On the Internet, your credit card number could pass through any number of nodes belonging to all kinds of people and on any one of them some unscrupulous hacker could pull out your credit card number. This is why you should send sensitive information only in encrypted form—and much effort is going into encryption technology for Web commercial transactions. It is also perhaps why French companies will continue to maintain their '3615' addresses until the public comes to trust Internet technology. As France Telecom is a direct intermediary between the information providers and the Minitel readers, it can also charge the readers for the information at a rate stipulated by the providers. This possibility for the author to sell information in small bits created a real market for content which has proved difficult to provide on the Web. Minitel therefore has an effective micropayment system that the Web does not yet have.

In the long term, however, Minitel is likely to be replaced by the World Wide Web. Just as the auditors predicted, a new technology has indeed come along to make the French system obsolete. The arrival of the Web with its high-quality graphics and multimedia was bound to challenge Minitel's dominance. The very fact that Minitel didn't spread beyond France is part of its problem: it may bring France to your home, but the Web brings you the world. It took the World Wide Web until July 1995 to surpass Minitel in terms of number of servers, but now it is slowly pulling away, and 'http' is beginning to supplant '3615' on French advertising hoardings even though Minitel continues to grow (1999) at three per cent a year and Minitel emulators are bundled with every computer modem sold in France.

Austria enters the game

Although France is without question the only country whose Videotex system achieved world fame, Sam Fedida's invention gave rise to innovative research in many other countries, notably Austria. There, a team lead by Hermann Maurer at the Institute for Information Processing in Graz was looking at ways to expand the appeal of Videotex. From the fate of Prestel, Maurer concluded that Videotex, which he called VTX, was not going to be an overnight success but he wasn't deterred. At a 1982 conference in New York entitled 'Videotex—Key to the Information Revolution', he declared, 'the thrust now is to concentrate on finding special interest groups which find VTX useful as it stands, and to upgrade VTX to make it attractive to a wider and wider audience'.

The upgrade that Maurer believed could make the system fly was the microprocessor, which by 1982 was becoming widely available and even affordable. Maurer thought that by building a microprocessor into Videotex terminals, he could turn them into actual computers complete with modern features like word processing. 'Sam Fedida had the idea of a networked information system,' he explains, 'but we in Graz had the idea of networked personal computers, and this was before the first IBM PC existed and long before the World Wide Web.'

At the time of the New York conference, Austrian Videotex was much like its British and French counterparts. It used a television set as the display and carried the news, weather, and sports that formed the backbone of Prestel and Minitel. It also offered a kind of electronic mail, with users having mailboxes to which others on the system could send messages. There was little danger of mailboxes overflowing, however, since Austrian Videotex had even fewer users than Prestel, a mere 250. But things began to look up when Maurer introduced his system of networked personal computers, which he called MUPID. As well as copying information over the network, like Prestel or Minitel, a MUPID terminal could copy programs and run them. These could be as novel as singing postcards, as diverting as computer games, or as serious as programs that helped you figure out your income tax. He called the idea tele-software. The Web is just catching up: its equivalent goes by the name of Java applets.

Some 40 000 MUPID terminals were eventually sold, and Maurer still believes that it could have been much more had the European political will been stronger. MUPID was based on a European standard developed by the Conference Européene des Administrations des Postes et des Télécommunications, CEPT. 'It is typical for Europe that all countries signed the CEPT agreement but the UK never cared, Scandinavia bowed out, the French went their own way, and Holland gave up on the standard,' he explains. 'Finally only Germany and Austria upheld the standard for a while, leaving not a big enough market to start computer networks in the mid-80s. It is my belief that if all of Europe would have stuck to their CEPT resolution, Europe might have today its own microcomputer industry and a network superior to the World Wide Web.'

The original Videotex concept, dreamed up by Sam Fedida and developed by Hermann Maurer, was already capable of many of the things that were still giving Web developers headaches at the end of the 1990s. Things like microcharging and privacy were built in, so it is not surprising that delegates at the New York conference were upbeat. They came from around the globe, all of them convinced that they were on the verge of changing the world. The conference chairman described Videotex as 'the last great electronic adventure of the century'. 'Videotex is already sweeping post-industrial countries,' he said. 'Its leading edge is creating entirely new industries, communications, and computer technologies. It is influencing consumer lifestyles and traditional ways of doing business and catalysing a wave of social and legal concerns.' His comments were a little premature, but there was no denying the optimism. 'There is a strong intuition among its devotees that it will be as important an influence on mass communications as the telephone,' he concluded. Delegates went on to discuss electronic newspapers, advertising on Videotex, home banking, and educational applications. There were presentations about Chinese and Japanese Videotex services. One speaker gave a talk entitled 'Instant Information or Electronic Ennui'.

Little over a decade later, conference delegates would again be using such language and discussing such topics, and just like their predecessors they would be full of the altruistic optimism that they were on the verge of changing the world. But instead of Videotex conferences, they would be attending conferences about the World Wide Web. Sam Fedida's revolution is happening after all, even if the name has changed.

Getting personal

With the development of hypertext systems and networks, the Web had two of its principal ingredients, but there was a third. What allowed the Web to grow so quickly was personal computing. Macintoshes and PCs are so common today that it seems they have been around forever, but their development is surprisingly recent, and it didn't happen overnight.

When the first stored program computers were built back in the 1940s they were far too bulky, unreliable, and expensive for any individual to buy. Nobody seriously thought that one day we would all have computers in our homes and offices, and few could even imagine why we might want to. But as time passed, new technologies appeared, computers became more reliable, smaller, and more powerful, and they even became cheaper to buy. People started playing with them as a hobby, and eventually the individual computer evolved into a useful tool and a powerful toy. Businesses started to put computers on their employees' desks and people started buying them to use at home.

A computer is basically a series of switches; if you decide to do one thing, the switch stays open, and if you decide to do another, it closes. A modern computer is filled with tens of millions of switches. In the early days these were made up of electronic valves like the kind that used to glow orange in the backs of radios and television sets, and they were counted in thousands instead of millions. Valves are a bit like light bulbs except that an electric current flowing through them can easily be switched on and off. That means that they can be assembled in such a way as to talk a kind of binary language: a current flowing equals '1', no current equals '0'. Binary codes are the basis of all computer operations. But the problem with valves is that they are as big as light bulbs, they generate just as much heat, and they are just as likely to burn out. That limited the power of the early computers. Machines like the ACE needed an army of attendants to survey the valves and change them as soon as they burned out. Computers over a certain size were ruled out because it would simply be impossible to change the burned-out valves fast enough.

Two inventions were needed to change that. The first was the transistor, invented in December 1947 by William Shockley, Walter Brattain, and John Bardeen at Bell Labs, and winning them a Nobel Prize nine years later. The transistor does the same thing as a valve, but it doesn't give off as much heat, it is a lot smaller, it uses less energy, and it is much more reliable. It was a big step forward and allowed Ken Olsen to build his TX-0 at MIT in 1956. However, the TX-0 was still a big machine because there was still no compact way of connecting thousands of transistors together in a box that was small and could be produced cheaply and reliably.

The second invention, which solved this problem, was the integrated circuit (IC), a way of building several transistors into a single chip along with other components such as resistors. The first IC was built by Jack Kilby, an engineer working for Texas Instruments, in 1958. It was a modest affair with just five components on a wafer one centimetre long, but it set the scene for the personal computing revolution. Integrated circuits quickly shrank and were soon carrying ten elements on a wafer roughly three millimetres square. By the mid-1960s, the co-founder of Intel, Gordon Moore, made the observation that every year since the IC was invented the number of elements per square inch on a chip had doubled. That observation has since become known as Moore's Law, and it still holds true today, though the doubling time has been revised upwards to 18 months. Put simply, it states that no sooner has a computer been produced than it is out of date.

Where transistors improved the reliability of computers and made them smaller and easier to maintain, ICs made them smaller still and easier to build. The next big step forward would be to put a whole computer on a single chip, and it was Moore's company, Intel, that did that in response to a request from a Japanese company that wanted to make an electronic calculator. The request came in 1969, and two years later, Intel unveiled the world's first microprocessor, the Intel 4004. It was the first time that all the elements needed for the operation of a computer had been built into a single chip.

A computer, however, cannot live on microprocessor chips alone. While advances were being made in computing circuitry, similar developments were afoot in computer memory. The magnetic ferrite memories that had made the ACE computer obsolete in the late 1950s were still relatively cumbersome devices. They stored the computer's code of 1s and 0s in magnetizable doughnut-shaped iron rings with wires passing horizontally and vertically through them. Currents in the wires could cause the magnetism in the rings to run clockwise or anticlockwise to store either a 1 or a 0. With the arrival of integrated circuits, however, it wasn't long before people realized that computer memory could also be stored on a chip. In parallel with the work on the 4004, Intel decided to do just that, and by 1972 they were producing memory chips that could store 4096 bits for less money than much larger magnetic ferrite memory. With IBM's new floppy discs for carrying information from one computer to another appearing around the same time, all the ingredients of a modern personal computer were in place.

It was much earlier, however, that the concept of personal computing was first developed at Lincoln Labs by Wesley Clark, the man who came up with the idea of the sub-net for the ARPANET in 1967. That little foray into networking had been a bit of an exception for Clark, whose real interests lay with the computers themselves. In 1962, he had developed what many people consider to be the first personal computer. Called the LINC, for Laboratory Instrument Computer, it was the first computer to combat what J. C. R. Licklider had called the 'neighbourhood dry cleaner' approach to computing where people would have to drop their computing tasks off and pick the results up later. With a LINC in their laboratory, scientists had direct access to the computer themselves for the first time. About sixty were built in the summer of 1963 at Lincoln Labs by the same researchers who would then take them back to their own laboratories and use them there. Although too big to be considered a personal computer by today's standards, the LINC was considerably smaller than the behemoths that inhabited university computing centres. The LINCs proved to be extremely long-lived machines in computing terms, with the last one not being switched off until 1992.

Although novel in its small size and approachability, there was nothing unusual about the kind of people who were using the LINC and what they were using it for. It was still a tool for scientists to crunch numbers on. Although the idea that computers might also make powerful non-numerical tools was in the air, only a handful of people were actively doing anything about it. But as the end of the 1960s approached, the powers that be at Xerox were beginning to think there might be something in the idea. Xerox made office photocopiers and nothing else, a situation its managers felt was becoming too precarious for comfort. They concluded that the company needed to diversify, so they bought a computer firm and set up an advanced computer research laboratory, the Xerox Palo Alto Research Center (PARC), far away from the photocopier labs.

Bob Taylor was brought in to recruit PARC's brainpower. Taylor's tenure at ARPA had put in him contact with most of the researchers in the still fledgling field of computer science, and the incentive of plenty of research money coupled with the freedom to develop their research interests proved an irresistible lure to many of them. By 1972 they were on their way to designing the Alto, a personal computer intended for ordinary people to use, and one that we would still recognize as such today.

The first Alto was finished in 1973 and development continued through the 70s. By the time it was finished, Xerox PARC had invented the office of the future. People sat at their desks and worked on Alto computers, networked using Bob Metcalfe's Ethernet. The Altos incorporated many of the features that had been developed for Doug Engelbart's NLS, including the mouse and the key set. Instead of a simple cathode ray tube display that could just show lines of characters, they had a graphical user interface (GUI), not dissimilar to those on Macintoshes and PCs today, complete with overlapping windows, pull-down menus, and icons. Before the Alto, everything was done on a command-line model, and graphics were something you had to go to a special terminal to look at. There was even a built-in word processor that worked on the principle of What You See Is What You Get (WYSIWYG, pronounced wizzywig), meaning that you saw on the screen a good approximation of what you would get on the printed page. One of the reasons the Alto was so advanced was the team's realization that the cost of memory chips was going to keep falling. 'We threw memory at any problem we could find,' recalls one team member. People outside the lab thought they were crazy. The Alto's 128k memory cost $7 000 at the time, which seemed extravagant for the needs of a single person.

By the late 1970s, Xerox was poised to revolutionize the office environment, but they didn't. The cost of memory did indeed fall, but the Alto was still expensive. When the company tried to sell a machine that had evolved from the Alto, the Xerox Star, in the early 1980s, they found that people weren't prepared to pay the $18 000 price tag they were asking. To make matters worse, in those days businesses did not put a computer on everyone's desk, and the Star was so slow that almost no one could see the point. And to compound Xerox's misfortune, PARC had become more like an academic institution than a corporate R&D base, and many of the best ideas leaked out to be developed by others. The office of the future was one of those ideas, and Xerox would be destined to continue primarily as a manufacturer of copiers and printers, but they didn't quite lose everything from the Alto project. Thanks in part to Bob Metcalfe's Ethernet and to the development of personal computing based in no small part on the Alto, the market for printers was much bigger than it had been when PARC was founded.

Homebrew

While the professionals were burning the midnight oil at Xerox PARC, another group of keen computer enthusiasts was blossoming on the West Coast. But they were birds of a different feather, and by PARC's standards a very amateurish bunch. There were scant few Ph.D.s among their number, many being too young for that. There were high school students, university students, university drop-outs, and anyone, in fact who liked tinkering with electronics. In March 1975, thirty-two of them met in a garage and formed what became known as the Homebrew Computer Club whose purpose was to form a meeting point to share ideas about and problems with electronics in general and computers in particular. Many of the club's members were eagerly awaiting the delivery of a product launched in January 1975 that would bring their dream of owing a computer to reality. It was called the Altair 8800.

Named by the 12-year-old daughter of the publisher of *Popular Electronics* magazine after a planet visited by the crew of the Star Ship *Enterprise*, the Altair was a build-it-yourself computer based on Intel's 8080 microprocessor chip. It was designed by MITS (Micro Instrumentation Telemetry Systems), a company that started by building radio kits for model aeroplanes and moved on to build-it-yourself calculators. The Altair was the next logical step. The computer was featured on the front cover of *Popular Electronics* in January 1975 and sold for a paltry $397. MITS soon found itself swamped by more orders than it could fill, with a fair number coming from future Homebrew members.

With computers, as with most things, you get what you pay, for so it was not surprising that the Altair couldn't do very much. If you managed to put it together correctly, it was not even obvious that you would know. To program an Altair, you had to flick switches in an arcane but logical sequence to load in your program. If you got it right, your efforts would be rewarded by nothing more than a few flashing lights. For Homebrew members, that was a wonderful beginning to their computing adventure, but the Altair's popularity ensured that there would be much more to come. A cottage industry sprang up to produce add-ons for the Altair in a bid to make it useful. One of these industries soon outgrew its cottage. The company's product was a system to allow the

Altair to be programmed in the BASIC programming language, and the boys who wrote it were none other than Bill Gates and Paul Allen. They called their nascent company Micro-soft. From those humble origins, Microsoft (they eventually dropped the hyphen) has gone on to become the world's dominant software company.

Gates wasn't a Homebrew member. He grew up in Seattle and briefly studied law at Harvard before deciding there might be money to be made from computers. But Gates wasn't the only one to found an empire on the back of Homebrew computing. Steve Wozniak was at that first Homebrew meeting. He had been interested in electronics since he was a child and it was at that meeting that he found out about the Altair. 'All of a sudden,' he remembers, 'I discovered that the prices of some parts called "microprocessors" and "memory chips" had gotten so low that, with maybe a month's salary, if I saved for a while, I could afford to design and build my own computer.' So he saved for a while and set himself the task of making something that was better than the Altair. By January 1976, he had succeeded in making a Homebrew computer that was actually useful. 'I actually brought it into work and solved some engineering and design problems I was working on, so I knew I had something good,' he says.

Steve Wozniak had a friend that he had known from high school who shared his love of computers. Five years Wozniak's junior, Steve Jobs would drop in to the Homebrew Computer Club from time to time to see what was going on. When he saw his old friend's computer he was impressed.

Jobs wasn't as much of an engineer as Wozniak but he was no slouch. He supported himself by writing computer games and he had an eye for business. It was Jobs who saw the commercial potential of Wozniak's computer, and on April Fool's Day 1976, he and Wozniak founded a company. They were both Beatles fans; Jobs might have been working in an orchard as well as writing games. No one really remembers why any more, but they called their company Apple. Wozniak immediately set about improving on his newly-named Apple computer. Hand assembled in Jobs' parent's garage, the Apple II was launched at the West Coast Computer Faire, and sold for $1 300. The era of the personal computer was about to begin. When the Apple II hit the shops in May 1977, it was not alone. The Commodore Personal Electronic Transactor, better known as the PET, had also been launched at the West Coast Computer Faire and both machines sold like hot cakes. Tandy's TRS-80 followed in August, priced at a mere $399, and soon companies were springing up all over the place to produce software from games to spreadsheets for the new machines.

Despite the diversity of products hitting the market, there was nothing approaching the power of Xerox's Alto, but few people outside Xerox knew anything about it. Steve Jobs and number of other Apple engineers got their chance to come face to face with Xerox PARC's office of the future in 1979 when Xerox decided to invest in Apple. They put $1 million of capital into the young company in exchange for 100 000 shares, and offered Jobs a tour of the fabled research centre. He was amazed by what he saw. 'Why aren't you doing anything with this?' he cried. 'This is the greatest thing! This is revolutionary!' And he went back to Apple with a clear vision of where he wanted his company to go. Apple would produce a computer that put the power of the Alto within reach of ordinary people.

It was five years before Jobs's vision became reality. Meanwhile, both Xerox and Apple had launched unsuccessful versions of the Alto. The Apple Lisa cost close to $12 000, and it joined the Xerox Star which was priced at $18 000 for a basic model. Both machines were far too expensive for the home market. The office market wasn't convinced that Stars and Lisas could do anything more than the big centralized computers it was already using, and with that kind of price tag it wasn't about to take a risk to find out. It would be Apple's next computer that brought Xerox technology to the people.

Jef Raskin was an Apple engineer who liked apples. He had started the project to produce a computer that would make the Alto's technology affordable. He wasn't at all in favour of naming computers after women, considering that a sexist thing to do, so he gave the project the code name of one of his favourite kinds of apple, the Macintosh. Asked to see what kind of computer he could come up with for $500, he replied, 'for a thousand I could give you something that could be dynamite.' Then he sat down to write the book of Macintosh. 'The purpose of this design is to create a low-cost portable computer so useful that its owner misses it when it's not around,' he wrote, 'even if the owner is not a computer freak.'

When the Macintosh was released in 1984 it was a revelation to all who saw it. Even today people speak in hushed tones about their first encounter with the new computer. 'And then I read the specs of the Mac and made a down payment without even seeing one,' remembers one early Mac fan. 'You lugged this thing around with you in what one friend called a "Mac Back Pack" but you certainly never let it out of your sight.' But despite the love it inspired in some, the Mac wasn't an overnight success. It sold well for the first month but then sales practically stopped, hovering at around 10 per cent of what Jobs had predicted. Joanna Hoffmann, who marketed the first Macintosh, isn't surprised. 'It's a miracle that it sold anything at all,' she says. 'This was a computer with a single disk drive, no memory capacity, and almost no applications.' The people who bought the Macintosh bought it because of what it represented, not because of what it could do. The Macintosh had the capacity to be dynamite, or even 'insanely great' as Steve Jobs would have it, but not as it was when first put on the market.

The Macintosh nearly spelled the end for Apple instead of a beginning. What kept it alive was its user interface. The Mac's WYSIWYG inspired the development of desktop publishing software that had the capacity to turn individuals into publishers without the investment of tens of thousands of dollars. Within a couple of years, a revamped Mac with more memory, a hard disk drive for storage, and a printer designed specifically for it secured the Macintosh a corner of the market where it is still unrivalled today.

So the Macintosh lived to see another day, but Apple's tribulations were far from over. The next few years saw a series of questionable management decisions at Apple, that nearly sunk the company. One wrong turning was setting a price. To the people at Apple the Mac was clearly so much better than its competition in other personal computers that people would surely be prepared to pay more for it. They weren't. Another concerned the question of licensing. If Apple had chosen to license, other manufacturers could have started to produce Mac clones, and they would probably have been able to sell them for less than the original. On the other hand, there would have been more Mac-like computers around, and more people writing software for them. Apple chose not to dilute the brand and kept the technology to itself. That meant that if you wanted a Macintosh, you had to buy it from Apple, and if you wanted software other than for desktop publishing, you probably bought something else. In the short term, at least, it was the wrong decision.

One company that chose the other route was IBM. Having built its strength in computing around big number-crunching mainframes, IBM was a relative latecomer to the personal computer game. But having decided that the future of computing lay with smaller machines, Big Blue acted decisively. Just one year after the company decided to build a personal computer, the first IBM PC, based on the Intel 8088 chip, was launched in 1981. At $2 800 it was not a cheap machine, but businesses loved it; IBM does stand for International Business Machines, after all. IBM was a company that people had learned to trust, and it was a company to be taken seriously. The IBM PC may have cost more than its competition, but the fact that it bore the IBM label said that here was a serious machine, not a toy, and that it had the backing of one of the world's biggest companies, not a garage full of hackers. Demand was so high that IBM increased the PC's production by a factor of four only a few days after it was launched. Pretty soon other companies were cashing in too, producing 'IBM clones' that looked remarkably like the IBM and could run the same software.

The IBM PC soon became the office standard, along with the operating system, MS-DOS, that came with it. IBM had decided not to develop software for its personal computers in-house, even though it was successful at writing software for its larger computers. Instead, IBM asked Bill Gates and Paul Allen if they could provide an operating system for the new PC. The two men agreed, even though they didn't have anything like an operating system in the works. What they did instead was buy one from another company for $30 000, and then rather than simply selling it on to IBM at a profit, they licensed it. This astute move proved to be the making of Microsoft; for every one of the millions of IBMs and IBM clones that have been sold, Microsoft has made between $10 and $50.

In 1982, *Time* magazine underlined the fact that personal computing had arrived by choosing not to elect its traditional Man of the Year. Instead, *Time* bestowed that honour on the PC. 'The enduring American love affairs with the automobile and the television set are now being transformed into a giddy passion for the personal computer,' said the first issue of 1983. 'It is the end result of a technological revolution that has been in the making for four decades and is now, quite literally, hitting home.'

Time magazine was right about the revolution, but they had missed the people that really made it happen. With NLS, Doug Engelbart had laid the foundations upon which the edifice of modern desktop computing would be built. Xerox PARC added the graphical user interface and networks, and Apple was the first to make it a commercial reality. Engelbart would have to wait a little longer for recognition to come his way, but come it eventually did. When the film of his 1968 demonstration was shown at the fourth World Wide Web conference in 1995, the audience sat through it in stunned silence then gave him a several-minute standing ovation. 'It was actually pretty moving,' one delegate later recalled. Formal recognition came soon after when in 1997 Engelbart was awarded the 'Nobel Prize' of computer science—the ACM's Turing Award.

The rise and fall of the British personal computer

American companies may dominate the personal computer market today, but things haven't always been that way. The first microprocessor-based computer was not American but French. And when personal computing was still in its youth, it was the British who embraced the new technology faster than anyone else. At the beginning of the 1980s, per-capita ownership of computers in Britain was higher than anywhere else in the world and the British computer industry was booming.

Released in 1973, the pioneering French computer took its name from a French slang word for small: Micral. The Micral was immediately put to use in French motorway pay stations, but it didn't get much further than that. Across the Channel, however, a vibrant new industry was about to appear. The first British personal computer manufacturer was Acorn, founded by Hermann Hauser and Christopher Curry in 1978. Its first product was a kit computer, like the Altair. The second, the Acorn Atom, although more powerful, also had something in common with the Altair: it was a huge success. Acorn advertised it in *Practical Electronics* and waited to see what would happen. 'We put that ad out and we just couldn't shovel the cheques to the bank,' recalls Hauser. For a while it seemed that for Acorn the only way was up. 'From then onward, until we went public in 1984, the one problem with Acorn was producing enough,' explains Hauser. One year the company grew by a factor of five. 'In Silicon Valley this was not unusual but in Britain,' he says, 'there was no experience of a company growing that fast.'

In 1981, Acorn won the contract that would make its reputation. Two years earlier the BBC had decided to make an educational series about computers. The idea was that they would commission a manufacturer to build a demonstration computer that the series would revolve around. It would have to be affordable so that viewers could have one at home to try out the things they had seen on the television, but it would also have to be powerful and versatile enough to make the series worthwhile. 'It was just typical BBC,' says Hauser. 'It was way over the top in every way: the amount of processing power, the integrated graphics, the connectivity it had to have for the rest of the world, the printers ... Basically they wanted to make a programme about the computer industry, so this thing had to do everything that you'd ever thought of.' It was a tall order, and by 1981, the company chosen by the BBC had failed to deliver, so Acorn stepped in to save the day. The result was the BBC Micro, a computer that fulfilled all the BBC's wild expectations. It was powerful, it had graphics, and thanks to the Acorn's proximity to

Cambridge it was ready to be networked using the Cambridge Ring local area network system.

The BBC Micro made it into homes and schools across the country, and Acorn eventually sold 1.5 million of them. Even America started to notice it. 'Bill Gates tried to talk me into adopting his MS-DOS,' says Hauser. 'He came to Cambridge and gave me a big spiel.'

Acorn was soon joined by a host of other companies producing computers for the home and office market. Among them was Apricot Computers, which for a while produced the best-selling computer in Britain. Apricot had begun life as Applied Computer Techniques (ACT), a Birmingham-based firm that bought a big computer in 1965 and rented out time on it. By 1982, ACT was selling a computer called the Sirius 1, but it wasn't a machine the company had made itself. The Sirius 1 had been designed by American Chuck Peddle, the same man who had designed the Commodore PET, and it dominated the UK and European markets until the IBM PC was launched.

Partly because of the success of the IBM in the United States, Peddle's company began to look shaky, and it eventually went bankrupt in 1983. But in 1982, ACT, buoyed up by the success of the Sirius, decided to start building computers itself. The direction that personal computing was going to take was not yet clear. Apple and IBM were both doing well in the States, but so were others like Commodore and Tandy. In Europe, you couldn't even buy an IBM PC. After abortive negotiations with Tandy, ACT decided to go it alone. They started work on a new computer that would be compatible with the Sirius 1, and not with the IBM PC. The result was the Apricot, launched in Summer 1983, the machine the company changed its name for. Apricot built a new factory in Glenrothes and the area around it soon became known as Silicon Glen because of the number of high-tech companies that were choosing to set up there. The Apricot picked up where the Sirius 1 had left off, but its success was short lived. A few months before its release, IBM had started selling its PC in Europe. In the USA, most manufacturers, other than the die-hard Apple, had started to produce IBM clones, and Apricot soon lost its leading position in Europe. By 1986, the company had accepted the inevitable and the Glenrothes factory was turning out IBM clones like everyone else. Had Apricot decided from the beginning to make its computer IBM compatible it might still be a dominant force in computer manufacturing. But it misjudged the prevailing winds, and with the production of the Apricot began its slow slide into oblivion. The company was snapped up by Mitsubishi in 1990 and the Glenrothes factory was shut down and sold off in 1999.

Another famous name in British Computing is Sir Clive Sinclair. Born at the beginning of the Second World War, Sinclair grew up with a love and a gift for electronics. He started his first company, Sinclair Radionics Ltd, in 1961, and among other things, he used discarded transistors to produce miniature transistor radios. Making things small had always been his passion. He brought digital watches and pocket calculators to Britain, so it is no surprise that when he saw the start of the personal computer industry he wanted to make a small computer. Sinclair Research's ZX80 was launched in January 1980, and it was at the time the world's smallest and cheapest computer, costing £99.95 assembled, or £79 if you bought it as a kit. Like many of the first computers it was an instant success among hobbyists, although it could do little more than add a few numbers or write 'Hello World' on a TV screen. The ZX80 was quickly followed by the ZX81 and the Sinclair Spectrum, both more powerful and selling for under £200. Then came the QL, short for Quantum Leap, but that was to be the last of Sinclair Research's computers. Sir Clive was about to take a leap of his own, and it proved to be his undoing. The result of a long-standing interest in electric vehicles, the Sinclair C5, an electric-powered tricycle, was launched in 1985 to cries of disbelief. How could someone who had brought us first the pocket calculator and then the personal computer have got it so wrong, people were asking? Sinclair advised not using the C5 in heavy traffic. 'I would not want to drive a C5 in any traffic,' quipped the *Daily Telegraph*, and Sinclair's reputation was shot. The C5 was a costly failure, and in 1986 Sinclair was forced to sell up to a trading company by the name of Alan Michael Sugar Trading, Amstrad for short, a successful computer company in its own right. He wasn't too upset, however, because he had grown disappointed at the sort of things people were using computers for. 'It had become a games thing,' he says, 'and from my point of view that's tiresome.' Sinclair shouldn't have been surprised by the popularity of computer games. Even Charles Babbage, the father of all computers, had foreseen that they would one day be used for that. Nevertheless, Sinclair went off to pursue another line of research, this time into fold-away and electric bicycles, a business that continues to this day.

By the end of the decade, the British personal computing adventure was almost at an end. The mainstream manufacturers had all folded or been taken over for one reason or another. The home market had collapsed just as the US market was taking off. Acorn, having become accustomed to cranking up the production rate, suddenly found itself with a glut of computers that nobody wanted, and the ailing company was snapped up by Olivetti. Apricot fell into the arms of Mitsubishi and Sinclair devoted himself to his bicycles. But not everyone was a loser. Amstrad is still a successful business. Psion, a company founded in London in 1980, identified a niche for really tiny portable computers that came to be known as organizers, and went on to become the world leader in that field. And ARM, a company spun off Acorn to produce high-performance computer chips is still thriving, albeit in a lower-profile sector of the computer industry than home computers.

Hop, skip, and a link

Andy van Dam's interest in hypertext didn't end with FRESS. That project continued for over a decade, making him, and as a result Brown University, a world leader in hypertext system development. In 1983, van Dam teamed up with William S. Shipp and Norman Meyrowitz to found the Institute for Research in Information and Scholarship (IRIS). By 1985, IRIS had a staff of thirty and its first project was to build a hypertext system for Macintosh computers. The result was Intermedia, an extremely sophisticated hypertext system developed at Brown and converted to Macintosh by 1987.

Intermedia was put together by a team of over twenty young software developers, most of them fresh out of college like Nicole Yankelovich. 'Our IBM sponsors used to refer to us as the "children's crusade",' she says. Like FRESS before it, Intermedia was a system that allowed people to 'write in the margins' of what they were reading. The viewing program was also an editing program, and it was built around the simple concept of cut and paste so that linking would be easy. 'You should be able to select any object and link it to any other', says Yankelovich, 'regardless of what type of editor was used to create that object.' One of the ways that Intermedia managed this was by keeping the links in a separate database. 'Another nice feature of the link database,' she points out, 'was that you could move files around to different folders and all the links would automatically update.'

Andy van Dam goes a step further. 'The beauty of having the separate links database is not only that you can use the database management system to manage them, but more importantly you have multiple webs over the same source material,' he explains. With the World Wide Web you can put one-directional links from your home page to any pages you are interested in. But what if you want to link from one of those pages directly to another? In the Web, you have to go back to your home page and then go out again, but if you store links in a database you can create any web of links you want. 'So you could support multiple points of view without messing up the original source material,' says van Dam, 'and that's a wonderful thing.'

The idea of keeping links in a database so that they would always be up to date became a cornerstone of hypertext dogma, but it also ensured that hypertext remained confined to small systems. 'Of course, in retrospect we realize that we failed to address the scaling issue,' says Yankelovich. Intermedia worked fine on a small network of computers with the same operating system. But it couldn't work across networks of different computers, as the link database would soon become unmanageably large. For the Intermedia team, however, that wasn't an issue. 'Our user population was classrooms of students. In the mid-80s we were definitely not thinking on a world-wide scale.'

Brown University eventually spun off a hypertext company, Electronic Book Technologies, which produced a successful commercial hypertext product called DynaText, but it was not the first. From 1987, anyone buying a Macintosh got a rudimentary hypertext system for free. HyperCard was invented by Bill Atkinson, who was also the author of the Macintosh's drawing program, MacPaint, and it was probably the first system to bring hypertext into people's homes. HyperCard looks like a stack of index cards. The difference, however, is that with HyperCard you can store a vast amount of information on your stack of cards, and because of the searching tools you can also find it again quickly. Not only that, HyperCard also allows you to make links between cards.

Atkinson had high hopes for HyperCard. 'HyperCard, acting like a software erector set, really opens up Macintosh software architecture to where individual people can make their own customized information environment, and interactive information and applications, without having to know any programming languages,' he says. 'It's the original Macintosh dream of making the power of personal computers accessible to individuals.'

HyperCard may have been the first widespread hypertext program, but it wasn't the first commercial product. That honour belongs to Guide, a hypertext editing program developed by Edinburgh-based company Office Workstations Limited (OWL). Guide ran on both Macs and PCs, and provided the world's computing community with its first introduction to hypertext. It was through Guide that Wendy Hall first encountered hypertext. Based at the University of Southampton, Hall had been trying to figure out how to organize historical archives. 'I'd got the challenge from our archivist,' she recalls, 'who said, "We've got all this stuff about Lord Mountbatten and we want to be able to link it all together."' Guide convinced her that hypertext was the way to go.

From the beginning, because she was dealing with such a wide variety of material, Hall wanted links to be able to bridge between applications. 'Whatever system I was using, whether it was Word or a database or a spreadsheet or whatever, I wanted links that went across those processes, across the applications. So I thought of links as being separate entities that you could apply.' She wanted to be able to link letters, pictures, and diaries in the Mountbatten archives with each other as well as external documents. 'What if someone's written an essay or a criticism,' she says, 'or there's a textbook about Mountbatten? We want to link to that as well, you know. Those were the problems I was trying to solve.' The solution she came up with is Microcosm.

Microcosm is in a way more powerful and versatile than the World Wide Web has turned out to be. Rather than just allowing you to click on a well-defined hypertext link to go from page A to page B like the Web, Microcosm links take you to a whole range of pages about the subject you are interested in. Like Intermedia before it, Microcosm separates links from documents, storing the links in managed databases. 'But we took it a step further using dynamic linking,' explains Hall. Microcosm knows how to find all kinds of documents, and all kinds of places within those documents on the fly. That means that if you know that there is a textbook on Mountbatten with a particularly good account of the Burma campaigns, a request to Microcosm to find links about those campaigns could take you to the precise page of that textbook; it will also take you to any photographs that were taken, and to any sound or video material that the Microcosm linkbase knows about. And if you try the same request some time later, after someone has added a map of the Burma campaigns, dynamic linking means that Microcosm will now find that too.

But Microcosm's strength was also its weakness. Like Intermedia, it didn't scale easily, unlike the World Wide Web where there are no linkbases to manage. If you want to point to a link on the Web, you just go ahead and do it. And if someone removes the page your link points to, too bad. With Microcosm on the Internet, such dangling links would not have been allowed to happen, as linkbase managers would have had to make sure that all the linkbases were kept up to date all the time. 'By the time we got round to thinking about that,' says Hall, 'the Web was already dominant, so we moved our work to the Web and started developing the Distributed Link Service, a sort of Microcosm on the Web.'

When they started out, Wendy Hall and her team at Southampton were interested in elegant hypertext first and networked hypertext second. But what was true of Microcosm wasn't true of Hyper-G, another hypertext system being developed around the same time by Hermann Maurer's group at Graz. The Graz team's efforts with MUPID meant that they were already seriously plugged in to distributed information systems, so it was a natural step for them to hop on the hypertext bandwagon with the idea of networking it firmly in mind. 'Around '89 we wondered', recalls Frank Kappe, one of Maurer's graduate students, 'what would happen if we designed the ultimate hypermedia system?' They decided to find out. The result was Hyper-G, a sort of halfway house between Microcosm and the Web.

Hyper-G's link management was not as comprehensive as Microcosm's, but its reach was greater. It was built to overcome the weaknesses of the Videotex systems the Graz group had previously worked with, and it introduced many of the features now taken for granted in the World Wide Web. An inability to search for the information you wanted was one of Videotex's shortcomings, so Hyper-G had sophisticated search capabilities built in. As well as full-text searching, Hyper-G documents came complete with 'metadata', information about the document that a casual user would never see but that could help the computer to locate the right information. Another weakness of Videotex was its link management. If a page was removed there was no way for the system to know about it. This is a feature of today's World Wide Web and appears as the familiar 'Error 404'. With the Web, 404s are an accepted fact of life that we live with as a consequence of the Web's global reach, but Hyper-G proposed a solution. There was an automatic exchange of link information between sites that attempted to correct broken links.

The Videotex experience also taught the Graz team the importance of separating content from presentation. 'In Videotex, you would find phrases like "Press 1 to order" directly in the content of a page,' explains Kappe. 'Later, when graphical input devices, mice essentially, became popular, one would have liked to have "Click here to order" appear on a terminal with a mouse, and "Press 1 to order" on others, but this was not possible because the presentation was handled right in the content.' In Hyper-G, the author provided the content but the way it was presented was part of the system, and this problem was overcome.

By 1995, Hyper-G was a highly developed system capable of handling sound, images, video, and even 3-D pictures as well as just text. All of these could contain hyperlinks, so a video clip, for example, could have a link built in. But by this time the Web had taken off, and the Graz team pragmatically recast their system as a Web-based product called Hyper-

Wave, designed to help companies to manage their Web information. 'Finally, some sorely needed structure for the Wild Web,' was the way one critic put it when Maurer's book about HyperWave was released in 1996.

By 1987, there were so many hypertext research efforts going on that someone had the bright idea they should all meet. The first World Wide Hypertext conference was held in Chapel Hill, North Carolina, in November of that year, and three hundred delegates attended. Andy van Dam gave a keynote speech. His opening was apparently modest. 'I'm a Johnny-come-lately to hypertext,' he said, 'I didn't get started until 1967.' But he knew his audience and that was just his opening ploy. 'I was being cute and I got a big laugh,' he explains. 'The reason was, of course, that except from the three of us most everyone there was a kid of 20-something and they were the Johnny-come-latelys.' He went on to pay tribute to Vannevar Bush, and described Doug Engelbart and Ted Nelson as 'the two real trailblazers who have inspired me and hordes of my students who have gone off to do their own independent hypertext projects'.

Van Dam gave credit for the inspiration of FRESS to Doug Engelbart. He had seen Engelbart's demo in 1968, and described it as a tour de force. 'Later that year I went on with my students to design FRESS,' he says. 'My design goal was to steal or improve on the best ideas from Doug's NLS and put in some things we really liked from the Hypertext Editing System.' He also thanked Nelson for introducing him to hypertext in the first place, calling him 'a self-proclaimed visionary who deserves the title'. Van Dam learned a lot from Nelson, in particular, that he mustn't get stuck in old ruts. 'One of the most important things he taught me,' he said, 'was that this is a new medium and you really can't be constrained to thinking about it in the old ways. Don't copy old bad habits; think about new organizations, new ways of doing things, and take advantage of this new medium.'

Van Dam ended his talk with a list of nine key items he wanted people to think about at the conference. One of them was prophetic. 'Ted talks a lot about the docuverse,' he said, 'a mythical entity out there that is all-inclusive and contains everything. But instead, right now, we are building docu-islands.' He also talked about size. 'We are still in the toy problem stage. There has not been a decent-sized hypertext built yet.' It was clear that the time was ripe for a hypertext system that addressed these problems. Little did van Dam know that a mere three years later, Tim Berners-Lee's World Wide Web would provide the answer to both.

Finding your way

The World Wide Web wasn't the first system to make information available on the Internet easy to access. Far from it. The Web made it child's play, but there was no shortage of other systems springing up around the same time. As the Internet expanded, it became clear to many people that some kind of map was needed to find all the information it held. So it is not surprising that in 1989, when Tim Berners-Lee submitted his first Web proposal, several other systems were also germinating in the minds of their inventors. Archie and WAIS were both conceived in 1989, with gopher following in 1991. The first one to work and find widespread acceptance was archie.

Archie is not a comic-book character

Archie grew out of a program written by Alan Emtage when he was a student at McGill University in Montreal, Canada. It was a so-called client–server system. The server lives on the computer providing the service, and it dishes up documents in response to requests from the client. Emtage, born in Barbados, had moved to Montreal in 1983 to study computing science. He remembers finding the change in climate 'a little bit of a shock to the system'. But the urban setting of McGill and the cosmopolitan environment made up for Montreal's cold and snowy winters. Two years later, during his third year at university, he started getting involved in the system administration of the department's computers.

'The first Internet link into eastern Canada was brought in about the same time,' he recalls, 'and I was one of the people who managed it.' But that wasn't all he was meant to do. 'One of the things I was responsible for was finding software for the students and the faculty,' he remembers. He found himself trawling the Internet for free software. 'It's one of the really bizarre situations in academia that the funding agencies are more than happy to pay for capital purchases,' says Emtage. 'So they'll buy you a $150 000 parallel processing machine and they will pay absolutely no money for the software or the systems staff to run it.' As a result, Emtage was spending too much of his time using FTP to visit Internet sites and search them for useful, free, software. A year or so later, when he got fed up with doing his searching by hand, he wrote a computer program to do it for him. 'After a while,' he says, 'it got a little tedious to have to go out there and list all the sites. So I basically created a set of shell scripts that would wake up every night and go to a bunch of sites that I had discovered and list all the contents of those sites.' A shell script is Unix-speak for a kind of program that automatically performs a set of commands. He would come in the next day to find a list of what was on those sites, but that is all it was, a list of names. There was often no indication of what the names meant, so finding the program he was looking for could be tricky. 'A lot of it was guesswork, obviously,' he says. 'So I need a program which does such and such, what could they possibly have called it!' If he were looking for a clock program, for example, he would hope that it was called something like clock, instead of something more cryptic, like Ben.

Alan Emtage's searching program might have remained his personal tool forever had it not been for his boss at the time, Peter Deutsch. Deutsch was the manager of the systems group and had recently found out about Emtage's lists of files. He had also recently seen a question asked on a newsgroup, and wondered if Emtage knew of anything that might be able to answer it. Sure enough, Emtage did, and Deutsch posted the result to the newsgroup. Pretty soon, remembers Emtage, 'he started getting other questions. You know, "Oh, you found that, well can you do this ... can you look for this for me?"' Answering other people's questions rapidly became just as tedious as searching the net by hand for software. So in the end Emtage and Deutsch decided, 'Why not give people the access to it themselves?' That is why, at the end of 1989, Alan Emtage found himself working with another McGill computer scientist, Bill Heelan. Together, and with some help from Deutsch, they rewrote Emtage's simple program and made it something that could be used by anyone.

Sometime in its development, it became clear that the program needed a name. Emtage remembers wandering into Deutsch's office late one evening. 'We've got to name this thing,' he said. 'We bounced around a few [names] at the time,' says Emtage, 'and I don't remember what we came up with but they all sucked! And then I said "Well, how about archie, because it's archive without the v?"' Deutsch agreed, but the name would eventually get them into trouble, because to many people, archie conjured up images of the carrot-topped comic-book character of the same name. Emtage swears that this was not their intention. 'I loathe the comic-strip character,' he says, 'I cannot tell you the depth of my disdain and contempt for that particular comic strip,' adding, 'it never occurred to me that people would have associated anything with that name.' But they certainly did, to the extent that Emtage and Deutsch found themselves embroiled in copyright disputes with comic's owners when archie went commercial.

Emtage enjoyed working with Heelan. 'Bill is one of those elegant programmers, you know,' he says. 'I'm a grunt programmer, on the other hand; I just bang it out.' Within three weeks they were ready to install the archie server on the dedicated computer Deutsch had provided for it. It was an instant success. 'I remember when it first hit a hundred people that day,' says Emtage, 'we were like, "Oh my god, there's a lot of people using this service!"' Little did he know that that was just the tip of the iceberg, before long the archie server at McGill was sucking up most of the bandwidth into eastern Canada. Archie quickly rose to fame outside McGill, but no one had bothered to tell the university's computing science department about it. 'The first that the head of our department heard about it,' recalls Emtage, 'was at a conference and somebody came over and congratulated him. He had no idea what they were talking about! So he came back to us and said, "What the hell's going on?"'

That first version of archie just served up lists of documents or programs on the Internet that were available for free. You could ask the archie server to give you a list of programs containing the word 'Ben', for example, and in time back would come the list. You would then use FTP to copy the things you wanted from the sites where archie had found them. It was a tool designed by system administrators, for system administrators and it wasn't renowned for its user-friendliness. That started to change when Clifford Neuman, a Ph.D. student at the University of Washington, came across it shortly after its release. Neuman remembers those early days when archie was painfully slow to use. 'What archie provided was very useful,' he says, 'it was just a pain to get at the data.' Neuman thought he knew how to solve archie's speed problem. He had been working on something called Prospero that was designed to make the whole Internet look like one single computer. Instead of using FTP to get from place to place, Prospero made it as easy as just changing directory. There was a hitch, however. For Prospero to work, all the computers on the Internet had to be running a Prospero server, something that Neuman knew would be a long time in coming. 'It was great for organizing data that was on sites that had bought in,' he explains, 'but to have any hope of reaching critical mass, we needed a way to access files even on systems that weren't running Prospero.' So his idea to improve archie wasn't purely altruistic; he was hoping for a symbiotic relationship.

'Archie was the answer,' says Neuman. If he could use Prospero to organize archie's files then that would give him access to a large chunk of the Internet, so he set about canvassing Deutsch and Emtage. But they proved hard to convince. 'To be honest, we didn't get it,' says Emtage. 'Cliff kept saying, "You've got to do this," and we didn't realize that the marriage was going to work.' But eventually Neuman won them over, and soon people were accessing archie through Prospero. Although archie's rising popularity meant that archie servers still got overloaded, it didn't happen anywhere nearly as quickly. Moreover, Prospero also gave the long list of files found by archie a structure, making it easier for anyone who knew Unix to find what they were looking for.

Brewster's way

While archie grew out of a system administration tool at an academic institution, the Wide Area Information Servers (WAIS, pronounced 'ways'), was a commercial venture from the start. Brewster Kahle, working for supercomputer company Thinking Machines, was head of the project, and he was a big fan of Minitel. 'The monopolistic aspect and the lack of development, the non-openness to it, was sort of a problem,' he concedes, but he didn't let these details cloud what he considered to be the main issue. 'They did think through trying to help people make money by publishing on the net.' For Kahle, it was Minitel's business model that made it great, and his plan was to emulate it over the Internet.

Kahle liked the fact that people paid to use Minitel, 'because otherwise you're going to end up with advertising supported media,' he explains, and that was something he hoped the Internet could avoid. He got together with people from Dow Jones, Apple, and KPMG Peat Marwick, the accounting firm, to set up an experiment. The idea was that Thinking Machines' supercomputer, the Connection Machine, would house a database of information provided by Dow Jones. Apple Computer would build the user interface and Peat Marwick would be the customer.

WAIS was a bit like a modern search engine. You didn't have to know any obscure computer commands to use WAIS because you could enter your query in plain English. Files were described by keywords, which meant that you could search for images and sounds as well as just text. Eventually, Kahle hoped, an industry would grow up based on the model he was testing, with a variety of content providers and customers, including home users, all of whom would use WAIS clients to access information stored on WAIS servers on Connection Machines across the United States. 'One of the mottoes for the project,' remembers Kahle, 'was to catalyse a market for information servers.'

With the experiment judged a success, the first version of the WAIS client was released. As with archie, the news spread fast. 'I posted the first notice in April '91 about the freeware version of WAIS to one list and just watched it spreading from list to list to list and getting downloads and people starting to use it and port it to different things,' recalls Kahle, still sounding thrilled. 'It was an amazing experience for me to see what the freeware world was all about.' But he didn't intend to stop with freeware, and in the summer of 1992, he started a company, WAIS Incorporated, to market a commercial version. 'It wasn't easy,' he says, 'because basically we had to have a profitable company in a non-market' But Kahle was determined. 'I also wanted to prove that you could make an Internet company,' he explains; 'people just thought I was crazy.' He certainly proved them wrong. WAIS Inc. achieved considerable success, tripling in size every year. Among Kahle's customers were the US government, the Library of Congress, and *Encyclopedia Britannica*, as well as a host of publishing companies. In 1995, it was bought by America Online for $15 million, leaving Kahle free to pursue other things.

Gopher

WAIS may have been more intuitive than archie, but both required more than a superficial knowledge of computers to use. Then in 1991, an application came along that was to open up the Internet to anyone. It was developed at the University of Minnesota in response to a quest for the ultimate Campus Wide Information System (CWIS), and was called gopher.

CWISes were all the rage at American universities in the early 1990s, and the University of Minnesota was no exception. Mark McCahill, who worked in the microcomputing division of the university's computing centre, remembers it well. 'There was a big push at conferences ... that "computer centres, what you should be doing is finding ways to make the network and computers act kind of like bulletin boards",' he recalls. 'The big slogan was Campus Wide Information Systems. Those were the neat things that you should be doing.' McCahill was happy enough to work on new projects, as he likes learning new things. But what he remembers most about the CWIS quest was how political it was. 'This became the contentious topic inside the computer centre of who was going to get to do the Campus Wide Information System, because if you got to do this, hey, that was the big thing. You got the hot project. So there's this big fight brewing.'

A lot of people wanted to get involved with Minnesota's CWIS project, so a committee was formed to design the ideal system. To McCahill, this was where the problem began. 'Twenty-five people can't design software in my opinion, or at least not very well,' he explains. But the committee came up with a design that most of them liked, and McCahill had to go away and do something about it. 'It was a mess,' he says. 'I went to probably my best programmer, Farhad Anklesaria.' But Anklesaria took one look at it and said, 'I'm not doing it.'

Farhad Anklesaria was born and raised in India and came to Minneapolis to go to university. He was doing a doctorate in population genetics and found that he had to use the computer a lot. 'I had to write a tool that simulated population in a sense, on a computer,' he says. 'And as time went on the tool and its problems got more interesting than the research it was supposed to solve.' As a result, as well as getting his Ph.D., Anklesaria also picked up a Masters' degree in computer science. After a couple of years working in Chicago, he wanted to go back to Minneapolis. So he called up the director of the micro group. 'I basically called him up and said, "Hey, this is who I am and I need a job."'

He got one, which is why, in August 1990, Anklesaria found himself staring at a set of programming specifications that made no sense. 'I couldn't quite understand how all this would fit together,' he recalls. 'I must have been kind of stupid.' But he knew that at the next meeting he would have to produce something, even if it was not the committee-designed software the university wanted. 'I came up with something very simple, extremely simple,' he says, 'that I could actually implement.' His idea was so simple, in fact, that he wasn't allowed to present it; he had to keep trying to work with the original specifications. As the months passed, the committee's design grew in complexity, and the final product was due in December. 'December came and went,' recalls Anklesaria, 'and I would say "I think it can't be done," and miss the deadlines.' By February 1991 things were getting desperate. 'So I said OK. I have about a week or ten days to go before everybody gets really upset.' What he decided to do was go back to his original, simple design.

Anklesaria was able to come up with a working system pretty quickly, largely because of a system he and McCahill had built a few years earlier called Popmail. Back in the late '80s, even using e-mail took some computer know-how. At the time, McCahill remembers, they thought 'e-mail is kind of useful for us geeks, but our secretary can never stand to use it'. So he and Anklesaria built a system they called Popmail that put a user-friendly interface for a Unix mailer onto Macintoshes.

Popmail came in handy for Anklesaria's CWIS. 'I patched together a server using bits and pieces of tools that we built for Popmail,' he says. 'And then I wrote the client, both on the Macintosh, and then I got them talking to each other ... And there it was.' When he had the Mac system working, with about a week to the deadline, he showed it to McCahill.

At this point, a couple of other people joined the effort and before long they had produced versions of the program that ran on PC and Unix machines.

Anklesaria decided early on to call his program gopher. 'The name "gopher" is Farhad's,' says McCahill. 'He came up with it because he thought it would sell.' There are a number of reasons why Anklesaria thought the name 'gopher' would appeal to the committee members. 'The mascot of the University of Minnesota is the golden gopher,' says McCahill, 'so all the sports teams are gophers.' The state of Minnesota is known as the Gopher State as well, 'so to be a loyal Minnesotan you'd have to like something that was a gopher.' But it was also a pun on the word 'gopher', which sounds like 'go for'. 'So this is the idea of a little thing that can go get things for you,' explains McCahill, 'that also led to stupid jokes about tunnelling through the Internet with gopher.'

The gopher design was easy to use. 'Farhad's original take was "I'll have a menu of items"', says McCahill. 'You can pick off the menu and you'll get that thing. That thing could be another menu or an object like a document or a picture or something. And the information for any given item is enough to identify the server it's on.' This was a key design feature. It meant that the information didn't have to live on the computer you were using; it could be anywhere. They knew that this would cause a problem when they presented it to the CWIS committee since the people who ran the campus's mainframe wanted it to house the CWIS. But at the same time it would solve one, since every department wanted to control the top-level menu of the CWIS. Gopher meant that there could be any number of CWIS starting points and top-level menus, all interconnected.

McCahill thought this might just be enough to win the day at the next CWIS committee meeting. But there was still something lacking. 'The one thing that Farhad's original design was missing was some sort of database search,' he explains. The committee wanted keyword searches for documents, and McCahill knew gopher would have no chance without some sort of searchable index. So McCahill and Anklesaria built an interface between gopher and a full-text search engine, giving them a system that combined distributed servers, document browsing, and full-text searches.

The two men went to the next CWIS committee meeting pleased with their handiwork but prepared for a rough ride nevertheless. 'The ugliest meeting I've ever been in in my life was the meeting where we showed these guys what we'd done,' remembers McCahill. 'They just about came over the table after us.' Anklesaria's memory is equally graphic. 'We went and threw it in there,' he says, 'and it was ... it was one of the most awful times we have had. We were yelled at and screamed at and nobody was happy because their thumbprint wasn't on it and we hadn't been obeying their dictates and we hadn't followed their charge except in the highest spirit of things. And there was a lot of yelling and screaming, and there was nothing else. It was ugly.'

They had presented the committee with a system that worked on Macintosh, PC, and Unix, but it wasn't the system the committee had designed. The committee was unhappy. 'The person at the helm was convinced by the other people not to let us release this,' recalls Anklesaria. But the gopher team had a powerful ally. The man who had hired Anklesaria some years earlier told that committee that unless they allowed gopher to be released he would say that the team had been on vacation for the last two months so that their creation was theirs to do with as they wished. This didn't go down well either but, Anklesaria says, 'there was a lot of yelling and screaming and, um, there was nothing else they could do.'

So while the University of Minnesota ignored its own creation, the rest of the world was allowed to use it. Gopher was released in June 1991, and being a rodent, it multiplied quite quickly. McCahill credits this to its ease of installation, and also to people's love of food. 'One of the things we did to jumpstart gopher acceptance was stupid stuff like taking the Usenet cookbook and putting a server up that had all the recipes with a full-text search engine.' And although they didn't expect it to take off, they were happy that it did. 'At first it was, "Get ten other people using it"', says McCahill. 'Then it was, "Get 100." Then it was, "Wow, this is kind of cool, how can we keep this going?"' Enough American universities liked gopher sufficiently to start using it as their CWIS and eventually word got back to University of Minnesota that gopher was the system to use. 'We started getting people above us hearing from outside that the university had a cool campus wide information system,' says McCahill. Where McCahill and Anklesaria had failed to convince the powers that be at Minnesota, word from outside succeeded and gopher was finally installed on the University of Minnesota campus.

In 1992, Anklesaria and McCahill went to their first IETF meeting in San Diego to present gopher officially to the Internet world. A year later, in March, they released RFC 1436, entitled 'The Internet Gopher Protocol'. This document has a curious introduction, reading like a dictionary definition: 'Gopher n. 1. Any of various short tailed, burrowing mammals of the family Geomyidae, of North America. 2. (Amer. colloq.)

Native or inhabitant of Minnesota: the Gopher State. 3. (Amer. colloq.) One who runs errands, does odd-jobs, fetches or delivers documents for office staff. 4. (computer tech.) software following a simple protocol for burrowing through a TCP/IP internet.'

By 1993, gopher growth was hitting the exponential. In April of that year, there were just over 460 registered gopher servers; by December there were over 4 800. One of the factors that made gopher so popular was a search engine that could search all gopher servers. Called Veronica, it was developed at the University of Nevada in 1992 . The name was the gopher team's idea. 'When Farhad and I first started going to IETFs the guys who had, at that point, the application that was really peaking and really hot were Peter Deutsch and Alan Emtage, who'd done archie,' remembers McCahill. And because he knew how much the archie team hated any association with the comic book character, they thought they would rub it in by calling the search engine for the gopher world Veronica. 'Because Veronica in the comic strip is cooler than Archie, Archie's kind of a dummy,' he says with a smile. To make it official, the people in Nevada afterwards came up with the acronym Very Easy Rodent Oriented Net-wide Index to Computerized Archives.

But 1993 was the same year that the World Wide Web began to hit the Internet scene in a big way, and it was also the year that gopher servers stopped being given away for free to anyone who wanted one. One of the reasons was that the gopher team was approached by large companies like Schlumberger wanting to use gopher for their internal information distribution system. 'A corporation like that wants you to charge them,' says McCahill, adding, 'It's hard to charge them if I'm not charging the other people.' So they decided on a model where they would charge for-profit companies around $500 for the server, but still give it away to non-profits and educational institutions. The browser would still be free to anyone. But it wasn't a popular move. 'I couldn't believe how much we got flamed,' says McCahill, still amazed at the Internet community's reaction.

For a while, gopher was the most popular Internet application around. It made the Net easy to navigate; hopping from one machine to the next was as easy as pointing and clicking. It could serve up all kinds of documents, text, pictures, and movies, and even served up Web documents by launching a Web browser when it recognized HTML. There were gopher conferences where hundreds of people came to listen to and present new gopher features. But eventually gopher was overhauled by the Web. McCahill remembers feeling a little disappointed when gopher stopped being the coolest thing around. 'I was sorry that gopher wasn't a big deal forever,' he says, 'but on the other hand I wasn't that sorry.' Gopher had begun to take over his life. Now, several years later, and involved in new projects, he says, 'I was sad, but not that sad, and now I don't care.'

4 Enquire Within Upon Everything

Tim Berners-Lee crossed the border into Switzerland in June 1980 to take up his first job at CERN. He had been hired on a six-month contract to write programs to control the particle accelerators of the laboratory's Proton Synchrotron (PS) complex. Although he didn't stay long on this first visit to CERN, he made a big impression and took the first concrete steps towards building the World Wide Web.

Computerizing the PS

Berners-Lee had been brought in as part of a team to help with a large improvement programme for the control system of the PS and a number of smaller accelerators that made up the PS complex. The older of CERN's two main accelerators, the PS was built before computerization was a viable option. Operators controlled the machine by pushing hundreds of buttons and tweaking a plethora of knobs that were arranged on panels set in almost a hundred meters of racks along the walls of the control room. The PS had been running this way for six years before its first computer was introduced in 1966. Since then, a number of small computers had been added, each with its own specialized task, but there was no overall control system in place. Small computers seemed to grow organically in between racks and on top of shelves, but they were added as special projects or as experiments. There was no overall scheme for controlling the accelerator with computers. 'Each piece of hardware had some piece of panel in the control room and the integration of the machine was done in the heads of the operators,' explains Berend Kuiper, head of a team put together in the mid-1970s to bring the PS controls system up to date. Kuiper was an old hand at CERN, a specialist in the magnets used in particle accelerators to constrain particle beams to a circular orbit. He had little experience with computers, but he knew exactly how an accelerator should work and he had made his reputation as a solid project manager. 'I was dragged in because there was a sort of management crisis in PS about controls,' he explains, 'so they took a guy out of another field who had some experience in accelerator operation.'

Kuiper joined the PS when construction of the new Super Proton Synchrotron (SPS), complete with a fully computerized controls system running over Jacques Altaber's TITN network, was well advanced. There was a lot of political pressure for Kuiper's team to adopt the SPS system and adapt it to the PS, but there was also a good reason not to. Back in the mid-1970s, although the SPS system was almost brand new, computer technology was already capable of better things. On top of that, while the PS may have been an older machine than the SPS, the arrival of the newer machine meant that the PS was being asked to do more and more. At the beginning of its life, the PS's job was to deliver beams of protons to experiments, full stop. When the SPS arrived, the PS had to pre-accelerate protons for the big new machine. And when the plan to convert the SPS into a proton–antiproton collider was approved in 1978, the PS would have to accelerate antiprotons as well. By the mid-1980s, the PS had added heavy ions, electrons, and positrons to its repertoire, making it the world's most versatile particle juggler.

All that was yet to come, but even with the addition of just protons for the SPS, the PS was being asked to react extremely quickly. The SPS controls system, on the other hand, had been designed to do things at a far more leisurely pace. It used a computer language that was interpreted, meaning that instructions typed in by operators at a control console would be sent across the network and interpreted in real time by the computer at the other end. This language was called NODAL, and it was developed in house. It worked in much the same way as Java, the modern language responsible for the scrolling banners, interactive crosswords, and sports results services, amongst other things, that are widespread on the Web today. Unlike Java, however, which can run on many different kinds of computers, NODAL was implemented only for the Norwegian Norsk Data computers used in the SPS controls system.

At the beginning of 1975, Kuiper started putting together a team to design the new PS controls system. He brought in Axel Daneels to run the applications programs section and Brian Carpenter to look after the systems software. Fabien Perriollat completed the team with his hardware section. His job was to put together a network of computers to control the accelerator. Carpenter had the task of writing the network software that would then allow Daneels's team to write the applications that would actually be used to control the accelerators of the PS complex. If the controls system were compared to a Macintosh or PC, Perriollat would have had responsibility for the actual computer, Carpenter for the operating system, Windows or MacOS, for example, and Daneels for the applications like word processors and spreadsheets. Daneels's applications, however, would do things like pump air out of the accelerators and switch on magnets instead of balance the household accounts.

Kuiper's team wanted to start from a clean slate, but political pressure decreed otherwise. After lengthy negotiations, what they eventually adopted was a compromise. 'Norsk Data computers were imposed on us,' explains Christian Serre, Axel Daneels's next-in-command, 'because they were European so it was them we had to have.' However, the team was in for a pleasant surprise. They soon found that the ND machines were perfectly capable of performing the task and at least as good as the competition. Kuiper's team was asked to copy as much of the SPS system as they could, but once they had got it they could do essentially whatever they pleased with it. NODAL was one of the first casualties. 'It was very easy to work with, simple to use, it's true,' explains Serre, 'but on the other hand we had problems from the point of view of speed.' In the PS, one complete cycle of particle creation, acceleration, and extraction for delivery to experiments or to the SPS took just 1.2 seconds. 'To stick to those 1.2 seconds with programs written in NODAL was very difficult,' says Serre.

The immediate solution was to use another language, called Nord Programming Language (N-PL), for the most time-critical applications. This was faster because it was a concise language closely related to what is called assembly language, a step in the translation process from so-called high-level computer languages that humans can understand to the electronic code used by computers. In assembly language, instructions are given to the computer in very terse codes; for example, 'LDA ADR1' might mean 'Put whatever number is at the memory location "ADR1" into register A,' a place in the computer's central processing unit (CPU) where the actual computing takes place. A simple program to add two numbers stored at ADR1 and ADR2 and store the result in ADR3 might then look like:

```
 LDA   ADR1
ADDA   ADR2
 STA   ADR3
```

In N-PL it would have been:

$$ADR3 := ADR1 + ADR2;$$

The program that turns languages like N-PL into executable code is called a compiler, and the closer a language is to the computer's electronic code, the easier it is to write. From Christian Serre's point of view, a crucial difference between a simple compiled language like N-PL and an interpreted language like NODAL is that a compiled language is translated into computer code just once. With an interpreted language, programs are translated every time they are used, and that is one of the things that made NODAL so slow. That is not to say, however, that compiled languages are automatically better. An efficient interpreter might be faster than an inefficient compiler. Writing compilers to convert high-level languages into computer code is not an easy task, which is why there were few compilers around when Christian Serre's team was putting together the PS controls system. A good compiler for N-PL existed precisely because N-PL is very close to the computer's electronic code, so translating it into that code was relatively easy.

Nowadays efficient compilers for high-level languages are two a penny, many are even clever enough to remove inefficiencies from the programs they are asked to compile, and few programmers have to worry about assembly language. Most would probably find N-PL programming daunting, but in Christian Serre's team, 'it didn't bother anyone,' he remembers, 'because we were all used to working in assembler.' Before compilers for high-level languages came along, they didn't have the option.

Questions of language were all very well, but without a network they would be rather moot. So whilst the applications team was busy worrying about the drawbacks of NODAL, Perriollat's computer network was rapidly taking shape. It was effectively a custom-designed local area network that looked very unlike either an Ethernet or a Ring network. If anything, it was a bit like the network Donald Davies had built at the National Physical Laboratory, in that it had a star-shaped configuration. There were two sets of computers, one used by accelerator operators in the control room and another attached to accelerator components to do the actual controlling. In between was a message-handling computer whose job was to link one of the control-room computers to one of the computers attached to a piece of accelerator hardware.

By 1980, the hardware was in place and Carpenter's system software was up and running. It was time to get down to writing the applications

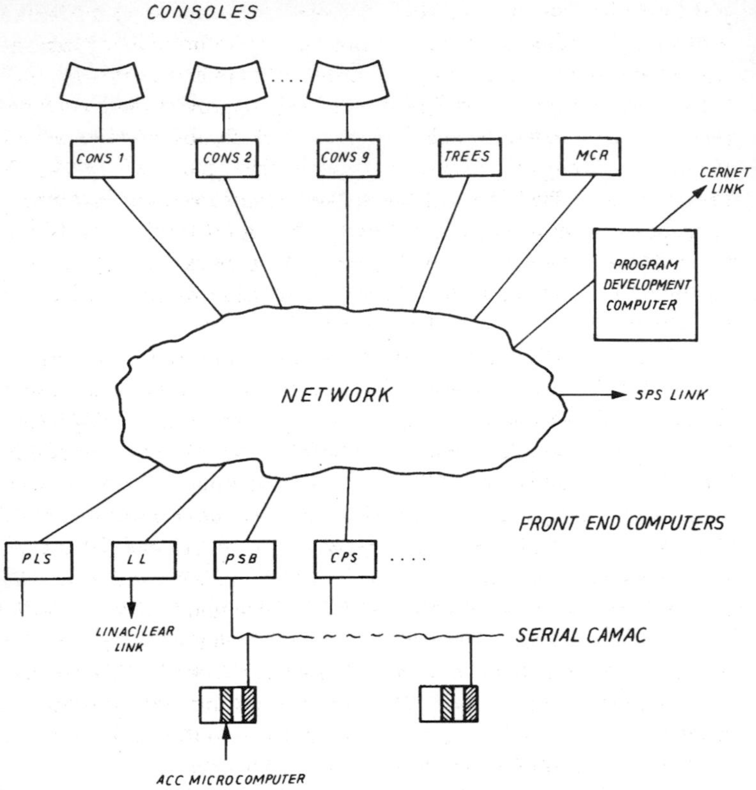

Figure 14: Brian Carpenter's drawing of the PS control system represented the network as a blob with computers radiating from it. Those above are the computers the accelerator operators would interact with. Those below are the computers attached to the accelerator itself. (From CERN Yellow Report 84-16)

programs that would be used to control the PS complex. Kuiper had estimated the project at around 150 man years of effort and he had been assigned manpower accordingly, but then a spanner was thrown into the works. In 1978, CERN's governing body approved the ambitious project that was to lead to Nobel prizes for Carlo Rubbia and Simon van der Meer by giving the green light to turning the SPS into a matter–antimatter collider. The SPS would get the glamorous role of colliding protons and their antimatter counterparts, antiprotons, but it would be up to CERN's unsung workhorse, the PS, to create, stock, and pre-accelerate both proton and antiproton beams. PS division was plunged into a manpower crisis.

Finding protons is a relatively easy task, as they are one of the principal constituents of matter. A litre of air, for example, contains a hundred thousand billion billion of them, and techniques for extracting them from everyday matter are routine. Antiprotons, on the other hand, presented a bigger problem for CERN's PS team. It is one of the great mysteries of physics that there is apparently no antimatter in the universe. If physicists are right about the Big Bang, then matter and antimatter should have been created in equal amounts when the universe was born. But as anyone who has ever read science fiction knows very well, matter and antimatter annihilate on contact, so all the stuff that came out of the Big Bang should have disappeared just as quickly. Clearly that hasn't happened. Instead, we are left with a vast universe filled exclusively with matter. Working out what happened to the antimatter is a pretty esoteric problem for particle physicists to deal with.

By comparison, the problem faced by the PS controls team was much more down to earth: they just had to make a little antimatter for the new collider programme. They did so by smashing protons into a target to produce a plethora of new particles, including some antiprotons, and then selecting just the antiprotons. When protons strike a target, all kinds of new particles are produced. Some are heavy, some are light. Some are positively charged, some negatively, and some are neutral. Charged particles follow curved paths in magnetic fields, with positive particles bending one way and negative ones the other. Their radius of curvature depends on their mass, so by judicious use of magnets, just antiprotons with their unique combination of charge and mass can be selected from the particle zoo emerging from the initial proton collision.

Collecting antiprotons is a slow process, so a new machine was needed to accumulate and store them up until enough had been made to transfer to the SPS. This machine was called the Antiproton Accumulator, and to many on Kuiper's promised team it presented a much more exciting project than the computerization of PS controls. Kuiper found himself with too few people to complete the task, particularly on the applications programming front. He had to find a new source of programmers. 'We tried fellowships and associateships and this-ships and that-ships,' remembers Brian Carpenter, 'and in the end, at one point, we were just hiring consultants—programmers from industry.'

These programmers were hired for short periods at key stages of the project, the first batch coming for the second half of 1980 when the first control consoles had been installed in the PS control room. A Europe-wide call to tender resulted in a company from Southampton called Benney Electronics clinching the deal to supply contract programmers to CERN and after consulting CVs, Berend Kuiper and Axel Daneels enlisted a number of new recruits. Among them was 25-year-old Oxford graduate Tim Berners-Lee.

The Web master

Dance halls were jumping to Bill Haley's 'Rock Around the Clock', James Dean was a Rebel Without a Cause, and in a quiet south London suburb, the future inventor of the World Wide Web was born in to one of the country's first fully computer-literate families. The year was 1955, the Warsaw pact had just been signed, West Germany had joined NATO, and the Suez Crisis was creeping up on Britain's new Prime Minister, Anthony Eden. Such concerns were far from the minds of Tim Berners-Lee's parents, Mary Lee and Conway Berners-Lee, who were riding a wave of optimism at the vanguard of Britain's blossoming computer industry. Back then, if the word 'computer' meant anything to most people it meant the armies of human calculators, mostly women, who churned out calculations by hand. Donald Davies, who was working on the ACE project at the National Physical Laboratory at the time, used to complain that every time he gave a talk he had to spend the first half explaining what a computer was before he could get down to what he really wanted to say.

Mary Lee and Conway Berners-Lee would have been people he could talk to. They had both trained as mathematicians and had met whilst working on the world's first commercial computer, the Ferranti Mark 1. This was a machine modelled on the Manchester Mark 1 built by Tom Kilburn's team at Manchester University. In 1949, the Manchester Mark 1 had been pipped to the post by Maurice Wilkes's EDSAC in Cambridge as the world's first practical stored program computer. Manchester, however, proudly celebrated the fiftieth anniversary of stored program computers in 1998, because the Mark 1 had been preceded by a small experimental version, nicknamed 'the Baby', that was working a year before the full-scale version. Earlier computers, like the wartime code-breaking Colossus at Bletchley Park, the first fully operational digital computer, were designed to perform a single specific task and could not be programmed to do anything else. Others, such as the Americans' postwar computer the ENIAC, which was used to calculate ballistic missile trajectories, were programmable in principle but programming required rewiring at worst or feeding programs in on punched tapes at best. They could not store a program in their own memory as every modern computer can. If stored programs had not come along, the world of computing would be a very different place. There would be no friendly smile as you switched on your Mac, nor 'Start' button on your Windows PC, because those are features of the computer's operating system, a program stored in memory that starts up automatically when you switch on your computer.

The spark of inspiration that led to modern programmable computers was provided by John von Neumann, a Hungarian mathematician who had moved to the United States in his twenties because the career prospects for academic mathematicians were better there than in Europe. Working on the atomic bomb project during the war, he became frustrated at the time it took to do the necessary calculations. When he learned about the ENIAC, he was very excited but at the same time frustrated that reprogramming it was such a labour. To von Neumann, who was renowned in Budapest society for his ability at the age of six to share jokes in classical Greek with his father and commit the telephone book to memory, the idea for the stored program computer must have seemed quite natural. Word about his idea rapidly spread, leading to stored program computer projects in the US and at Manchester and Cambridge in England. The English teams narrowly won the race to get the first machines working, with the American EDVAC being delivered about three months after Maurice Wilkes's machine performed its first calculations.

Decades later, Tim Berners-Lee was in Germany when Konrad Zuse's daughter presented him with a book about another claimant to have built the first computer, her father, who had started to build a computer as early as 1936. 'That made me realize how many groups were making these discoveries in parallel,' he says. The story shows that in the early days of computing, things were moving very fast, there was a lot of creativity, and new 'firsts' were not uncommon. When Berners-Lee himself came to invent the World Wide Web four decades after those pioneering stored program computers had run their first programs, the pace had hardly slowed down at all.

The Ferranti Mark 1 improved on the Manchester Mark 1 by, among other things, upping the speed from 1.8 milliseconds per instruction to 1.2 milliseconds. Put another way, it worked at just over 833 operations per second, 833 hertz (Hz). This meant that the machine could do about the same amount of calculation in two seconds as a human could do in a day. 'In a day it could do more arithmetic than the average man could do in many years,' said an early sales brochure, 'and will make fewer mistakes.' It could solve differential equations with such esoteric applications as binary star formation and Schrödinger's equation for the helium atom. It could even be asked to solve chess problems, or play draughts against a human opponent, fulfilling Charles Babbage's 115-year-old prediction. The Ferranti Mark 1 was built in two cabinets each 16 feet long, 8 feet high, and 4 feet wide, with a separate operating console. It consumed 27 kilowatts of power, about the same as five electric cookers running full blast, and its thousands of components were connected by 6 miles of wire.

Programming the Mark 1 was a black art compared to modern standards. There was no easy language for programmers to use with a compiler to convert their code into a form the machine would understand. They had to talk to the machine in its own language. The Mark 1 worked in base 32 rather than base 10, with the numbers 0 to 31 being mapped onto the keyboard as:

```
/E@A:SIU½DRJNFCKTZLWHYPQOBG"MXV£
```

The Mark 1 was state of the art for its time but positively slow compared to the hundreds of megahertz operation of even the most modest of modern desktop computers. The first Mark 1 was delivered to Manchester University in February 1951 and Mary Lee Berners-Lee went with it to set it up. 'My mother has been dubbed the first commercial computer programmer,' says Tim with a touch of pride. Ferranti went on to sell nine Mark 1s including three for export, a major success story for the time, and Tim Berners-Lee's parents stayed with Ferranti as the company developed successors to that first commercial computer.

His parents' career had a profound effect on Tim Berners-Lee's childhood. The older of two boys, Tim recalls maths being part of everyday life. 'We learned to enjoy mathematics wherever it cropped up,' he explains, 'and learned that it cropped up everywhere.' He recalls teasing his younger brother, then in primary school, with the concept of imaginary numbers at the breakfast table. 'He could multiply and he'd just figured out negative numbers,' recalls Tim, but even for a primary-school Berners-Lee, the square root of minus one proved a bit much. Computing was also a familiar subject in Tim's childhood. He would visit his parents at work and then come home and make Blue-Peter-style models of the latest Ferranti computers out of old cardboard boxes and sticky-back plastic. 'I have seen photographs of the mock-up I made out of cardboard boxes when I came home,' he recalls, 'and the main features were that you could push paper tape in one side and pull paper tape out of the other side, and there was a clock in the middle. And that's a pretty good model for a computer.'

Typically for the time, Tim Berners-Lee's upbringing was informal Church of England, but he soon tired of the conventional Christian dogma and as an adult adopted the more open Unitarian Universalist approach to religion. Formed from the union of two organizations, the Unitarian Universalist Association is perhaps the freest of the churches with a Christian heritage. Unitarianism has its origins in sixteenth-century England when Christian thinkers began to question the idea of the Holy Trinity and instead stressed the unity of God. The first Unitarian Church was established in 1773 by Theophilus Lindsey in London, but soon ran into official opposition. Holding Unitarian views was technically an offence in Britain until 1813, and the church had to wait for the nonconformist movement of the Victorian era before it could grow there. In the United States, however, Unitarianism enjoyed greater success, particularly in New England, and no fewer than five US Presidents have been Unitarians. In 1961, the Unitarians merged with the Universalist movement to form the Unitarian Universalist Association in Boston, Unitarianism's heartland. Universalist ideas have popped up several times in Christian history but the modern version was founded in the United States in the eighteenth century on the belief that everyone will eventually be saved, no matter what religious opinions they hold.

For Tim Berners-Lee, the appeal of Unitarian Universalism is that it believes in 'the inherent dignity of people and in working together to achieve harmony and understanding'. It accepts the notion of divinity, but in an abstract way. 'It tackles the spiritual side of people's lives,' explains Tim, 'but it doesn't require you to believe six impossible things before breakfast.' The modern Unitarian Universalist Association allows its members to think whatever they want as long as they believe in a spiritual dimension to human existence, an ideal doctrine for Tim Berners-Lee, who believes that there is 'more than just biology', but that whatever divinity is, it doesn't involve 'characters with beards'.

Emanuel School

In 1594, Anne Sackville, Lady Dacre, wrote in her will, 'I will and devise that myne executors shall cause to be erected and builte a meete and convenient house with rooms of habitation for twentie poor folkes, and twentie other poor children.' That is how Emanuel Hospital, now Emanuel School in Wandsworth, South London, came to be. Lady Dacre had the fortune to be cousin to Queen Elizabeth I, who ensured that funds were available for the will to be executed. Emanuel initially occupied premises in Westminster and moved to its present site on Wandsworth Common in 1883.

Tim Berners-Lee went to Emanuel from 1966 to 1973 and remembers two of his old teachers with particular fondness. 'Frank Grundy taught maths,' he recalls. 'He didn't keep a whole lot of order but he'd give the class problems and what was good was that he would quietly help people who needed more help and to those who'd done the problems, he would throw little extensions with a little bit of a wink. You know: "Demonstrate that the following formula is true for n = 6; is that true for any n?" Something like that.' Frank Grundy was also a keen bridge player, and the brightest of his pupils, those like Tim who frequently managed to prove the case for any n, would often find themselves sitting in their maths class playing cards.

Frank Grundy was also famed within the school for his mental agility. 'When required to find the square root of an arbitrary number,' recalls Tim, 'he would do binomial approximations in his head really fast. He could generally outpace somebody with log tables or slide rule and so people wanted to know, "How do you do it? How do you work out the square root of 50 like that?"' Grundy would explain, 'Well, you know what the square root of 49 is, right? And so what's going to be the difference between the square root of 49 and the square root of 50?' By showing off his agility at mental arithmetic, Frank Grundy was trying to encourage his students to exercise their brains by learning the mathematical technique of binomial expansions rather than resorting immediately to tables and slide rules.

Tim's other favourite teacher was Derek Pennel. Known to his students as Daffy because of his initials, D. A. F., it was thanks to Pennel that Tim ended up with four A-levels instead of the more conventional three. In Emanuel's sixth form, 'there were two choices,' explains Tim, 'maths, chemistry, and physics, or double maths and physics, and I thought I wanted to do maths at that point so I had to do double maths and physics.' But Daffy Pennel didn't want to lose a good pupil, so he said to Tim, 'Well, look, why don't we make arrangements for you to fit in some more maths and then you can go to maths, physics, and chemistry classes. I will not require you to hand in anything on the chemistry side, but I'd like you to come.' Tim took that advice, sat in the front row, listened through Pennel's classes, and went on to get straight As in double maths, chemistry, and physics, ensuring his place at one of the country's most prestigious universities.

The Queen's College

Elizabeth I proved a recurring theme in Tim's education, since a decade before Emanuel school was founded in London, she had granted The Queen's College, Oxford, a new charter. Tim Berners-Lee began his undergraduate physics degree at Queen's under the tutelage of John Moffatt in 1973. He had chosen to read physics as a compromise between maths and his hobby of electronics, subjects that for him represented the theoretical and practical sides of the same thing. 'It turned out not to be that,' he says without regret, 'but to be something special and wonderful in itself.' Over the course of his three years at Oxford, he developed a lot of respect for his tutor. 'John Moffatt had a rare talent for being able to understand not only the physics itself but also my tangled, misguided attempts at it,' explains Tim, 'and then show me in my terms using my strange symbols and vocabulary where I had gone wrong. Many people can only explain the world from their own point of view.' The respect was mutual, with John Moffatt recognizing his student's outstanding ability, and his unorthodox approach. 'He had an original mind,' says Moffatt, 'and often adopted an unconventional approach to a problem. This sometimes led him astray but often produced an interesting and illuminating solution.'

Despite the fact that physics didn't offer the compromise he had wished for between theory and practice, Tim Berners-Lee didn't abandon his hobby. At a time when personal computers were beginning to appear in kit form, Tim ended up building his own from scratch. 'It sort of came in a rather long, extended period of time,' he explains. During one of the university vacations he was working in a sawmill to earn some extra cash and using his spare time to build a Visual Display Unit (VDU) that he could attach to one of the university's computers as his own personal terminal. He went to a television shop in search of a broken television set and spent five of his hard-earned pounds on one that was no good as a television but that suited his purposes. All television sets at the time were built in much the same way and, of particular interest to Tim Berners-Lee, they all had something called a video 1 volt point where video signals could be injected. This he learned from a friend who knew televisions. 'The guy would say, "Take the back off the television ... here you are, that's got to be this valve, and that's got to be this valve, and that's got to be this valve, and this has got to be the video 1 volt point,"' says Tim, with clear excitement at the memory. 'And then I started playing with circuits,' he continues, 'so I got first horizontal bars and then vertical bars and then eventually ended up putting logic on it to give patterns.' That was the first component of his home-made computer. The second came by pure chance: 'And then meanwhile in the sawmill I was climbing up a pile of wood to this huge skip,' explains Tim, 'and I was just about to pour all the sawdust out of the garbage can on my back, and there was this funny box sitting right in the middle of it.' The sawmill's office had thrown away an old adding machine, which wasn't much use to Tim as an adding machine, but it had something like a keyboard attached to it. 'It had ten rows of ten buttons, so when you wanted to multiply you would put 6 2 8 4 2, and then you'd press a button and put it in a register, and then you'd press another thing, and then it would whirr and whirr. It was like an electronic version of ...,' he stops to think, 'well, whatever it was it had a huge number of buttons on it and I took the buttons home and reassembled them into a QWERTY keyboard.' And that is how the second component of Tim's computer came to be. When he then bought a device to generate characters so that he could type and see the characters come up on the screen, his initial goal was accomplished. 'I had my own terminal,' he explains, 'and then just as I left Oxford the 6800 microprocessor came out and I got an evaluation kit.' That kit teamed up with the VDU he had just made to become Tim Berners-Lee's first computer.

When he left university with first-class honours in 1976, Tim knew he didn't want to do research physics. 'I didn't have any role models for that,' he says. 'At Oxford I didn't know anybody who had gone into research and had fun.' But while he may have had no role models in physics, he had two clear role models in computer science in the form of his parents. In the family home, problems in the emerging field of computer science had been the stuff of dinner-table conversations for as long as Tim could remember. This, combined with a clear aptitude and the fun he had had building his own computer from scratch, led him to choose a career in computing, making him among the world's first second-generation computer scientists. 'I joined Plessey Data Systems,' he explains. 'Of the companies doing the "Milk Round" interviews, the Poole, Dorset, site won hands down in terms of the sea and the countryside!'

At CERN for the first time

By 1980, Tim Berners-Lee was based in Southampton. He had left Plessey in 1978 to join a young company called D. G. Nash Limited that made intelligent printers. Tim's job was microprocessor software development. 'Those who got into designing microprocessor hardware and software,' he recalls fondly, 'rode the crest of the wave of the deployment of microprocessor technology.' Soon after, when he began the work that led to the World Wide Web, it felt like the same thing all over again. 'The thought of building an abstract information space,' he says, 'had the same sort of kick.'

At the time CERN enlisted Southampton company Benney Electronics to provide its extra manpower for the PS controls project, Tim was off on a consulting job in Zug, Switzerland, but a friend spotted Benney's advertisement and they both applied. Soon After, Tim found himself on a train to Geneva to meet his future employers.

Although he may never have planned to be a research physicist, Tim still managed to find his way to the laboratory that was preparing for the most exciting particle physics project of the early 1980s. He arrived at CERN on 23 June 1980. 'There was Axel Daneels and Christian Serre,' he remembers of his first days in Switzerland. 'They'd just ripped out all the hardware controls system for the PS and put in a sort of clone of the SPS controls system with Norsk Data machines and there was a whole lot of control monitoring programs to write.' He had arrived at the moment when the new controls system was in place and all that was lacking was applications programs to do the actual controlling. He worked on an accelerator in the PS complex called the booster, so called because its job was to boost the intensity of beams injected into the PS.

The booster's importance at CERN is illustrated by the fact that there is a road named after it. Just about every other road at the laboratory is named after an illustrious figure from the history of physics. There is a Route Einstein, for example, and a Route Curie. The most recently named road is Route Salam, named after the Pakistani physicist who won the Nobel Prize for his work on unifying electromagnetic and weak forces, and who did much to further opportunities for scientists from the developing world.

One of Tim's tasks was to write the programs that would control the vacuum inside the booster. There was a console in the control room that was used for this function. It had a principal display screen, four smaller screens, a tracker ball to move a pointer around the screens, and a number of dials that could be used to set up the operating parameters of the

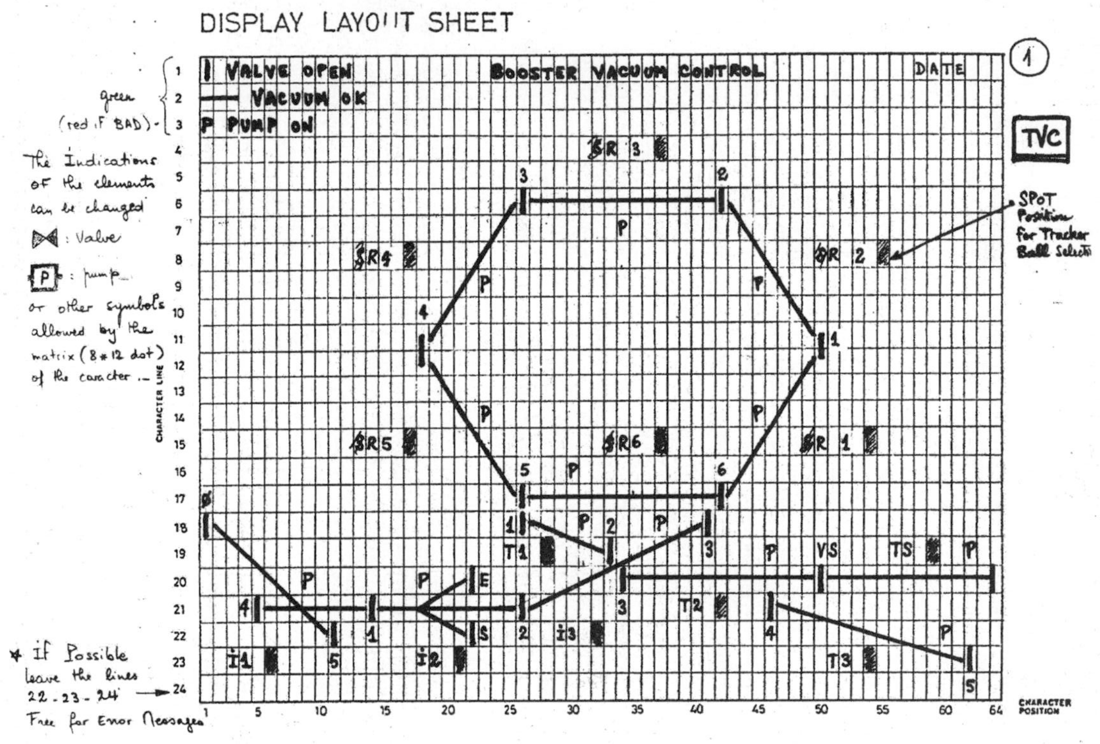
DISPLAY LAYOUT SHEET
VALVE OPEN
VACUUM OK
P PUMP ON
BOOSTER VACUUM CONTROL
DATE
green
(red if BAD)
The Indications of the elements can be changed
: Valve
P : pump
or other symbols allowed by the matrix (8*12 dot) of the caracter
TVC
SPOT Position for Tracker Ball Selection
CHARACTER LINE
CHARACTER POSITION
* If Possible leave the lines 22-23-24 Free for Error Messages
SR 1
SR 2
SR 3
SR4
SR5
SR6
T1
T2
T3
TS
VS
I1
I2
I3
E
S

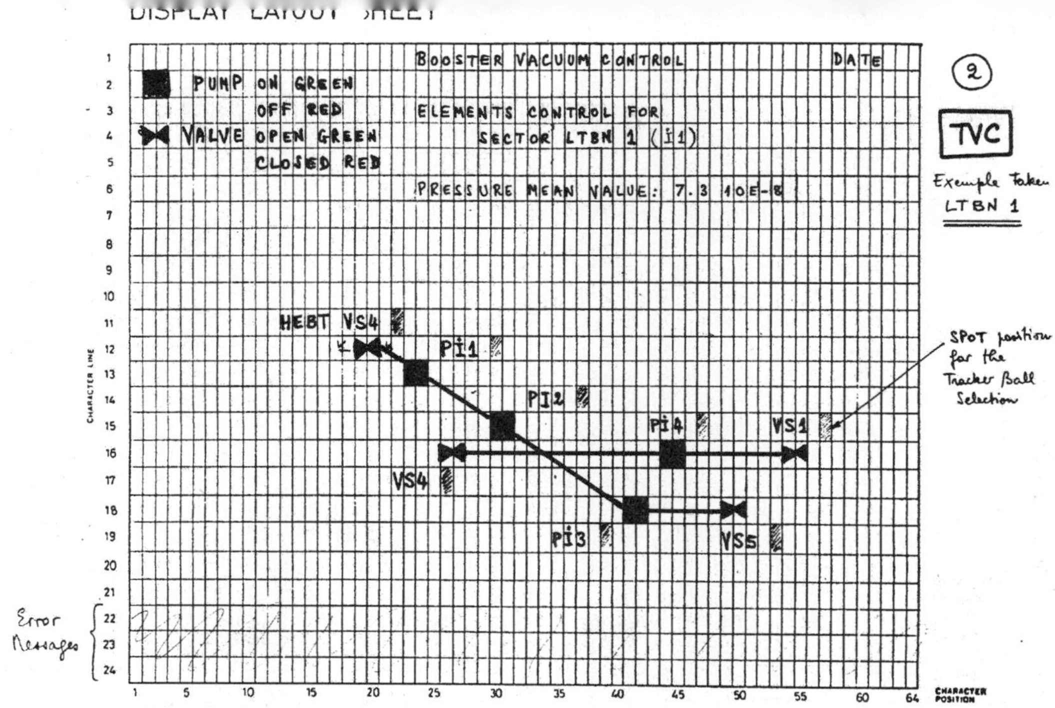

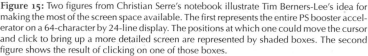

Figure 15: Two figures from Christian Serre's notebook illustrate Tim Berners-Lee's idea for making the most of the screen space available. The first represents the entire PS booster accelerator on a 64-character by 24-line display. The positions at which one could move the cursor and click to bring up a more detailed screen are represented by shaded boxes. The second figure shows the result of clicking on one of those boxes.

vacuum system. The whole control room was reminiscent of NASA mission control at the time of the early moon shots. It looked pretty high-tech, but in reality the consoles that applications programmers had to work with were still quite primitive. 'We were lucky enough to have colour,' says Christian Serre of the principal screens, 'but on the other hand it was a terminal that had 64 characters and 24 lines.' That meant that an applications programmer like Tim Berners-Lee had to cram all the information the accelerator operators would need to run his programs into that tiny space. Standard information like the date and time had to be there. A space had to be left free for the programs to post messages about the state of the system and another had to be reserved for error messages. That didn't leave much room for anything else, so programmers were forced to devise very concise ways of displaying information. Tim Berners-Lee, however, had other ideas.

'He was 25 then,' remembers Christian Serre, 'he was full of enthusiasm, and he worked very fast, and above all he had these new ideas that he brought with him.' The unconventional approach that John Moffatt had remarked upon led Tim to come up with new ways of doing things that none of his colleagues had thought of. 'His ideas,' says Serre, 'were sometimes completely wacky and sometimes quite brilliant.' One brilliant one was to modify the four smaller screens so that the tracker ball could move a pointer between them all. This made it easier for operators to select information from any of the screens for further investigation or modification. 'That,' says Serre, 'was something that hadn't been imagined before.'

Another Berners-Lee idea looks, with hindsight, suspiciously like hypertext. It concerned the 64-character by 24-line main display screen. Tim's task was to give operators a user-friendly way to control all of the pieces of equipment in the booster's vacuum system, but there was not enough space on the screen for all the components to be shown at once. His solution was to start with a very simple schematic of the whole system. When an operator pointed and clicked on the part of the system they wanted to work on, a new screen would be displayed zooming in on just that part. From there individual components could be selected. It wasn't quite hypertext because it was hierarchical—clicks took you up and down a well-defined structure, whereas in hypertext they can take you anywhere—but the point-and-click method of navigating your way through it was already there.

The organizer

Although neither of them realized it at the time, there was another member of the PS controls team who was destined to play an important role in getting Tim Berners-Lee's brainchild, the World Wide Web, accepted at CERN. Robert Cailliau was eight years older than Tim; he had first come to CERN in 1974 and by 1980 was member of the laboratory's permanent staff. Robert had studied electrical engineering at the University of Ghent, and after taking an M.Sc. in Michigan had returned to Ghent to work in the university's hybrid computing laboratory. Soon after he arrived, he had a call from Axel Daneels at CERN. Daneels was also a Ghent graduate, so when he had a problem to solve with the PS booster's power supplies, but no manpower to deal with it, he had the idea of asking his old professor if he could give the problem to a student at Ghent to solve as part of a Master's thesis. 'That's interesting,' said the professor, 'You should discuss it with Robert Cailliau.'

Robert found a student and together they started working on the problem. They would do the thinking in Ghent and then go to CERN to test out their ideas. 'I knew about CERN and I knew that they were working there on nuclear physics,' says Robert, 'but when I actually went I saw that there was an incredible amount of computing going on and so I thought, "Hey! This is a very interesting place to be."' He applied for a CERN fellowship, a highly sought-after position with the reputation of being a launch pad to a successful career in whatever field you happened to be in: physics, computing, or any of the other subjects that came together at CERN to fuel the demands of pure research. His application was successful, but before he could take up his position there was the little question of military service. Robert was hauled off to the infirmary of the Royal Military Academy in Brussels, where he was earmarked to work as an auxiliary nurse for a year. Luckily for Robert, however, the infirmary was physically attached to the School of War, which had a need for capable computer scientists. Robert soon engineered an escape from his nursing duties. 'When there was slack at work,' he explains, 'rather than sit in the infirmary twiddling my thumbs I went and got myself some time on the computer there, and soon they noticed that I could actually program these things, so they switched me over to the School of War because they needed a programmer.' Consequently Robert spent his military service playing computer war games, modelling NATO troop movements and battlefield scenarios, 'which was great fun,' he recalls. His student in the meantime finished solving Axel Daneels's problem at CERN and passed his Master's with flying colours.

Robert's war-gaming days came to an end just in time for him to join Brian Carpenter's systems software team at the beginning of the PS controls project. Robert was a meticulous organizer, going to great lengths to introduce methodical programming techniques and documentation. 'He set up all kinds of little tools to help people to program, documented in—he called it a Cookbook,' recalls Berend Kuiper. 'That contributed to uniformity and reliability, so it was extremely useful.' Robert's other main contributions early on in the project were also project management tools: one was a kind of early word-processing program called Report that he wrote with fellow CERN newcomer David Bates, another was a new way of planning out a computer program called a Program Structure Diagram (PSD). The Cookbook itself was where you would find Report and PSDs documented, along with all kinds of other tools that could help applications programmers with their jobs.

Report

Before the days of WYSIWYG word-processing programs like WordPerfect and Word, if you wanted to write an attractive printable document on a computer you had to use something called a markup language. Even today, markups have their champions, and for certain things they are more flexible than word-processing packages because they put more power in the hands of the user. The downside is that markups take more time to learn. Report was the first markup language that ran on Norsk Data computers and so had an important part to play in documenting the PS controls project.

In a markup language you use 'tags' to define how the text should appear. Sometimes these are distinguished from the text by putting them in angle brackets, for example, <TITLE> might tell the computer that the following text is a title, with </TITLE> marking the end of the title. Angle brackets are a feature of a markup language called Standard Generalized Markup Language (SGML) that evolved from another called GML. GML itself was invented at an IBM research lab in 1969 by Charles Goldfarb, Edward Mosher, and Raymond Lorie, whose surname initials just happened to spell out GML.

SGML has become a very popular markup language running on a wide variety of computers. One of SGML's most appealing features remains that it is free. In fact, it played an important role in establishing the modern freeware and shareware movement, peopled by idealists who believe that software is an essential commodity that should be freely available to anyone and not owned by big corporations. In the 1980s, SGML became very popular in computing circles at CERN, and it was the officially supported markup language at the laboratory. So when Tim Berners-Lee was writing the markup language for Web documents, it was natural that SGML should serve as the model for his

Hypertext Markup Language (HTML), the 'language' in which all Web pages are written.

Despite SGML's official support, however, CERN's physicists tended to prefer a markup called TEX because it is very good at doing equations. TEX, which was published by Donald Knuth at Stanford in 1979, is pronounced 'teck' because, despite appearances, the letters really represent the upper-case Greek characters tau, epsilon, and chi, τεχ. Knuth gave his markup a Greek name because English words like 'technology' stem from a Greek root beginning τεχ, and the same Greek word means 'art' as well as 'technology'. TEX was designed to produce documents that are works of art, but for physicists it is the powerful mathematical ability of the markup that appeals. TEX, as the original manual points out, rhymes with 'blecchhh', which has led to speculation that this was Knuth's reaction on seeing what typesetting technology was capable of before he invented TEX. The ambiguity in its pronunciation has provided hours of fun for manual writers, whose products range from Knuth's own *Texbook* through guides for 'texnicians' to *The Joy of Tex*. TEX uses the dollar sign to tell the computer that what follows is maths. For example,

```
$\int{x^2}dx={{x^3}/3}$
```

would tell the computer to print:

$$\int x^2\, dx = x^3/3$$

It is possible to do that with a WYSIWYG word processor, but any competent 'texpert' could do it much faster, which goes some way to explaining why markups are still favoured by technical writers.

When Robert Cailliau joined the PS controls project, an easy way of producing documentation simply wasn't available. Despite their later popularity, both SGML and TEX were relatively unknown at CERN, and WYSIWYG programs were well in the future. Robert Cailliau and David Bates identified a niche that needed to be filled, so they devised their own markup language. In Report they called the tags 'directives' and delimited them by the % or @ characters. A piece of text marked up in Report for the 'User's Guide' Robert and colleagues put out in September 1977 looked like:

```
%ds=@%
@ch=Summary of Most Useful Directives
The length of the previous chapter may give the
```

```
impression that use of Report is rather
complicated.

However, most of the directives described are
for creating special layouts, modifying default
parameters and also for specifying the standard
PS/CCI Cover page. The beginner need not bother
with these extras and can manage well with the 5
basic directives briefly repeated below:

@lm=+7@ @rm=+7

@ip=1) @Chapter (%CH=String%)

@p@ Used when a new chapter is required.
"String" is the new chapter name, which will be
automatically numbered.

@ip=2) @Section Down (%SD=String%)

@p@ Used when a new section is required, one
level down. "String" is the new section name
which will be automatically numbered and
indented.

@ip=3) @Section (%SE=String%)

@p@ Used when a new section is required on same
level as previous section. "String" is the new
section name which will be automatically
numbered and indented.

@ip=4) @Section Up (%SU=String%)

@p@ Used when a new section is required, one or
more levels up than previous section. The
special case %SU% must be used to move up more
than one level before printing a new section
heading.

@ip=5) @Paragraph (%P%)

@p@ Used to specify that following text should
begin a new paragraph.

@bl=3@ @a@
```

And it would tell the computer to print a page that looked like:

```
7. Summary of Most Useful Directives

The length of the previous chapter may give the
```

impression that use of Report is rather complicated. However, most of the directives described are for creating special layouts, modifying default parameters and also for specifying the standard PS/CCI Cover page. The beginner need not bother with these extras and can manage well with the 5 basic directives briefly repeated below:

1) Chapter (%CH=String%)

Used when a new chapter is required. "String" is the new chapter name, which will be automatically numbered.

2) Section Down (%SD=String%)

Used when a new section is required, one level down. "String" is the new section name which will be automatically numbered and indented.

3) Section (%SE=String%)

Used when a new section is required on same level as previous section. "String" is the new section name which will be automatically numbered and indented.

4) Section Up (%SU=String%)

Used when a new section is required, one or more levels up than previous section. The special case %SU% must be used to move up more than one level before printing a new section heading.

5) Paragraph (%P%)

Used to specify that following text should begin a new paragraph.

Report and other markup languages like it were a lot less intuitive than modern word-processing programs, and since Report was written before the days of modern printers, only a standard typewriter typeface was available. Nevertheless, Tim Berners-Lee chose to use a markup for Web documents because by doing so he ensured that, no matter what kind of computer you had, an HTML page would be understandable, even if it didn't look exactly the same on all computers.

Report was first written for DEC computers. Robert Cailliau was hoping that the PS controls team would be given carte blanche and if they were, DEC machines would have been the computers of choice. When politics dictated that Norsk Data machines would be used, Robert Cailliau and David Bates recast Report to run on them, and in doing so they filled an empty niche in the markup market and gave Norsk Data a lucrative new product into the bargain. Norsk Data eventually succumbed to the competition from Macintoshes and PCs, but ran a profitable business for many years selling office computer systems. In a typical Norsk Data package there would be a central computer with several terminals attached to it, and a software bundle including Report came as standard with the system.

Program Structure Diagrams

For Robert Cailliau, planning was all important, and just as clear documentation was essential, so was a systematic method of designing programs. PSDs were his answer. Before he came up with PSDs, the standard way of designing a program would be to write down what information you had to start with and what you needed to have at the end, and to draw a straight line between them. PSDs allowed program designers to produce graphical representations of the programs they were about to write in a kind of hierarchical tree structure. 'The arrival of these PSDs was something new that allowed us to represent, graphically and in a compact form that could be extended later as one wished, all the information about a program,' explains Christian Serre.

PSDs were rapidly adopted by the PS controls system's applications programmers, with one notable exception. When looking through old files years later, Christian Serre was amused to find his initials at the top of the PSDs that described Tim Berners-Lee's programs. 'Look, it's even me who did the PSDs!' he exclaims. But there was no bitterness: Tim Berners-Lee simply did not manage to get the documentation done. 'Of course not,' says Serre, 'because that locked him in to something and he always wanted to escape.'

Robert's recipes

Robert Cailliau's Cookbook was the ever-expanding document that contained all you would ever want to know about Report, PSDs, or any other tools of use to PS applications programmers. It contained the recipes for all sorts of things that people writing PS applications programs might need to do. Robert, as a member of the systems team, was well aware of the gap that existed between the systems programmers and the applications team. Systems programmers tended to be professional computer scientists, whereas the applications programmers were often accelerator physicists or engineers, who knew more about particle beams than computer chips, supplemented by contract programmers like Tim Berners-Lee. The Cookbook was Robert's way of plugging the cultural gap between them. It contained all sorts of tips for applications programmers about how the system worked and it was constantly growing. 'If you had such and such a problem,' explains Christian Serre, 'you looked at this, you did that, and you got to there. If you had another problem, you tried to resolve it in such and such a fashion. When you wanted, for example, to post some piece of information on the screen, then you'd take this function, or this function, or this function. So all these recipes made our lives easier and allowed us to realize a large number of applications programs quite rapidly.' Robert's Cookbook became such an important part of the PS controls group landscape that Report even had a special directive, %CB%, to tell the Report program that the document in question was a Cookbook document. 'Without a doubt,' says Christian Serre, 'for us application programmers the Cookbook was invaluable because it allowed us to communicate with the system guys.'

He fell in love with the language

The tools Robert Cailliau had produced had helped to oil the wheels of the PS controls project. 'But then,' remembers Berend Kuiper, 'he fell in love with the language.' The language in question was a relatively new computer programming language called Pascal defined by Swiss computer scientist Niklaus Wirth in 1970.

By the time the PS controls project came along, Norsk Data had a well-developed operating system called Sintran-III, and Norsk Data computers also came with the compiled Nord Programming Language. That, along with NODAL, was what was used at first for the PS controls system's applications programs. NODAL served for the less time-critical applications, Nord Programming Language for those that needed to be executed quickly. But both of these languages had their shortcomings, and Pascal looked as though it might offer a solution. 'Pascal,' recalls Christian Serre, 'was at that time the language that you found in schools and through which one learned programming.' It soon became clear, however, that for computer control applications Pascal wasn't up to the task. 'We found that Pascal was lacking in a number of gadgets that were necessary for programming a controls system,' explains Berend Kuiper. Robert had the idea of taking Pascal and building it up into a language that would be well adapted to real-time controls systems.

But despite Berend Kuiper's worries, Robert's main argument in promoting his idea had nothing to do with gadgets. It was his organizational passion again that convinced him that a higher-level language than Nord Programming Language was needed. 'I had been saying,' he recalls, 'how important it was not to program in assembly language if you wanted to do ten to twenty years' maintenance.' Because higher-level languages are much closer to the way humans think than the way computers operate, it would be much easier for subsequent generations of programmers to work out what their predecessors had done if everything were written in a high-level language. And since no suitable high-level language existed at the time, Robert decided to write one. 'So he sold us the idea,' says Kuiper, 'to make a project that he called P+, Pascal-plus, which would be a Pascal-oriented language that would include a number of modifications that would make it useful for accelerator controls.' A professor at ETH in Zurich, Niklaus Wirth, wasn't far away, so the CERN people decided to pay him a visit to see if he would like to work with them on the project. Wirth declined, and some years later, Berend Kuiper remembers finding out why. 'Secretly he was doing exactly the same,' he says. Wirth, it turned out, was working on his own language based on Pascal called Modula, which he released in 1976.

Wirth's refusal didn't dampen Robert's ardour and before long he had convinced Kuiper that his Pascal-plus was the thing to do. Kuiper, being a pragmatic man, accepted the proposal on one condition: that the manual be written before the language. By this time, Robert had enlisted the help of his boss, Brian Carpenter, and together they set about writing a manual which they handed to Kuiper just as he was about leave for a holiday in Spain. 'It was a very good manual,' remembers Kuiper: 'Even I could understand everything!' On the strength of that, he gave the go-ahead for Robert to write his language.

By 1981, applications programmers for the PS were producing code in P+, but little known to them, its days had been numbered from the start. A programming language called C was beginning to make its presence felt. C had the same heritage as Unix and was just as quirky. Nowadays, C is the language most Unix operating systems are written in. It was derived, logically enough, from a language called B, which was itself probably derived from a mid-60s language called BCPL that had been developed as part of the Multics project. BCPL was in its turn the successor to what else but ACPL, 'A Computer Programming Language'.

When Unix came along, BCPL became the Unix hacker's language of choice, so it was natural that the language of Unix should be derived from it. An alternative theory, however, has B being derived from a language called Bon, also created during the Multics days and named either after its author's wife, Bonnie, or a pre-Buddhist Tibetan animist religion called Bon whose rituals involve the murmuring of magic formulae. Whatever the truth, B was crammed into a tiny 8 kilobytes of memory and its compactness set the standard for C.

The first book on C was published in 1978 by the language's authors, Brian Kernighan and Dennis Ritchie, and served as its standard for a decade. But by the mid-1980s, C programming had become so widespread that the American National Standards Institute (ANSI) started to look at it and eventually published a new standard in 1989. 'C is quirky, flawed, and an enormous success,' says Dennis Ritchie. 'While accidents of history surely helped, it evidently satisfied a need for a system implementation language efficient enough to displace assembly language, yet sufficiently abstract and fluent to describe algorithms and interactions in a wide variety of environments.' C was very concise to write, which meant that once you knew the language you could do a lot with it, but it also meant that C programs could quickly become very difficult to follow. C initially polarized the programming world, but it rapidly caught on. Before long it had not only sent Pascal-plus to an early grave, it had taken over; among the new generation of programmers, if you didn't know C, you were nobody.

What divided the computing community about C was its structure. It was a bit like TCP/IP versus OSI all over again. Traditional languages like Pascal were well structured, designed first and then implemented. They corresponded to the same school of thought that had produced the infamous OSI seven-layer model of computer networking: design the perfect system and then go away and build it. C, on the other hand, was the TCP/IP of languages. It had little structure and tended to grow organically. 'A parsimonious, pragmatic approach influenced the things that went into C,' says Ritchie. 'It covers the essential needs of many programmers, but does not try to supply too much.'

To the highly organized mind of Robert Cailliau, C was a disaster. 'It's like you take a box, a huge box of random Lego bricks, and you dump it on the floor. That's the impression C gives you,' he despairs. But just about anything can be built from Lego given enough imagination, enough effort, and enough bricks. Years later, when Tim and Robert teamed up to work on the World Wide Web, C would be the language Tim chose to write the world's first Web server and browser. Although he would have preferred to use a structured language like Pascal, pragmatism guided Tim to the all-pervasive C. Robert, with his distaste for C, instead devoted his energies to convincing a sceptical CERN management that here was a project worthy of their support.

Together they made an improbable but irresistible team. In their attitudes to organization, Tim Berners-Lee and Robert Cailliau are perfect opposites. For Robert, the natural organizer, everything had to be planned and documented to the smallest detail. Tim, on the other hand, had no time for administration. He was too busy achieving his grand vision. Tim Berners-Lee made the Web, but without Robert Cailliau to deal with the administration and sell the project to CERN's management in terms they could deal with, he may well not have had the chance.

Enquire within

Applications programming for the PS was Tim Berners-Lee's job, but it wasn't all he did during his six months at CERN. 'Tim, being what he was, could do his assigned work in about half an hour in the morning so he had the rest of the day to think,' says Brian Carpenter. One of the things he thought about was a program called Enquire, designed to help him organize his thoughts. 'Enquire was something I found useful for keeping track of all the random associations one comes across in real life and brains are supposed to be so good at remembering but sometimes mine wouldn't,' he explains. He had come to the same conclusion as Vannevar Bush had done thirty-five years before.

Tim Berners-Lee's father, Conway, had been interested in the way brains worked for as long as Tim could remember, and in particular how they were good at different things than computers. 'Computers had always been good at storing things in tables and not storing random associations,' explains Tim. For example, if you happen to be out to lunch in Toronto with a person who orders something unusual like the Swiss national dish, your brain will always associate Rösti with Canada, a not altogether obvious link. Or if you visit a friend's house just after they have arranged a vase of fragrant roses, the smell of those flowers will always take you back to that house. Computers, on the other hand, would be good at arranging things in a hierarchical structure: Cuisine—Swiss—Rösti, for example, or Plants—Flowering—Roses. What Tim wanted to do with Enquire was use computers to store those kinds of random association that brains are supposed to be good at but his wasn't.

His school maths teacher, Frank Grundy, might well have served as inspiration too. Despite his prodigious skill at mental arithmetic,

Grundy was in possession of a famously absent-minded brain. 'And how many times did he mislay his briefcase?' wondered a fellow teacher on Grundy's retirement. 'Not to mention his ever-elusive spectacles and pen: "Now, what have I done with my spectacles?" And there they are pushed up on his forehead. Or, "What on earth have I done with my pen?" And there it is firmly clamped between his teeth.' Enquire did not aspire to offer a cure for absent-mindedness, but it was Tim Berners-Lee's first attempt to use computers to help overcome some of the shortcomings of the human brain.

The program took its name from a book Tim remembers from his childhood. *Enquire Within Upon Everything* was an almanac first produced in Victorian times and was full of potential random associations. 'Whether you wish to model a flower in wax; to study the rules of etiquette; to serve a relish for breakfast or supper; to plan a dinner for a large party or a small one; to cure a headache; to make a will; to get married; to bury a relative; whatever you may wish to do, make, or to enjoy, provided your desire has relation to the necessities of life, I hope you will not fail to "Enquire Within",' wrote the editor of the 1875 edition. Within its 400 pages, the book contained advice to young ladies on rules of conduct: 'If you have pretty hands and arms there can be no objection to your playing on the harp if you play well. If they are disposed to be clumsy, work tapestry.' On etiquette: 'A gentleman walking should always wear gloves, this being one of the characteristics of good breeding.' Some of the advice *Enquire Within Upon Everything* dispensed to Victorians is as valid today as it was then. At balls and evening parties, it recommends, 'avoid political and religious discussions. If you have a hobby, keep it to yourself.' There were cures for every ailment under the sun, mostly involving leeches, and hints on parlour games including a long list of words suitable for charades, 'ba-boon', 'ham-let', 'wed-lock'.

'It has little aphorisms at the top of each page,' remembers Tim. 'Never open the door to a little vice,' warns one, 'lest a great one should enter also.' 'Read not books alone, but also men; and above all, read thyself.' Some have survived: 'Take care of the pence and the pounds will take care of themselves,' or 'Every man's house is his castle.' 'Idle folks take the most pains,' cautioned one, while 'fools have an abundance of vanity.' A young lady agonizing over whether to take up the harp or resign herself stoically to tapestry might glance at the top of the page to learn that 'An hour in the morning is worth two at night', thus forming a random association between a major life decision and the Victorian work ethic.

Tim Berners-Lee doesn't wear gloves when out walking and doesn't remember much about *Enquire Within Upon Everything*, but one thing about the book stuck in his mind. 'Well, the title was pretty good,' he says. 'I didn't use the book, but the title stuck!' And that title became the name of the program he wrote, largely for his own benefit, to document the programs he was writing. Later on he built a help file into Enquire and made it available to anyone who was interested. 'Enquire,' says the help file, 'allows one to find information about people, things, software and concepts involved in a project and the relationships between them.' At the time Enquire was written, a computer screen would typically present you with a $ sign, called a prompt, and nothing else. The $ sign was the computer's way of prompting you to give it a command and you would simply type an instruction next to it. If you typed 'Enquire' on the computer Tim used, then the computer would display a list of topics for you to choose from.

'Enquire,' said the help file significantly, 'allows information to be structured in any arbitrary way. It does not have to be forced into a tree structure or a set of tables.' That feature made Enquire good at describing random associations. As if to prove the point, Tim made lots of labyrinthine hyper-routes in Enquire that served no better purpose that to exploit the program's capacity for making them. 'I made mazes of twisty passages all alike,' he explains, 'in honour of Adventure.' He had never met Will Crowther, but one of the things Tim had done with the home-brew computer he built at Oxford was play the world's first ever computer game. Enquire's lack of hierarchical structure, Tim believed, could lead a user 'to information which he did not realize he needed to know'. An example given in the program's help file runs as follows:

Enquire might tell you

That	A. Smith is part of DD division
and that	DD division is part of CERN
and that	A. Smith designed the "worsel mangler"
and that	the "worsel mangler" uses FASTBUS
and that	FASTBUS is described by the FASTBUS spec, ISBN 471-84472-1

Furthermore, if in an evolving project B. Jones later went on to update the worsel mangler, Enquire could easily carry that information too. A good indication of where Tim's thinking was leading can be had from the section headed 'new user' in Enquire's help file, which gave the advice, 'it is not particularly complicated, so the best way to get to know it is to play.' Another feature of Enquire that later fed into Tim's designs for the World Wide Web was its interactive nature: it was just as easy to add material as to read it.

When he went to CERN in 1980, Tim Berners-Lee had never heard of the pioneers of hypertext, but he knew that computers could be used to make up for the shortcomings of his brain. In that sense, he had a lot in common with Vannevar Bush, Doug Engelbart, and J. C. R. Licklider. Like them, he saw computers as a way to make life better for everyone. When he wrote Enquire, he was in some ways reinventing the wheel, but unlike his predecessors he had modern technology on his side. Enquire was a powerful program, but it was initially confined to the Norsk Data computers of the PS controls system. Later, Tim made versions to work on other computers (and it is from one of those that the above extracts from the help file have been taken), but nevertheless Enquire was still limited to single computers. 'This proved to be a debilitating problem,' says Tim. 'The whole point about hypertext was that it could model a changing morass of relationships which characterized most real environments I knew, and certainly CERN! Only allowing links within distinct boxes killed that.' Later on, these limitations would lead him to make the intellectual jump of putting hypertext on the Internet and giving everyone the means to enquire through the World Wide Web.

5 What Are We Going to Call This Thing?

Whilst Tim Berners-Lee was working at CERN, things had been moving back in Southampton. D. G. Nash Limited was run by two of Tim's friends, Dennis Nash and John Poole, and once the company was up and running, Poole decided to set up on his own. Tim had briefly helped Poole before he left for CERN and when his six months were up, Poole invited him back as a director of the new company, Image Computer Systems Limited. Tim was responsible for software development and made a profound impact on the company's future success. 'Most of my company's products,' Poole would later recall, 'are the result of his extensive involvement in their conception and implementation.' Over the years Image Computer Systems has evolved to become a successful specialist in the systems for printing labels and for making and reading bar codes. But Tim didn't stay to share in its success. By 1983 he was looking for new challenges and he remembered his old job at CERN.

By then CERN's matter–antimatter collider was in full swing and had made the discoveries that would bring the Nobel Prize to the laboratory for the first time. The laboratory was moving on to new challenges and the future Large Electron Positron collider project (LEP) was picking up steam. Tim had enjoyed working on the PS and he thought that if that had been fun then the much bigger LEP accelerator would be even more fun. He applied for a prestigious CERN fellowship, citing John Moffatt, Christian Serre, and John Poole as referees. 'Without just seeming to give a glowing reference for someone I know and like,' wrote Poole, 'I hope that I can impress on you the exceptional ability of Tim.' For his part, Christian Serre noted that all the software Tim had written in his six months at CERN in 1980 was still in use. 'He was an intense, efficient and creative worker,' he wrote. When he found out what Tim's other referees had written, he was amused to find they had all used the same three adjectives.

When Tim got back to Geneva, he found that CERN was still a chaotic mish-mash of different computers and networking systems. What had changed was the number of people around. The LEP project meant that CERN's already cosmopolitan mix of scientists from around the world was growing faster than ever before. It all added up to fertile ground for Tim's maturing dreams of a global hypertext system to come to fruition.

1984

Tim Berners-Lee's CERN fellowship application was successful, but the job he was offered wasn't quite what he had been hoping for. He had been pretty vague on the part of his application form that asked him to define what he would like to do. 'Computer technology: Networking, telecommunications, modular real-time systems, man/machine interface,' he had written. Building databases for the massive civil engineering project underway at CERN to dig the 27-kilometre tunnel that would house the laboratory's new accelerator was what he was offered. But managing mud was not Tim's idea of fun, so while accepting the offer he wrote a long letter to CERN setting out more precisely what he wanted to do. The result was a job in Peggie Rimmer's section of the laboratory's On-line Computing group, where he would work on an up-and-coming high-speed computer-controlled electronic system called Fastbus that had first seen the light of day in 1982 and was fast making inroads at CERN.

Peggie Rimmer had been working with Fastbus right from the start, with a view to developing it for the experiments that would be using LEP when it started up in 1989. Another Oxford physicist, she had joined CERN in the late 1960s to continue her research, but she soon moved into electronics and in particular the area of data acquisition (DAQ) systems. These are the pieces of electronic wizardry that physicists use to collect the raw data from their particle detectors: electrical pulses signalling the passage of tiny particles. A DAQ system converts these signals into computer-understandable form that tells the physicists things like where the particles went and how much energy they had. Fastbus was a powerful new system for DAQ, and when it was first proposed in the United States, Peggie dived into the nuts and bolts of designing the system. At a conference in 1983, she pinned her colours to the mast, calling for standardization so that no matter how many companies you bought your Fastbus hardware and software components from, you could be confident that they would all work together.

Tim arrived back at CERN on 1 September 1984 just as the standardization process was getting under way. The laboratory was still using a huge range of different kinds of computers and whilst most physicists were still working in a computer language called FORTRAN, a few were moving over to C because it was closer to the hardware. For Peggie Rimmer's Fastbus team this meant more work, because the Fastbus standards had to work with whatever language the physicists might use. She assigned a language to each member of her section, and much to his chagrin Tim wound up with FORTRAN.

Enquire again

Tim soon re-established his reputation as a brilliant and enthusiastic programmer, if something of a loose cannon. Sometimes in meetings his ideas would come faster than anyone could follow them, and asking him to slow down didn't seem to have any effect. 'We actually got sheets of paper,' remembers Peggie Rimmer, 'which we used to hold up saying, "Tim Slow Down".' Tim was always full of good ideas and he would implement them faster than anyone could keep up with, which was a little frustrating to his colleagues. 'The ground was constantly shifting under their feet,' remembers Peggie. 'You came back on Monday and the standard package, version 1.6.11 or whatever, had gone up to 1.6.21 and nobody knew why or when or what had been put in. But he always insisted that the ideas were so good that he couldn't possibly not put them in.' While he always had time for program modifications, however, he rarely had time to write them up. But Rimmer was a stickler for documentation and she insisted he did. In any standardization process, she reasoned, good, clear documentation is essential. 'You had to write an English sentence,' she explains, 'which would go to ISO or something and be read three years later by somebody in Bolivia, and what they did would be exactly what you wanted them to do having read that English sentence.'

Tim was always a bit restive in the standardization meetings, always wanting to get back to work. 'I found that I did not like working on the Fastbus standard,' he explains. 'It was tedious because you had to try to get the darn thing right.' Through those meetings, however, he learned to respect the importance of standards and in time became an acknowledged expert in the Fastbus field. 'It was a really good education for building standards and writing specifications,' he continues. 'Peggie's tutoring on what makes a specification and what doesn't was good.' Later on when it came to standardizing the Web, that experience would stand him in good stead.

But the mundane Fastbus standardization process wasn't enough for Tim, and he soon found other outlets for his creativity. One was an interesting idea that had been gathering momentum since the mid-1970s, when microcomputers were just a little cloud on the horizon of mainframe computer dominance. The idea was called Remote Procedure Call (RPC), and it was a way of distributing a single program around several microcomputers. Bruce Nelson, a graduate student who divided his time between Xerox PARC and Carnegie-Mellon University, was the first to give RPC a thorough treatment in his 1981 dissertation, which he dedicated to the islands of the South Pacific. Each chapter was headed with a set of geographical coordinates and a little snippet of information about the island to be found there. Nelson's acknowledgements began with the words, 'Writing my dissertation was a voyage of discovery through a sea of detail,' and closed by wishing a 'Bon voyage' to future travellers who would follow his journey and perhaps use it as the basis for an expedition of their own.

Sailing through a sea of detail

Tim charted a course for RPC into the unknown waters of data acquisition systems for the big experiments in preparation for CERN's new LEP accelerator. There were to be four experiments, each with a particle detector as big as a three-storey house and packed with electronics. These detectors were being built in a modular fashion all around the world, the plan being that all the different 'sub-detector' modules would arrive at CERN to be assembled ready for LEP start-up in 1989. Even the simplest of the four experiments, known as OPAL for 'Omni-Purpose Apparatus at LEP', was made up of some fifteen sub-detectors each under the control of a microcomputer. All of these would be commanded by another computer called the run-controller whose role was akin to the captain of a ship. Tim saw RPC as being the ideal candidate for first mate, running around making sure the captain's orders got implemented.

At the beginning of February 1985, the On-line Computing group got a new leader. Mike Sendall was already a good friend of Peggie Rimmer's, and Tim soon came to appreciate his sound common sense, good judgement, and wry, understated sense of humour. Before long, the three were bouncing Tim's RPC ideas around. 'I remember Tim would passionately educate us about its importance,' recalled Mike, 'in particular trying to convince me, who believed at the time that real programmers did not need RPC.' Mike took some convincing, but with a little help from Ben Segal, Tim would eventually win him over. Segal, who was still trying to persuade CERN to adopt TCP/IP, was keen to embrace new ideas, so when Tim asked him to have a word in Mike's ear, he was only too happy to oblige. 'What I was basically telling Mike,' says Segal, 'was, "Look, this guy seems to have got a real nuts-and-bolts approach and he's capable of putting RPC out in the experiments. Give him some resources."' And eventually, Mike did.

Computer programs are built up of distinct blocks that perform specific tasks. These are called procedures, and they are generally used for tasks that are repeated often. They are a way of keeping the code compact. Just as a sailing ship's captain is likely to have one basic command for hoisting sails, 'Hoist the mainsail,' or 'Hoist the stay sail,' a program that needs to open windows on a screen is likely to have one procedure whose job is to do just that. It might say, 'Open the text window,' or 'Open the graphics window'. And just as the command 'Hoist' is never likely to be used to move the ship's rudder, the procedure 'Open' is never used to do anything other than open windows.

Breaking up programs into procedures is easy when the whole program is executed on one computer, but the advent of microprocessors changed all that. Small affordable micros introduced the concept of distributed processing, where several computers work together: a program in one computer can call procedures in others. The problem was how to send instructions and data between the various computers of a distributed system; most programming languages were not designed to do that.

CERN was a pioneer of distributed computing, and Tim had been involved almost from the start. NODAL was the first distributed system at the laboratory in the 1970s. A NODAL command issued on one computer could be executed on another. Later, when Tim was writing applications programs for the PS controls in 1980, he had also confronted the problem. The solution the PS controls team adopted was to design tailor-made interfaces between each controlling program and each remote procedure. This led to a plethora of different interfaces for programmers to learn: they had to know all about networks as well as all about programming. As far as Tim was concerned, there had to be a better way, and he said as much in his parting shot to the laboratory when he went back to Britain at the end of 1980. In a note he penned just before he left, he outlined some rough ideas about how the PS's distributed programming might be streamlined, but they were never seriously developed. By the time he came back, however, a solution was at hand in the form of RPC. An RPC system would allow people who could write programs for a single computer to behave as if their programs were actually running on a single computer; it effectively made the network of distributed computers invisible. Tim realized that for programmers writing data acquisition systems for the big LEP experiments, RPC could make life much easier. They could stick to programming and wouldn't have to become network experts as well.

By August 1985, Mike was slowly being won over by Tim's argument. His softening opinion was reflected in the title of a note he wrote to Tim: 'Real Programmers Don't Use Remote Procedure Calls . . . (But Maybe They Should).' Tim grasped the opportunity to drive home his point and fired back a memo to Mike three days later confronting his boss's remaining worries. This time Mike was convinced. 'In general my gut feeling is that we should have RPC available for those applications where it is appropriate,' he replied, and Tim immediately set about converting his ideas into a concrete system. 'He developed a system single-handed that was simple and straightforward, and it ran not only on all these implementations but it also ran on every networking support you could think of,' explains Ben Segal. By 1987, Tim's RPC was ready to be presented at a conference, and the LEP experiments soon took note. Soon afterwards, programmers on OPAL were busily writing their data acquisition software using RPC, and Tim himself had been assigned to help implement the system in another experiment called DELPHI. When the experiments started two years later, RPC had become a CERN standard.

Tim's implementation of RPC was based on a client–server model. A client, like the run controller, would send off an RPC to a server, which might be one of the computers controlling a sub-detector. The server would then perform some task and return information to the client. From the programmer's point of view it would look just as if the program had called a local procedure with no network in between. By the time Tim finished his RPC, it system was running over TCP/IP and the germ of an idea had been sown. 'It was the second ingredient of the Web,' believes Segal; 'the hypertext was already in his head.'

CERNDOC

Keeping track of documents at CERN was an old problem, but one that was growing fast, as the complexity of the laboratory's experiments grew along with the number of scientists using the laboratory's facilities. To compound the problem, the CERN fellowship programme ensured that there was a constant turnover of talented people like Tim Berners-Lee. Although many fellows went on to secure permanent contracts at CERN, and Tim would be one of them, many more left to pursue careers in industry. To compound the problem further, most of the scientists who came to CERN were only there for as long as it took them to collect their experimental data. It wasn't that nobody documented what they did, so much as that there was no coherent way of keeping track of all the documentation they produced, so a great deal was being lost.

In 1984, CERN started a project to address the documentation problem. It took a piece of software developed at the Rutherford Laboratory in Oxfordshire and tailored it to CERN's needs. The result was a system called CERNDOC that ran on the laboratory's big central IBM computer. CERNDOC's goal was ambitious: to store tens of thousands of documents in a hierarchical tree structure with keyword searching and the ability to display documents on a screen or send them to a printer. At the heart of CERNDOC was SGML, by this time rapidly progressing on its way to becoming an international standard.

Eric van Herwijnen was an SGML expert and one of the programmers who had put CERNDOC together. He had put a lot of effort into CERNDOC, but unfortunately for him it was doomed before it got off the ground. The whole system had been conceived for big, central computing facilities where you would access the computer through a primitive terminal that could only display text. There were no windows, no different typefaces, and no graphics. Everything appeared in the classic `courier typeface` adopted from typewriters. Back then, the coolest thing hackers could do to text was make it appear twice the normal size or make it blink on and off on the screen. That was about the limit of what could be done. But the year the CERNDOC project was launched was also the year that the wraps were coming off the Apple Macintosh. With the desktop publishing revolution that followed, people would soon be expecting to have control over every aspect of their documentation. They would want to include graphs in-line with the text, and when they sent things to print, they would want to get on paper exactly what they saw on the screen. The term WYSIWYG was about to enter the English language.

Nevertheless, CERNDOC played an important role at CERN well into the 1990s, when the big IBM was finally supplanted by small desktop computers. The On-line Computing group started to put its documentation into CERNDOC in October 1987, and that set Tim Berners-Lee thinking. By this time he had resurrected an old friend. 'I missed

Enquire,' he recalls, 'so I therefore produced a version for VMS and used it to keep track of projects, people, groups, experiments, software modules, and hardware devices with which I worked.' VMS was the operating system of the Digital Equipment Corporation's VAX computers that were popular in research circles at the time. They weren't microcomputers, but neither were they so big that a major laboratory like CERN had to share just one. VAXes were minicomputers, small enough for a modestly sized team to afford but powerful enough to run a fairly complex experiment. They were also particularly good at running programs written in FORTRAN, physicists' favourite computer language.

To Tim, the contrast between CERNDOC and Enquire was striking. CERNDOC was doing the kind of things that computers were traditionally good at, storing information in a hierarchical structure, and not storing the kind of random associations that brains were supposed to, for which he had written Enquire. CERNDOC was good as far as it went; but what if you made your way down to the bottom of one tree in the hierarchy to find a document written by A. Smith, and you wanted to find out what else A. Smith had done? The only way to do that in CERNDOC would be to climb all the way to the top of the tree and start searching all over again. With Enquire, all you would have to do would be to ask the program to take you to the other information it had about A. Smith. There was a lesson in that for Tim, but he knew that Enquire wasn't the answer. 'I had lost the source of Enquire and rewritten it and never got around to coding up the external links,' he remembers. 'I recognized that external links were very important and in fact that internal links could best be seen as special cases of external links that just happened to be in the same document.' So the version of Enquire he had resurrected on VMS was fine as a sort of personal aide-mémoire, but if more people started to create their own aides-mémoires, it would be impossible to link them together. In other words, Enquire wouldn't scale up.

By 1989, all the ingredients to build the Web were in place at CERN. The lab's computing requirements were increasingly being supplied by a lot of small computers instead of a single big one. TCP/IP networking was gradually becoming a de facto standard, complete with its scalable addressing scheme, the Domain Name System, and serious thought was going into document handling through CERNDOC. Tim himself had practised with client-server architecture in his RPC project. He had reinstated Enquire and fretted about the inadequacies of CERNDOC, and he had gained a good deal of respect for the standardization procedure through his work with Fastbus. All that was missing was the tool to allow him to pull all these strands together. That would soon be provided by a new kind of computer called NeXT.

Vague but exciting...

In December 1989, Berners-Lee announced that that RPC is 'now fairly stable', and that 'there are no plans to extend its functionality significantly'. The LEP experiments had got going earlier that year, the first beams being circulated in the new machine with a great sense of theatre on Bastille Day, 14 July, and the first electron–positron collisions following one month later. With the advent of LEP, CERN was entering a new era. One by one the old pioneering systems were being turned off. OMNET had switched its last packets at the end of 1986, and with the rise of TCP/IP, CERNET was also switched off in December 1989. The computing and networking technologies CERN had helped to pioneer were now in the hands of industry, and CERN was just a customer like any other. A brave new world was being ushered in with TCP/IP, Ethernet for local networks, Fastbus for data acquisition hardware, and RPC to control the hugely complicated distributed data acquisition systems.

As the RPC project reached maturity, Tim was finding himself with more time to devote to the dream he had been nurturing for over a decade. In March, he had sent a memo off to Mike Sendall with the title, 'Information Management: A Proposal'. On the cover was a bewildering array of bubbles with arrows pointing between them. Inside was the first draft of Tim's blueprint for the World Wide Web.

Information management: A proposal

'When I read Tim's proposal,' remembered Mike, 'I could not figure out what it was but I thought it was great.' Peggie Rimmer didn't even get that far. 'I've looked repeatedly at that March paper,' she says, 'and I couldn't honestly tell you even now that it's about the World Wide Web, but somehow Mike could.' Back in 1989, what Tim was proposing was so far removed from anything people were used to that few could figure out what he was driving at. He was lucky that he had the boss he had. Mike Sendall had a reputation for knowing a good idea when he saw one, and even if he didn't quite understand it, Tim's proposal looked to him like a good idea. 'Vague,' he scribbled on the cover, 'but exciting.'

Everything one needed to know about the proposal was encapsulated in the bubble and arrow diagram on the cover. Tim's name appeared at the bottom right embedded in CERN's organizational hierarchy. An

Pl.1 Nobel Prize-winning French physicist Louis de Broglie was the first proponent of a world-class European physics laboratory. His dream was realized in 1954 with the foundation of CERN.

Pl.2 British network pioneer Donald Davies (right) with European Informatics Network (EIN) project leader Derek Barber (centre) and Roger Scantlebury pictured with the National Physical Laboratory's EIN node.

PL.3 Louis Pouzin (left) with members of the Cyclades team (left to right) Jean-Louis Grangé, Najah Naffah, Hubert Zimmermann, and Jean Le Bihan on the occasion of Naffah's election to the French Ordre du Mérite in 1984. Fifteen years later honour was again bestowed on the Cyclades team when Pouzin was elected to the prestigious Legion d'Honneur in recognition of his pioneering work on computer networks.

PL.4 Vannevar Bush contemplating his differential analyzer, the mechanical computer that he patented in 1935.

PL.5 The first computer mouse in the hand of its inventor, Doug Engelbart.

PL.6 A screen shot from Doug Engelbart's legendary 1968 demonstration of NLS at the Fall Joint Computer Conference. Note the mixture of video and text.

PL.7 A networking tour de force at the International Conference on Computer Communication '76. The European Informatics Network was used to pipe Ceefax pages through to Toronto. Many delegates used the demonstration for checking the latest cricket scores.

PL.8 The control room for CERN's PS accelerator in 1980, scene of Tim Berners-Lee's first steps into hyperspace with his Enquire program.

PL.9 Mike Sendall collects an award on behalf of Tim Berners-Lee at the Prix Ars-Electronica 1995 award ceremony in Linz, Austria.

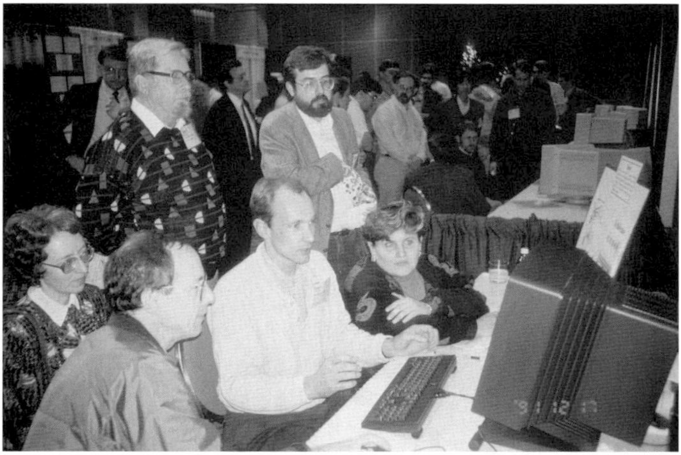

PL.10 After having his paper rejected, Tim Berners-Lee demonstrates the World Wide Web to delegates at the Hypertext '91 conference in San Antonio, Texas.

PL.11 Tim Berners-Lee with Nicola Pellow, the reluctant revolutionary who wrote the line-mode browser for the World Wide Web. They are pictured with the NeXT computer on which Tim wrote the original World Wide Web software.

PL.12 A gathering of WWW Wizards. Standing left to right, Louise Addis, George Crane, Tony Johnson, Joan Winters. Seated, Paul Kunz.

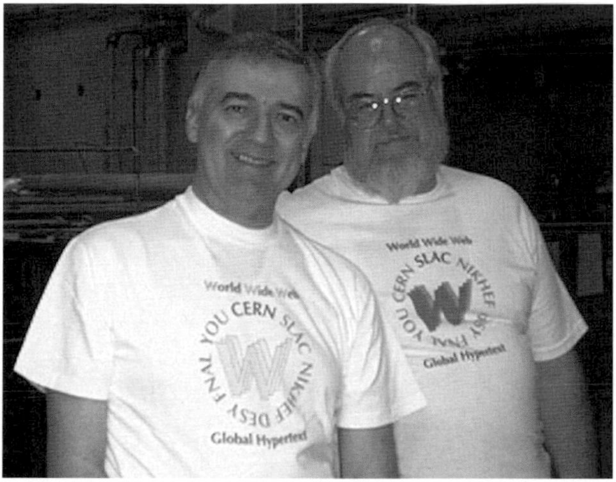

PL.13 Robert Cailliau (left) and Bebo White modelling the CERN and SLAC versions of the original World Wide Web T-shirt at SLAC.

PL.14 The Norwegian team that put up the 1994 Lillehammer Winter Olympics Web site, described by Tim Berners-Lee as the one that demonstrated how a site could become overloaded. Steinar Kjærnsrød is top left.

PL.15 The prodigal son. Tim Berners-Lee returns to CERN in 1998 as keynote speaker at the 'Internet, Web, What's Next' event.

PL.16 Tim Berners-Lee (left) and Ted Nelson (right) square off as Robert Cailliau plays to the camera.

Vague but exciting ...

CERN DD/OC

Information Management: A Proposal

Tim Berners-Lee, CERN/DD

March 1989

Information Management: A Proposal

Abstract

This proposal concerns the management of general information about accelerators and experiments at CERN. It discusses the problems of loss of information about complex evolving systems and derives a solution based on a distributed hypertext sytstem.

Keywords: Hypertext, Computer conferencing, Document retrieval, Information management, Project control

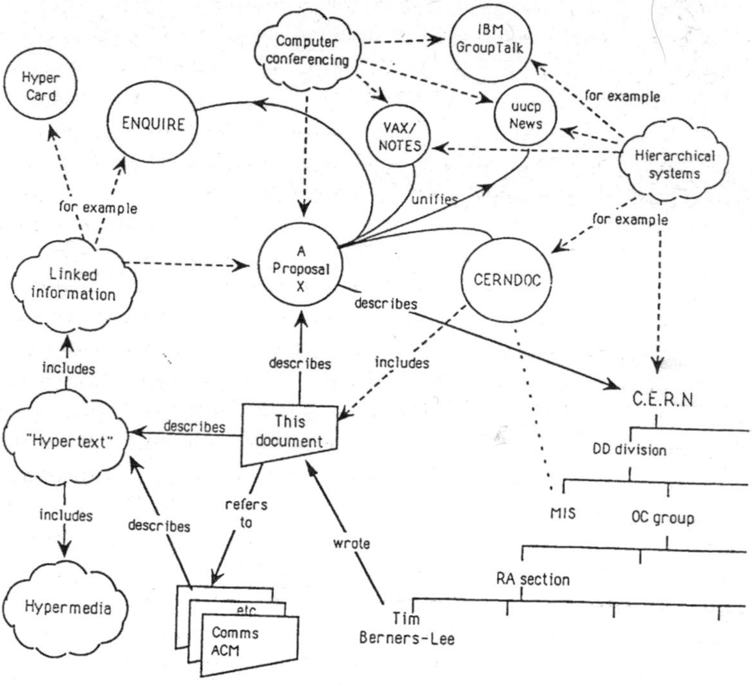

Figure 16: The cover of the original proposal for the World Wide Web with Mike Sendall's comment top right: 'Vague but exciting ...'

arrow labelled 'wrote' pointed from Tim to a box labelled 'This document'. The document itself described a proposal which itself described the CERN hierarchy. The proposal aimed to provide a unifying interface to all kinds of information management systems, including CERNDOC, of which the document itself was a part. In short, Tim's proposal described a system to bring Enquire out of its box: it was a proposal to make hypertext global.

'CERN is a wonderful organisation,' Tim began. 'It involves several thousand people, many of them very creative, all working towards the same common goals.' These people were all organized into a hierarchical structure, but Tim had noticed that in practice people didn't always work that way. 'The actual observed working structure of the organisation is a multiply connected "web" whose interconnections evolve with time,' he noted. To Tim, it seemed natural that the documentation system for such an organization should also be a constantly evolving web. Such a system would solve the problems of information loss caused by rapid turnover of people and a plethora of different information handling systems that couldn't talk to each other. Moreover, although Tim was proposing a solution to CERN's problems, he was already looking beyond the walls of the laboratory. 'The problems of information loss may be particularly acute at CERN,' he pointed out, 'but in this case CERN is a model in miniature for the rest of the world in a few year's time.' It had been almost a decade since he first came to CERN, and he had already noticed how CERN's position at the high-tech frontier led to the laboratory's solving problems in computing a few years before the rest of the world caught up. It had happened with networks, it had happened with distributed programming systems like RPC, and now Tim believed it was going to happen again with distributed information systems. 'CERN meets now the problems the rest of the world will have to face soon,' he concluded.

The main problem Tim had with hierarchical information systems was that they placed restraints on the information itself. 'This is why a "web" of notes with links between them is far more useful than a fixed hierarchical system,' he claimed. A common technique for making sense of a complex problem, like a proposal for an information management system or a plan for a wedding, is to jot down a diagram of circles and arrows. On a wedding plan, the circles might contain words like 'Send out invitations', 'Organize caterers', 'Speeches', and 'Ceremony'. An arrow labelled 'must be done before' could join 'Send out invitations' to 'Organize caterers'. Another labelled 'includes' might join 'Ceremony' to 'Speeches'. Tim had made his circle and arrow diagram for information management the cover of the proposal, and inside he explained why. 'The system we need,' he said, 'is like a diagram of circles and arrows, where circles and arrows can stand for anything.' Circles might be people, concepts, documents, or projects. Arrows could mean that circle A depends on circle B, or that it is part of B, or that it made B, and so on.

He hadn't made up his mind about the technology he would use to develop his system, but the proposal contained all the ideas that would eventually make the World Wide Web. It even anticipated the sort of problems the Web would encounter as it spread about the globe. With systems like CERNDOC, for example, keywords were used for searching. 'The usual problem with keywords,' Tim pointed out, 'is that two people never choose the same keywords.' And while people may recognize similarities in meaning between words, computers do not. A person wishing to buy a yellow car in Massachusetts, for example, would recognize that a primrose Ford in Boston matched his needs, but a computer would not equate primrose with yellow or Boston with Massachusetts.

Digital already had a solution to the keyword problem for its VAX NOTES system. That required keywords to be registered so that there would only be a restricted list to choose from. That was fine as far as it went, but a little impractical for a widely distributed system such as Tim envisaged. His conceptual solution was to define 'circles' as keywords and point them to any other documents to which they were relevant. The difficulties of implementing this idea in practice were still troubling Web developers a decade later.

All the ingredients to make Tim's dream come true were in his March 1989 note to Mike Sendall. He listed the system's requirements. First on the list was the requirement that it be accessible across networks. It should also be able to access and provide data between different computer systems. It should be distributed so that anyone could put up information and make sure that it stayed up to date. There should be private links so that people could generate their own webs of information for private use. Tim's initial vision was not just for one great amorphous Web, but for countless related webs. Putting information on to the Web, for general consumption or for the use of a small group like a distributed family, should be just as easy as looking at information that had been put there by others. The Web we have today still has some way to go before that vision will be realized.

Tim's remaining requirements were purely pragmatic. He proposed to build a system that would provide access to existing data so that people would quickly start to use it and realize how useful it was. It would also be low on functionality at first. Just the bare minimum would be implemented so that it could be swiftly deployed. Bells and whistles could wait. Mike Sendall was bemused but impressed. 'And now?' he scribbled at the end of the proposal, little realizing what he was about to unleash by giving Tim the space to develop his ideas.

The next step

'Hi, I'm at Fermilab. Everything's fine, I'm finding out about their DAQ systems and their RPC project,' Tim wrote to Mike Sendall on 4 January 1990. 'I hope you had a pleasant Christmas.' He himself had spent a very pleasant one with his American fiancée's family and had taken the opportunity of being in the United States to visit one of America's leading particle physics research laboratories. CERN was still closed after the Christmas holidays but the United States takes shorter vacations than Europe and Fermilab staff were already back at their desks. Tim wanted to be sure that his message would be in Mike's mailbox as soon as he got back to work, because there was another reason he was staying a bit longer in the USA. The National Institute of Standards in Technology (NIST) was organizing a workshop on hypertext in Gaithersburg, Maryland, and he wanted to go. All he was asking for was the time. 'Fermilab are paying my board out here,' he said. 'I could pay for myself if necessary in Gaithersburg, and I will pay the conference registration fee if I go. I've already paid the transatlantic air fare.' Tim was desperate to go. 'I am in need of something refreshing and a bit different,' he said, 'after four years working on RPC.' On terms like that, Mike could hardly say 'no'. Twelve days later Tim was in Gaithersburg.

As someone who had been working with hypertext for nearly a decade, Tim needed no further convincing about its value. Nevertheless, he came back to CERN more sure than ever that distributed hypertext was what the laboratory needed. 'I feel that CERN, more than most organizations, needs hypertext,' he told his colleagues. The problem was that it was unlikely that a suitable system would be available off the shelf any time soon. 'The question,' he said, 'is whether we can wait until commercial products become available.' Tim certainly didn't think so. He had hoped to learn at the workshop that a standard server was just around the corner, one that would allow something like CERNDOC to be made available across networks and in hypertext format. 'This may happen in a few years,' he believed, 'but not earlier without some encouragement.' Tim Berners-Lee was keen to do the encouraging, but he needed a computer on which he could develop his ideas quickly into a working prototype. By this time he had a good idea what that computer might be.

Life after Mac

In September 1985 Steve Jobs left Apple following an acrimonious boardroom scuffle and the following year he set up a new company called NeXT. It was an audacious move. The market for desktop computers was already overcrowded, and if Jobs wanted to succeed, he would have to offer something very special to tempt prospective buyers. The days of personal computers being confined to a few geeks were rapidly passing, so it was no longer enough just to offer the latest, fastest chip or a few more kilobytes of RAM. What ordinary people wanted was applications: spreadsheets, word processors, games.

Jobs decided that the best way to break into the market was to come out with a machine that had lots of great applications. That redefined his potential market. Instead of trying to appeal to end users, he would make a machine that appealed to the program developers who wrote the sexy applications that would persuade the end users to buy his machines. That, however, was easier said than done. Developers are the kinds of people who spend days and nights in front of their screens learning every little detail about the way their computer works. Theirs is a fervour bordering on religion and, appropriately enough, they have their own 'bible'. Everything a developer might ever need to know about the particular computer system they specialize in is contained in the book of APIs, Application Program Interfaces. APIs specify all the built-in functions in the system. If such things existed for household appliances in Britain, there would be one saying that to make any appliance work, you take the square-shaped object with three metal prongs, defined as 'plug', and push it into the three similarly disposed holes in the wall, defined as 'socket'. It is not necessary to redesign plugs and sockets for each new appliance we buy; they are part of the system. In a computer, APIs play a similar role. For example, a developer writing a spreadsheet program for doing the household accounts does not have to invent a range of colours to allow users of his program to colour in spreadsheet cells. That is built into the system and there is an API to describe it.

Most computers have thousands of APIs and most good developers know them all by heart. Moreover, experience shared with fellow developers has told them what works and what doesn't. That represents a considerable investment of time and is not something to be given up easily. What Jobs had to do was convince the developers that his computer had something to make it worthwhile starting all over again. He was putting his money on the marriage of Unix's power with the ease of use of the Macintosh. And he stirred into that a programming technique that goes by the misleading name of 'oops'.

Oops

There is nothing haphazard about Object-Oriented Programming Systems (OOPS); they take the concept of dividing a program up into discrete specialized chunks to its ultimate conclusion. The idea goes back to 1965 when two Norwegian researchers, Ole-Johan Dahl and Kristen Nygaard, invented a style of programming that was radically different from what had gone before.

Instead of treating a program as a monolithic system designed for a specific task, Dahl and Nygaard proposed a more modular approach. Unlike a procedure in an ordinary program, an object in an object-oriented program is a combination of code and data. The object 'Shep' for example, might contain all the data describing Shep; a three-year-old border collie weighing fourteen kilograms. It might also contain the things that Shep can do: bark, run, roll over, for example. Shep in turn might be one instance of a particular object class called 'dog' which could include 'Rover' and 'Spot' as well, both of whom would inherit the standard dog-like characteristics from the basic 'dog' object. The programmer would interact with the objects by sending them messages that all objects of the same class would understand. Objects of the class 'dog' would understand messages like 'bark', 'run', and 'roll over'.

This may all sound a bit esoteric, but the point of it is that once an object has been defined it is not just confined to a single program: it can be reused. 'Shep', for example, would be just as useful to a programmer writing a 'round up sheep' application as to one writing a 'fetch sticks' application.

The idea took a long time to catch on, perhaps because it was so far removed from the one-step-after-another way that humans tend to think, but once people realized how powerful the technique could be, object-oriented programming was quick to take off. The first serious devotee was the same Alan Kay who had been so impressed with Doug Engelbart's 1968 demonstration of NLS. Now at Xerox PARC, Kay had even invented the term 'object-oriented'. He wanted to develop a language that could turn children into sophisticated applications programmers, and the object-oriented approach seemed to be the way to do it. The result was Smalltalk, a programming language that had objects for windows, icons, and menus. While it was being developed,

Xerox PARC would invite children in from local schools to try it out on Saturday mornings, just to make sure that it really was something they could understand. Something we have learned since then is that children aren't the problem; nowadays if someone could come up with a programming language that their *parents* can handle, then we might be making progress.

Smalltalk introduced all the features of a modern graphical user interface (GUI) such as you now see whenever you switch on a Macintosh or PC, and it was all in place by 1979. The similarity is no accident: it was Smalltalk that inspired the developers of the original Macintosh. Apple had been running for three years by the time Steve Jobs sold Xerox 100 000 Apple shares for $1 million and a peek at Xerox PARC. They showed him their network of Alto computers and they showed him object-oriented programming, but first they showed him the Smalltalk graphical user interface. 'I thought it was the best thing I'd ever seen in my life,' he later remarked. 'Within, you know, ten minutes it was obvious to me that computers would all work like this some day.' And he determined that Apple would be the company to bring Kay's invention to market.

Alan Kay is famous for saying, 'The best way to predict the future is to invent it. Really smart people with reasonable funding can do just about anything that doesn't violate too many of Newton's laws!' That was at a Xerox PARC planning meeting in 1971. By the end of the decade, he had invented the future, and four years further on, Steve Jobs deployed it on the screen of the new Macintosh computer. But all Jobs had taken was the GUI; he left half the power of Smalltalk behind. So impressed had he been with the Smalltalk GUI on his visit to Xerox PARC that he had hardly noticed the language. It wouldn't have made much difference if he had, as the sort of power the Apple team could put into the first Macintosh wouldn't have been enough to run a system like Smalltalk anyway.

And that in a way was a pity, because Alan Kay had succeeded in developing a system his children could get to grips with, not just to run applications, but to build them. Smalltalk's objects for things like menus and windows meant that any prospective programmer could take those same objects and build them into applications of their own. Not for the first time in the history of computing, Smalltalk was an idea well before its time. But its time would come.

Monsieur Hullot's holiday

Jean-Marie Hullot had got his Ph.D. in computer science from the University of Paris at Orsay in 1981. He had shared his time between the university and INRIA, which had evolved from IRIA and was just across the road in Rocquencourt, and because his supervisor went for a sabbatical year at SRI, Hullot went too. Like Alan Kay, Jean-Marie Hullot was an early fan of object-oriented programming. 'For me it's very intuitive,' he says. So intuitive, in fact, that he rediscovered the concept himself, but to him that is no big deal. 'You automatically come to it,' he explains, 'whenever you get a programming language that allows you to do it.'

The language he was working with was one that was deeply imbued with the object-oriented culture; you didn't have to use it that way, but if you wanted to, it was easy to do. Hullot was using a Macintosh, and like many developers, he rapidly found that although the Mac's GUI might have been brilliant, it was a pig of a machine to write applications on. 'When the Macintosh was invented,' he explains, 'suddenly, compared to what you had to do before, you had to add at least 60 or 70 per cent of your time to make the user interface.' Before the Macintosh, the interface was pretty basic—you would just type a line of text and the computer would respond with successive lines scrolling up the screen—but that meant that programmers didn't have to worry about it. All the windows and menus that came with the Mac were great for the people who used the end applications, but for the people who had to write them they were a nightmare. Each time they wanted a menu or a window in their application, they had to program it in from scratch. Hullot's big idea was to turn the problem into a simple question of drawing lines on the screen. He made a palette of objects for things like menu items and windows. Then to build the outline of an application you would simply take objects from the palette and draw lines between them. So, for example, you could pick up a menu object, and then by drawing lines from other objects like 'Open' or 'Print', you would put those functions into the menu.

Hullot called his invention the Interface Builder. It was a powerful tool that, like Smalltalk, put the power of objects at the developer's disposal. 'I realized quite fast that I had something, you know, really hot on my hands,' he says. 'And I also realized that if I stayed at INRIA I would get ten people using it, I would make a publication, and that would be all that I could get out of it.' Soon after, however, he found a way to get the Interface Builder the kind of exposure he thought it deserved. He went to an Apple University Consortium meeting in Cambridge. 'The people from Apple really loved what I was doing,' he recalls, 'and they wanted me to meet Jean-Louis Gassée.'

A fellow Frenchman, Gassée was head of research and development at Apple, and he persuaded Hullot to go to the United States. California was no stranger to him by this time, so soon after he jumped on a plane at Charles de Gaulle airport bound for San Francisco. When he arrived, however, he found that Apple was not the sort of place he wanted to work. It was already a big corporation. 'It was impossible really to do something new,' explains Hullot, 'so what I decided was not to work with them and to find somebody to sell this product for me in the United States.' So he touted his Interface Builder around and eventually wound up at a software house called ExperTelligence in Santa Barbara. ExperTelligence was looking for new partnerships and so was Hullot, by this time back in France. He suggested to his Santa Barbara colleagues that they give NeXT a call.

Hullot and two colleagues from ExperTelligence soon found themselves demonstrating the Interface Builder to someone from product marketing at NeXT's Palo Alto headquarters. He was sufficiently impressed to call in Steve Jobs, so Hullot began the demonstration all over again. Jobs gave the impression of being nonplussed by it all and the ExperTelligence trio left. 'And when we reached the parking lot,' Hullot recalls, 'the guy from product marketing came and said, "OK, you come back."' Hullot did as he was asked and left his colleagues in the parking lot. When he got back to the NeXT building, he found Steve Jobs waiting for him. 'When do you start working for us?' he asked. Hullot explained that he was leaving the following day for a well-earned vacation. 'I'll call you in two weeks,' said Jobs. 'No, Steve,' replied Hullot, 'it's not a US vacation, it's a European vacation. Call me in seven weeks.' Jobs didn't forget, and no sooner was Hullot back from his vacation than the phone rang. The next day Hullot was back on the plane to California. He agreed to go to NeXT for six months, and ended up staying for ten years. His Interface Builder became the heart of NeXTStep, the GUI and development platform he developed along with others for the NeXT computer. It ran on top of the NeXT's underlying Unix operating system.

Unix was an operating system for hackers; its commands were very terse and not always intuitive, so you had to learn them all by heart. But unlike other operating systems for desktop computers at the time, it was multi-tasking. That meant it could so several things at once: you could be working in one application whilst another one was printing something out or doing some calculations in the background. That was the feature that Jobs wanted for his new machine. The NeXTStep user interface allowed him to harness that power to the intuitiveness of the Mac's graphical user interface, and the Interface Builder made life easier for applications developers into the bargain. It was a very powerful combination and it looked like taking the desktop market by storm. Jobs had succeeded in what he set out to do. He had produced a computer that would appeal to the developers.

Commercial success, however, was not to be. 'NeXT was never really good at marketing,' explains Hullot. 'We got lots of praise from the press and everything,' he continues, 'as we say in French, "le succès d'estime".' One magazine even called NeXTStep the best piece of software on the planet. But the sales didn't follow. Over the company's ten-year life, NeXT went from being a company that sold a complete package of computer, operating system and software to one that just sold software, NeXTStep. It was finally sold to Apple in 1997, and Steve Jobs resumed the helm of the company he had originally founded. Apple was in the doldrums and Jobs planned to put it back on the rails. Drawing a salary of just $1 per year, Jobs had taken his payment in share options so he would get his reward if he managed to turn the company round. A couple of years later, people were snapping up Apple's new iMac faster than the company could make them, and Apple developers were working on a new operating system for the company's computers. Called MacOS X, it would be based on NeXTStep. Nearly thirty years on, the idea pioneered by Alan Kay to make programming simple for children, and independently by Jean-Marie Hullot to make programming easier for himself, looks finally set to hit the mainstream.

A new arrival

The first NeXT arrived at CERN in 1989, but it did not come to the computing division of the laboratory where Tim Berners-Lee worked. That division had strict rules about what computers you could and could not buy. There was a fine line being walked between giving people freedom of choice and having a chaotic unmanageable situation where everyone had a computer that was incompatible with everyone else's. NeXT computers were still new and relatively unknown. They were definitely not on the computing division's allowed shopping list. But CERN is not a monolithic place, and what is not allowed in one part of the laboratory often is in other parts. So it was left to Emilio Pagiola, a physicist who had a reputation as a bit of a technology junkie, to bring the first NeXT to CERN.

For weeks after Pagiola's NeXT arrived, curious computer scientists took the one-kilometre walk across the laboratory from the computer centre to the office where the NeXT was set up. Among them was Robert Cailliau. 'There was this black cube moulded in one piece from a magnesium alloy, vaguely reminiscent of something out of Star Wars,' he remembers. 'All of us who had a techie heart beating inside wanted to play with this box: Unix with a GUI interface, a read–write optical disk, Hullot's Interface Builder, Shakespeare's complete works in a corner of the disk somewhere, and Webster's dictionary as the spelling checker.' Robert became a big NeXT fan and later on, when it was clear that the company was not going to succeed, he added his voice to the chorus of reasons why. 'NeXT was a first-rate machine but with second-rate marketing,' he explains. 'Now we are stuck with second-rate machines with first-rate marketing.'

Most of CERN's computer scientists wandered sadly back to their offices, but not Tim Berners-Lee. He doesn't remember how he found out about the NeXT but as soon as he did he aimed to have one. With the NeXT's object library, he realized that he would be able to put together a prototype for his information management system faster than he could on any other computer. Remembering his ally from the RPC days, he stuck his head around Ben Segal's door. 'Tim asked me to go along with him to see Mike Sendall,' Segal remembers. 'He thought Mike would listen to me so I agreed to go.'

It was a day towards the end of March 1990 when the two men went off to see Mike. They were expecting to have a heavy sales job on their hands, but to their surprise, Mike just said 'yes' to Tim's request for two NeXT computers. He had done his homework, and like everyone else he had been down to look at Pagiola's NeXT, so he was expecting Tim's visit. As his visitors were leaving, Mike called after Tim, 'Why not try programming your hypertext thing on it?' 'I thought I saw a twinkle in his eye,' remembers Tim.

Mike asked Tim to spruce up his March 1989 proposal and argue the case for building such a system at CERN. An update duly landed on Mike's desk in May. Not much had changed. There was a new introduction that referred to the anticipated information management problems of CERN's proposed new accelerator, the Large Hadron Collider (LHC) that would bring together even bigger and even more distributed collaborations than LEP had done. 'Many of the discussions of the future at CERN and the LHC era,' Tim began, 'end with the question, "Yes, but how will we ever keep track of such a large project?" This proposal provides the answer,' he said. He was pitching the idea at a problem that CERN quite definitely had, and that was all the justification that Mike needed to buy the NeXTs.

Anticipating resistance from his divisional management, Mike decided that he would buy the machines through Pagiola. 'I don't think the management need be too concerned,' he wrote in a note to Pagiola at the beginning of April, in which he said he was ready to commit up to 20 000 Swiss francs to buy the new machines. Then he took off for four weeks, first to a conference and then on his honeymoon; he and Peggie Rimmer had just got married. When he got back, there was a reply waiting for him. 'There is an order fighting its way through the bureaucracy,' Pagiola told Mike. 'If CERN bureaucracy is prompt,' he added hopefully, 'delivery in two weeks. If . . .'

CERN bureaucracy wasn't prompt and Tim's NeXTs finally arrived in September. By this time, Mike was no longer Tim's boss. The arrival of a new Director General for the laboratory the year before had seen the usual new broom of a new management. Nobel Prizewinner Carlo Rubbia was the incoming Director General. He had been the driving force behind CERN's antimatter project and gone on to lead one of the experiments that studied collisions between matter and antimatter. That was one of the first really big experiments. Electronics and computing had played a vital role, and now Rubbia wanted to separate the desktop and off-line side of computing from the sort of computing that went right into the experiments. He set up a new division called Electronics and Computing for Physics (ECP) and Mike moved over. Tim and his NeXTs stayed behind in the old division.

By this time, Tim's name had been put forward for tenure at CERN. His friend Ben Segal had been among the many people to support his promotion from a short-term contract to an indefinite appointment. Segal's supporting letter described Tim's work on RPC and then went on to other things. 'Tim's is not at all a "one-track mind",' he wrote, 'and he has several other areas of interest which I believe to be important for CERN.' He singled out one in particular. 'The topic that I think he is ready to take up next is the use of hypertext techniques in data storage and retrieval. This could have repercussions on the widest scale at CERN.' By this time it wasn't only Mike Sendall who recognized the potential of Tim's proposal, but it was still not an officially supported project.

Tim spent long hours working on the NeXT and by Christmas he had put together a working prototype browser and server. He called it WorldWideWeb, but later it became known as Nexus when World Wide Web took on an altogether wider meaning. For a prototype, Tim's first browser was really quite special. Usually a prototype is riddled with problems and the version that follows is a great improvement. With the World Wide Web, the opposite is true. Tim's browser set the standard for everything that followed and nearly a decade later no other browser has been able to match it. The reason we are not all using it is the same reason that Tim was able to write it so quickly; it was a browser written for the NeXTStep system and only people with NeXTs could use it.

The way it worked was that every time you clicked on a link, a new window opened up on your screen with the page you'd requested in it. There was good reason for doing things that way. It was a system designed for scientists and scientists often have graphs and diagrams that they refer to throughout a long piece of text. With the NeXT browser, there were no images in-line with the text as is the case with most of today's browsers. Instead there would be a hypertext link that would open up another window with the image in it. That meant that you could keep the image on the screen whilst you scrolled through the text in another window. With a modern browser, you would have to keep scrolling up and down between text and image. They are designed to make Web pages look like the magazines that we are all used to, but as computing pioneers from Doug Engelbart on have been pointing out, there is no point inventing new media if we are just going to use them like the old ones.

Another big difference between Tim's first browser and modern ones is that with the NeXT browser it was just as easy to write pages as to read them. There were no bookmarks as there are in modern browsers; instead you would have a 'home page'. That would be the page that came up on your screen when you started the program and in it you would keep all the links to pages you visited frequently. When people say 'home page' today, they generally mean something rather different. If you know the address of a Web site but you don't know the name of the page you want, your browser will take you to a default page that generally says 'Welcome' on it. That is what we now call a home page, but in the original design it was a 'welcome page'. The original home page was something altogether more private. If you found a new page you liked, all you would have to do would be cut and paste the link into your home page, and if your home page got too crowded, you could make other pages of links and link to them from your home page. Creating a page was as easy as making three simple keystrokes, 'command-shift-n', which would create a fresh page with a link to the page you had just come from. So if the page you had just come from was your home page, you could call the link 'family', for example, and then keep links to the sites of your relatives wherever they might be on the new page. Or you could call it 'LHC' and have links to pages about CERN's new accelerator. Or you could call it 'news' and keep links to the pages of broadcasters and newspapers.

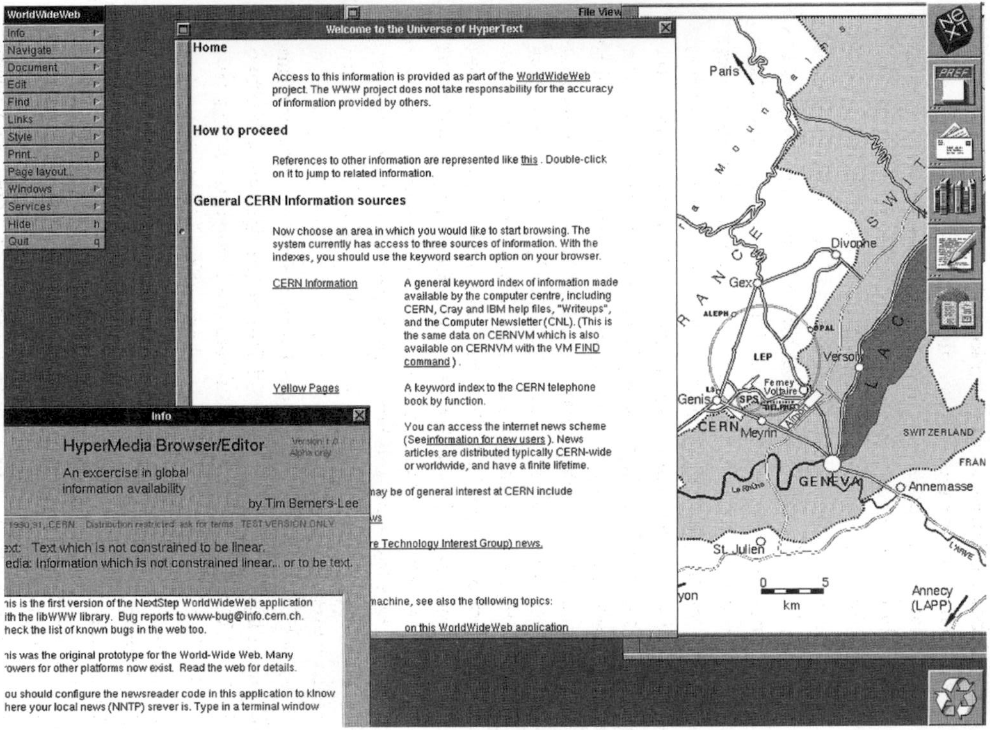

Figure 17: Tim Berners-Lee's first Web browser set the standard for everything to follow.

Of course at the time, no such things existed—all there was was a single Web site on Tim Berners-Lee's NeXT—but that was the idea. There wouldn't just be one Web, there would be many. People could create their own Webs for personal use among family and friends, or for community use among colleagues working on the same distributed project, or for global use like news organizations. Writing would be as easy as reading, which is another feature that is lost in most modern browsers. So once you had put all your favourite links into your home page you could type your own notes around them just as if you were using a powerful word processor. And in fact you were. Writing in the NeXT browser was something that anyone could do, thanks largely to the most complex of the objects that Jean-Marie Hullot had put into his Interface Builder, the editable text object. 'Editing text is the most common thing that you want to do in a work situation,' explains Hullot, but when he was writing his Interface Builder that was something you could only do inside a word processor. Hullot decided to put the power of a word processor at the disposal of application developers in the form of an object in his palette, so that whatever application they were writing, they could put full word-processing capability into it. An application programmer could take a window object and put the editable text object in it so that in the finished application whatever was in that window could be edited. 'You had the text editor for free,' says Hullot, and Tim Berners-Lee made full use of it. Every window that popped up in that first browser had the editable text object running behind it, so you could edit the text just as if you had a word processor in front of you with all the functionality that entails, like bold and italic, and different fonts, and cut and paste.

'Picture a scenario in which any note I write on my computer I can "publish" just by giving it a name,' said Tim in a magazine article two years later. 'In that note I can make references to any other article anywhere in the world in such a way that when reading my note you can click with your mouse and bring the referenced article up on your machine. Suppose, moreover, that everyone has this capability.' That was the original dream behind the Web. A distributed family could use the Web to plan their annual holiday. One member might write, 'Let's go to Cornwall, I know a lovely hotel.' The word 'hotel' might be a link that would take you to a picture of the hotel, or the hotel's own Web page. Then another member of the family might add, 'Yes, and there's the great scenery of the moors nearby; I was there last year and these are some pictures I took.' A community like a CERN collaboration could use it to store contact details for members of the collaboration, and because they were on-line, those details would always be up to date, unlike a paper phone book that only comes out once a year. At the global level, too, everything would always be up to date. There would be no need to wait for a news bulletin; you could get the latest news whenever you wanted it. Moreover, all these Webs, private, community, and global, would merge seamlessly together. But this was still 1990. The World Wide Web was still a single computer on a desk at CERN, and it still wasn't an officially approved project.

Before moving away from the computing division to ECP, Mike Sendall had bought the NeXT machines and let Tim quietly get on with developing his ideas. Mike had created the space for Tim to work and he had shielded him from the eyes of jealous physicists who might have seen his work as a diversion of vital resources that could have been better spent on physics. When Mike had gone, Tim had taken advantage of the grey twilight region between the computing division and ECP to put his prototype together. What was still missing was a real proposal. Tim's two drafts had been full of idealism: they had described a dream and hinted about how that dream might be realized. Since Mike was the only one to have seen that proposal, that was fine, but if 'Information Management' were to move from proposal to officially supported project, a detailed technical proposal would have to be put forward complete with time scales, milestones, and requirements for budget and manpower. That proposal landed on Tim's new boss's desk on 12 November 1990 and it carried two names, Tim Berners-Lee and Robert Cailliau.

A modest proposal

Tim describes Robert as Best Man at the marriage of hypertext and the Internet. The two men had worked together on the PS controls project back in 1980, but since then their careers had taken them in different directions. When Tim went back to England, Robert had stayed on at the PS. But when Tim came back to CERN a few years later, their paths would soon cross again.

The year that Tim came back to CERN was also the year that Brian Carpenter, head of the PS control system software group, moved across to the laboratory's computing division and Robert took a step up the CERN career ladder. By this time, his P+ language had become the standard language for PS with about thirty programmers writing applications in it. The controls project was largely complete and the job Robert inherited from Carpenter was no longer at the head of an exciting new project; it was more of a maintenance operation. Nevertheless, running a service was something that suited Robert's methodical mind, and he stuck with it until 1987 when he followed Brian Carpenter over to the computing division.

This was the time when you could pick up a typewriter for next to nothing as ordinary people cleared their desks to make way for computers. CERN had created a new outfit to handle the office computing revolution, called Management Information Systems, and it had two groups within it. One was concerned with Administrative Data Processing and was headed by the flamboyant Italian Vittorio Frigo, whose wild Einsteinian locks and electric guitar were rapidly earning him a reputation as CERN's leading rock star. Robert, whose sobriety couldn't have contrasted more sharply with Frigo, headed the other group, which went under the name of Office Computing Systems.

Robert's job was to develop the computing systems that the laboratory's administrators and secretaries would use, and towards the end of the 1980s that meant Macintoshes. The administration divisions at CERN had gone into Macintosh in a big way and, unlike the rest of the laboratory, they had a pretty uniform system of Macs and nothing else. Robert was already a confirmed Mac lover and dived headlong into HyperCard. He kept his group's accounts in HyperCard, he used it for his trip reports, and he made a HyperCard application for making presentations. It looked a bit like a black and white version of today's Microsoft PowerPoint. After a while, however, he ran into the same barrier that Tim Berners-Lee had with his Enquire programme on the VAX. HyperCard was great, but it only worked on one machine. If Robert were working on someone else's Mac and he wanted to link from somewhere in one of their HyperCard stacks to somewhere in one of his own, he couldn't do it, even though there was Apple's proprietary AppleTalk network running between the two computers. And that wasn't the only thing that Robert thought was missing from CERN's office AppleTalk network. 'Why should we have a report that is done by secretary X in any other place than on her machine?' he wondered. 'We'd just link to it so that you'd sort of suck it over.' He tried to sell the idea, but CERN was heavily into CERNDOC. The time wasn't right, but networked HyperCard lingered at the back of his mind.

At the end of 1989, Robert was having coffee with Mike Sendall. Mike had already decided that the new ECP division was where the computing action would be, and he persuaded Robert to move across with him when the division got off the ground in the middle of the following year. So Robert set about cleaning up his office in the computer centre and handing over his responsibilities to someone else. And it was then that the answer came to him. 'Why not put HyperCard over AppleTalk?' he thought. He mulled it over and started to jot down some notes for a proposal. 'This may sound somewhat frivolous,' he began, 'but I believe that for LHC we should start now having all information computer based and inter-linked.' When he got to the new division he found himself having coffee with Mike again, and they got to talking about Robert's ideas. They must have sounded pretty familiar to Mike, who had not long before signed the order to buy NeXT computers for Tim Berners-Lee to write his prototype on. 'There's someone you should talk to,' he told Robert.

So Robert wandered up the hill to see what his old colleague from the PS days was up to. There he found Tim with a prototype that was close to completion. 'So I immediately dropped my proposal,' Robert explains, 'because Tim's was a lot more detailed and further ahead than mine, and he already had some code running.' And that's how one of the most unlikely collaborations in the history of computing was born. It was a collaboration that was poised to bring the power of the Internet within reach of just about anyone. Robert freely admits that the pace of development in computing was leaving him behind. He had already begun to develop a healthy dislike of C back in 1980, but C had won out and was the language people were using. So Robert assigned himself the task of taking Tim's evolving project and turning it into a reliable service. 'I believe this is Robert's important contribution to the success of the Web,' explained Mike Sendall. 'Robert understood the importance of clearly distinguishing the constantly evolving software development environment from setting up and running a reliable, user-friendly service, which he knew a lot about.' As the project evolved, Robert became its evangelist. He fought hard to get resources, he set up the first ever welcome page for CERN, and he made sure that when the Web was offered as a service for physicists, it was reliable and well run. Tim, on the other hand, was content to bury his head in the bits and develop his software. Not for him the planning and organization that Robert thrived on. 'I remember a day when I tried to sit down with Tim and make a project plan,' recalls Robert. 'He just did not understand the concept!'

Despite their differences, however, Mike thought they made a complementary team. 'They were both brilliant, enthusiastic, innovative, and, by and large, uncontrollable,' he said. And that Robert ended up being the closest thing the Web project at CERN ever came to a project manager was probably for the best in Mike's opinion. 'Robert may have been the one with better management skills,' he explained. 'Mais n'exagérons pas!' he concluded, switching into French for dramatic effect: 'Let's not get carried away!' So the Web team was born, with two temperamentally opposite men in two different divisions as its members. The first thing they had to do was turn Tim's twilight hacking into a project. They went to see Mike's successor as Tim's boss in the computing division, René Brun. He took a look at Tim's vague but exciting proposal and told them to go away and write a new one. What he was after was something that administrators could understand, something that would tell them exactly what they stood to gain and exactly what it would cost them. This was just the kind of thing Robert was good at, so with Tim looking over his shoulder, he set to work.

The first thing to go was the title. Information management sounded too dry; they needed something a bit more sexy. One possibility Tim had considered was 'Mine Of Information,' but 'MOI, c'est un peu égoïste,' he explains, adopting Mike Sendall's technique. 'The Information Mine' was another, but that abbreviates to 'TIM, even more egocentric!' Yet another was 'Information Mesh,' but Tim decided that sounded too much like 'mess'. By the time he and Robert sat down to put a name to their proposal, Tim knew the name he wanted. He listened to Robert explaining what sort of name he didn't want before putting forward his proposal. 'I want some concise name,' said Robert, 'I don't want another Greek god or Egyptian pharaoh.' CERN was known for its penchant for classical acronyms. 'World Wide Web,' said Tim. 'We can't call it that,' replied Robert, 'because the abbreviation WWW sounds longer than the full name!' 'But it sounds good,' argued Tim. 'OK,' said Robert. And so before the Web stretched even from one office to the next, its global intentions were stated.

The joint proposal

'WorldWideWeb: Proposal for a HyperText Project' was less vague than Tim's original but none the less exciting for that. It laid out clearly the cost, manpower requirements, time scales, and project deliverables. In short, six months, five staff including themselves, and 80 000 Swiss francs were what they were asking for. For that, CERN would get a single information management system giving access to all the computer-stored information at the laboratory through a single easy-to-use interface.

In a first three-month phase, Tim would polish his NeXT prototype while Robert would go around the laboratory discussing the needs of the big new experimental collaborations and start working on a browser for Macintosh computers. A student, Nicola Pellow, would write a very simple browser that would work on any computer with absolutely no frills, just to get the Web off the ground. Bernd Pollermann, who had already built an interface called XFIND to all the information held on CERN's big IBM computer, would write a gateway to make all that information available on the Web, and another gateway would provide access to the world of Usenet news.

At the end of these three months, anyone at CERN on any computer would be able to access a limited but useful range of information on the Web. Then a second, more ambitious, phase would get underway whose goal would be to produce browser/editors with all the power of Tim's prototype for a range of different computers. At the end of this phase, people would be publishing on the Web as well as reading. Nicola Pellow's browser would have served its purpose for most people as fully functional browsers appeared for the IBM, Macintoshes, and a system that was becoming increasingly popular among physicists called X-Window. A hyper-librarian would be assigned to keep track of the mushrooming amount of information that Tim and Robert were sure would rapidly become available if they were given the resources they had asked for.

Tim and Robert sat back and waited to see what kind of reception their proposal would get. Not for the last time, they were to be disappointed by the management's response: the project could go ahead, but with much lower resources than they had wanted. Tim and Robert could work on the project full time and Nicola Pellow could write a simple browser as her sandwich course project. Bernd Pollermann would be able to use some of his time to write the interface to XFIND. But that would be it. There would be no resources released for a hyper-librarian or for someone who knew X-Window. Later on, this was to prove a crucial point. The longer the project went on, the clearer it became that an X-browser was a vital missing ingredient, and although Tim had been happy to learn the API bible for the NeXT, he wasn't prepared to delve into the X-Window API library, which ran to several thick volumes.

CERN's management was wary of committing resources to projects outside the laboratory's core area of physics research. The new LHC accelerator was not yet approved by the laboratory's member states, the Americans were planning to build a similar machine, and management's main priority was convincing member state governments that Europe really did need another billion-dollar atom smasher. They were keen to be seen to be spending the taxpayers' money wisely, and pumping resources into what they saw as no more than an interesting curiosity did not look like the way to do it. Because despite Robert's attentions, the new proposal had failed to convince many people at CERN that the Web was needed. They could see that it might be another useful tool to put alongside FTP, e-mail, and Usenet news, but if you knew all those things, what was the use of another? The number of people who believed in the Web at the end of 1990 could still be counted on the fingers of one hand.

It is not surprising that so few people fully understood Tim's dream. Neither hypertext nor networks were new ideas. They had both been around since the 1960s, but nobody had put them together to make a global hypertext system before. Now it seems hard to believe that the benefits wouldn't have been obvious, but they weren't. A lot of bright people had worked on the two systems over the years and putting them together just hadn't occurred to anyone except perhaps one. 'Ted Nelson had thought about this forty years ago,' Mike Sendall pointed out, 'but it was Tim who went and did it!' When the information superhighway was still little more than a country lane, Tim Berners-Lee had invented the networking equivalent of the Formula 1 racing car when everyone else was still pottering around in Austin Sevens. No wonder people didn't understand.

With hindsight, the attitude of CERN's management seems hard to understand. By withholding the cost of a couple of members of staff in an organization of close to 3 000, they had put the brakes on Tim Berners-Lee's dream. But CERN's management had to examine dozens of requests for manpower every week. This was against a backdrop of increasing scrutiny from member state governments, the lobbying for money to build the LHC, and pressure from the laboratory's physics community to spend every available penny on physics. But although CERN's management may not have taken the bold step of giving Tim all the backing he wanted, they had given him the breathing space he needed to nurture his dream. At the end of 1990, the World Wide Web project was on the road.

6 Sharing What We Know

Over the next two years, the World Wide Web bandwagon steadily gathered momentum. A constant trickle of students and enthusiastic young programmers passed through CERN, each making their own piece of Web history before moving on to other things. Tim Berners-Lee and Robert Cailliau argued tirelessly for resources from CERN but never got quite what they asked for. The laboratory didn't feel that it could give them all they wanted, but nor did it refuse them completely. Tim soon realized, however, that with the support he was getting his project would never really fly. So he adopted another strategy. Instead of trying to develop browsers for popular computer systems like X-Window, Macintosh, and PC at CERN, he concentrated on building a sort of tool-kit that would allow others to build them elsewhere. He then persuaded the laboratory's management to let him release the tool-kit for free. Within a year, there was a choice of browsers for X-Window, and the first Macintosh and PC browsers were starting to appear.

Meanwhile the body of information available over the Web also started to grow. The CERN server, http://info.cern.ch, went public before Christmas 1990. By the end of 1991 there were servers in other physics labs around Europe. Herman Maurer's group in Graz had set one up which offered, among other things, a dictionary of computer geek shorthand. There you could find out that IMHO means 'in my humble opinion', or that KUTGW means 'keep up the good work'. Another recurring theme in Tim and Robert's appeals to their bosses was for a 'virtual librarian' to catalogue the growing amount of information available. With just a dozen servers up and running by the end of 1991, including the first one in the United States at the Stanford Linear Accelerator Center in California, a librarian might have seemed a dispensable luxury. Soon, however, keeping track of the explosion of information on the Web would become one of Tim's biggest headaches.

What use is one Web site?

A Web site is a bit like a telephone: if there's only one it's not much use. But Mike Sendall had bought two NeXTs, not just one. The second was installed in Robert's office, allowing Tim and Robert to become the world's very first Web surfers at the end of 1990. They used Tim's invention for what it was intended for: managing their project. They may have been in separate buildings, but the Web allowed them to keep in touch.

The unlikely revolutionary

The Web project's first recruit, Nicola Pellow, is an unlikely revolutionary. A maths student at Leicester Polytechnic on a sandwich course, she had landed a one-year work placement at CERN and turned up at the computing division in September 1990. 'At the time I had no knowledge of any computing languages really,' she remembers, 'apart from using a bit of Pascal and FORTRAN as part of my degree course.' Nevertheless, it was to Pellow that the task of getting the Web out of Tim's NeXT and onto people's computer screens fell. After a crash course in C programming, she was given the job of writing a very simple browser that anyone could run on any computer or terminal. The idea was that even if you didn't have the browser running on your own computer, as long as you had a network connection you could use Telnet to login to a computer at CERN where you would be presented with Pellow's browser. It was to be the vehicle that allowed the Web to take its first tentative step on to the world stage, but Pellow was unfazed. She was given the task and she simply sat down to do it, little realizing the enormity of what she was about to unleash, but that was enough for Tim. 'She wasn't full of the passion of hypertext,' he remembers, 'but she produced this code.' The only thing she found daunting was keeping up with Tim. 'His brain works faster than he talks,' she explains. 'It was kind of a steep learning curve at first just trying to get my head round what Tim was trying to come up with.' Nevertheless, Nicola Pellow's line mode browser was ready for testing by spring 1991. It was nothing like the Web browsers of today. It had been designed for computers with a so-called command line interface where you typed on a single line and things scrolled up the screen. There was no mouse to point and click; instead, the line mode browser presented you with a list of numbered choices and you would type in the number of where you wanted to go.

Pellow's browser gave anyone with an Internet connection access to the world of information that resided on the World Wide Web. The problem was that in early 1991, that consisted of a few pages on Tim

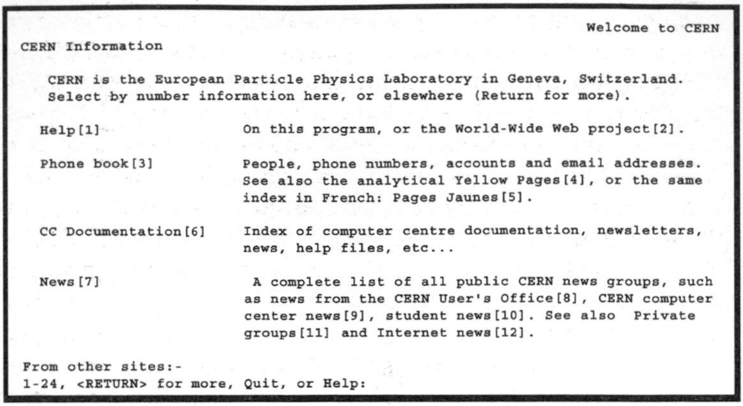

Welcome to CERN
CERN Information
CERN is the European Particle Physics Laboratory in Geneva, Switzerland.
Select by number information here, or elsewhere (Return for more).
Help[1]
On this program, or the World-Wide Web project[2].
Phone book[3]
People, phone numbers, accounts and email addresses.
See also the analytical Yellow Pages[4], or the same
index in French: Pages Jaunes[5].
CC Documentation[6]
Index of computer centre documentation, newsletters,
news, help files, etc...
News[7]
A complete list of all public CERN news groups, such
as news from the CERN User's Office[8], CERN computer
center news[9], student news[10]. See also Private
groups[11] and Internet news[12].
From other sites:-
1-24, <RETURN> for more, Quit, or Help:

Figure 18: A screen shot from Nicola Pellow's line mode browser.

Berners-Lee's NeXT describing the Web project itself. Tim knew that the way to convince people that they really needed the Web was to give them access to information they couldn't live without. One day, he described his dilemma to a colleague, Bernd Pollermann, who turned out to be exactly the person who could help.

Like Pellow, Pollermann was impressed with the way Tim talked. 'He spoke about twice as fast as anybody else,' he explains. But Pollermann got the drift. He was an old hand at CERN, and in the early 1980s he had developed a system for storing information on the laboratory's big IBM computer. XFIND had evolved to contain all kinds of indispensable information like program write-ups and explanations of the often-cryptic error messages the computer would give you if your code didn't work. The only limitation with XFIND was that you had to logon to the IBM to look at it. Together Berners-Lee and Pollermann hatched the idea of writing a gateway that would make all this information available anywhere. 'And that was the really convincing thing,' explains Pollermann, 'it helped to get over the threshold.'

The announcement of Pellow's line mode browser was made to a group of 'guinea pigs' on 8 April 1991. By this time, the amount of information available was already beginning to spread. The CERN phone book had been linked in through XFIND and Mike Sendall had set up an experimental server for a new group he had formed called the Software Technology Interest Group, STING. As a forum for anyone interested in state-of-the-art software, the World Wide Web was the natural place for it to live.

The guinea pigs soon started to use the Web, but their reactions were mixed. The line mode browser was a simple piece of software designed to get the Web deployed fast, and it served that purpose admirably, but it also had its shortcomings. 'People who did not understand the whole thing,' explains Pollermann, 'were not impressed with the line mode browser.' Mike Sendall had some sympathy with this point of view. NeXT computers hadn't really caught on and there were just a few at CERN. That meant that if you weren't up to following Tim's whirlwind description of his Web vision, and few were, then the only place to see it was on a NeXT. 'We actually had to invite people here to show them what wonderful things we could do on the Web,' recalled Mike, 'and that was not the original idea now, was it?' Mike was beginning to have second thoughts about the wisdom of buying the NeXTs. They had allowed Tim to rustle up a prototype that set the standard for everything to follow, but it was clear that a comparable browser for the sort of computers that people actually used was needed. Until that came along, Tim's vision would belong to a select few who either had the foresight themselves to grasp what Tim was saying, or the privilege to see the NeXT prototype in action.

Among physicists who relied on XFIND, however, the line mode browser was impressive enough to get the Web noticed. Bernd Pollermann remembers one visiting scientist from the German particle physics laboratory DESY in Hamburg. A big fan of XFIND, he used it extensively when he was at CERN, but using it from DESY was not easy. He had to Telnet to CERN, login to the IBM, and then delve into XFIND for the information he needed. The link was slow and the connection would often be lost before he got what he wanted. So he took the line mode browser back to DESY and used it from there. Soon after he took up a job in industry, but before he left he helped the Web to spread beyond the walls of CERN by setting up the one of the first servers outside the laboratory on DESY's IBM.

The first Web consultant

The second student to join the team was Jean-François Groff, a young telecommunications engineer who had come through the prestigious French Grandes Écoles system. When the time came for his military service he signed up for a programme that gave bright young Frenchmen an alternative. 'We got to serve our country using our brains instead of our legs', Groff explains. He arrived at CERN in December 1990 and joined Peggie Rimmer's group in the new ECP division. But he wasn't there for long. Soon after he arrived, Ben Segal introduced him to Tim

Berners-Lee, and before long Rimmer agreed to let Jean-François work for Tim. Groff was one of the privileged few to see Tim's NeXT prototype in action and he was very impressed with what he saw. 'Everything was in it,' Groff recalls, 'all the foundations of the Web.'

The three defining features of the World Wide Web are the Uniform Resource Locators (URLs) that form its addresses, the Hypertext Transfer Protocol (HTTP) that allows hypertext to be transported over networks, and the Hypertext Markup Language (HTML) that is the language of Web documents. These were all already there in Tim's prototype browser/editor, although you didn't have to know about any of them. Thanks to Jean-Marie Hullot's editable text object, creating a Web document was as simple as typing. The browser/editor took care of arranging what you had written into HTML for other browsers to interpret. URLs weren't displayed; if you really wanted to see one, or type one in explicitly, you had to open a special window. The idea was that using the Web would be as close as possible to people's everyday experience of computers, and they wouldn't have to learn anything new. But inside the URL, which Tim initially called a Universal Document Identifier (UDI), was hidden all the power of the Web. The URL built on the Domain Name System invented nearly two decades before by Paul Mockapetris, and because of that, it was scalable. No matter how big the Web became, there would always be enough URLs to go round. The URL got its present name in 1992 when Tim tried to get his Universal Document Identifier accepted by the IETF as a recognized Internet standard. The Internet crowd thought it was a bit much for this young upstart to be calling his invention universal, so after some protracted wrangling they settled on uniform instead; but they didn't change the basic idea. With the subsequent spread of the Web, things don't come more universal than the URL, but the IETF weren't the only ones to have missed the significance of Tim's deceptively simple idea of building on the Domain Name System. At first, Robert Cailliau missed it too and wondered why Tim was so insistent on using the Internet protocols. But as the Web exploded, he would come to look back on the URL as Tim's single most important idea. 'To look that far into the future,' he says, 'that, I think, was remarkable.'

Jean-François Groff immediately set about helping his new guru, and one of the first things he did was to start writing an interface to another popular source of information at CERN, the 'help' system on Digital VAX computers, VMS help. That would give physicists another reason to start using the Web, but still they only had Nicola Pellow's line mode browser to access information with. The need for more sophisticated browsers for X-terminals, Macintoshes, and PCs was becoming acute, and on 17 May, Tim made a presentation to the top brass of CERN computing explaining where things were and what was needed. The centrepiece of his presentation was a diagram that was to see a lot of use over the coming months and years. Labelled 'development status', it showed what existed and what, in Tim's view, was missing.

In the middle of Tim's diagram was a two-headed arrow representing the network and all the things that the Web would make transparent to users. The UDI addressing scheme was already in place, as was the HTTP common protocol. Another phrase in the arrow, however, 'format negotiation', was inside brackets to show that it was not yet implemented. Format negotiation was high on Tim's agenda of things to do.

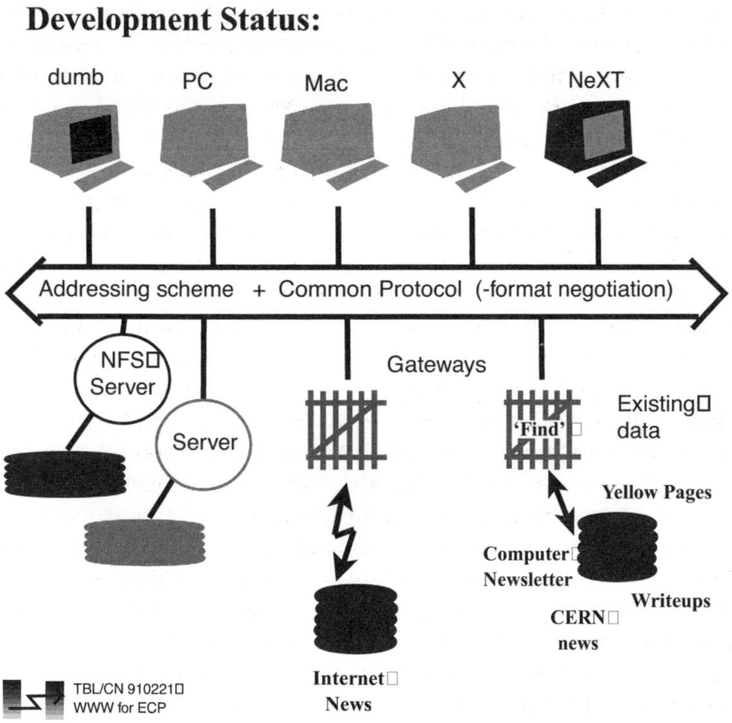

Figure 19: The diagram Tim Berners-Lee presented to CERN management on 17 May 1991 showing the Web's structure.

It would mean, for example, that if a server held a document in a format other than HTML and a browser that could only display HTML asked for that document, the browser and server would negotiate and the server would convert the information to HTML before sending it.

Below the arrow were the sources of information. There were information servers like the one Tim had installed on his NeXT and there were the gateways to Bernd Pollermann's XFIND and Usenet news. Above the arrow were the browsers. There were five drawn but three were represented as ghostly outlines because they didn't yet exist. The existing pair consisted of Tim's sophisticated NeXT browser/editor and Nicola Pellow's line mode browser, labelled 'dumb' because it could run on anything, even a so-called 'dumb' terminal with no computing power built in. The three that were missing were PC, Macintosh, and X. Robert Cailliau had started to work on a browser for the Macintosh, Tim told the meeting, but there was so far no effort going into X, which Tim highlighted as 'essential'.

'I would have written it,' says Jean-François Groff from the safe distance of several years. He had had a bit of training in X-Window and was not one to shy away from a challenge, but Tim had other plans for him. He was beginning to realize that getting a fully fledged X-programmer out of the CERN management in the laboratory's current political climate was not likely to happen. What he had to do was find another way to get an X-programmer working on the Web. Tim Berners-Lee decided that if he couldn't get an X-programmer at CERN, he would have to take the Web to the X-programmers.

What's GNU? GNU's Not Unix

On 26 June a prophet came to CERN. Complete with long hair and a bushy unkempt beard, Richard Stallman looked every bit the part. His message was that software should be free. In 1983, alarmed at the growing commercialization of the computer software industry, Stallman had set up the GNU project to bring back 'the cooperative spirit that prevailed in the computing community in earlier days'. That spirit had been destroyed, as he saw it, by proprietary software, and since every computer needs an operating system, providing a free one became Stallman's first objective. He and a like-minded band of followers collaborating over the Internet had therefore set themselves the goal of replacing Unix with a compatible, better, and free alternative. They called it GNU, for Gnu's Not Unix, and founded the Free Software Foundation to grant a GNU General Public License to anyone who wanted to use the code as long as it was not commercially exploited.

Tim had long been an admirer of Richard Stallman. GNU had quickly come up with software that outperformed many commercial alternatives, and since NeXT had been one of the companies to distribute some of it freely, Tim had had the chance to use it. The year before Stallman came to CERN, Tim had published a note in a CERN computing newsletter drawing the laboratory's attention to GNU. 'A source of much debate over recent years has been whether to write software in-house or buy it from commercial suppliers,' he began. 'Now, a third alternative is becoming significant in what some see as a revolution in software supply. Richard Stallman's almost religious campaign for usable free software led to the creation of the Free Software Foundation and the GNU General Public License. This defines software which is free, but at the same time attaches enough strings to ensure that it cannot ever be charged for, and that any improvements on it must be made public in the same way.' The GNU General Public License exemplified the idealism of the generation of computer programmers that had grown up with the Internet. 'When we speak of free software,' it says in the License documents, 'we are referring to freedom, not price.' But it was not just the ideal that had impressed Tim; it was the way that Stallman had harnessed the power of the geeks to put it into practice. He had followed the lead of the early Internet pioneers and used the network as a way of getting a widely distributed group of people to work together. Tim was beginning to wonder whether he might be able to do the same thing himself with the World Wide Web. 'Just as we publish physics for free, should we not in certain cases "publish" our software?' he wondered.

So instead of asking Jean-François Groff to put his limited X experience to work in designing an X-browser, Tim instead set him to work on the core Web software. Together they broke down the code into individual bricks that could be bundled together into a software library for others to use as the foundations of Web browsers and servers. The result was called libwww and it became part of the publicly available CERN program library by August.

But the CERN program library was a library of software used by physicists who weren't, for the most part, the kind of people who would be likely to start building X-browsers for the World Wide Web. Tim wanted make the code available to the geeks on the Net, but first he had to convince CERN's management that it would be worth their while. He argued that since the World Wide Web promotes the free interchange of information, it was following a proud academic tradition, and he urged that the software be made freely available under the terms of the

GNU General Public License. The laboratory's management looked at the Web and decided that trying to charge for it would not be worth the paperwork—100–200 Swiss francs was the price they put on it—so they gave Tim permission to put libwww up for free distribution on the Internet. Soon after, Tim announced it to the world in the form of postings to newsgroups, such as 'alt.hypertext' and 'comp.sys.next', and through a new mailing list he had asked Groff to set up called 'www-talk'. In an echo of his earlier advice to users of Enquire that the best way to learn about it was to play with it, the announcement invited people just to try it. They could pick up the code from the CERN Web server, info.cern.ch, and it wasn't long before the geeks latched on. By the end of the year X-browsers were under development in places as far flung as Finland and California.

The X step

Tim Berners-Lee wasn't the only one to write fast code. Barely one year after he had started work on his NeXT to get a prototype Web browser/editor ready for Christmas, hackers around the world were beginning to tap out X-browsers with equal speed. By the end of 1991, there were no fewer than three in the making.

One of the first to get off the ground was a browser that went by the unlikely name of 'Erwise'. Produced by a team of undergraduate students at the Helsinki University of Technology (HUT) as a final-year project, Erwise took its name from the Finnish title for the project part of their course, 'Ohjelmatyö', which translates roughly to 'programming work' and abbreviates to 'oht'. Roll that up with an English word meaning something like 'alternative', and you get oht-erwise. From there it's just a short jump to 'otherwise', the name Kim Nyberg, Teemu Rantanen, Kati Suominen, and Kari Sydänmaanlakka chose to work under, and 'erwise', the name they gave to their browser.

The 'otherwise' team had a strong tradition in computing and networking behind them. Ever since the first ARPANET site outside the United States had come on-line in 1973, the Nordic countries had gained a well-deserved reputation for being among Europe's most wired, and Finland was no exception. It was among the first to set up an academic network, funet, the Finnish university and research network, in 1984, and at the beginning of the 1990s Finland was a hotbed of innovation. It was at Oulu University that Jarkko Oikarinen invented Internet Relay Chat (IRC) in 1988, a way for chatting over the Net. And Helsinki University student Linus Torvalds became the hero of the Free Software movement when he wrote the Linux operating system, now the core of the GNU software. Folklore has it that Torvalds himself found the name Linux a little egocentric and would have preferred something else, but Ari Lemmke liked the name, and since he was the one who put it out on funet for the first time in 1991, that is the name that stuck.

Lemmke was a computer scientist at HUT and his students were constantly on the lookout for new things to hack with, so it came as no surprise when the 'otherwise' team came to him in summer 1991 talking about this thing called the World Wide Web. He approved their project, and the Erwise X-browser was announced by Lemmke on www-talk on 26 July 1992. Back at CERN, Tim Berners-Lee was impressed. 'Erwise looks very smart,' he remarked. But Erwise didn't get much further than that. The 'otherwise' team finished their degrees and went on to other things, leaving no one to pick up the project. 'Certainly I couldn't continue it,' says Tim, 'all the code was documented in Finnish!' The Erwise team may have earned themselves little more than a footnote in the history of the World Wide Web, but Erwise didn't do their academic careers any harm. 'The group got five out of five points out of it,' says Lemmke.

Take the A tag

Another early starter that never saw the light of day came from young computer scientists at the Convex Computer Corporation in Richardson, Texas. Convex built what it called minisupercomputers, and it had a policy of allowing free rein to its brightest programmers. Dan Connolly was one of them, 'I didn't realize until after I left,' he recalls, 'how rare Convex was in saying "As long as you get the work done that's assigned to you we don't care how you do it, what you wear, when you come into work."' Connolly certainly got the work done and Convex even gave him an award for it. 'By intelligently borrowing from public domain software and sharing your experience and discoveries with others,' said the citation, 'you have made great strides in providing usable on-line documentation for Convex customers.'

Documentation was one of Connolly's big interests and he had been looking at SGML, so when the Web came along with an SGML-based markup language behind it, he was curious. He started to follow www-talk and at the end of October 1991 told Tim that he had an X-browser working. 'This code is not in any shape to distribute, or even show to anybody,' he said. 'But it works and it's pretty speedy. That's enough to encourage me to polish it off.'

Connolly saw immediately that just reading on the Web was not enough. What was needed for X was a browser/editor like the one Tim had on his NeXT machine. The problem was that there was no practical equivalent to Jean-Marie Hullot's editable text object for X, so he set about writing one himself. His 'RichText widget' was eventually published and released into the public domain, but the browser/editor never joined it. The reason why is that Connolly found something else that needed to be done first. 'You need a DTD,' he wrote to Tim on 28 November.

Document Type Definitions are an important part of SGML and HTML didn't have one. They define the features of any class of documents. For example, you might have a DTD for letters since all letters have essentially the same structure. They have addresses and the date at the top, a line beginning 'Dear', at least one paragraph, and a signature at the bottom. The DTD for letters would contain tags to do all these things, <ADDRESS>, <DATE>, <DEAR>, <P>, and <SIGNATURE>, and it would also contain the rules about how letters should appear on the page. The fact that the address comes above the date, for example, would be in the DTD.

The advantage of having a DTD is that once you have one, everyone writing in that DTD knows the rules and every program designed to display the markup, a browser for example, knows them too. That means there is no risk of someone going off in their own direction and writing things into their documents that other people's browsers don't understand.

Dan Connolly recognized that HTML was really nothing more than a DTD of SGML, with the defining feature that it had a tag called 'anchor' to support hypertext. A line in an HTML document reading '<A HREF="http://www.cern.ch"> Come to the home of the Web!</A>,' for example, would appear as the phrase 'Come to the home of the Web!' underlined to show that it is a hyperlink.

The problem with HTML was that nobody had actually written down the HTML DTD. The SGML community had learned the importance of DTDs the hard way, and Connolly could see the consequences of not having one for HTML. 'I saw an SGML DTD as just a means to an end,' he explains. 'The end goal was interoperability and structured information exchange: not just publish/browse but read/write on both ends.' Without a DTD everyone would rush off to write browsers and whenever they thought of some nice new feature they would like to add they would just write the tag for it. Then if you wanted to see that feature you would have to use their browser. The nightmare scenario was that you would have to have a plethora of different browsers for looking at all these different kinds of pages. Over the next few years, Dan Connolly made it his job to ensure that didn't happen. He wrote the DTD for HTML. As far as he was concerned, getting that right had to come before writing browsers. But that didn't stop other people from writing them in the meantime.

Viola

Pei Wei didn't play the viola, it just happened to make a snappy abbreviation of Visually Interactive Object-oriented Language and Application, a project he was working on in his spare time while a geography student at Berkeley. Taiwanese by birth, Wei had moved to California when his parents decided to immigrate in 1980. They set themselves up two blocks away from the University of California's Berkeley campus, so when he was old enough to go to university, that is where he went. He chose geography as a meeting point between the sciences and the arts, but computing was his true love. Each summer he would look around for a new project to work on, and in 1989 HyperCard caught his eye. 'HyperCard was very compelling back then, you know graphically, this hyperlink thing, it was just not very global and it only worked on Mac,' he recalls. 'And I didn't even have a Mac.'

The sort of machines he did have access to were X-terminals, and that gave him the idea for his project. 'I got a HyperCard manual and looked at it and just basically took the concepts and implemented them in X-windows,' he says. But the reality wasn't quite as easy as that. There were two approaches he could have taken. The direct route would have been to write all the code in C and build a one-off HyperCard-like application for X-Window. The second approach, and the one he took, was far more ambitious. He started by writing a new computer language, something not unlike Jean-Marie Hullot's Interface Builder but for X-Window instead of NeXT. That is what Viola was in 1990, and the HyperCard-like application was the first thing that Wei did with it.

In 1991, as Pei Wei was graduating, he released Viola 0.8, but unlike the 'otherwise'-people he wasn't ready to leave his project behind. Rather than get a real job, he did what any self-respecting geek at the time would have done. He got himself access to the latest computing hardware. Berkeley's Experimental Computing Facility, where Wei had been developing Viola, was open to suggestions, and if you made them a proposal they liked, they would let you loose on their computers. That was all the salary Pei Wei needed. He worked for a few months at an Internet Service Provider start-up company and then he got an advance from a publisher called O'Reilly and Associates to write a book about

Viola. 'My dad owned an apartment building in Berkeley that I helped to manage,' he says, 'so that nicely took care of the rent.'

So although Wei didn't starve, Viola was basically a labour of love. Getting his HyperCard-like application running was just the start. What Pei Wei wanted to do next was run it over the Internet. X-Window was a Unix-based system so it had TCP/IP built in and the Internet was a logical step. The question Wei had to answer was how to transport his Viola pages across the Internet. He was on the verge of an independent invention of networked hypertext. 'And that's when I read Tim's e-mail about the World Wide Web,' he explains. 'The URL was very, very clever, it was perfectly what I needed.'

He dropped Tim a line saying that he was thinking of writing a browser for X. 'Sounds like a good idea,' said Tim in a reply posted to www-talk on 9 December. Four days later, Pei Wei told www-talk that he had made a browser. 'It's not very sophisticated at this point,' he said, 'a one-night hack.' What made it possible for him to do it so fast was the fact that he had taken the more adventurous approach to writing his HyperCard-like application. All he had had to do was plug the line mode browser code into Viola and he had a rudimentary X-browser.

There was much more to come from Pei Wei. Viola was to become the first X-browser to make any impact, but even his early versions went down well at CERN. 'ViolaWWW works great,' exclaimed Tim on 24 January 1992. But there was one thing about it that disturbed Tim. 'A strange thing is,' he said, 'that it seems to be so fast—a search in the CERN phone book seems to be instantaneous!' Not only had Pei Wei produced a working X-browser in record time, he had also made it the fastest.

Over the next few months, Pei Wei rewrote Viola and refined the browser that had so impressed Tim. As this ViolaWWW developed, it was to set the standard for everything to follow. It had a bookmark facility so that you could keep track of your favourite pages. It had buttons for going backwards and forwards and a history feature to keep track of the places you had been. As time went on, it acquired tables and graphics and by May 1993 it could even run programs. 'The Web back then was basically like reading a book, a really big book,' explains Wei, 'but nothing was really interactive.' His idea was to add interactivity to the Web so that it actually became the graphical user interface. You wouldn't need to have different programs to do spreadsheets or word processing or surfing the Web, you would do it all in ViolaWWW. And just as with documents, you wouldn't need to know whether the application you were running was on your machine or somewhere else. In

Wei's ideal world, you would never find a file you couldn't open because you didn't have the right program; the program would just come down the wire along with the information. A click could take you to a program on some other computer that would be loaded into your ViolaWWW browser and run there. If this all sounds familiar it is because today we have a name for such programs: they are called applets.

With Erwise and Viola both shaping up, Tim Berners-Lee was in buoyant mood in early 1992. 'The World Wide Web bounds into spring,' he wrote in CERN's computing newsletter, 'with some exciting client software releases from outside CERN.' His ploy to harness the geeks had borne fruit, just as he expected. It was Viola, however, that was to become the standard bearer for the Web on X-Window. By 15 May, Pei Wei had got his rewritten ViolaWWW into good shape and Tim wrote a review of it for the growing Web community. 'A very neat browser usable by anyone,' he said, 'very intuitive and straightforward. The extra features are probably more than 90 per cent of real users will actually use but just the things which an experienced user will want.'

Things were looking up for Pei Wei too. O'Reilly and Associates, the computing publishers who had commissioned a book from him, were looking into putting some of their books on-line. 'Dale Dougherty at O'Reilly Associates saw the browser,' remembers Wei, 'so we went to lunch and he hired me.' Wei's policy of eschewing a real job and getting by on what he could while enjoying his time on the computers at the Experimental Computing Facility was paying off. Now he had a real job where he could continue to play with computers.

Viola made the task O'Reilly gave Wei easy for him, so he had plenty of time to keep working on ViolaWWW. O'Reilly was interested in stand-alone electronic versions of its books. With Viola, it took just a few lines of code to put a 'button' object on the screen with a word or two inside it and have that button link through to somewhere else. So before long there were electronic O'Reilly publications with clickable buttons to guide you through them. And all the while, Wei was refining ViolaWWW. He came up with 'mini-applications', applets to all intents and purposes, to do a whole range of things. There was one that just sat in the window constantly monitoring network traffic and presenting it in a graph. Another was a chessboard on which you could move the pieces around. There was a chat application that not only let you send lines of text to someone on another computer, but also let you draw things on your screen that would then appear on theirs. And there were applications that would allow you to formulate computations and have them executed on a more powerful computer somewhere else. One that has stuck with Tim Berners-Lee is the one of the early demos that Wei wrote to demonstrate the idea. 'When you first got to Viola you had a little puppet show,' Tim recalls, 'with curtains that would open dramatically on the screen and all these animations would happen.'

All this was highly prophetic, but the only person writing mini-applications at the time was Pei Wei and the only browser that could run them was ViolaWWW. In May 1993, however, he and colleagues from O'Reilly had a visit from people from Sun microsystems and showed them what mini-applications in ViolaWWW could do. The application

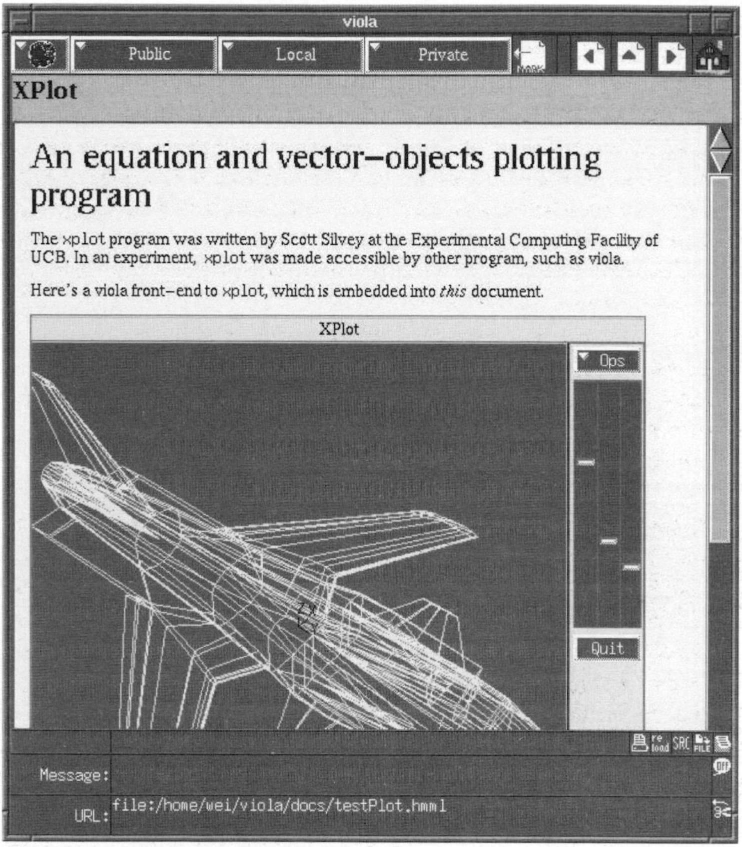

Figure 20: Pei Wei's ViolaWWW browser was the first to be able to download programs across the network and run them.
http://www.xcf.berkeley.edu/~wei/viola/violaScreenDumps2/testPlot.jpg

they demonstrated was a drawing tool called xplot. Two years later Sun released the Java language, complete with applets, to great fanfare, but Pei Wei had been there first.

The time for applets would come, but in the middle of 1992, just having an X-browser at all was providing a major shot in the arm for the Web. Tim was really excited about it and started discussions with Pei Wei about cross-licensing software. Wei could make free use of the CERN code and CERN could use Viola as long as neither tried to make a profit at the other's expense. It was an arrangement in the spirit of GNU General Public License and it was just what the Web needed. CERN soon had the ViolaWWW code sitting on the info.cern.ch server free for anyone to download.

The last release of ViolaWWW came in March 1994, because by then a browser called Netscape was taking the Web by storm. 'That's when I threw in the towel and gave up on developing Web browsers,' says Wei, 'because, you know, they've got this whole company, they're doing a good job, let them do it.' He moved on to other things, but looking back he can't help thinking how things might have turned out differently. 'Boy, would I have loved to have known some technology investors then,' he sighs.

Crossing the Atlantic

In August 1991, the World Wide Web was just a handful of servers, mostly in physics laboratories and none outside Europe. It was a Web of few strands, but Paul Kunz was about to change that. After his exploits on BITNET in the mid-1980s, he had shifted to the Internet when he got a NeXT computer in 1989. He followed the NeXT-related newsgroups to see if anything interesting would turn up, and when Tim announced the Web he thought it was anything but. 'What are these crazy CERN people up to now?' he thought as he skipped to the next message and forgot all about it.

The following month, however, Kunz was at CERN for some meetings and Tim wasn't about to let the opportunity pass. 'I had a pretty full schedule,' remembers Kunz, 'but he caught up with me by telephone and twisted my arm and insisted that I come and see him.' That Friday afternoon, Kunz found himself sitting in Tim's office listening to what he thought was just some boring stuff about documentation. 'But then he showed me something that opened my eyes,' he remembers. 'He showed me that from the Web interface on the NeXT machine he was able to access the help system that was sitting on the IBM.' Tim's demonstration of the XFIND gateway he had cobbled together with Bernd

Pollermann turned out to offer the solution to a problem that had been at the back of Kunz's mind for some time.

The Web inspires

Preprints are the advance copies of the scientific world, a way for scientists to let other scientists see their papers without having to wait for the lengthy peer review process of scientific journals. Of course, that means that they don't have quite the same authority as published papers, so scientists treat them with a little more caution, but the speed more than compensates for that. The SLAC library had been collecting preprints since 1962, and by the 1970s was developing a system for storing bibliographic information about them on computers. In 1974 the laboratory launched what it called the Standard Public Information Retrieval System (SPIRES) preprint database, which rapidly became the most valuable information source in the world of particle physics. The people at SLAC estimated that some 5 000 entries ought to be big enough, but by the following year that estimate was already beginning to look a little modest. The physics community had enthusiastically embraced SPIRES and physicists were sending in preprints at the rate of around 70 a week. By 1980 that number had risen to 100.

By that time, SLAC was running SPIRES on the same kind of IBM computer as the one at CERN, and while Bernd Pollermann was writing his XFIND system, half a world away Paul Kunz was developing a way of accessing SPIRES for people who didn't have an account on the SLAC IBM. Being a BITNET enthusiast, Kunz had invented an interface called QSPIRES that allowed people to send queries to SPIRES over BITNET and get back the information they wanted without actually logging on to the SLAC IBM. That worked fine until physicists started to desert BITNET for the Internet; then the only way to access SPIRES remotely was to send it an e-mail and wait for it to reply. Kunz was sure there had to be a better way, and when he saw Tim Berners-Lee querying XFIND from his NeXT, he knew what it was.

Before leaving Tim's office at CERN, Paul Kunz asked for one more demonstration. He was fairly impressed that the Web worked within CERN, but what would really impress him was a demonstration of it working across the network. So they sent Tim's browser over to Kunz's NeXT in California and set it up to display on Tim's NeXT at CERN. Sure enough, when they made enquiries from Kunz's machine, the output appeared in the window that the browser in California had opened up on the computer in Tim's office. What was even more impressive was that the information seemed to be making the round trip from Geneva to California surprisingly fast. 'So now I was really excited,' admits Kunz. 'I told Tim I was going to put SLAC's SPIRES database on the Web as soon as I got home.'

The following morning he was on the flight to San Francisco and as soon as he got back to work he went off to see Louise Addis, SLAC's librarian. 'Paul dropped in,' she remembers, 'and he said, "I've just been at CERN and I found this wonderful thing that a guy named Tim Berners-Lee is developing. It's called the World Wide Web and it's just the ticket for what you guys need for your database."' Kunz gave Addis a demonstration using the browser he had installed with Tim a few days earlier. This time the Web pages were just making a one-way trip, however, from Europe to California. 'She was really surprised,' he remembers, 'we were all surprised at how fast it was.'

'Would you like me to start a server?' Kunz asked Addis. 'Yes! By all means,' came the reply. But Paul Kunz wasn't excited enough about the Web to do it himself, so he passed it on to someone else. 'I was too busy with what I thought was my more important project,' he laughs, unable to recall exactly what that project was. Tim Berners-Lee and Louise Addis didn't forget his promise, however, and prompted by them he helped finish the job. On 12 December, http://slacvm.slac.stanford.edu/ became the first Web server in the United States, just in time for Tim Berners-Lee to demonstrate it at the Hypertext '91 conference that started in San Antonio, Texas, three days later.

San Antonio

The paper Tim and Robert submitted to Hypertext '91 was rejected by the conference committee. 'They must have felt like the guys who rejected the Beatles,' said a slightly amused Wendy Hall years later. Nevertheless, Tim and Robert did get the chance to demonstrate the Web in San Antonio. 'They have chutzpah,' one delegate was heard to exclaim, 'calling that the World Wide Web!'

The hypertext community was not impressed with the Web. What they were looking for was bells and whistles. Even Wendy Hall, taking time out from her own demo, found herself thinking, 'Where's the hypertext in that?' The Web was just too simple for the academics at Hypertext '91. It was so simple, in fact, that nobody had done it before and few realized that the Web's simplicity was its strength. The hypertext community had got embroiled in making sure that hypertext systems were all-singing and all-dancing, with their links in a database so they would update automatically whenever a document was moved or deleted. Tim's design dispensed with that piece of hypertext dogma completely. Web links are in the document and if someone moves or deletes a document to which you have a link, your link will just point nowhere and you will get a message saying that the document you wanted could not be found. Tim had realized that such dangling links were the price that had to be paid for scalability.

But there was at least one delegate at San Antonio who was impressed by the Web. 'It was sort of an interesting weekend,' recalls Dan Connolly. 'The same weekend I met the girl who's now my wife, I met the guy who's now my employer!' A girl at a party had made a bee-line across the room for him and handed him a jello shot. Three years later they were married with a young child and on a flight to Boston where Connolly was due to take up a new appointment. Tim Berners-Lee had become the Director of the World Wide Web Consortium based at MIT and Connolly was one of its first employees. He wasn't too keen on leaving Texas, but when he told his old professors from the University of Texas that he had the chance to move to Boston, they replied, 'You have an opportunity to go to MIT and you're not already on the plane? This is the Grand Central Station of computer science, go!' The young family stayed in Boston for two years until the call of home became too strong and they moved back to Texas, from where Connolly now telecommutes.

Airborne

The end of 1991 saw the World Wide Web team of Tim Berners-Lee and Robert Cailliau still working in different divisions and in different buildings. It was about a ten-minute walk along Route Rutherford and down Route Democritus to get from Tim's office to Robert's. Moreover, despite the lab's notional approval of the Web project, there were no extra resources allocated for its development. 'We need to strengthen the team,' they had pleaded in a regular trickle of status reports and action plans, all of which went unheeded. CERN management was suffering from tunnel vision, the tunnel in question being the one that housed the laboratory's LEP accelerator and the vision being LEP's successor the LHC. The laboratory, they believed, was a physics research establishment. Sure, computers and networks were necessary, but they were secondary to the laboratory's primary mission of doing physics. And despite LEP's great success in the world of research, bringing prestige to Europe and fundamental knowledge to all of humanity, some of the laboratory's member states were looking jealously at CERN's budget. For CERN's physicists and management, the LHC was all there was. Getting it approved by the member states had to take priority over everything else, and with the laboratory's budget increasingly squeezed, the last thing the physicists wanted to see was any of their precious resources being funnelled off into some little computing project. Little matter that less than five years later, CERN's Director General Chris Llewellyn-Smith worked out that the Web was already worth more than the member states had put into CERN since the laboratory was founded almost half a century before.

Mike Sendall was still the Web's only truly committed supporter and his office became Tim's and Robert's sounding board. 'They would charge into my office and enthusiastically explain their new ideas on my blackboard using coloured diagrams,' he explained. 'Tim would elaborate on his "round green entity" whereas Robert would have his "blue amoeba" and I would be caught in between asking how Tim's green entity related to Robert's amoeba. It was all quite dynamic.' Unlike the delegates at Hypertext '91, Mike realized that the apparent simplicity of the Web belied a clever strategy on the part of its inventor. 'Tim situated the innovations at the right level, not too clever, not too simple,' explained Mike. 'The level of technology was just right, it was good enough to fly.'

It may not have reached Mach 1, but at the end of 1991 the Web was at least off the ground. There were three X-browsers in the pipeline and Robert was still thinking of writing one for Macintoshes. There were about a dozen institutions serving up information onto the Web, including the SLAC bridgehead in the United States. And it wasn't only Web servers that you could access through the Web. Since his presentation to CERN's computing top brass in May, Tim had added more gateways, so that with a Web browser you could now access information on FTP, WAIS, and archie servers as well as HTTP servers. The World Wide Web was beginning to live up to its name. 'A world of information is now available online from any computer platform,' announced Tim in the October–December 1991 issue of CERN's computing newsletter. 'Information sources at CERN and across the world span subjects from poetry to biochemistry and supercomputing.'

The second year

The year 1992 was one of consolidation for the World Wide Web. It became a recognized service at CERN with information about how to use it being distributed to new arrivals at the laboratory. More X-browsers appeared. Robert started work on his Mac browser and a couple of projects sprang up to write browsers for PCs. The number of servers grew steadily through the year as the CERN Web team travelled the world on evangelizing tours to conferences, laboratories, and universities. Hot on the heels of the San Antonio demonstration came a workshop at the French south coast town of La Londe-les-Maures. 'It was a workshop with the longest title you could possibly imagine,' remembers Paul Kunz, who was pleased to find Tim there demonstrating SPIRES access through the Web.

The workshop's full name was the Second International Workshop on Software Engineering, Artificial Intelligence, and Expert Systems in High Energy and Nuclear Physics. With an all-embracing title like that, it had attracted an eclectic group of attendees, and in his talk Tim was able to tell them that Web traffic was growing steadily. He flashed up a graph showing the number of documents downloaded from info.cern.ch from July 1991. There was a blip in August when he'd

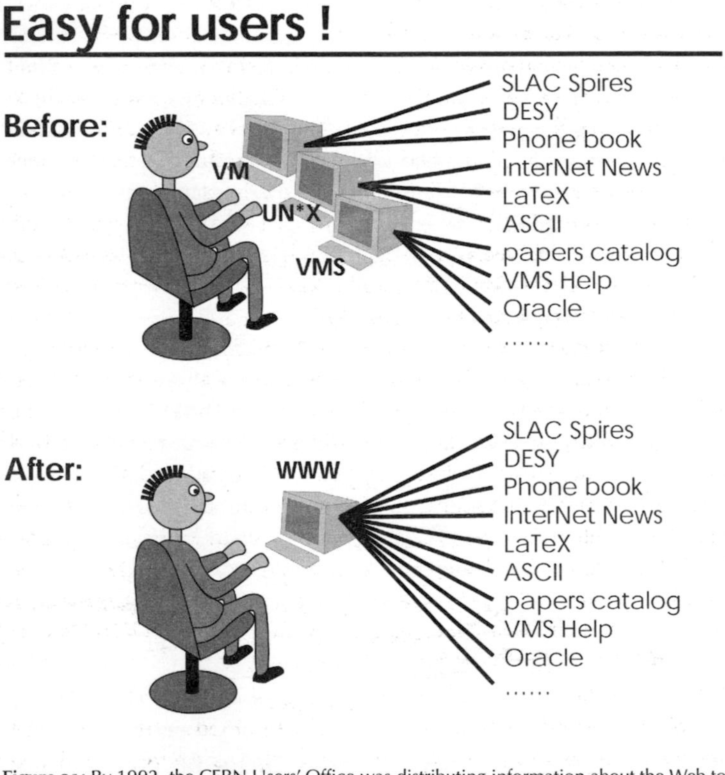

Figure 21: By 1992, the CERN Users' Office was distributing information about the Web to scientists visiting CERN. The cover showed the remarkable change the Web was already beginning to have on working practices.

announced the Web on the newsgroups, a lull in September, but since then Web use had been rising steadily.

As the year wore on, the CERN team busily accumulated air miles as they went from conference to conference spreading the word. La Londe-les-Maures was just the beginning. By the end of the year, Tim would have spent three months in the United States touting the Web from coast to coast, while Robert and Jean-François Groff trod the conference circuit in Europe. In May, Jean-François demonstrated the Web at the Joint European Networking Conference, JENC '92 in Innsbruck. Two months later, when his CERN contract came to an end, Groff headed north to work on a Web project for a university in Denmark. 'That went down as probably the first paid Web services consulting in history,' he recalls. But his evangelizing continued at conferences in Pisa and Helsinki.

A landmark for Robert was the Computing in High Energy Physics conference, CHEP '92, held in the French town of Annecy in September. 'That was where we had our first Web T shirts,' remembers Bebo White, a friend of Robert's from SLAC who was helping to run the server that Paul Kunz had put up there. On an earlier visit to CERN, White had installed something called IBM Grouptalk on the laboratory's main computer. It never had much impact but was immortalized as one of the bubbles in the bubble and arrow diagram of Tim's 1989 proposal. The CHEP '92 T shirts featured the names of the first particle physics Web sites like CERN, DESY, FNAL, and SLAC, and they were one-offs. Robert's had the WWW logo in green because he is a 'victim' of the relatively mild condition of synaesthesia, which means that he sees each letter in a different colour, and Ws are green. Bebo White had no such constraints and so his Ws were red, but his T shirt had SLAC at the top instead of CERN. At the time they could afford to make personalized T shirts for every single Web site, and Bebo White used to joke, 'Maybe some day there'll be enough sites to go around our chests.' The Web team's evangelistic tourism had the desired effect. Summing up after CHEP '92, one of the closing speakers remarked that 'if there is one thing everyone should carry away with them from the conference, it is the World Wide Web,' and he urged people to go off and install it.

WWW wizards

One of the earliest converts was an Oxford-trained particle physicist who had moved to California after finishing his doctorate and had never returned. To subsequent generations of Oxford particle physics graduate students, however, Tony Johnson was well known. Buried on

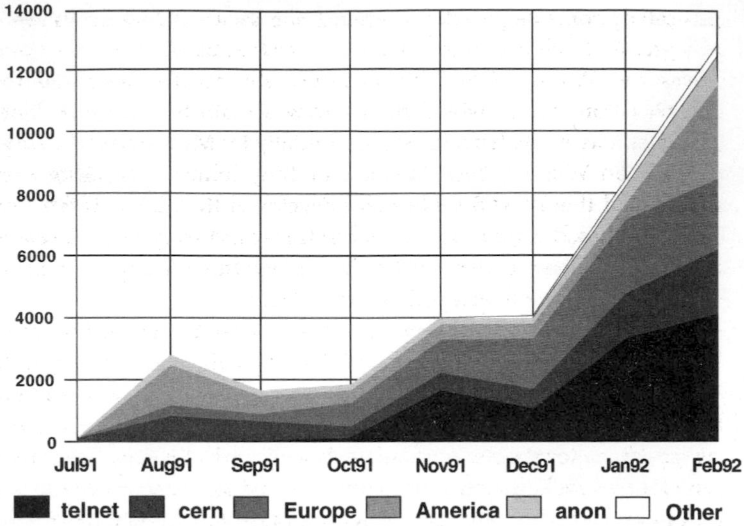

Figure 22: By early 1992, Web use was rising sharply. From a trickle in July 1991, the number of documents downloaded from the CERN server at info.cern.ch had risen to over 12 000 per month. (Graph on p. 163 of AIHEP Proceedings.)

the Oxford department's VAX computer there was a directory of files entitled 'Johnson hangovers'. In it were all manner of little programs to make the VAX's operating system display text in huge characters, to put text in a box, or to make text blink on and off. None of this was absolutely necessary, but back in the days when computer displays were simply screens of scrolling text everyone thought it was rather fun, and 'Johnson hangovers' got copied by each new generation of graduate students for as long as Oxford kept its VAX. A SLAC physicist like Paul Kunz, Johnson had nevertheless been unaware of the excitement over the first Web server in the United States, and he had to come back to Europe before he first encountered the Web at La Londe-les-Maures. He and a group of colleagues were planning to set up a bigger, better version of the CERN program library that supplied free code of use to physicists. They had a name for their project, FREEHEP, but they hadn't worked out how to distribute it. After La Londe-les-Maures, the answer was obvious. 'We decided to use the SPIRES database,' he explains, 'and to use the same Web interface that Paul had set up.'

By this time, Paul Kunz had left his server in the hands of Louise Addis and had gone back to his more important projects. Since she couldn't just call up some help desk for support, she decided to set up an informal group of volunteers to support the Web at SLAC. 'We called ourselves the World Wide Web Wizards,' she recalls, 'much to the consternation of some who thought that was a little too informal.' Chief sorceress was Addis herself, assisted initially by Mark Barnett, George Crane, Joan Winters, Bebo White, and Tony Johnson. Together they maintained the SPIRES service and developed the SLAC server. 'You could do a broad search and then add extra terms to narrow your search as you went along,' explains Johnson. 'I guess this was one of the first examples of a Web interface that allowed that.'

But Johnson's main claim to fame isn't the SLAC server, but an X-browser called Midas. Like Viola, Midas originally had nothing to do with the Web; it had started life as a language Johnson had written to help him write X-Window applications. Johnson's experiment had a system that allowed physicists to analyse their data interactively, they called it IDA for Interactive Data Analysis and Johnson worked on the user interface for it. He called it Midas for Motif Interactive Data Analysis Shell, Motif being a popular system for showing X-Window displays at the time. 'I'd been writing that for quite a while,' recalls Johnson, 'getting frustrated at how difficult it was to program X-Window on Motif.' He wanted to build in a 'help' system to Midas and started to look at the Web as a possible solution. He started by using Viola but eventually decided that wasn't quite what he wanted. 'I decided that maybe I could just write something myself,' he explains, 'typical physicist style!'

Just like Pei Wei before him, Johnson already had the tools. Where Wei had cobbled the first version of ViolaWWW together overnight by plugging the line mode browser into Viola, Johnson had his Midas toolkit with which to build a browser. Tim Berners-Lee saw Midas before he left for his three-month trip to the United States, and a visit to SLAC was on his agenda. He wanted to persuade Johnson to put more effort into Midas, but he didn't succeed. 'Tony was and is first and foremost a physicist,' he says, 'and he didn't like the idea of supporting Midas for a group any wider than that of his colleagues.' Nevertheless Johnson announced MidasWWW on www-talk on 16 November and people, especially physicists, rapidly started to download it. By this time, a colleague of his had translated it to run on VAX computers, so Midas became the first, and one of very few, dedicated browsers for VAXes, which were beginning to lose ground, even in their academic strongholds, to X-terminals, Macintoshes, and PCs.

In its first release, MidasWWW didn't do much that other browsers weren't already doing. 'I think its one claim to fame is that the links changed colour when you clicked on them,' explains Johnson. 'I think it was the first Web browser to do that.' But as time went on, Tony Johnson's browser evolved in a different way from its main competitor, ViolaWWW. Where Pei Wei was trying to blur the boundaries between files and applications with his downloadable apps, Johnson was developing the feature that ensured MidasWWW would become the favourite browser of the world's particle physics community. MidasWWW was the first browser to make use of 'plug-ins': programs that could literally be plugged into the browser for dealing with formats that the browser couldn't understand on its own.

The first ever plug-in was inspired by SPIRES. Johnson was still a WWW Wizard, and SLAC librarian Louise Addis was still chief wizard. She explained to Johnson that she wanted to make the full text of preprints available through the Web. Up to then, physicists could search for preprints on a particular subject, but once they had found them they would have to download the preprint as a computer-readable file, run it through a program on their own computers, and send it to a printer. Addis wanted to be able to display the whole preprint in the browser. Tony Johnson didn't relish all the work entailed in making his browser do that, so he came up with a better idea. All the preprints on the SPIRES database were in the form of TEX files, written using the physicists' favourite markup, and the standard way of printing them out was to use a commercial system called PostScript. The problem with PostScript, however, was that it turned TEX files into files that printers could understand without going through the step of showing you what the printed output would look like. That meant that producing attractive documents using TEX was something of a hit-and-miss affair. There was a burning need for an intermediate step, a program that would display PostScript on the screen so you could look at your documents before printing them off. Tony Johnson knew of a program that did just that, called Ghostscript, and he realized that the simplest way to satisfy Addis's request would be to plug Ghostscript into MidasWWW. All he would have to do was check incoming files to see if they were PostScript, and if they were, launch Ghostscript and have it display the files inside the browser. It was a whole lot easier than writing a PostScript display package from scratch. 'We were ecstatic,' says Addis. 'This was an absolutely stupendous development for us and our users.'

If there is one thing that sold the Web to the particle physics community, it was the fact that physicists could use it to get at the SPIRES database. And the relationship wasn't all one-way. Partly thanks to the Web, SPIRES remains the most important source of on-line information for particle physicists. By 1999, it had overrun the initial estimate of 5 000 records by a factor of 80; SPIRES counted no fewer than 400 000 records. Preprints were coming in at several hundred per month, although most of them by now were e-prints. Physicists had by this time largely deserted the paper world and were submitting their preprints electronically.

Would you like a demo?

Robert Cailliau couldn't suppress a smile when Brian Kelly asked him if he would like a demo of the World Wide Web. He had found himself at a loose end in Leeds whilst visiting his partner's family and decided to do a little PR for the Web at the local university. He found his way to the university's computing help desk and asked, 'Does anybody know about the World Wide Web?' They looked at him blankly, consulted their list of supported systems, and said 'No, what is it?' Robert explained that the Web was a distributed hypertext information system. 'Ah, information,' they said, 'we'll take you to our information officer.' That was Brian Kelly, who received his unexpected visitor with a healthy dose of scepticism. 'Have you heard of the World Wide Web?' repeated Robert. 'Yeah, it's great,' replied Kelly, 'would you like a demo?' Kelly has never forgotten Robert's response. 'Well I'm Robert Cailliau,' he began, 'and I work with Tim Berners-Lee at CERN, and I'm helping to build the Web.'

'I must admit,' says Kelly, 'that I thought, "This is a crank, this is a wind-up."' But Robert explained that he was visiting his partner's father in Leeds and, suffering from a pressing need to talk shop, had escaped for a couple of hours to put in a plug for the Web at the local university. Kelly was still unconvinced, so he called his colleague Andrew Cole to see if he had ever heard of Robert. 'Oh yeah,' replied Cole, 'he works with Tim Berners-Lee.'

It turned out that Robert's visit couldn't have been better timed. John McMillan, a Leeds physicist, had been at the workshop in La Londe-les-Maures and had been impressed with Tim's demonstration. McMillan was into Unix, and when he got back to Leeds he told his fellow Unix geeks all about it. They came from many departments at the university, brought together by their common interest in Unix. At this time, Unix and the Internet were still intimately linked thanks to the early deployment of TCP/IP on Unix, so the Unix geeks had a head start. At Leeds, they decided to organize an Internet day on 9 December 1992. They demonstrated archie and gopher and the World Wide Web through ViolaWWW. 'This was the first time I saw it,' remembers Kelly, 'and I thought, "Wow, this is great, this is the future!"' Kelly was one of the team that had been charged with developing a Campus Wide Information System (CWIS) at Leeds. He went back to his colleagues and said, 'This is the thing we should be using, it's clearly superior to gopher.'

It was on 1 March the following year that Robert Cailliau turned up at the Leeds computing help desk. The university still hadn't decided how to run its CWIS and his visit was to prove decisive. Kelly organized a meeting for Robert to explain to everyone at Leeds what the Web was and why they should be using it. He put on a good show, but Kelly was a difficult customer. 'How many people are working on the Web at CERN?' he asked. Robert had to admit that despite its growing importance around the world, the Web was still a very small part of CERN's activity. 'There was Tim and Robert, and there was a student and a cleaner or something,' remembers Kelly, 'sort of about three and a half people.' Kelly was worried, he had a service to run, so he asked Robert what would happen of they were all knocked down by a bus. 'And Robert told us they'd entered into discussions with an organization in the States called NCSA.' The National Center for Supercomputing Applications in Urbana-Champaign, Illinois, was in the middle of developing a suite of browsers called Mosaic that would eclipse everything that went before and put the Internet firmly on the map. Robert knew about Mosaic and he told the people at Leeds where they could find it.

The university's administration was slow to embrace the information age but the rest of the university was quick to catch on. Nicos Drakos in the computer-based learning unit wrote a program to convert $\TeX$ files into HTML. 'So you'd be over in the States,' remembers Kelly, 'and you'd recognise documents converted by Nicos's program.' The university's music department was the first of its kind to be up on the Web, with a server coming on-line on April Fool's Day 1993. And the information office where Brian Kelly worked put up on the Web any information it could get its hands on. They made sure that Leeds was the first UK university to put its computing service newsletter on the Web in November 1993. John McMillan had an article in that newsletter, complete with a picture of what the Web looked like. The information he chose to show underlined the physics origins of the World Wide Web: it was a page dedicated to a piece of hardware being planned for the Large Hadron Collider. Another page reproduced in the newsletter, however, showed the way the Web was heading. The computing service put in an article about the new World Wide Web service at Leeds complete with a picture showing their Web page. They had managed to convince the university's administration to jump aboard the Web, and Leeds University became the first institution in the UK to have an officially sanctioned Web presence. Their welcome page contained information about the university and included links to all the departments that had a resident geek to write the HTML.

Robert's visit tipped the balance at Leeds in the Web's direction, and he was impressed with the result. 'Leeds had one of the best early sites,' he says, 'and they were first in Britain.' To cap it all, the father of the Web, Tim Berners-Lee, made a point of visiting Leeds to give a talk in April 1995, by which time his invention had seen off all comers and was the de facto standard for the Internet. His talk was entitled 'Future Directions of the World Wide Web'. By that time, he knew that his invention had a future, but back in 1992, when Leeds jumped aboard, there was still some way to go before he could sound so confident.

Port 80

The URL of that pioneering Leeds University page was

http://gps.leeds.ac.uk:80/

The 80 at the end represented something called the port number where

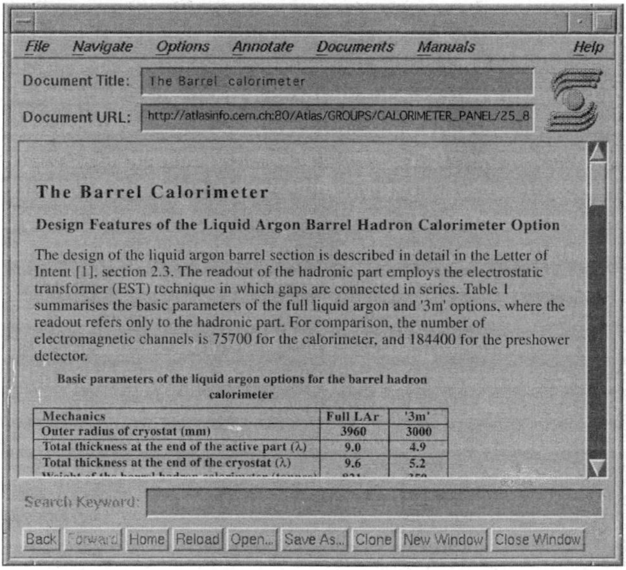

Figure 23: The example Web page, displayed in Mosaic, published in the Leeds University computing newsletter showed the Web's physics origins.
(From http://www.leeds.ac.uk/ucs/newsletter/news209/news209.html)

the Leeds information was available. Brian Kelly and his colleagues were being particularly cautious in specifying it explicitly because the Web had had an official home port for nearly a year by the time they had launched their server.

Nowadays it is rare to see a port number in a URL. Browsers automatically use port 80 unless they are specifically instructed to use a different one. If you have ever stumbled across a Web site with a URL like http://www.site.domain:8080/, it probably belongs to someone developing a new site, or revamping one that already exists. Try adding ':8080' to the URL of your favourite Web sites and see what you find. More likely than not, you will get a message saying something like 'page not found', but you never know.

An officially assigned port meant that you were officially accepted by the Internet crowd, at least insofar as the Internet crowd was capable of being official. The bodies set up to govern the Net back in the 1970s were still as informal as they had ever been; the difference in the 1990s was that instead of being a bunch of academics working in some backwater, their pronouncements ruled the world of data communications. The geeks had supplanted the power of the telecommunications monopolies and the Web was their ultimate form of expression. It was a classic case of people power, and years later, at the 8th World Wide Web conference, their quiet revolution would be complete when a Vice-President of IBM, the archetypal industrial behemoth, gave a talk on the theme of 'Power to the People'.

By early 1992, the Web had been assigned port 80, and from that moment on it has been hard-coded in any software to come out of CERN or any of the other places working on the Web. A port is like a post office counter: there is one for letters and one for parcels; others might deal with savings accounts. On the Internet, ports 0–1023 are reserved for recognized services. FTP is on ports 20 and 21, Telnet on port 23. For years, ports were assigned by Jon Postel whose selfless efforts had ensured the smooth running of the Domain Name System. Postel had acquired the status of a benevolent emperor, presiding over the nomenclature of the Internet. For Postel to assign a port to a new Internet service is a sign that that service has come of age, so when the Web was given port 80 it was a time for celebration, at least for Robert Cailliau. 'When Tim told me we'd got port 80 I was amazed,' he recalls. Ports with low numbers were scarce and that we'd been given one meant we were being taken seriously.' Tim, however, took it all in his stride. 'He was completely unfazed,' said Robert, 'he seemed to expect it.'

Badgering the gophers

There are a lot of animals that prey on gophers, and that presented a bit of a problem for Lou Montulli. An undergraduate student at the University of Kansas, Montulli was trying to come up with a name for a CWIS he had written for the university, and since gopher was the main competition, he wanted a name that said he meant business. 'So our original name was badger,' he laughs, 'because it went around killing gophers.' That name stuck for about a month until Montulli's colleague, Charles Rezak, came up with something better, and by the time the University of Kansas' Campus Wide Information System was released to the world it went under the name of Lynx.

The idea of building a CWIS at Kansas had been around since 1989, and by the time Montulli came along there was an attempt to set something up using gopher. 'Gopher was interesting in that it was the first real client–server application on the Net,' he explains. 'The concept really intrigued me but I really hated the visual implementation.' He had recently come across hypertext in the form of something that was being used by the university's library, and he thought that looked much better. Called HYPERREZ, it had also inspired the first hypertext system for the Internet, HYTELNET. Written by Peter Scott at the University of Saskatchewan, HYTELNET was first deployed in 1990, predating the Web by several months, but it was more limited in scope. It was a hypertext catalogue of all the Internet sites that you could use telnet to logon to. By this time, telnet was being used to allow access for people to search catalogues, for example, so HYTELNET was popular with libraries. Its interface looked a lot like the CERN line mode browser, and it would show you a hierarchically arranged catalogue of telnet sites. When you found the one you wanted you would telnet to it and search the catalogue.

To Lou Montulli, hypertext and networks seemed to belong together and he decided he would just get on and do it. 'It's easier to ask for forgiveness than permission right?' he says with a mischievous chuckle. 'And you know, the vigour of youth, you could stay up all night and work on things and you'd get things going, and really I knew once people saw what it did that people would be pretty excited about it, and lo and behold they were.'

One of the most excited people was Michael Grobe, Montulli's manager. He liked Montulli's hypertext interface and he began to think about linking it in with the work of another student, Charles Rezak, who had been working on setting up a gopher-based CWIS. 'Finally, one day in 1992, I had the idea of grafting the gopher client Net management routines onto Lynx to merge the two tools,' remembers Grobe. 'Lou and Charles thanked me for finally catching on, pointing out that they'd been suggesting just that for a week.'

So with his boss's approval, Montulli got down to work, and by July 1992, Kansas had its own distributed hypertext system. What Montulli had put together was effectively the World Wide Web by another name. Instead of HTTP, it used the gopher protocol, and instead of HTML, it had its own hypertext language developed from HYPERREZ. 'There's no such thing as original thought,' Montulli was later to claim, going on to explain that the pieces just happened to fall together for him just as they had for Tim Berners-Lee nearly two years earlier.

Kansas released Lynx to the world and universities started to adopt it for their CWISes, but the Web had a head start and it soon came to Montulli's attention. In October, a colleague had been to a big Internet conference where he had learned that libwww was available from CERN for free. On returning from the conference, he suggested that Lou add it to Lynx, and one week later Lynx had become a Web browser.

This was the first version to come to the attention of the people at CERN, and to them it just looked like a fancier version of the line mode browser. Like the line mode browser, it just handled text, but it did so in a more sophisticated way. Lynx had been written using a system called 'curses' that allowed you to move a cursor around the screen using arrows on your keyboard. That meant that instead of being confined to typing in numbers corresponding to the links you wanted to use, with Lynx you could move the cursor to the link and then hit the carriage return to 'click' on it. It was the next best thing to having a mouse and it worked on all the same kinds of 'dumb' terminals as the line mode browser. As time progressed, colleagues of Montulli began producing Lynx browsers for different platforms. Garrett Blythe wrote DosLynx for PCs and Foteos Macrides produced a version for VAXes. Eventually there were so many different versions that someone set up the Lynx Binary Distribution Outlet, Lybido for short, with links to the places you could find them all. The Macintosh version resides at http://www.lirmm.fr/maclynx and its author, Ol Gutknecht, has added an interesting twist to the Free Software movement. Maclynx is neither freeware nor shareware, it is postcardware. 'If you like it,' says Gutknecht, 'please send me a postcard of your town!'

Montulli himself had plans to write an X-Window version of Lynx. 'Lynx was always designed to be multi-platform,' he explains. 'I'd done the text version first because it was the most ubiquitous.' But then

NCSA released the Mosaic X-browser. 'And I saw that and realized that it could take the place of the X-client I was working on because it basically did exactly the same thing,' Montulli explains. 'I'm not one for doing work for work's sake!' The X Mosaic browser was released in January 1993 and it went on to become the World Wide Web's killer application, the one that definitively dragged the Web out of academia and dropped it centre stage.

The end of the beginning

At the end of 1992, World Wide Web traffic on the Internet was still a barely discernible trickle, but the foundations for growth were in place. Pei Wei's ViolaWWW X-browser had been joined by Tony Johnson's MidasWWW and there were more on the way. Joseph Wang at MIT had announced another X-browser called tkWWW on www-talk at the end of July. SLAC had been joined by other American institutions on the Web. At the end of the year in which the number of Internet sites broke one million, Robert estimates that there were about fifty Web servers worldwide. The effort that Tim, Robert, and Jean-François had put into touring conferences had borne fruit as more and more people had seen the Web and taken it home with them. The same trip that took Tim to SLAC, where he first saw MidasWWW, had also taken him to Fermilab, where he helped Jonathan Streets and Ruth Pordes to set up a server. Streets had been at La Londe-Les-Maures, and when he got back to Illinois, he told his colleagues that the Web was 'the best thing around'.

With Pei Wei working at O'Reilly, the first glimmerings of the Web's commercial potential were in the air, and the prospects of Tim's original dream being realized looked high. With a stable income at last, Wei was able to give his Viola a mass of innovative features, and Tim was hoping that a built-in editor to give it the same browser/editor functionality as his original NeXT prototype would soon be forthcoming. The first browsers were also in the offing for Macintoshes and PCs. Nicola Pellow had come back to CERN after finishing her degree and she was helping Robert with the Mac browser, which by this time had acquired the name Samba, neither Greek deity nor Egyptian Pharaoh. For Pellow, progress in getting Samba up and running was slow, because after every few links it would crash and nobody could work out why. 'The Mac browser is still in a buggy form,' lamented Tim in a September '92 newsletter. 'A W3 T shirt to the first one to bring it up and running!' he announced. The T shirt duly went to Fermilab's John Streets, who tracked down the bug, allowing Nicola Pellow to get on with producing a usable version of Samba.

Another recurring theme of 1992 was the periodic requests for resources that Tim and Robert would make to their hierarchy, and CERN's continuing lack of response. There was one in July. 'CERN is expending considerably less effort on improving access to information than it is on producing, hand-distributing and searching for that information,' it pointed out. And there was another in December reiterating the request for a virtual librarian and an X-programmer. For Mike Sendall, who by this time had achieved the status of the Web's godfather, managing the Web was a delicate balancing act. At one point towards the end of the project's life at CERN, he had been asked to work out how much the laboratory had actually put into the project. 'That was not an easy task,' he explained, 'but I ended up counting some 20 man-years effort in total.' Neither Tim, nor Robert, nor their managers believed him. Management said, 'That's too much, cut back,' Tim and Robert said 'It's nowhere near that, give us more!' 'So I must have been quite close to the real figure,' concluded Mike.

At one point in 1992, Tim and Robert had pondered setting up a company called Websoft. Robert saw it as a possible way of getting the resources that CERN was unable to provide, but the thought was quickly dismissed. For Tim Berners-Lee, cashing-in would have been tantamount to betraying his instincts. He may have become rich, but his World Wide Web would never have grown into the free and open standard that it is today. If Tim had set that kind of precedent, he believes we would now be stuck in a world where you needed ten different pieces of software to browse instead of a single browser, because his company would soon have been joined by others before an agreed standard had been set. 'I was still looking after it because it was my baby,' explains Tim. 'I'm not sure anybody else had that much attachment to it to actually hold the technology together.' Robert reluctantly agreed, and they left the name Websoft for some future entrepreneur to snap up. 'Tim's not in it for the money,' says Robert. 'He accepts a much wider range of hotel-room facilities than a CEO would.' He says it with admiration for his ex-colleague, but he is still not convinced that they made the right choice back in 1992. 'It could have given us the resources we needed,' he explains, 'and anyway, look at all the plug-ins you need to do anything nowadays.' As he sees it, the balkanization of the Web that Tim's idealism was trying to avoid has happened to some extent anyway.

Two more important US servers to come up before the end of 1992 were NCSA at the University of Illinois, Urbana-Champaign, and the Cornell Law School, which started putting up all kinds of legal documents on the Web. 'As law tends to be mostly cross-reference,' noted

Tim, 'hypertext makes a lot of sense here!' Another thing that made a lot of sense to Tom Bruce, the person behind the Cornell server, was a browser for PCs, since those were the computers that lawyers tended to use. The result was a PC browser called Cello, released on 8 June 1993, which was soon being downloaded at a rate of 500 copies a day. With Cello and Samba, the Web was making its first appearance on the sort of computers that you find in people's homes. But even with the kind of take-up rate Cello was enjoying, its success would be short-lived. Mac and PC versions of Mosaic were about to arrive.

7 The Beginning of the Future

With the circle of Web developers growing daily, it could only be a matter of time before the Web left home, and in 1993, with the release of the Mosaic browsers by the National Center for Supercomputing Applications (NCSA) at the University of Illinois, the inevitable happened. The Web became accessible to anyone using a Macintosh or Microsoft Windows and it took off like a rocket. Browsers were downloaded by computer enthusiasts at the rate of several thousand per day. Nerds and neophytes alike were riveted to their computer screens. The European Commission began to take notice, prompted partly by a Web-based dinosaur exhibition produced by Kevin Hughes at Honolulu Community College in Hawaii. This exhibition became the yardstick of what the Web could do, and even prompted the bureaucrats of an EU project coordination group to shift their meeting from their not-yet-wired administrative buildings to a nearby university's computer science laboratory so Robert Cailliau could show it to them. So impressed were they with Hughes's dinosaurs that they agreed to fund a Web-based project Cailliau had gone to Brussels to promote. Known as WISE, this project would take the Web to small and medium-sized companies in Europe's poorer regions. More importantly for Cailliau, however, it was a foot in the door of a funding agency that might be able to deliver where CERN had not. But WISE was to prove too little, too late, as Mosaic took off, driving the Web's expansion at the breathtaking rate of 341 634 per cent in 1994 compared to archrival gopher, which only grew at the relatively leisurely pace of 997 per cent that year.

Mosaic

The spark that lit the Web's explosive growth in 1993 came out of NCSA at the University of Illinois at Urbana-Champaign, about 120 miles south of Chicago in the heart of America's prairies. NCSA had been set up in 1985 by astrophysicist Larry Smarr as part of the National Science Foundation initiative to make supercomputing power available to all of America's academic community. In the mid-1980s, Smarr was head of a local group called the Illinois Alliance to Prevent Nuclear War, and there he met Joseph Hardin, a sociologist who was studying arms control lobby groups. 'Larry asked me to help with getting the center off the ground,' remembers Hardin, who soon found himself head of NCSA's software development group. His brief was to combine the supercomputing revolution with the rapidly emerging desktop computing revolution, bringing desktop access to supercomputing facilities.

NCSA's zeitgeist was established along with its first product, NCSA Telnet, a very successful implementation of the telnet protocol that lets you logon remotely to a distant computer. NCSA Telnet clearly meshed very well with the goal of providing remote access to powerful computers, and in an age where software was either highly polished and reliable commercial stuff or impenetrable and often unreliable academic stuff, it took a middle line. NCSA Telnet was easy to install and use and it was pretty robust, but it didn't come with the kind of backup you would expect if you had bought it in a shrink-wrapped box at your local computer shop. It also established another NCSA tradition, being released for a number of different computers ranging from the powerful Unix machines used in academia to the Macintoshes and PCs in people's homes.

NCSA's offices were crammed with the latest powerful Unix machines, and just as at Berkeley's Experimental Computing Facility where Pei Wei had developed his ViolaWWW browser, they acted like a magnet drawing in undergraduate geeks keen to get access to these machines and earn a little extra pocket money into the bargain. One of these was Marc Andreessen, a strapping 6'4" local boy hired by Ping Fu to work on visualization tools.

Ping Fu had an eclectic mixture of talents: a Ph.D. in Chinese literature and a flair for scientific visualization projects on computers. When she joined NCSA in 1990, she worked on the morphing for the film 'Terminator 2' before settling down to more academic pursuits. She teamed up with geometer Herbert Edelsbrunner, who had been a student of Herman Maurer's in Graz, and eventually they combined their talents by getting married and setting up a company with the delightful name of 'Raindrop Geomagic' to develop 3-D modelling software. But that was later. In the early 1990s, Ping Fu needed someone to work with her on visualization projects and she hired Andreessen.

Andreessen had earned himself a reputation as a bit of a whiz at graphical interfaces, and that is what Ping Fu wanted him to work on. 'How about you write a graphical interface for a browser?' she suggested. 'What's a browser?' came the reply. This was before the Web had reached central Illinois, but through her husband's Graz connection, Ping Fu had seen Hyper-G when Maurer had visited NCSA, and had been impressed. She demonstrated that to Andreessen. Her idea was that Andreessen would write a tool that would allow people to download any free software that anyone put up on the Net just by clicking on a button. Andreessen was not impressed. 'He said, "Isn't that just a hard-code FTP?"' recalls Fu, who replied 'Marc, you can do something more intelligent than that!'

Soon after, Dave Thompson, another NCSA staff member was sifting through his mail one morning when he came across a flyer from O'Reilly and Associates advertising new booklets they had on offer. One of them concerned 'WWW: a hypertext retrieval system for the Internet', and it caught Thompson's eye. Instead of ordering the booklet from O'Reilly, however, Thompson did an archie search on the term 'WWW' and found Nicola Pellow's line mode browser and Pei Wei's ViolaWWW available for downloading at info.cern.ch. 'Both were buggy and not easy to get going,' he recalls, 'but they demonstrated the technology.' That was on 9 November 1992, and two days later Thompson was riding in Joseph Hardin's pick-up truck to a small Internet start-up company called Spyglass that NCSA had spun off two years before. He told him about his find. Hardin was pretty excited because it looked like the solution to a problem he had been worrying about. NCSA had recently put out a product called NCSA Collage that allowed several people in different places to work on the same documents. 'Scientists wanted to be able to go to FTP servers where papers by their colleagues resided and pull those papers down into an NCSA Collage session,' he explains. 'And we said, "Gee, that's a good idea. We don't have a good way to do that but let's think about it."' It looked as though O'Reilly's mail shot might have done his thinking for him.

Back at NCSA the next day, Thompson demonstrated the Web to a group of people including Andreessen, who saw it as perhaps a way into the 'more intelligent' thing Ping Fu had urged him to do. He immediately started to investigate further by plugging himself into the www-talk newsgroup. As chance would have it, this was just a few days before Tony Johnson announced the first public release of MidasWWW on www-talk, putting the code up on FREEHEP, and Andreessen was among of the first to download it. 'MidasWWW is superb! Fantastic!

Stunning! Impressive as hell!' he mailed Johnson at 16.44 on 17 November. After explaining who he was and what NCSA was, Andreessen laid out the potential improvements he had in mind; WYSIWYG hypertext editing, inclusion and accessing of graphics, animations, and scientific data files were on the list. Andreessen suggested they collaborate on developing a Web browser with all these features and closed his message with a long list of bugs he had found in Johnson's code. Johnson was at first receptive to the idea and replied to Andreessen at 18.24. 'If there is some possibility of collaboration,' he said, 'then I would certainly be interested in pursuing it.' At 20.12, there was long reply from Andreessen in Johnson's mailbox describing at length what NCSA did and pointing out that 'MidasWWW doesn't talk gopher or FTP yet; are you planning to add that in the near future?' Marc Andreessen was going through MidasWWW with a fine-tooth comb and it came as something of a shock for Tony Johnson. Another message arrived at 22.13 pointing out more bugs in MidasWWW, then things went quiet until the following day. At 10.44 Johnson pointed out that MidasWWW did talk to gopher and FTP through a gateway that had been down the previous day. Then he sat back to see what would happen next. He had to wait until nearly ten past four in the afternoon, but then the floodgates opened. Andreessen sent messages at 16.09, 16.19, and 16.29 asking questions, suggesting modifications, and pointing out more bugs. Andreessen had got the bit between his teeth and he was establishing the work pattern that would contribute to making NCSA Mosaic the great success that it was. But for Tony Johnson, a mixture of bewilderment, pique, and simple desire to get on with his day job led him to think twice about collaborating with NCSA. 'So I sent back a message saying, 'Well, I'm not sure I want to change everything, I'm happy with it the way it is",' he recalls. 'Very expensive e-mail,' he added later. 'If I'd have answered, "Yes, yes, I want to collaborate with you, let's scrap it all and start again!" maybe I'd be a millionaire by now.'

After that Marc Andreessen left Tony Johnson in peace, asked NCSA staffer Eric Bina to help him, and set about writing his own X-browser. They worked around the clock until it was done. 'Haunts were the local twenty-four-hour convenience store for Marc's cookies and milk, my Skittles and Mountain Dew,' remembers Bina. It didn't take long for them to come up with a working browser. They picked up libwww and on 23 January 1993 they had released X-Mosaic 0.5. 'By the power vested in me by nobody in particular,' posted Andreessen on www-talk, 'X-Mosaic is hereby released.' Tim Berners-Lee was thrilled. 'Brilliant!' he told Marc in a message posted to www-talk two days later. 'Every new browser is sexier than the last. There is a lot of cross-fertilization going on, which is very good. KUTGW everyone.'

Tim added X-Mosaic to the line mode browser and ViolaWWW on info.cern.ch for people to download. The striking thing about it was that unlike all the earlier X-browsers, it was all contained in a single file. Installing it was as simple as pulling it across the network and running it. Later on, Mosaic would rise to fame because of the <IMG> tag that allowed you to put images inline for the first time, rather than having them pop up in a different window like Tim's original NeXT browser did. That made it easier for people to make Web pages look more like the familiar print media they were used to; not everyone's idea of a brave new world, but it certainly got Mosaic noticed. For Tim, though, it was not the <IMG> tag that made Mosaic great. 'What I think Marc did really well,' he explains, 'is make it very easy to install, and he supported it by fixing bugs via e-mail any time night or day. You'd send him a bug report and then two hours later he'd mail you a fix.'

Andreessen hadn't slowed down since the day he started bombarding Tony Johnson with e-mails and he wasn't about to stop now. X-Mosaic was downloaded from NCSA 145 times before the end of January. 'In February, the number of downloads was up to 1 161,' points out Dave Thompson. 'It grew quickly after that.' Joseph Hardin was well pleased with X-Mosaic. It fulfilled the NCSA design criterion of being somewhere in between academic and commercial software, and it solved the problem that had been worrying him about NCSA Collage. 'The earliest versions of NCSA Mosaic in the Unix environment had a "collaborate" button on the menu bar,' he explains. 'You could download a document from anywhere on the Web and just pipe it right into a Collage session and share it with people.' Early versions of Mosaic also had an 'annotate' feature to allow collaborative work (see Figure 23). You could pick up a Web page from anywhere and add your own annotations. These could either be for your own personal use or for the use of a well-defined group of collaborators; they would be linked in as a hyperlink at the bottom of the page. In that way it was a bit like Brown University's FRESS system, which allowed hypertext annotation. The idea was partly inspired by the Usenet news system, which allowed people to post messages as replies to other ones so that threads of messages on a certain theme would build up, but it was more sophisticated. Mosaic's annotate feature wasn't exactly the browse/edit capability that Tim Berners-Lee had implemented on his NeXT computer, but it was the first attempt since then to make the Web a collaborative space.

'By February or March I've got the Mac and the Windows guys moving their effort over from Collage to building their versions of NCSA Mosaic,' says Hardin, following the NCSA tradition of making its software available for several different kinds of computers. The principal 'Mac guy' was Aleks Totic, whilst the 'PC guys' were Chris Wilson and Jon Mittelhauser. For them, the race was to catch up first with the functionality of X-Mosaic. For Andreessen and Bina, the goal was to stay one step ahead of both of them. They were all in for a frantic few months. 'It was five or six guys sitting around in the basement of this building and working in the middle of the night,' remembers Mittelhauser. 'Soda cans piled up, empty pizza boxes all over the place, and just having a lot of fun. Going to class or sleeping during the day, whichever was more convenient, which was usually sleep.'

By the summer, all three versions of Mosaic were ready, and NCSA officially released them to the world in November. The effect was remarkable. A widely reported response was that NCSA had fired 'the shot heard around the world', and Mosaic browsers for X-Window, Macintosh, and PC were downloaded in their thousands. They were even joined later by a version for the Commodore Amiga, which like many early PCs still had a loyal following, although that version wasn't released by NCSA. Here at last were easy to install browsers for the kinds of computers that most people were using. The important thing was that NCSA's shot was heard way beyond the world of Unix.

NCSA was putting more and more effort into Mosaic, which by this time was the software development group's biggest project. The developers and their managers, like Hardin and Smarr, would expend considerable effort demonstrating Mosaic. 'I remember early on one time,' says Hardin with a smile, 'that a Vice President from Hewlett Packard and Larry and Marc and me and a couple of other people were down in the "fishbowl", which was the little round presentation room, giving a demo. And we'd shown some other stuff but we hadn't publicly shown Mosaic to anybody yet and I said to Marc, "Why don't we pull this up and see how it looks?" And Marc pulled it up and went to an HP site and it knocked the socks of the HP guy!' After the person from HP had left, Hardin remembers his boss saying, 'You know, this kind of thing only happens once in a while, that you get that kind of response from people, and this is going to be very big.'

Nobody knows how many copies of the Mosaic browsers were downloaded in total, but estimates of around a million are not uncommon. At the beginning of the year, there had been around fifty known Web servers and Web traffic was barely perceptible. By October, the Web accounted for 1 per cent of Internet traffic, 'which seemed like a lot in those days,' remembered Mike Sendall. At the end of the year, that had risen to 2.5 per cent and the number of servers had risen tenfold. To the NCSA team, it seemed like an explosion. Mike and the Web team back at CERN had a different impression: they had been watching the exponential rise of the Web for two years already.

CERN's Mac browser had been released a little earlier than Mac Mosaic and the laboratory was also getting involved with a PC browser. A French student called Alain Favre from the Conservatoire National des Arts et Métiers (CNAM), a sort of French equivalent of the British Open University, was working on a PC browser at CERN as a project for his course. Tom Bruce's Cello had been around for some time before PC Mosaic, and Tim had reviewed an advance copy in May 1993. 'And very nice it looks too,' he said. 'The catch? Tom doesn't want to let it out until he has polished it. He plans a July release.' Cello duly appeared in June and had some success, but by that time the NCSA juggernaut was rolling and there was nothing anyone could do about it. 'You cannot compete with a team of youngsters who sit in front of their machines day and night,' admits Cailliau. 'We released our Mac browser first, but when they came out with theirs it was obvious we didn't stand a chance.'

The difference between NCSA and everybody else was the idea that they would steer a middle line between commercial and academic approaches. Before Mosaic, all the browsers had been academic, so Mosaic was a new departure. Tim Berners-Lee was in Fermilab in the summer of 1993, visiting Ruth Pordes who had earlier been involved with setting up Fermilab's server when Tim had visited the laboratory in 1992. She suggested they drop into NCSA to see what was going on there. Tim was impressed. 'It was clear they were really going to market Mosaic,' recalls Pordes. 'That was the first time we realized that he [Berners-Lee] was really going to have a big success.'

That the Web was succeeding was clearly good news for Tim, but he had mixed feelings about Mosaic. For him, the ideal was still to provide a medium in which people could publish as easily as they could read, and Mosaic didn't look much like a browser/editor. That may have been one of Andreessen's goals when he first fired an e-mail off to Tony Johnson, but as Mosaic developed, presentation became more and more important to its developers. Andreessen remembers Tim's visit clearly. 'Tim bawled me out in the summer of '93 for adding images to the thing,' he later said. Tim does not see it quite that way; he remembers embracing the idea of images wholeheartedly. 'Of course we did approve of images, in fact we had images on the Web before anybody else,' he points out, 'like diagrams in talks, for example. The NeXT was set up to do all kinds of multimedia.' For him it was more a question of how to handle images than whether or not to do them. So Tim's pleasure at seeing the Web take off was tinged with regret that the vehicle for it had not been a browser/editor like his original NeXT prototype. With Mosaic on the loose, that idea would have to go on the back burner for a while, as the Web became another consumer medium with many readers but relatively few publishers. Even the 'annotate' feature disappeared from all but the earliest versions of Mosaic. Berners-Lee had been pinning his hopes on Pei Wei turning Viola into a browser/editor, but that was not to be. 'Viola was more advanced in many ways,' said Tim, 'but Mosaic was the easiest step onto the Web for a beginner and so was a critical element of the Web explosion.'

Life goes on

While the Mosaic tsunami was building up in Illinois, life at CERN went on much as before. Though by this time, Tim's and Robert's requests for more manpower were starting to bear fruit. Robert's boss, Paolo Palazzi, was one person who embraced the Web wholeheartedly. He set up a cluster of public Web terminals, the world's first, in the corridor outside his office. He suggested the 'HR' tag in HTML—any time you see a horizontal ruled line in a Web document, it is Palazzi you have to thank for it. He provided office space for the team, and last but not least he maintained a constant stream of students to keep the Web effort moving along. Carl Barker from Brunel University spent six months at CERN in 1992 working on the CERN server software. He arrived just as Jean-François Groff was leaving to do his Web consultancy work in Denmark. Arthur Secret, the son of French diplomats, also spent two months at the laboratory in 1992 before returning for a longer spell in 1993. Following Secret came a trio of Scandinavians, the Dane Henrik Frystyk Nielsen, the Norwegian Håkon Lie, and the Finn Ari Luotonen. Although the race to build popular browsers effectively came to an end with Mosaic in the middle of 1993, the CERN team still had much to contribute in refining the basic software, developing HTML, and cataloguing the growing World Wide Web.

The Secret service

Arthur Secret was studying for his Diplôme d'Ingénieur at a Grande École in Cergy-Pontoise, just north of Paris, and he came to CERN for his work placement. Earlier in the year, whilst visiting his mother, the French Consul in Geneva, Secret had taken the opportunity of dropping in to CERN to check out the possibilities of a work placement there. He had been introduced to Tim Berners-Lee. 'Nice to have you here,' Secret remembers Tim saying. 'Have you heard about the Internet?' 'No,' replied Secret, so Tim sent him off with a long reading list.

When Secret returned to CERN in July, he made his way up to Berners-Lee's office to find it empty. Tim had recently left for his three-month trip to the United States, but Secret found a piece of paper on Tim's desk with the name Robert Cailliau written on it. So with a leg in plaster from a recent accident, off he went along Route Rutherford and down Route Democritus to Cailliau's office, where he arrived just in time to hear Robert's new electronic diary going 'ping' to remind him that he had a meeting to go to. 'Come back in the morning!' said Cailliau, who was as fastidious about his timekeeping as he was about everything else. It was an inauspicious start for Secret, but he made the best of his time at CERN nonetheless.

Tim Berners-Lee arrived back at CERN just before Secret was due to leave. By that time, the Frenchman had cobbled together an interface between the CERN Web server, httpd, and a database system called Oracle that is widely used at CERN. The 'd' of 'httpd' stands for 'daemon', a word commonly used in computers and networks for things that lurk unseen behind the scenes and behave in an apparently intelligent way. After Cailliau had suggested that interfacing the Web to Oracle databases would be a good idea for a two-month project, Secret soon found himself wading through the Oracle manual trying to find the page that would tell him how Oracle made its data available to other programs. When he found the right page, all he had to do was copy a few lines of C code from it into httpd to make all the data held in Oracle databases available on the Web. Tim seemed suitably impressed, and when Secret confessed that all he had done was copy a few lines of code from a book, he replied, 'Oh, we all do that!'

Those few lines never made it into the official version of CERN's httpd, but they weren't Secret's only contribution to the Web. A year later, having finished his Diplôme d'Ingénieur, he found himself back at CERN again. During his first stay at the laboratory, he had been excited by the project and appalled at the lack of resources it was getting. He decided to go back to CERN and take away some of the growing administrative burden from Tim Berners-Lee. He found himself a grant and settled in at CERN in March 1993, staying until leadership of the World Wide Web project moved on.

When Secret arrived at CERN for the second time, the Mosaic browsers were still new and there was still some attempt to catch up. 'It was funny one time when they told me, "Look, Mosaic can do that, do

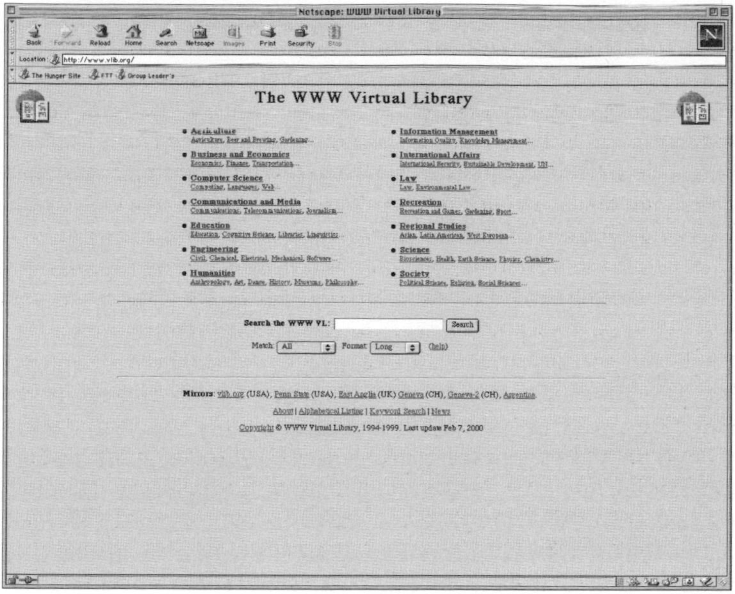

Figure 24: A page from the WWW Virtual Library.

it!" So I started to look in the Mosaic code,' he recalls, 'and it said "code from Lynx".' This was the cross-fertilization that Tim had been talking about, but soon after it was all Mosaic, and Secret settled into a more administrative role. He fielded e-mails to the Web team and he took over from Tim the increasingly important task of keeping track of the growing number of Web sites around the world. The Web finally had its virtual librarian.

At first that was a task that he could manage on his own, but the work soon became too much for one person to handle. 'Every few months the number of servers would double,' remembers Secret, 'everything doubled!' So he hit upon the idea of delegating. 'Lou Montulli contacted me,' he remembers, 'and said, "There's a history professor at my university who might be able to help you."' So Kansas took over responsibility for classifying the historical sites in the Virtual Library. Soon Secret had a network of volunteers helping him to maintain the Virtual Library, which for a while was the most important way of finding information on the Web. Soon, however, it would give way to commercial directories and search engines pioneered by two Stanford University graduate students Jerry Yang and David Filo. Starting life as a pooling of their bookmarks, towards the end of 1994 Yahoo! was valued in the millions. 'When I see now the sums that Yahoo has made,' sighs Secret, 'well, we were well positioned.' But he was talking about time, not geography. By 1994, the centre of gravity of the World Wide Web had crossed the Atlantic to a place where the entrepreneurial heart beats stronger. No one at CERN had even thought of cashing in on the Virtual Library and by the time Secret himself tried to set up a company around it, he had missed the boat by a very long way.

The arena or the market place

When the Scandinavians started to arrive, Arthur Secret became a bit of a novelty in the Web team at CERN. With the exception of Secret, they were all serious heads-down-in-the-bits computer programmers. Henrik Frystyk Nielsen turned up in February 1994 and spent a year working on libwww. He was joined soon after by Håkon Lie, whom Secret remembers catching fast asleep in his office at 5 a.m. one day. He had been living there for the last few months, only sleeping when he was too tired to work. Lie had been a geek for almost as long as he can remember and he was proud of it. 'I was 15 when I touched my first computer. That was in 1980,' he recounts. 'And you know, from the moment I sat down I realized this was going to change my life.'

Seeing HTML for the first time was a similar revelation, and he resolved to get to CERN somehow. So he scanned www-talk for jobs, and when Robert Cailliau announced there was something called an Associateship on offer, he applied and got it. An Associateship wasn't a real position—it was a kind of short-term detachment whereby you would keep your own job and CERN would top up your salary—but it showed that the laboratory's management was beginning to think that perhaps this Web thing was worth some more resources after all. When he arrived at CERN, Lie's pet subject was document presentation and in particular separating the presentation from the structure. There is a fine line between what constitutes structure and what constitutes style. A heading is a structural element of a document, for example, and HTML has tags for headings <H1> and subheadings <H2>, <H3>, but whether your heading appears in 12-point bold underlined Times font or 15-point Helvetica is a question of style. Moreover, you might want a different style for the screen, where bigger characters make text easier to read, than for a good-quality printed output where smaller characters might be just as readable. Developing standards that set the dividing line between presentation and structure is just as important as defining a DTD for HTML. Without it, people could just go off producing tags for style as well as structure and you could end up with several versions of HTML and several different browsers to view each one. Soon after Lie arrived, that started to happen. The Web didn't have any formal standards body or procedures, and HTML started to fracture. Web pages began to appear bearing the label 'Best viewed with such and such a browser', which was a big worry for Tim. 'Anyone who slaps a "this page is best viewed with Browser X" label on a Web page,' he wrote in 1996, 'appears to be yearning for the bad old days, before the Web, when you had very little chance of reading a document written on another computer, another word processor, or another network.'

Soon there would be a 'Viewable with any browser' campaign, launched by the purists, and Tim Berners-Lee himself would be heading an International World Wide Web Consortium to keep the Web free and open. But at the beginning of 1994, there was just Håkon Lie at CERN working on style sheets, recipes that could be applied to other documents and that determined how, for example, an <H1> heading should be presented. He wasn't working entirely alone, however; there was still Dan Connolly, the person who had first pointed out that HTML needed to be standardized if the Web was to grow in any sensible way, and there was an Englishman working at Hewlett Packard's laboratories in Bristol.

Dave Raggett was an Oxford-educated physicist like Tim Berners-Lee. He had gone up to Oxford in 1972, stayed on for a doctorate in astrophysics, and eventually wound up in Bristol after a stint of artificial intelligence research in Edinburgh. Raggett shared the same concerns as Dan Connolly about the non-standard nature of HTML, but the two hadn't had much to do with each other before they met at the first Web Conference at CERN in May 1994. 'It didn't become clear to me until I met him,' recalls Connolly, 'but he had all sorts of stuff he was thinking about and he would only spend a little bit of time writing it down for other people to look at, so if you just judged his work by the quality of the writing you sort of went, "Jeez, this guy isn't very serious, is he?"'

But Raggett certainly was serious, even if he came at HTML with a different perspective from Connolly. 'We sort of had to learn to appreciate each other's work,' says Connolly. 'He and I, throughout this design process of HTML, have always been the extremes,' he explains. 'I was always the minimalist, you know, you can get it done without that.' Raggett, on the other hand, wanted to expand everything. He had been working on a hypertext system of his own at Hewlett Packard and the company had implemented it for commercial use. 'It was used by sales staff,' says Raggett, 'to create quotes for HP's computer systems in response to telephone enquiries.'

Dave Raggett found out about the Web when he posted a proposal of his own for a networked hypertext system to alt.hypertext in 1992 and was soon directed to the work already in progress at CERN. His first impression was that the Web was becoming a purely academic tool. He wanted to add features and beef up the presentation to make it suitable for commercial use. 'Tim showed little apparent interest in these issues and, in my opinion, was out of touch with the commercial world,' he says. Nevertheless, Raggett recognized the potential of the Web and was soon on a plane to Geneva with his boss to discuss the possibility of spending a year at CERN with Tim Berners-Lee and Robert Cailliau. Robert remembers the meeting well. 'Knowing Tim,' he recounts, 'I felt that a demo of the Web by him might go into too much technical detail. I knew I had to get to Tim's office before they arrived.' But Robert hadn't counted on the plane arriving early, and when he got to Tim's office, Raggett and his boss were already there. 'There were Tim and Dave,' says Robert, ' almost hugging the NeXT screen, talking bits and bytes at light speed and Dave's boss dozing off in a corner.' But Robert's fears proved to be unfounded, and for a while it looked as though Raggett's secondment would go through. An administrative hiccup eventually put paid to that, however, and Raggett had to collaborate at a distance. 'We don't know what we may have missed there,' says Robert.

Dave Raggett essentially picked up where Dan Connolly had left off. Connolly had steered HTML towards being a real DTD, and that gave Raggett a solid foundation from which to develop it further. He started to lead the global effort on HTML and eventually came up with the HTML 3.0 specification. His work took him to CERN from time to time and during a visit in the second half of 1994 he brought with him an X-browser he had been working on. Mosaic may have been fine for most users of the Web, but for Raggett, who wanted to test all kinds of extensions to HTML, Mosaic wasn't enough. When he arrived with his new browser, it turned out to be just what Lie had been looking to test his style sheets. Raggett's browser was the first to have text flowing around pictures, background textures instead of just plain white, tables, and mathematical equations. In short, it was the perfect test bed for new Web features. Raggett and Lie started to work on it together, and they decided that it needed a name. They called it Arena, 'which doesn't really mean much,' says Lie, 'but we wanted to have a name.' Arena was the forum in which tables first made their Web appearance as Raggett developed his HTML 3.0. It also checked every page it displayed to make sure that it was valid HTML. When Tim's World Wide Web Consortium got off the ground, Arena would become its official test bed, but before that it had another role to play.

The name may not have meant much to Raggett and Lie, but to Arthur Secret, it reeked of elitism. Because his head was not down in the bits, Secret perhaps more than anyone had his finger on the pulse of who was actually using the Web, and more importantly, who wasn't. The number of computers on the Internet may have passed the two million mark at the beginning of 1994, when the number of Web servers was still under 1 000, but two million is a small number set against the population of the world, and most network users only had access to the Web by e-mail. Secret decided that he would have one more go at programming for the Web and produce a service for getting Web pages by e-mail. When it came to finding a name, Secret consulted his grandmother, a highly cultured lady with an interest in etymology. He wanted a name that would be the opposite of the elitism he saw in Arena. 'Well then, it has to be Agora,' said granny. Where an arena is a place the well-heeled go for entertainment, the agora was a market square, a common meeting place for everyone.

Secret was pleased with his creation and released it on to the Internet, where it was immediately seized upon by the disenfranchised e-mail-only denizens of the net. The way it worked was that you would e-mail a URL to Agora, which in turn would get that page from wherever it was on the Web and e-mail it back to you. Because Agora ran on a CERN computer, it would not only receive and reply to requests for documents from CERN's server, but it would also do all the fetching and sending of documents from all over the world. This meant that it could generate an enormous amount of Internet traffic for whoever was running the Agora service. When Agora was released, CERN's traffic rose dramatically and the laboratory developed a touch of Agoraphobia. 'What happened,' explains Secret, 'is that I started to develop far too much e-mail when compared to CERN's total e-mail volume and then it saturated the machine and they asked me to stop.' So as a popular uprising Agora was not the greatest of successes, but it still has its followers. 'I still get e-mails from this woman in Argentina,' said Mike Sendall, one of the original Agoraphobes, 'saying that she still uses Agora!'

Up, up, and away!

With Pei Wei busily developing his ViolaWWW browser at O'Reilly and Associates, the California-based publishing house was starting to take a keen interest in the World Wide Web. O'Reilly caters for geeks, specializing in books about Unix, X, and the Internet, and it was vital to their credibility that they maintained an image at the cutting edge. O'Reilly wanted to be the first publisher on the Web, and by employing Pei Wei they had made sure they would be. In September 1992, they brought out a book called *The Whole Internet User's Guide and Catalog* that rapidly became the network newcomer's bible. It contained articles about the origins of the network and descriptions of all the different protocols and how to use them, as well as descriptions of all the resources available on the Net. And buried within its 376 pages was one short chapter about the World Wide Web. One of Pei Wei's tasks had been to produce an electronic version of *The Whole Internet* in Viola and that quickly led to other things. O'Reilly aimed to position itself as a pioneer in online publishing, and on 1 October 1993 launched the Global Network Navigator, GNN, which it described as a free Internet-based information centre. GNN had regularly updated news pages to keep its readers abreast of events on the Net and the people who used it. It had a quarterly magazine with features and reviews of places to visit on the Net. There was a digital art gallery, a marketplace where companies could advertise, and there was the electronic version of *The Whole Internet.* Their logo was a hot air balloon with a map of the world on it, drifting off the top of the screen.

A prime mover behind GNN was Dale Dougherty, the same man who had hired Pei Wei in the first place. A couple of months before GNN was launched, he had sounded out the World Wide Web by organizing a meeting for Web developers in Boston. It seemed as though everyone who was anyone was there among the twenty-five or so people who turned up. Tim Berners-Lee had come over from CERN, and NCSA turned out in force. Pei Wei was there, as was Tom Bruce from Cornell and Lou Montulli and Michael Grobe from Kansas.

This was the first occasion that everyone who had been working on the Web had had to meet face to face, and Grobe looks back on it as the 'zeroth' World Wide Web Conference. They discussed where the Web was going and all agreed that some kind of coordination was needed. At one point, Berners-Lee scribbled 'Club Web' up on the whiteboard as a sort of embodiment of the kind of organization he foresaw steering the Web to maturity. Nothing was settled that day, but the message Tim took back to CERN was that the need for some kind of steering body was rapidly becoming urgent. It wouldn't be long before he acted.

The infomercial begins

O'Reilly and Associates weren't the only ones to be putting up exciting new Web sites in 1993. With the Web spreading rapidly and with the

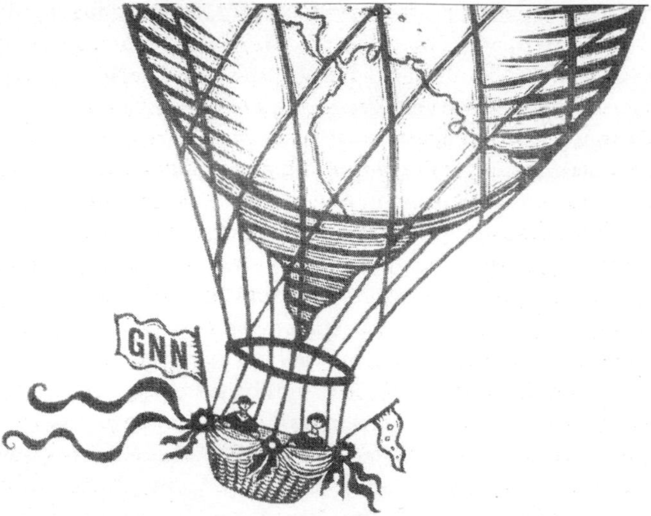

Figure 25: The GNN Logo.

advent of inline images, all sorts of people started to experiment with this new medium. There was a 'Web Louvre', where you could see digital versions of famous works of art, until the site's creator was obliged to close it down. 'A good story of missed opportunity,' believes Robert Cailliau. 'The correct action would have been to hire him rather than discourage him.' There was a hypertext version of an exhibition that the Vatican had lent to the US Library of Congress. Xerox PARC had a server that would deliver you a map in response to a click, and one Norwegian family turned their home into a Web site. There were articles about each member of the family and what they were up to, and you could click your way from room to room around the house. For years, owner Børre Ludvigsen could rightly maintain that the only other person with an interactive house on the Web was Bill Clinton.

One site that particularly impressed Robert Cailliau was put up by a commercial art student at Honolulu Community College. As a teenager, Kevin Hughes's goal was to become an industrial designer, worrying about such problems as how to make VCRs that anyone can programme or fridge doors that work equally well for left- and right-handed people. His master plan was to take an engineering degree at Berkeley followed by a course at art school in Pasadena, but that was not quite how it went. In 1989, he went up to Berkeley as planned. 'And I hated it,' he says. 'I decided to spend some time with my grandparents in Hawaii.' Industrial design was still on the agenda, because Honolulu Community College's commercial art courses had a good reputation, but it was going to be a longer route to Pasadena.

The college was on the university's main Manoa Valley campus where over two decades before, Norm Abramson had set up the ALOHANET to communicate with outlying campuses and research stations. The problems of keeping in touch were still high on the university's agenda, and soon Hughes was given the job of looking for tools on the Internet that could be used for on-line learning. He plugged himself into newsgroups and mailing lists and eventually a message landed on his computer saying, 'You should try out this program Mosaic, it looks really cool, check it out.' So he did. 'And the system was purporting to be this distributed multimedia thing and yet it was just text on a grey background,' he remembers. 'Very uninspiring.' He found his way to the CERN Virtual Library. 'And it was a very boring list,' he says, 'mathematics divisions of technical libraries and physicists and research papers.' He went to almost every site in the Virtual Library only to find more of the same boring text on a grey background. One Web site even just consisted of a link saying 'Welcome to our World Wide Web site, please click here to go to our gopher site.'

Thanks to the <IMG> tag that Marc Andreessen had proposed in February 1993, Web site designers had the potential to make their Web sites look more like glossy magazines, but no one had done that yet. Kevin Hughes decided to be the first. 'I went to my boss,' he explains, 'and said I'd like to try making a campus-wide information system out of this.' He started by making on-line versions of student and faculty publications, and he wandered around the campus with a camera taking pictures to build a virtual tour. And then he came across Rick Ziegler, who was responsible for a dinosaur exhibition that the university was holding, and asked if he could produce an interactive on-line version. The two of them wandered around the exhibition, Hughes holding a tape recorder while Ziegler described the exhibits. When that was over, Hughes transferred the tape to his computer and split it up into soundbites. On the finished dinosaur Web site, there were little pictures of the exhibits with explanatory paragraphs beside them. You could click on the picture to get a bigger version, or click on a little speaker icon to hear Ziegler's description of the exhibit. There were navigation buttons for going backwards and forwards, and there was even a movie. That is all common fare nowadays, but in 1993 it was a big change from plain text on a grey background.

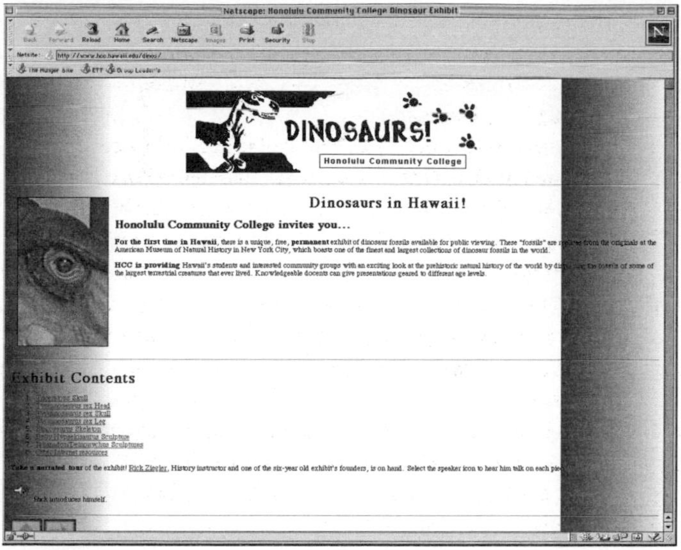

Figure 26: At http://www.hcc.hawaii.edu/dinos/dinos.1.html, Kevin Hughes' Dinosaur exhibit at Honolulu Community College is still a popular site on the World Wide Web.

Robert Cailliau was not the only one to be impressed with Kevin Hughes's dinosaur exhibit. The day Hughes turned on the server, people started coming to it from all over the world. 'Someday someone's going to write a book about this,' he thought as he checked the server's log files later that evening from his Macintosh at home. The site soon made it into a 'What's New' list that NCSA had set up on its server. 'At one point, one of the versions of Mosaic had Honolulu Community College hard-wired in one of its menus,' remembers Hughes, 'one of the hot places to go!' For Robert Cailliau, Hughes's dinosaurs might well have been the clincher that day in Brussels when he was trying to convince the European Union to fund the Web. He had not made much headway in explaining to his Brussels contacts what the Web was all about. 'So I proposed something very unusual,' he explains, 'to hold the next project meeting at the computing centre of the Vrije Universiteit Brussel.' The demonstration was a success and Robert's WISE project was duly funded.

Soon after, Hughes had a call from a small startup company called Enterprise Integration Technologies (EIT) in Palo Alto. The offer of a real salary proved too tempting, and soon after he was back in California, as the company's webmaster. It wasn't long before he started thinking about that book, but instead of going into print it seemed much more appropriate to set up a new Web site at http://www.web-history.org to chronicle the history of the World Wide Web. He never did get to Pasadena.

Another early Web site that caught the world's attention in a big way was set up by a small Norwegian company called Oslonett to cover the 1994 Lillehammer Winter Olympics. 'That demonstrated how a site can get overloaded,' remembers Tim Berners-Lee. When it was founded in 1991, Oslonett was Norway's first Internet company. 'We offered e-mail services to start with,' explains Steinar Kjærnsrød, one of the company's founders, and in 1993 they were planning to expand into the World Wide Web. The Winter Olympic Games gave them the ideal publicity opportunity. They signed a deal with Sun Microsystems, which was one of the game's sponsors, and with Norwegian TV, to put up a live results service along with pictures of the events. Two weeks into the Olympics, the Oslonett server and a 'mirror' at Sun in California had been accessed 1.3 million times by users on something between 20 000 and 30 000 computers in 42 countries. Oslonett had got the publicity it wanted, but one of the games' other sponsors was not at all amused. After shelling out to be a main sponsor of the games, IBM didn't like the glory that rival company Sun was getting on the cheap. 'They tried to stop it,' remembers Kjærnsrød, 'but it was completely legal, we'd made sure it was legal!'

With sites like GNN, Honolulu Community College, and the Lillehammer Olympics, the Web was entering the mainstream. Just before Christmas 1994, Robert Cailliau found himself in a surreal meeting with Mark McCahill in the departure lounge of Washington Dulles airport. He had just bought himself a piece of Americana to take home for Christmas. 'Ahh, but I have such fond memories of the strange irony of gopher and the Web joining hands to drag a plastic Christmas tree through the airport,' says McCahill. 'I think in a symbolic way it anticipated the Internet turning into the world's largest continuously running infomercial.' And if any further evidence were needed that that was where the Web was going, Mike Sendall used to joke about the Iceberg lettuce he had bought in the latter half of 1993. It came from Salinas, California, and its wrapper carried a URL. 'This must be it, it must have spread everywhere if it's on lettuce wrappers,' he told Robert. The very next day, that early networking pioneer, the Queen of England, opened her own Web site. The infomercial was about to begin.

Mozilla

Over the coming years, the Web was to win many awards, but one of the first went to Marc Andreessen and Eric Bina in 1994 for developing Mosaic. It was delivered by none other than Ethernet inventor Bob Metcalfe, who by this time had redefined himself as *InfoWorld* magazine's technology pundit. It was *InfoWorld*'s Industry Achievement award for 1993 that he went to Illinois to deliver, but he had some difficulty figuring out whom he should deliver it to. Metcalfe wanted the names of the five or so key players. 'And the University of Illinois refused,' he recalls. 'They gave me a list of 40 names!' Unknown to Metcalfe, tension had been rising for some time between the developers and the management at NCSA, and he had arrived just as it was coming to a head. 'A lot has to do with taking the credit for Mosaic,' explains Dave Thompson. 'While NCSA gave credit to NCSA as an organization, the developers preferred individual credit.'

Joseph Hardin was the person who had refused to give Metcalfe just a handful of names. 'We always looked upon it as a group effort,' he says, 'and as the head of the group, I was always interested in giving as much credit as possible to everybody who worked on it, including the Mac and PC people and all the support people who answered the phones and kept the servers running.' But that is not quite the way the developers saw things. In the early days, they were pretty much left to their own devices, 'and we liked it that way,' remembers Jon Mittelhauser. But as soon as Mosaic started to take off, things changed. 'We suddenly found ourselves in meetings with forty people planning our next features, as opposed to the five of us making plans at 2.00 a.m. over pizzas and Cokes. Aleks, who had basically done the Mac version, suddenly found that there were three or four other people working on it with him, according to NCSA. And they were, like, his bosses, telling him what to do and stuff. And how can I put this politely? We didn't think that any of them had Aleks' ability or foresight.'

Things really started to go awry when the *New York Times* got hold of Mosaic in December 1993. The newspaper's business section carried a big spread about Mosaic along with an equally big picture of Joseph Hardin and Larry Smarr, without a developer in sight. It was the newspaper that chose the photograph, but the damage was done. Andreessen was offered a job at NCSA when he graduated, but he turned it down and chose instead to try his luck in California. He took with him a share of *InfoWorld*'s award. 'Eventually I just put Andreessen and Bina as award recipients,' says Metcalfe, 'and alluded to the team effort at the University of Illinois. And then I gave a lecture to the University of Illinois and I said, "You should be happy, your job is to create people like Marc and send them off into the world!"'

Andreessen's first job was at EIT, the company that had lured Kevin Hughes back to the mainland, but he didn't stay there for long. On 19 April 1994, he was expected at a meeting organized by Bebo White at SLAC to discuss Web browsers. 'We had Tony Johnson, we had Pei Wei, and we also had via telephone Tom Bruce, the Cello guy,' explains White. The idea was that the developers of the most important Web browsers around would briefly discuss the features of their browsers and then go on to consider future directions Web browsers could take. EIT was just down the road from SLAC, so Andreessen didn't have far to go, but he got a more pressing invitation that day. 'He called and cancelled,' explains White, 'because he was having lunch that day with Jim Clark.'

Jim Clark was already a Silicon Valley legend. On the back of a chip he had invented while a lecturer at Stanford in the 1970s, he had set up a company called Silicon Graphics (SGI) which made powerful Unix workstations. Thirteen years later, in January 1994, and with a considerably healthier bank balance, he had left SGI and was on the lookout for new ideas. He was toying with the idea of starting a company to build a games network when a friend put him in touch with Marc Andreessen. They met a few times in Palo Alto's Café Verona, and eventually hit on the idea of setting up an Internet company to develop Web software and hiring the Mosaic team to do it. Andreessen sent off an e-mail to his former colleagues at NCSA telling them he was coming back to Urbana-Champaign with Jim Clark and a business proposition. Lou Montulli got the e-mail too, and jumped on a plane to Illinois. That evening, Clark and Andreessen outlined their business plan. It was pretty straightforward. They would do Mosaic all over again, but this time they would do it better; they would make a Mosaic-killer.

Soon after, the Mosaic Communications Corporation was in business, with the core of the NCSA Mosaic team once again hacking away at all hours of the day and night. The new company had established itself in Mountain View, and the developers all worked in one big room under the watchful gaze of Mozilla the Mosaic-Killer, a huge green Godzilla-like character who was the company's mascot. It was just like the old days for the developers. Pretty soon they had made browsers that were much faster than Mosaic had ever been, and then the challenge became to outdo each other. By and large, the old hands from NCSA got the same jobs they had had in Illinois. Jon Mittelhauser worked on the PC version and Aleks Totic on the Mac. 'And so we'd be there real late one night and we'd get something working,' remembers Mittelhauser. 'And Aleks would come in the next day and we'd go, "Ha, ha, look what we did," and we'd got images working. And so we'd go home and go to sleep. He's got to get images working now before he goes home or he's not going to be able to sleep.' It was high pressure, but they thrived on it, and by 13 October they were ready to release the first versions of their browsers. The developers put all three versions of Mosaic Netscape, Unix, Mac, and PC, up for FTP download and sat back to see what would happen. Time passed. 'And it was five minutes and we're sitting there. Nothing has happened,' explains Mittelhauser. 'And all of a sudden the first download happened. It was a guy from Japan. We swore we'd send him a T shirt!' But in the excitement, nobody thought to write down who it was. 'So there's some guy who we owe a T shirt to and obviously probably about 200 million people will claim it was them!' After a while, they decided to keep the spirit of competition alive by keeping a count of how many copies of each version were taken. They set up the servers to sound a bell when a copy of the Macintosh version was taken, the sound of an explosion for the Unix version, and a cow mooing for the PC version. 'So we're sitting here and there's downloads flying by and there's all these sounds going off. Finally the servers were crashing and too many people were coming and stuff, and finally morning came along and we just stumbled out of there and went home,' remembers Mittelhauser. 'It was a fun night, though.'

The developers may have been having the time of their lives, but the friction with NCSA was by no means over. The University of Illinois had been selling licenses for Mosaic, and one of the takers was Spyglass, the company that NCSA had spun off in 1990. Spyglass had paid $2 million for the name and the technology, and were none too happy that the original developers were setting themselves up with the name Mosaic in California. To them, it looked as though Mosaic Communications Corporation had taken a product for which Spyglass held the license, and was planning to launch it in competition with their own product. Clark remembers getting a strongly worded letter demanding that he change his company's name and stop distributing Mosaic Netscape. 'Fine,' he thought, 'I'll change the name.' But there was no way he was going to stop people downloading. He had made sure that his developers had really started from scratch so that no trace of the original Mosaic code would get into his company's browsers. 'I paid for the writing of this code,' he decided, 'I choose what I'm going to do with it.' So Mosaic

Communications Corporation became Netscape Communications Corporation, and the Netscape browser quickly went on to capture an estimated 95 per cent of the browser market.

NCSA and Netscape came to a settlement. Spyglass carved out a tidy little niche for itself, producing slimmed-down browsers for devices like telephones and pagers. And Netscape went on to have the most publicized launch on Wall Street ever, its stock tripling in value overnight when the company was floated in August 1995. NCSA is never likely to find itself with a Marc Andreessen Chair of Computer Science, but Joseph Hardin maintains that the university's position was always reasonable. They had licensed the software, after all, and as they saw it all they were trying to do was protect their licensees. 'Jim Clark's position on this was that NCSA was trying to stop them from developing. I don't think that was the case,' explains Hardin. 'The university and NCSA were just trying to realize some of the value.' He believed that the more browsers there were on the market, the better, and that three was the absolute minimum required. 'My position was to have as many successes as possible,' he says, adding that 'with only two browsers it's just a slug-fest'. In the light of what has happened since, it is hard to disagree. Rumour has it that the undisclosed settlement included stock options in Netscape, but the university chose cash instead. They might have realized more of the value if they hadn't.

With the battles behind them, Netscape could concentrate on carving out an unassailable position for itself in the Web market. When Jim Clark first met Marc Andreessen, Web traffic was at number eleven in the Internet charts. By the time the first version of Mosaic Netscape was released, it had moved up to number five, and in April 1995 the Web reached number one with over a fifth of all of Internet traffic, overhauling the long-time leader, FTP. The Internet was spreading like wildfire, and it was the Web that was driving it. Netscape's Navigator browser was still the number one, but the young company was having to gear up for another battle. Software giant Microsoft launched its Web browser, Explorer, developed using Mosaic technology licensed from Spyglass, in August 1995. Like the US satellite of the same name launched in 1958, Explorer came second, but it remains to be seen whether it will suffer the same fate as its pioneering namesake and get lost in the mists of time.

With the NCSA problem safely dispatched, the Netscape team set about improving their original product. Not all of the changes were a universal success. Chriss Neuss, a developer from Darmstadt, remembers one in particular that has entered the folklore of the Internet. 'The cross-Atlantic link during the daytime was completely unusable,' he remembers. 'And that was because Netscape, in order to load pages faster, would start off simultaneous TCP connections. The network would get saturated by TCP "open" packets, so without transferring any real information you would get a totally overloaded network, and that of course is a very, very bad design. Opening parallel TCP connections is really something you should not do, and the HTTP technicians still call this "marca mode"' (marca was Marc Andreessen's name on e-mail). Other Netscape innovations achieved notoriety for a variety of reasons, and one person in particular was behind the most notorious.

Like the NCSA team, Lou Montulli had accepted Jim Clark's job offer, but not being part of the original NCSA team, he had devoted his effort to general concepts rather than building the X, PC, or Mac version of Navigator. At the trivial end of the spectrum came 'The Amazing Fishcam'. The Netscape offices had a tropical fish tank, and Montulli had the idea of pointing a camera at it and posting a fresh picture of the fish on the Web every few minutes. The Amazing Fishcam site also gave descriptions of all the fish in the tank (it is still out there at http://www.netscape.com/fishcam/fishcam.html). But it was not the first camera on the Web. That honour belongs to a bevy of computer scientists at Cambridge University. Computer scientists had, of course, been among the Web's first users, and these had quickly realized the real potential of the new medium. They shared a common coffee pot that resided in a place dubbed 'the Trojan room', next door to the Titan room and just around the corner from Sleepy Hollow in the University's computer labs. Computer scientists were spending a lot of valuable time trudging down to the Trojan room only to find an empty coffee pot. The obvious solution was to point a camera at it so they could see from their browsers whether the walk was worth their while. Of course, the Web didn't solve the problem of who would actually make the coffee, but it did prevent a lot of wasted journeys. Montulli's Fishcam rose to fame in the United States through the David Letterman show, but Montulli is happy to give credit where credit's due. Had he heard about the Trojan room coffee pot? 'Oh, I knew about it at the time,' he readily admits.

Montulli's other early contributions to Netscape both gave rise to lengthy polemics. Most people agree that 'cookies', or something like them, are necessary, but opinions are much more divided when it come to his <BLINK> tag. Cookies are a way of storing information about what you have been doing on the Web. They are essential for things like shopping on the Web, because as you jump backwards and forwards through a shopping site filling up a virtual shopping basket, it is a cookie that will keep track of what you have been filling it with. The problem with cookies, however, is that they are behind the scenes so you can't see exactly what they are doing. That made some people nervous. 'You wouldn't believe the things I've had attributed to cookies,' says Montulli. 'I got a cookie and Microsoft Word stopped working,' was one. 'Cookies gave out my credit card number,' was another common complaint. But nevertheless, cookies have become the standard way of storing information about what you do on the Web. 'We actually did spend quite a bit of time trying to make sure that cookies did not reveal too much about you and didn't violate your security in any fundamental way,' says Montulli. Nevertheless, in later versions of Navigator he had to bow to pressure and build in a feature that allowed cookies to be switched off. All browsers these days allow you to reject cookies, but if you try to do any Internet shopping or newspaper reading with cookies off, you probably won't get very far.

The <BLINK> tag, which made a piece of text blink on and off, was interpreted by some as another reason why a steering body for the World Wide Web was needed. 'I think that's pretty funny,' says Montulli, who had implemented 'blink' because it was something he had come across when writing Lynx using the curses system. 'The only curses feature that Navigator didn't use up to this point was the blinking attribute,' he laughs. 'And therefore what we really needed was the blink tag, because that way it would be perfectly compatible with Lynx.' They didn't announce the blink tag. 'It was kind of an Easter egg in the product,' says Montulli, 'everybody just found it, right?'

Not everyone, however, liked what they found. Curses was a system designed for cursors, and whilst it is perfectly acceptable for cursors to blink on and off, some people found blinking text a bit much. 'The <BLINK> tag caused a real outcry from the Web developers and the purists,' says Robert Cailliau, '<BLINK> text was a real eye-sore. It appeared everywhere, every author used it, and every reader hated it.' For Tim Berners-Lee, the problem was not so much with the blinking text itself, but the fact that it had just appeared with no reference to any standardization procedure. He was beginning to think about how to set up some kind of consortium and the <BLINK> tag provided another argument for doing so. 'The consortium was not needed because the blink tag was not a good idea,' he explains. 'The consortium was needed if one person did blink and another person did flash.'

The real problem wasn't whether you liked it or not. After all, blinking text was nothing new; years earlier it had been one of the things bequeathed to Oxford physics graduate students in the 'Johnson hangovers' folder on the Oxford VAX computer. The real problem was that it had more to do with presentation than with structure. <BLINK> was accompanied by <I> and <B> for italic and bold face, features that should have been in style sheets and not HTML. Netscape's success was all the more reason to get some kind of standards organization for the Web going without delay.

Last days of empire

As time wore on, it became clear just how big the Web was going to be, and that it would need considerably more support than CERN had been able to give it. The crunch would come in 1994, but the signs were already there. At 400 000 bytes per second, the Web was carrying the equivalent of an Agatha Christie novel around the world every second of every day, and that was just the beginning.

Back at CERN, Eric van Herwijnen, the laboratory's SGML guru and the man who had built up the ill-fated CERNDOC system when big mainframe computers still ruled the roost, had left CERN to set up an Internet company in the neighbouring region of France. 'We were the first Internet Service Provider in the Pays de Gex,' he says proudly. Van Herwijnen and his partner had grand designs for their new company. 'We were going to do the Web in a Box,' says van Herwijnen, 'make a server, browser, you know, shrink-wrap it, package the lot for the PC and sell it.' They even offered Tim Berners-Lee a job. 'We offered him 30 per cent of our shares,' says van Herwijnen, 'but unfortunately Tim was too busy.' Berners-Lee had steered his vision of a free and open World Wide Web this far, and he was not about to cash in now and watch it break up into myriad proprietary protocols. In the end, however, van Herwijnen's efforts came to nought; he sold out to another local Internet Service Provider and went back to CERN. His timing was right, but he was in the wrong place. Europe simply wasn't ready. Van Herwijnen might have had a healthy dose of the entrepreneurial spirit, but the support he needed to get started wasn't there, and nor were the potential clients. They were all in America.

In April 1993, pushed on by Tim Berners-Lee and Robert Cailliau, CERN issued a statement putting the Web software in the public domain. By this time, Tim had gone one step further even than the GNU public license and CERN's statement carried no strings other than that CERN be given a mention whenever the code was used. The year 1993 was also when CERN caught up with SLAC and put its preprints on the Web. An up-and-coming Scotsman by the name of Mick Draper had taken over the project from Eric van Herwijnen when he had left to set up his company. At the time, the CERN preprint server used the SGML-based hypertext system DynaText marketed by Electronic Book Technologies, the company that had been spun off by Brown University, but Draper was soon convinced that the Web was a better way to go. By the following year, his team was serving CERN preprints up over the Web.

The last of the CERN Web recruits, Ari Luotonen, arrived at CERN in August 1993. He quickly established himself as a real programming wizard. Robert even remembers Henrik Frystyk Nielsen saying that Tim should just describe the ideas to Ari and let him do the programming. He worked on things like access protection so that you could ask for password access to a Web site, and something called a proxy server that makes Web use faster for most people without them even knowing it.

Robert had hired Luotonen after noticing that some of the early CERN collaborations that had been using the Web were beginning to desert it. They were not prepared to use the Web for their documentation unless they could protect it from the prying eyes of other physicists. 'The Web was doomed inside CERN,' he explains, 'unless that feature was established.' So Robert asked for resources to hire a programmer to implement it, and this time CERN was forthcoming. Finland had recently joined CERN, so Robert thought that might make a good hunting ground. 'I was invited to Finland in January 1993,' he remembers, 'and at Tampere University of Technology, with a temperature of minus 17°C outside, I found an interested team who were going to pick a star student for the job.' Ari Luotonen arrived in August, Robert explained the problem, and gave him six months to deliver. 'But in the middle of September it was ready,' exclaims Robert, and the star student moved on to other things. Basing his ideas on a concept called caching, Luotonen came up with the idea of the proxy server. A cache takes its name from the French verb *cacher*, to hide, and that is exactly what it does. Most Web browsers have a cache of documents that you have accessed recently so that if you want to go back to them, you don't have to fetch them across the network again. Luotonen took the idea a step further. He realized that in a big organization like CERN, everyone's caches might be holding the same documents, which was not very efficient. By allowing browsers to appoint a proxy, somewhere like CERN could be made to look like one, very active, browser to the outside world and everyone's recently accessed pages could sit on what he called the proxy server.

The idea of proxying went on to become crucial for the development of the Web. It is what allows organizations to screen incoming traffic, hiding their internal computers from the outside world. One day Robert Cailliau remembers Luotonen coming to ask if he could leave his contract early. 'Someone made you a job offer?' asked Robert. 'Yes, Netscape,' came the reply. 'There was of course no objection,' said Robert later. 'Ari had more than delivered! The only thing I impressed on him was to be sure that Netscape included a clause in his contract allowing him to go back to Finland and finish his degree in engineering. I was not so sure of the long-term future of these start-ups. Netscape did, and Ari was off to Silicon Valley.'

By the time he got there the Web was approaching the most critical stage of its existence. Netscape wasn't the only company marketing browsers and servers; giants like Microsoft were also limbering up to enter the fray. In 1994, it was as if several opposing teams were preparing to square off but there was no referee in sight. The need for a recognized arbiter of Web standards was becoming urgent if the Web was not to break up into so many fragments. Making sure that body came into being would be Tim Berners-Lee's next move. 'Time was slipping away,' he explains. 'During 1993 HTML was fragmented, during 1994 it was getting ridiculous.'

8 It's Official

Even before NCSA released the Mosaic browsers, the Web had begun to make its presence felt beyond the realms of particle physics. Web traffic overhauled WAIS in early 1993, by which time it was rising tenfold every few months. Companies, individuals, and government institutions were all putting up Web sites. By the end of the year even the White House had one, and everyone looked to Tim Berners-Lee at CERN for guidance. The world at large had the impression that there was a big, well-organized team at CERN looking after Web matters, but the reality couldn't have been more different. 'There were still just two staff members working on the Web,' remembers Robert Cailliau, 'and we were still in different divisions.' Tim and Robert were supported by their enthusiastic band of followers on temporary contracts, but the fact of the matter was that CERN had created something it didn't quite know how to handle. The Web had brought the laboratory into contact with a world it didn't normally have to deal with, and the result was not always plain sailing. For Tim, however, his vision had to come above all else, and as 1993 wore on, he decided that the crunch had come for CERN. Either the laboratory had to put serious resources into the Web, or the Web would have to find a new home.

Too hot to handle

While Tim Berners-Lee was winning over the hearts and minds of the international physics community, things were happening in America that were to change the course of Web history. The ideal that the Internet should be non-commercial was slowly being eroded, and in 1991 legislation preventing the commercial use of the Internet was dropped. One of the first companies to start using the Web commercially was Hewlett Packard, the computer manufacturer. HP had many customers in academia and they had tentatively asked whether they could offer customer support over the network, things like software updates and customer service. HP's request seems innocuous enough now, but at the time it was against the rules. When HP got the answer 'yes', the door to commercialization of the Internet opened a crack. With the 1991 legislation, it was thrown wide open. By 1994, CommerceNet had blazed a trail for today's Amazon-dot-coms and e-bays to follow. FirstVirtual had pioneered payment over the Net, and Pizza Hut had famously opened a Web site where you could order home delivery pizza on-line.

On the political front, Vice-President Al Gore, the son of the man behind America's network of Interstate highways, was taking a leaf out of his father's book and turning the Internet into what he called the Information Superhighway through the National Information Infrastructure initiative. Internet access was coming to schools and homes around the country faster than ever before. One big winner was Cisco, the company whose products years earlier had allowed Daniel Karrenberg to plant Trojan horses for TCP/IP around Europe. Cisco's founder, Len Bosack, had been bought out in 1990 for the tidy sum of $170 million. Three years after Gore's initiative, however, Cisco was valued at a whopping $3 billion. Whilst all this was going on, a dream was maturing in the mind of Michael Dertouzos, Director of MIT's Laboratory for Computer Science (MIT/LCS), which had evolved from J. C. R. Licklider's Project MAC.

The son of a Greek Admiral, Dertouzos grew up in Europe during the war. He excelled at school and after a spell in the Greek navy left for the United States on a Fulbright scholarship in 1954. 'I wanted to go to MIT,' he recalls, 'but so did everyone else and there was no room. Instead, I was sent to the University of Arkansas, which is Senator Fulbright's state. It was a marvellous way to enter America, far better than through an urban metropolis like Boston or New York which were similar to my home town, Athens, Greece, and less representative of this huge country.' A bachelor's degree at Arkansas was soon followed by a master's, but Dertouzos was still dreaming of MIT. As a teenager working in the United States Information Service Library in Athens he had stumbled across a paper describing a mechanical mouse that could navigate its way through mazes. 'My heart and mind were totally captured by this little machine,' he explains. 'I knew that designing mechanical mice at MIT was what I would do for a living.' And so Dertouzos moved to Boston for his doctorate. By 1968, he had the MIT faculty position he had dreamed of as well as his own successful company, Computek, which made intelligent terminals and was one of the first companies to produce a commercial version of Doug Engelbart's mouse. Six years later he sold the company to devote his energies to a new job: in September 1974 he had been appointed Director of the Laboratory for Computer Science.

But Michael Dertouzos didn't only dream of electric mice. One of his biggest dreams was something he called the 'information marketplace'. Dertouzos had followed the growth of networking from its early days and he knew that information would be exchanged over networks like eggs over supermarket counters as soon as all the ingredients were there. What he didn't know was that as early as 1980 a young applications programmer at CERN was taking the first concrete steps to building that marketplace. It took a chance encounter on a bus in northern England to put Dertouzos in touch with Tim Berners-Lee.

In late 1992, Tim was attending a conference at Newcastle University in the north of England. On a bus coming back from the conference dinner, Tim found himself sitting next to Dave Gifford, a professor at MIT/LCS, and they got to talking about the Web. By this time, Tim was already feeling seriously overstretched at CERN with the growing Web community looking exclusively to him for support. He knew that things could not go on as they were, and he told Gifford about his worries. Gifford immediately recognized Tim's ideas and suggested that he drop Michael Dertouzos a line at MIT. Dertouzos had been dreaming about his information marketplace for over a decade; perhaps the Web would turn out to be the vehicle to make it a reality.

On returning to CERN, Tim did as Gifford had suggested, but it wasn't until February 1994 that the he and Dertouzos found time in their overcrowded schedules to meet. Dertouzos was passing through Zurich on business and Tim joined him there for dinner. 'We exchanged views and for the first time I heard of Tim's concept that the Web could eventually evolve into a gigantic "brain", leveraging people's ideas,' remembers Dertouzos. 'I believe that Tim also heard for the first time my views on the information marketplace.' There was an obvious synergy between the two concepts. 'We both realized, and said so to one another, that our views and hopes for the world's information infrastructure were very similar, even though we used different names to describe it,' says Dertouzos. They discussed their ideas late into the evening and by the time they came to coffee, the idea of forming a World Wide Web Consortium at MIT/LCS had been hatched.

Forming consortia was nothing new for MIT/LCS. Six years earlier, the laboratory had taken an important step in standardizing the X-Window system. Like the Web, X-Window had been developed in academia and had gone on to attract interest from a broader community.

Seeing the growing importance of X-Window and the potential for disaster if manufacturers couldn't be persuaded to agree on standards, MIT/LCS decided to establish the X-Consortium. Companies were invited to join the consortium for a fee that depended on their size. In exchange, MIT/LCS provided expertise and a neutral forum for the industry to agree on standards rather than having them all rush off in their own directions to produce a plethora of incompatible products. The argument was the same one Bob Metcalfe had used almost two decades earlier when he insisted that the Ethernet standard be established before eager companies could start turning out products. That way, everyone benefits. The alternative is that everyone loses.

Industry was won over by MIT/LCS's reasoning, and soon the X-Consortium was up and running with its inventor Bob Scheifler as Director. After a few years, when MIT/LCS's enabling job was complete, the laboratory spun-off the consortium as an independent organization. The X-Consortium had been a very successful venture providing the right environment for a new technology to grow, so when Michael Dertouzos met Tim Berners-Lee in Zurich, the solution to Tim's problems seemed obvious to him. MIT/LCS would set up a World Wide Web Consortium and Tim would move to Boston to be its Director. It was a very enticing proposition but Tim remained true to his global vision. For him there had to be a European dimension too. Nevertheless, he went back to CERN confident in the knowledge that there was a good home for his invention across the Atlantic if CERN didn't deliver the resources he needed.

Some months before his meeting with Dertouzos, Tim had delivered CERN's management an ultimatum. He had been doing the best he could for the growing Web community with his ragged band of followers, but NCSA's release of the Mosaic browsers brought things to a head in 1993. Tim decided that it was make-or-break time for CERN. The laboratory had to act decisively one way or another: to keep the Web, or to let it go. He jotted down some notes about a possible World Wide Web Consortium. 'Commercial, educational and government bodies are all rushing to get on board,' he said. These people, he went on, 'are calling for a central body to define the Web, ensure its stability and smooth progression through continued technological innovation.' He had been playing with the idea of some kind of consortium for some time and his ideas were beginning to crystallize. The sort of organization he envisaged would build on the altruism inherent in the Web. It would promote the use of the Web all over the world and across all layers of society. And it would make sure that the Web became a great leveller.

The way it would do this would be by coordinating development of standards so that anyone anywhere could use the Web. There was even a special clause saying that it would devote some of its efforts to helping less technically developed countries to use the Web. In an echo of the Internet creed, Tim's rough notes said that although technical design would be coordinated by the new body, 'decisions will be taken by rough consensus among participants'.

The greater penetration of the Internet in the United States, coupled with its growing commercial and public use there, meant that already the Web was much bigger in the USA than it was in its European birthplace. Tim was well aware that the action was in America and that it was likely to remain there for some time. The directions taken by commercial application of the Web would lock the Web's development for years, so it was very important to guide the early activity from its centre. He jotted down a suggestion that the new consortium might be constituted as a non-profit organization in the United States with an office or subsidiary organization in Europe. Moving to the centre of Web gravity must have been tempting to Tim, but he took care to state that the new organization would have a European branch, that it would be financially independent, and that as the need developed, new branches on other continents might be added.

By October 1993, Tim had converted his jottings into a proposal. He now had a clear vision of where he wanted the Web to go. The question was, would CERN share that vision? With just Tim and Robert, separated by the vast chasm of inter-divisional boundaries in CERN's rigid hierarchy and supported only by students and short-term staff, the set-up at CERN was hardly what was needed to manage and oversee a technological revolution. And nor was that likely to change in the near future; CERN's managers had their minds on other things. The laboratory's flagship research instrument, the Large Electron Positron collider (LEP), was scheduled to be shut down in 2000, by which time it would have served its purpose. With the lead time for a replacement likely to be over a decade, now was the time to start work if CERN were to have a viable future at all. A successor accelerator, the Large Hadron Collider (LHC), had been proposed a few years before and all the technical details had been worked out. CERN knew it could build the LHC if the laboratory's member states would agree to fund it. In 1993, CERN's management was asking for the money. They knew they were in for a struggle. In CERN's early days, the laboratory enjoyed the unstinting support of its member states. It was a model of international collaboration, it was a centre of excellence that was keeping bright young minds in Europe, and physics seemed to hold out the promise of a brighter tomorrow. But as the years rolled on, physics research at CERN became more and more expensive, and although the field was delivering the new technologies its early promise had suggested, they were going largely unnoticed by CERN's paymasters. To compound the issue, a new way of thinking about research funding was afoot. The new rationale questioned the received wisdom that innovations came through pure research and dared to suggest that a better approach would be to channel funding to applied areas. Instead of funding particle physics and waiting to see what happened, the new approach would be to try and predict something like the Web and then send computer scientists out to build it. 'Technology foresight' was one of the names given to this approach, and armies of anonymous civil servants were deployed to gaze into crystal balls in a bid to predict the technologies of tomorrow.

To scientists at CERN this looked like bureaucratic folly at its most idiotic. At a stretch, they argued, you might just imagine such an approach working for the Web at the end of the 1980s. By then, academic research had already provided the basic ingredients for that particular advance, but what about the totally unforeseeable things? A favourite example was Michael Faraday and his early experiments on electricity. The story goes that Faraday was demonstrating his invention for generating electricity to Chancellor of the Exchequer William Gladstone when Gladstone asked him what was the practical worth of it. 'One day, sir, you may tax it,' Faraday reputedly replied. Faraday was working from curiosity, not because someone picked him out as a likely inventor of the electricity generator.

If you don't know what you want to develop, reasoned the scientists, you can't fund it, and from the wheel to the Web the most important advances have come about as the result of pure curiosity. Scientists may have found such arguments very persuasive, but to governments with domestic budgets to balance, the bill for the LHC looked frighteningly large. As CERN's management saw it, if they wanted to get the funding for the LHC, the laboratory would have to demonstrate a clear focus and a serious desire to keep costs to a minimum. Launching a major new activity in computer science could easily send out the wrong message.

Tim's design for the new body bears witness to his growing frustration at CERN's apparent inability or unwillingness to give the Web the resources he thought it deserved, but nevertheless, when he turned his ideas into a concrete proposal, it was to CERN's management that he submitted it. He had resolved to give CERN the chance to decide whether to grasp the opportunity to make a go of the Web or to let it go and actively help transfer Web technology from CERN to another organization. As he saw it, there were no other alternatives. One day in October, Tim's memo, 'World Wide Web Decision Point for CERN,' landed on the desks of CERN's computing coordinators marked 'for discussion at 15.00'. Tim had thrown down the gauntlet; the question now was would CERN dare to pick it up with crucial decisions on the LHC looming.

Tim fervently believed that his proposal would be in CERN's best interest. After all, thanks to the policy of keeping the software free, the laboratory's support for the Web had already paid dividends. 'NCSA's Mosaic project and BSDi's Plexus server, to name but two, have now returned more to CERN and CERN's users than a local development would ever have done,' explained Tim. If the software hadn't been in the public domain, there would have been no Mosaic and the Web might well have languished in the backwaters of academia. But now it was out there, what further role did CERN have to play? Tim argued that by staying involved, CERN could ensure that the Web developed in a way that would keep it useful for physicists.

That alone would not be a strong enough argument to win the laboratory's management over, but Tim thought he had a better one. It was a version of the same argument that others were using to keep a lid on CERN's Web activities. What CERN needed was to be seen as a place not only where scientists do incomprehensible things with tiny bits of matter, but also where their efforts give rise to useful spin-offs. In that, Tim agreed with CERN's management. Where he differed, however, was in believing that the Web could bring that sort of kudos to CERN. 'The W3 technology is an economic catalyst which has been compared to the invention of railways and motor transport,' he pointed out. Far from sending out the wrong message, Tim believed that 'the member states will be seen to benefit from CERN's work.' The Web had the potential to show once and for all that pure scientific research did produce tangible benefits for all mankind as well as enriching the pool of human knowledge.

Having presented his case, Tim concluded by laying his cards on the table. 'If serious manpower is not directed to the project now, CERN's role in W3 development will by Christmas be purely historical,' he warned. 'CERN has to decide whether its charter to further science by the dissemination of knowledge and promotion of scholarly communication allows, or indeed requires, it to actively develop the Web.' He had at least one supporter, his stalwart ally Robert Cailliau, who had been sending the same message to CERN management since 1991. Cailliau was by this time also being driven by a vision. But whilst sharing the same basic ideals, Tim and Robert diverged in the detail. Where Tim saw global, Robert saw an opportunity for Europe to make up some lost ground on the USA.

Alexandria

CERN's management may have had other things on their minds, but Robert Cailliau didn't. For him, the Web was a now-or-never opportunity for Europe and he lost no time in spreading the word. To his frustration, however, Cailliau's word often fell on deaf ears. 'At a lunch I sat next to a France Telecom person,' recalls Robert. 'I asked for his e-mail address on the Internet and he said, "Monsieur, vous ne pensez quand-même pas que France Telecom va soutenir l'Internet? [Sir, you surely don't expect France Telecom to support the Internet?]"' Robert's boss, Pier Giorgio Innocenti, had a similar experience when he tried to sell the idea in his native Italy. He contacted the Italian PTT and was politely told that the Web was a niche product that was only good for physicists. 'And now they're marketing it,' he laughs. In a Europe where networking had been slow to get established, it seemed no one could see what was coming.

It didn't take Robert long to realize that just touting the idea vaguely from one company to another was not the answer. What he had to do was produce a concrete proposal and put it before the European Union. He developed the idea of a European centre dedicated to furthering the Web. It would do all the things Tim thought were necessary but it would do them in Europe. In choosing the name 'Alexandria' for his proposal, Robert was thinking big. He had done nothing less than adopt the name of the greatest library of the ancient world. With some half a million volumes in its possession, at around 300 BC the library at Alexandria was unrivalled. Ships entering the harbour would be obliged to surrender any books they were carrying so that copies could be deposited in the library. Because of its library, Alexandria became a great centre of learning. Robert's dream was to recreate the glory that was Alexandria in Europe by building a centre that would turn the Web into the greatest library of the modern world.

In January 1994, Robert sent his Alexandria proposal to the European Commission in Brussels. 'In a fashion so characteristic of Robert,' laughed Mike Sendall, 'he would send this 50-page initiative called "Alexandria" straight to Jacques Delors and to a few other important people in Europe.' But Mike had no objections. There was certainly no harm in trying and Robert had good reason to be optimistic; his earlier proposal to the European Union had resulted in the 'WISE' project being funded in October 1993. WISE was an acronym concatenated with typical Brussels ingenuity from 'World wide Information System for support of R&D Efforts'. Funded by the EU's information technology directorate, DG XIII, WISE had the goal of using the Web to spread information to small and medium-sized enterprises in Europe's least favoured regions. Robert saw the WISE project as a foot in the EU's door. Alexandria would be the real test of Europe's commitment.

'Enclosed you will find a proposal,' began Robert, 'to keep Europe at the forefront of an initiative called the World Wide Web, originated at CERN, and for which urgent action is now required.' And he went on to explain why. 'The World Wide Web,' he said, 'is the most powerful and efficient software for networked information distribution on the Internet.' That it was relatively unheard of in Europe was a consequence of past mistakes, he explained. The local power of the European telecommunications monopolies in the 1970s and '80s coupled with the leisurely perfectionism of the CCITT and ISO had set computer communications in Europe back by decades. America had not suffered as much as Europe from the TCP/IP versus OSI wars; as a result, the Internet was far better established there and the Web was spreading like wildfire. Europe's data communications, on the other hand, were still fragmented.

In Britain, Prestel had failed but teletext was flourishing under the names of Ceefax and Oracle. In France, some five million homes were equipped with Minitel and using it had become as natural as using the telephone. There was even talk of developing a kind of high-definition Minitel, which would have looked much like the Web of today, although since it would have followed Sam Fedida's model instead of Tim Berners-Lee's, it would have been much more centralized. The pros and cons of that can be hotly debated, but the fact is that with the arrival of the Web, high-definition Minitel was a non-starter. Minitel was France Telecom's proprietary standard. It worked in France but nowhere else and the popular groundswell behind the Web would eventually leave Minitel in its wake. But the fact that teletext and Minitel were so well established delayed the uptake of the Web. Paradoxically, without the early lead they seemed to confer, Europe might have been faster to latch on to the Web. As it was, the existence of established information systems slowed down the spread of a new one.

Robert looked across the Atlantic with a combination of envy and dismay. But all was not lost. By 1994, European telecommunications monopolies were on their way out. The playing field was being levelled and Robert saw a chance, by seizing the Web initiative, for Europe to close its gap with the United States in the information revolution. 'This is an appeal for help,' he said. 'The opportunities for government, education and business should not be lost!' But for Robert Cailliau, the months that followed were to prove deeply frustrating, as Europe failed to heed the message he was delivering before, as he saw it, it was all too late. It was an impassioned appeal. 'CERN, as a laboratory with physics as its main mission, cannot and should not support development of networked information systems,' he declared. 'We appeal to the European Union to exploit this very important technology for the benefit of its own governments, its businesses and the education of its children.'

The bottom line was 2.84 million ECU per year, or about what it cost to run a typical university computer science department. For that, Europe would have a centre of excellence with a staff of 32 defining the standards of the twenty-first century's first blockbuster technology. To Robert, it seemed a small price to pay and he had it all planned out. For the first year—1994, as Robert didn't want to waste any time—Alexandria would be hosted at CERN. Once the new organization was up and running, a thriving new technology park just a few kilometres away in France could provide a suitable home.

'The existence of the Alexandria centre will provide the critical mass needed to get Europe to the forefront of developments in multimedia networked information systems,' said Robert. But his dream was not to be. The real world often reserves its heaviest blows for idealists like Robert, and the harsh political reality of the next few months was to see a transatlantic tussle for the heart of the Web. Ultimately the honours were to come out even, but Robert's Alexandria proposal was an early casualty. With Tim already frustrated at CERN's foot-dragging and beginning to think transatlantic, Robert's case was looking weak from the start. 'He never heard from Delors,' added Mike Sendall, 'which was a shame, really.'

Transatlantic tussles

Things soon started to move so fast that Europe's cumbersome bureaucracy could not keep up. Exactly a month after Robert had sent his Alexandria proposal to Brussels, Tim Berners-Lee's tentative first contact with Michael Dertouzos bore its first fruit in the form of a draft agreement between the World Wide Web initiative, represented by Tim, and MIT/LCS, in the form of Michael Dertouzos. By this time, nonstandard items like Lou Montulli's notorious blink tag were starting to proliferate and Dertouzos decided there was no more time to lose. He summoned his associate director, Al Vezza.

Vezza was a hard talking veteran of the networking world who had cut his Internet teeth back in 1972 as Bob Kahn's right-hand man in the build up to the milestone ARPANET demonstration at the ICCC conference in Washington. He had gone on to start a company that sold interactive fiction, even persuading Douglas Adams to produce an interactive version of the *Hitch Hiker's Guide to the Galaxy*. By the time he sold the company in 1986, his biggest title, the *Zork* trilogy, had sold a million copies. Later on, Vezza had played a part in setting up the X-Consortium, and when the talk at MIT/LCS got round to doing the same thing for the Web, he knew exactly what had to be done. 'I said, "Look, guys, the consortium worked really well because we had the inventor of X here",' he explains, 'and everybody looked at each other and said, "Well, maybe we should talk to this guy Tim."' Al Vezza booked himself a ticket to Geneva.

Tim Berners-Lee already had the idea of moving to Boston in his head from his earlier meetings with Michael Dertouzos in Zurich and a couple more when he had flown over to MIT/LCS to discuss things further. Vezza's job when he went to CERN in May 1994 was to make it stick. Tim and his wife took Vezza out to dinner at the Auberge des Chasseurs, a discreet village inn popular with CERN people, and Vezza tried to persuade them that a move to Boston was their best option. Knowing Vezza's jetsetting schedule, the Berners-Lees had carefully chosen the country auberge to give him a bit of a rest. But there was to be no peace for Al Vezza. 'The people there thought he was pretty funny,' remembers Tim, 'because this American was getting faxes all the time.'

Vezza went back to MIT with his mission accomplished, and he sent Tim a fax with a job offer a few weeks later. To the Berners-Lees, it seemed like an offer to good to refuse. Tim was tentatively due to start his new job in October. For Vezza, however, there remained the little problem of how to pay his new recruit. He went to see his dean at MIT to plead his case. 'This is a famous guy,' he argued, to which he remembers the dean replying 'Ah, famous guys, we got all kinds of famous guys here.' So getting Tim a salary was Vezza's problem. As far as Tim was concerned, he could go into work armed with the knowledge that if CERN were not forthcoming, he and the Web had somewhere to go.

The draft agreement Tim had signed on his own initiative with Michael Dertouzos aimed to make the Web the vehicle for the information marketplace. It was every bit as idealistic as Robert's Alexandria proposal, but without the purely European angle. 'The international information infrastructure,' it said, 'is envisioned as a highly scalable information market where information and services can be purchased, sold, or exchanged freely so as to improve the economic well being and the quality of life of people throughout the world; as an educational medium and as a means of exploring, nourishing and sharing cultures.' These were grand words indeed for something that began life as a simple computer program to help physicists to talk to each other, and they showed a global vision on MIT/LCS's part that was slower to develop in Europe's corridors of power.

Ever since the days of project MAC, the MIT lab had enjoyed an enviable reputation in the computer science world. It had been associated with a host of important advances. 'This lab's motto,' says Dertouzos, 'is to make the technology useful to humanity.' Nevertheless, MIT/LCS remained largely out of the public eye, while MIT's other computer science lab, the relatively young upstart Media Lab, founded in the 1980s, was rarely out of the news. Under the charismatic leadership of Nicholas Negroponte, the Media Lab had grabbed the headlines with its work on robots and artificial intelligence. The Web brought a bit of glamour to MIT/LCS's portfolio, and some people were suggesting that grabbing a little of the Media Lab's limelight might have been on Dertouzos's agenda in bringing the Web to his laboratory. Dertouzos, however, has none of that. 'A journalistic artifice to cause adrenal secretions,' he says. 'It's total nonsense. I conceived of the information marketplace twenty years ago and set the goal at LCS of architecting tomorrow's information infrastructures.' He saw the Web as a realization of what he had been prophesying for so long, and bringing it to MIT/LCS was the natural thing to do.

Tim's agreement with Dertouzos stated the intention to form a W3 Organization (W3O) to define the World Wide Web and provide the point of reference for it. The organization would also coordinate the definition and development of the World Wide Web protocols. It would edit the standards, provide freely available reference code in support of the standards, and it would provide help to all users of the standards, including non-technical people, throughout the world. In short, W3O would be a truly altruistic organization. Through it Tim Berners-Lee would see his dream through to fruition and MIT/LCS would gain respect as the world authority on an information revolution.

Speed was of the essence to keep the Web going where Tim wanted it to go. 'This was a battle to see whether we could hold the Web together to let it really take off,' he reflected later. 'It was a battle to form common languages for HTML and HTTP and URLs before the Web disintegrated into a mass of incompatible parts.' To realize that goal, Tim was quite happy to move to wherever he could make the greatest impact. 'Whether it happened in the US or Europe was largely predetermined by where the Internet was largely deployed and where the existing software companies were,' he explains. 'That was a strategic fact which put the focus of Web development in the US whether you liked it or not.'

Tim, however, was not abandoning Europe. His resolute insistence on keeping the Web global was reflected in the agreement. 'The W3 Organization,' it said, 'shall be a collaboration between W3 America (W3A), administratively within MIT/LCS, and W3 Europe (W3E), administratively within a host organization such as CERN.'

Apart from the fact that Tim would be the head of the new organization and he would be based in Boston, there didn't seem much to choose between his draft agreement with Michael Dertouzos and Robert's Alexandria proposal; the Alexandria centre equated pretty well with W3E. But nevertheless Tim waited to see what CERN's management would do with his earlier ultimatum before making any move. The deal with MIT/LCS put him in a no-lose situation. If CERN rose to the challenge, he would be able to negotiate with MIT/LCS from a position of strength. If not, he would be able to leave with a clear conscience knowing that CERN had had the opportunity to capitalize on his invention and had chosen to pass it up and concentrate on other things.

Taken at face value, W3E would give Europe an equal partnership with the United States in the Web; an equitable arrangement between the place where it was born and the place where it grew up. Europe wouldn't seize the Web quite as firmly as Robert would have liked, but nor would it lose it. On closer inspection, however, Tim's agreement with Michael Dertouzos would have put the Web's centre of gravity somewhat further to the west of the mid-Atlantic ridge than Robert felt comfortable with. Of the W3O's technical board, four would be selected by the organization's membership, four by the director, and four by MIT/LCS. Seen through US eyes, that seemed entirely reasonable, but when Tim showed Robert the agreement, that apparent US bias was a bitter pill to swallow. And it didn't end there. Although funding was to be split equitably between the United States and Europe—ARPA would fund W3A, the European Union's ESPRIT programme would fund W3E, and both would be backed up by industrial members of a World Wide Web Consortium (W3C)—financial management would be entirely in the hands of MIT/LCS. Membership of the proposed W3C would be open to 'any organization willing to execute a participation agreement with MIT', rather than with the global W3O. Moreover, the agreement stipulated that part or all of the European funds would be deposited with a European bank through an arrangement whereby they would be released 'on the instruction of MIT/LCS and the W3 leadership for use by W3E and W3A'. In other words, the European Union would be asked to hand over money to US control, an unprecedented situation and potential political dynamite in Europe.

Nevertheless, when Tim presented the idea, CERN agreed to work with MIT/LCS towards a global World Wide Web Organization, and on the basis of Tim's agreement with Michael Dertouzos, MIT/LCS started to put together a draft proposal for CERN to send to the European Union. The draft was prepared at the beginning of 1994 but it was never sent. When Tim showed it to his colleagues at CERN, Mike Sendall immediately saw its shortcomings. 'It was one of the few occasions I've seen Mike with steam coming out of his ears,' recalls Robert Cailliau. The idea of a global W3O with American and European branches struck the Europeans as a good one. The idea that European funding would be controlled by MIT/LCS, however, was seen as entirely unacceptable by Robert and Mike. 'We read those paragraphs several times,' says Robert, 'to make sure our eyes had seen it right.' They could see what the MIT/LCS people couldn't: such a proposal would be more likely to cause a diplomatic incident than secure funding for a brave new world. So they immediately set to work on a new draft.

The resulting document was based largely on the MIT/LCS draft but with the important difference that EU funding was channelled directly to W3E. Robert drew up a 'half-moon' diagram showing MIT/LCS and CERN as equal partners with US public funds going to MIT/LCS and European funds to CERN. An industrial consortium also figured in Robert's diagram, made up of the companies that would benefit from the work of W3O and a society of individual users. How the consortium would fit in financially with W3O was left undefined, however, an oversight that later came close to scuppering the entire W3O project.

By 6 June, CERN's proposal to the European Union was ready and the laboratory's Research and Technical Director, German physicist Horst Wenninger, sent it off to John Powers at the EU's industry directorate, DG III, despite Cailliau's foot in the door at the information technology directorate, DG XIII. With Michael Dertouzos already talking to George Metakides in the industry directorate that was where the proposal had to go. 'CERN seems to us a natural candidate for the role of European coordinator,' Wenninger began, 'in view of the fact that the project originated here and also because of CERN's international character and excellent networking infrastructure.' Serving as a member of the direc-

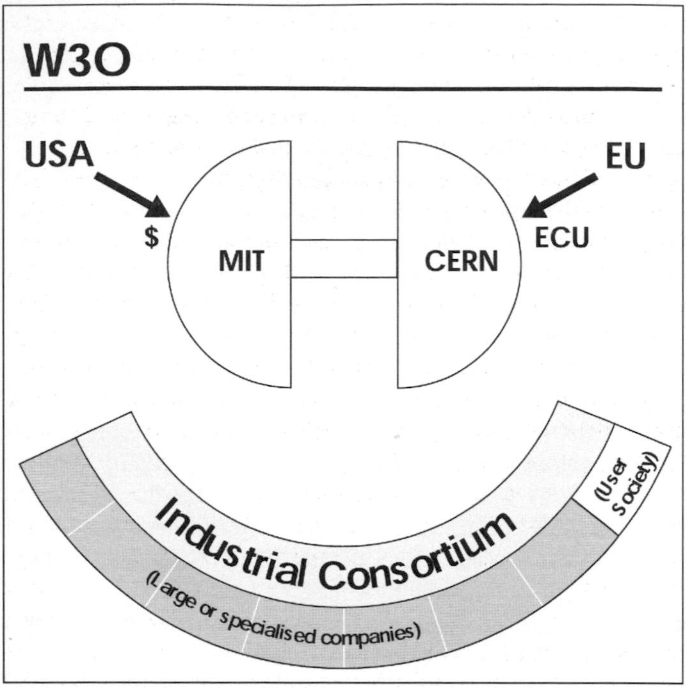

World-Wide Web© CERN—W30

Figure 27: Robert Cailliau's half-moon diagram. In the original agreement signed between Tim Berners-Lee and Michael Dertouzos, the EU arrow would have pointed to MIT.

torate of an organization funded by nineteen different countries had taught Wenninger to tread gingerly when dealing with multinational bodies like the European Union. There was no mention of funding being managed from anywhere other than Europe. Pointing out that CERN was already an international organization proved to be an astute move. Brussels funding was well known to favour international groupings rather than individual EU member states. These European sensibilities were unknown to the Americans, who were happy to go along with CERN's approach.

The proposal carried the names of Tim Berners-Lee, Robert Cailliau, and Mike Sendall. It was broadly in agreement with MIT/LCS and much of the wording was lifted directly from the original draft Tim had signed with Michael Dertouzos. The differences were subtle and came through in the form of a peppering of phrases chosen to appeal to the prevailing political climate in Brussels. The Web, explained the proposal, would 'help the European Community to take advantage of the new international information world'. It would 'improve the economic well being and quality of life of people in Europe and throughout the world', and it provided 'a means of nurturing and integrating different cultures'. These are all concepts central to the European ideal.

The proposal pointed to the Web's staggering 350 per cent growth in 1993, which had happened largely in the United States, but it branded the Web as European technology. It was a proposal designed to convince Brussels that by acting fast, Europe's lag with respect to the USA could be made good. The Web, it stressed, had been invented by an Englishman at a European laboratory and brought to fruition through twenty man-years of effort at that laboratory. Even that icon of American prowess in data communications, the Internet, was portrayed as something that might one day become dispensable to the all-conquering World Wide Web. 'The Internet,' it said, 'is the substrate over which WWW is growing rapidly, although other global networks might also be used to support the Web.' This would have been welcome news in Brussels, hinting that Europe's deficit might only be a temporary blip. In promoting the collaboration with MIT/LCS, however, to develop a single set of world standards there was an implicit warning that not doing so would again leave Europe lagging behind. 'A combined effort in Europe and the US has the further advantage,' the proposal pointed out, 'of providing one common international standard, since as has become evident with the Internet, information infrastructures will invariably cross international boundaries.'

It was a skilfully composed document designed to press all the right buttons in Brussels and success seemed almost guaranteed, but it left one important ingredient curiously ill-defined: the industrial consortium that Robert had left floating detached below his half-moons of MIT and CERN. 'It is the intent that an international consortium of industrial partners shall be formed, to provide a forum for mutual guidance, and to progressively take over funding of the project's activities,' said the proposal. Funding from this consortium would match EU funding after two years and replace it completely after five. What is curious is that there was no description of how this consortium would be formed, or of how it would be managed. Perhaps CERN considered that level of information to be unnecessary for Brussels or something that could be worked out later, but to the Americans it was taken as a green light to get to work on setting up the consortium.

The announcement of a CERN–MIT link-up came at the first International World Wide Web conference held at CERN in May 1994. Robert Cailliau had first raised the possibility of holding a conference the year before, when he had asked Horst Wenninger if CERN could host one. 'I asked him how many people he thought might come,' remembers Wenninger, 'and I think he more or less guessed there would be maybe a hundred.' As it turns out, over four hundred people came to the conference that was soon being labelled the Woodstock of the Web, and CERN was having to turn people away. Even Robert Cailliau, the Web's strongest advocate, had no idea how fast the Web was growing. 'When I came out of the Seattle Hypertext conference in 1993, I was convinced that it was high time to hold a conference on Web technologies,' he explains. 'I had calculated to break even at 65 participants, started from absolutely zero financing, and had over 600 people wanting to come.' Robert was overwhelmed. 'People wrote desperate e-mails saying things like "I must be there, I don't need food, I don't need lodging, I'll sit on the steps, but please let me in."' Robert was obliged to turn them down and even people from CERN found themselves being refused entry. 'I was told off by several CERN people who expected to be able to attend for free and were not pleased to be turned back at the doors,' he remembers.

Tim Berners-Lee's talk at the conference was billed as 'The Future of the Web', and he desperately wanted to be able to announce the new organization. But in Brussels, the administrators were still picking over the details. They were keen to support CERN's proposal but they weren't quite ready to make the announcement. The telephone lines were buzzing between Geneva and Brussels and eventually a compromise was reached. Tim would be able to say something, but he couldn't call it an announcement. He devoted his talk to the problems that existed with the Web, the kind of problems that needed some kind of Web organization to sort them out. It was a long list and it ended up with the question of scalability, 'so we don't, in two years time,' explained Tim, 'have to say "Stop! On Tuesday you will all have to put a seven in front of your URL when you're dialling from out of town."' That got a big laugh and gave him the opening he needed to make his statement. 'The answer is there is an effort to solve that,' he began. 'It is a fairly substantial effort. It has taken a certain amount of setting up and I cannot talk a lot about it now because some of the funding which we hope to be involved has not been defined so that is sub judice. So this is not an announcement,' he announced. 'However, what I can tell you is that there will be a W3 Organization. It will be completely international and it will be open, so it is not going to be a centre to develop all the software everybody's going to be using for the next decade. It is going to be a meeting point. It is going to be a centre for stability. But it'll never be able to do all the development, of course, and it wouldn't want to. So it is going to be a place where institutes and companies meet. It is going to be vendor neutral.' He then moved onto the structure of the new organization. 'CERN has decided that it will take on the role of being the European focal point,' he said. 'It will do this in collaboration with other institutes. We've been talking to a lot of other institutes who are very very keen to get this going straight away, so we will be linking in other institutes. But from the point of view of being a pan-European meeting point, CERN will take this role. This wasn't clear earlier and in fact in talks perhaps a year ago you'll have heard me say that CERN has expressed the opinion that it is there to do high-energy physics. CERN is now willing to take on this role and the Massachusetts Institute of Technology will be the focal point in the US in collaboration, of course, with a lot of other people, a lot of companies, NCSA obviously. And there will be a strong link between CERN and MIT and between CERN and MIT respectively and organizations on each continent.' He went on to mention the industrial consortium that would eventually take over funding after public money had got the new organization off the ground, but not how it would be managed. 'So that's the W3 Organization un-announcement,' he concluded, 'and that wraps up my talk for today.' He was greeted with the kind of reception more appropriate to a rock concert than to the main auditorium of a physics laboratory. There were claps, cheers, and whistles, and when it all died down, just one question: when would the real announcement come? 'July', Tim replied, when all the founder members were on board.

It doesn't look like so much now, given what has happened to the Web, but the CERN proposal to Brussels was big money for a first project. It would be worth some 1.6 million ECU, close to $2 million, over 18 months, and as such would be one of the flagships of the ESPRIT programme and a model for transatlantic collaboration. Everything seemed to be going according to the timetable Tim had announced at the CERN conference. On 7 July, right on schedule, an MIT/LCS press conference announced that 'The Massachusetts Institute of Technology (MIT) and the European Laboratory for Particle Physics (CERN) will co-operate in the further development and standardization of the World Wide Web to make the world computer network easier to use for research, commercial use, and future applications.' At the beginning of October, soon after Tim Berners-Lee had taken up his appointment in Boston and while the European Union was still mulling over the CERN proposal, MIT/LCS sent out letters inviting companies to join the 'MIT World Wide Web Consortium' (W3C) with effect from 1 October. 'MIT will collaborate,' it said, 'with other organizations in the development of the W3 protocol. In particular CERN in Europe, EIT and CommerceNet, OSF, NCSA, Spyglass, Inc., and others.' CERN had been cast in the same breath as a string of US organizations, a far cry from equal partnership, and the CERN people didn't like it one bit. CERN wanted to be an equal partner in the organization, not simply a sub-contractor.

When Mike Sendall and Robert Cailliau got wind of what had happened, a flurry of e-mails, letters, and faxes flew between Geneva and Boston. A second Web conference, this time to be held in Chicago at the end of the month, was looming and both sides were keen to avoid any potentially damaging public split. But MIT/LCS's decision to launch the consortium had raised hackles at CERN. In Boston, however, Tim Berners-Lee seemed genuinely surprised at his former colleagues' reaction. MIT/LCS had sent draft W3C contracts to Mike Sendall at CERN in advance, but Mike had not felt the same sense of urgency that was building at MIT, and so had not replied immediately. Back in Boston, no reply was taken to mean no objection, so the contracts went out.

Mike did not conceal the sense of bemusement he felt at MIT/LCS's action. 'I must say right away,' he e-mailed Tim, 'that I don't understand what you think the relation between W3C and W3O is.' 'We have been working here setting things up essentially along the lines you proposed, and this looks very like an alternative way of doing things,' he added. His incomprehension was underlined later in his message: 'Brussels is prepared to spend nearly $2M on the W3O proposal, as they (and we) understood it, but not necessarily on something different. If I show them your contracts as they stand, I don't know what their reaction will be.' But Tim couldn't see what all the fuss was about. 'I don't think you need to show Brussels the contract,' he replied. As far as he was concerned, what MIT/LCS had done was entirely within the letter of CERN's proposal to Brussels, and to underline his confidence that everything was above board, he fired off a copy of the contract to Robert for distribution to potential European members. Forewarned of the potential reaction this would provoke, he pre-empted Robert's question about the distribution of W3C funds. 'People will ask about funds split,' he began, 'and we can't commit to spending in Europe exactly what we get in contributions in Europe.' But to put Robert's mind at rest, he cited the example of the X-Consortium where MIT had contracted a lot of work to Europe despite relatively few European contributions. That was just the way it turned out. Tim's point was that the money should go where it could be put to best use and that this was dictated by having to react fast in the business environment into which the Web was moving. In such an environment it would be impossible for W3C to make commitments in advance.

Mike and Tim both wanted the same thing for the Web—an organization that would ensure its continued development in a non-proprietary way—but the misunderstanding over the W3C contracts had sown the seeds of mistrust between CERN and MIT. Seen from MIT, speed was the most important factor. The people there could see the Web exploding all around them. It was clear they needed to launch the consortium as quickly as possible and start enrolling companies that would sign up to an open standard before someone else did—or, worse, before one company launched a proprietary alternative to the Web. That is why MIT/LCS lost no time in sending out invitations to join the MIT W3C.

In Europe, the Web had not yet become the cultural force it already was in the United States, and the need for action did not seem so pressing. The people at CERN had been taken off guard by MIT/LCS's action and after four months of patient negotiation they felt hurt by what appeared to be a betrayal. They set about analysing the MIT W3C contract and didn't like what they found. To them, it seemed that MIT would get the credit for the work that had been done at CERN. Companies would sign a contract with MIT and not the W3O, and copyrights on Web software would refer exclusively to MIT. But by this time the consortium was a fact, and like it or not, CERN would have to live with it. As Mike Sendall later pointed out, 'You had two options, either you could cooperate with the Americans, or you could take them on and lose. What we almost ended up doing is cooperating with them and losing!' Mike Sendall said this when the dust had settled, and he said it with a smile, because what did eventually transpire was a World Wide Web Consortium that both CERN and MIT could be proud of, and for most people all that was left of the misunderstanding was a sense of bemusement that it had ever happened at all. But in October there was a long way to go before an equitable solution would be found.

Things came to a head around the time of the second World Wide Web conference in Chicago. Tim Berners-Lee was attending the conference, as were Robert Cailliau and François Fluckiger, the person who had been nominated to assume responsibility for the Web at CERN when Tim had left. Fluckiger hadn't been much involved with the Web before, but he knew all about networks. He had a lifetime's experience in networking behind him, having worked on Transpac, the French PTT network that had superseded Louis Pouzin's Cyclades, before moving to CERN.

A press conference was scheduled at which the consortium was bound to come up and Cailliau was wondering what he could say to reassure people that CERN and MIT/LCS were still working in harmony. On 17 October, he found an urgent fax from CERN waiting in his room at the Ramada Congress Hotel where the conference was being held. It contained the faxes and e-mails between Boston and Geneva since Robert had left for the conference, prefaced by a covering note from Mike Sendall. Mike had had to warn the European Union that there had been a hiccup, but he had been vague on details. He advised Robert to take the same approach. 'Have a good conference,' he closed, 'and a "vague et souriant" [vague and smiling] press event.'

Three days earlier, Mike had set down CERN's worries in a faxed letter to Tim Berners-Lee and Al Vezza. In it he explained with the utmost diplomacy that CERN had assumed that the relationship between the industrial consortium and W3O would be explicit, which didn't seem to be the case in MIT's contracts. He had also assumed that mechanisms for sharing resources would be discussed. 'It seems to me,' he concluded, 'that we cannot just go ahead with things as they are. We therefore need clear and speedy notice of your intentions, and in particular to know if MIT is still interested in building W3O with us.' In closing, Mike said, 'I feel there is no time to be lost if we are to ensure the continuity of service and effort we all wish to see.'

Tim's reply, e-mailed back the same day, tried to put Mike's worries to rest. 'I read your fax as being a bit miffed,' said Tim, 'so we need to sort this out.' He tried to explain why there was no reference from W3C to W3O in the MIT/LCS contracts. What it boiled down to is that as far as MIT/LCS saw things, the time scales that government and industry work to are incompatible, and mentioning a government-sponsored body in the W3C contracts would only have served to frighten industry away. MIT/LCS was convinced that time was of the essence and they had no intention of wasting any. 'Industry is interested in results,' said Tim. 'Industry can't wait for anything which has to get government approval.' So MIT/LCS wanted to keep the government-supported W3O entirely separate from the industry-supported W3C, even if the same people were involved in both. Mike was not convinced. 'You seem to be setting up two independent bodies at the same time, with no connection between them, to do the same job,' he replied. 'This doesn't make sense to me.'

Another thing that didn't make sense to Mike, and suggested that the problem was less serious than it seemed at first sight, was that in launching W3C when they had, MIT/LCS had put at risk nearly $2 million of funding from the European Union. Perhaps, after all, it was just cultural differences that were at the root of the misunderstanding.

In his Chicago hotel room, Robert read all the faxes and e-mails with consternation and started to jot down some suitably vague and smiling things to say during the press event. 'Mechanisms of allocating income generated by W3C to the different W3O partners are under discussion,' he wrote, and he sketched a modified half-moon diagram. This version had an arrow pointing upwards from the W3C to some indistinct place in between the half-moons of MIT/LCS and CERN. But he never showed it. When it came to the press conference, Cailliau and Fluckiger let Tim do the talking to avoid any possible contradiction. The following day, all three boarded a plane for Boston where they had scheduled a meeting with Al Vezza to try and clear up their misunderstandings.

Robert had noticed at the conference that Joseph Hardin, of the National Center for Supercomputing Applications (NCSA) at the University of Illinois, did not seem happy with MIT's de facto domination of the Web, and began to regret his earlier mistrust of NCSA. Because of the limelight that fell on Urbana-Champaign when Mosaic was released, NCSA had for a time become the centre of gravity of Web development. CERN's role faded into the background as the media hyped Mosaic as the 'killer app' for the Internet, conveniently ignoring the fact that Mosaic couldn't have happened without the Web. There had even been a move to call the Chicago conference not the 2nd World Wide Web conference but the 1st Mosaic Conference. That had raised European hackles, but the situation was happily resolved. Both CERN and NCSA had had the idea of holding a conference at the same time, but Cailliau had got his announcement out first. 'I announced at the end of December,' he recalls, 'and instantly got NCSA on the line.' Joseph Hardin had called Robert as soon as he received his invitation to the CERN conference and, presented with a fait accompli, agreed to postpone his own conference, which became the 2nd World Wide Web conference. Cailliau and Hardin joined forces in August 1994 to form the International World Wide Web Conference Committee (IW3C2). Should they also have seized the initiative and set up W3O themselves? mused Cailliau. They very nearly had. Back in February, Robert Cailliau and Tim Berners-Lee had even got as far as drawing up a draft agreement with Joseph Hardin, but then Tim had chosen the cosmopolitan bustle of Boston over the plains of rural Illinois. For Cailliau, this was a time for 'what ifs?' He was ruing the fact that MIT/LCS's nimbleness in getting things moving had effectively killed his own dream, the Alexandria proposal.

But there was no point dwelling on the past. If Cailliau were to keep his European dream alive, he would have to start matching MIT/LCS's nimbleness. In Boston, Cailliau and Fluckiger had found Al Vezza in confident mood, keen to get on with W3C, but with little enthusiasm for W3O. When Fluckiger pointed out that CERN resources were going into providing the services promised by MIT/LCS in the W3C contract, Robert remembers Vezza responding, 'If you are in pain, we will pay for your pain.' It was abundantly clear that MIT/LCS just wanted to get down to business. To Vezza, CERN's attitude seemed like so much petty mumbling. MIT/LCS would run the consortium, CERN could be a partner if it wanted, and the money would be spent where MIT/LCS, and Tim Berners-Lee in particular, thought it would be put to best use. Where was the problem with that? After all, CERN had had exclusive control of the Web since 1990. That had been plenty of time to set up its own consortium if that was what the laboratory had wanted to do. Vezza simply wasn't convinced that CERN's heart was in it, and he may have been right. Even Cailliau could see his point. 'There is a credibility gap,' he explained to his colleagues at CERN, 'which CERN by itself cannot fill: expertise, intention and vision must be seen to come from non-physics communities also.' He strongly recommended striking up liaisons with other organizations such as France's national research institute for computer science, INRIA, to give Europe a stronger case.

When CERN had celebrated its 40th anniversary in September, the press release of scientific highlights made no mention of the World Wide Web. That didn't do anything to close the credibility gap, but for CERN's management there were bigger fish to fry. The laboratory's make-or-break point was looming ever closer, with CERN Council due to vote on the LHC in December, and the Web didn't quite fit in. As a tool for physicists, the Web was great for CERN, but despite going along with the idea originally, the laboratory's management was beginning to question whether supporting a W3C or a W3O or a W3-anything was really its job. By now it was becoming obvious how big the Web was going to be even in Europe, and CERN's management was backing off. The ideal situation, as they saw it, might after all be for CERN to let the Web go, as long as they could somehow let the world know that it had been invented at CERN. The Web was set to be the most valuable spin-off from fundamental science ever, and the political value of that was what mattered most to CERN's management.

But at the time Cailliau and Fluckiger returned from the United States, all that was still left unsaid and for the people at CERN who were directly involved in Web work there was no question that the laboratory didn't have a role to play in the Web's future. Cailliau's action plan was to inform the European Union immediately of exactly what the situation was and to take measures to put CERN back on equal terms with MIT/LCS. He recommended that CERN should immediately withdraw MIT's write access to the CERN server, and start to negotiate terms. He also recommended that the laboratory take out copyright on the name 'World Wide Web'. Far from clearing up any misunderstandings, the meeting in Boston had only made things worse. Cailliau even recommended a thorough examination of the information available from the CERN server to make sure that MIT/LCS hadn't added anything CERN wouldn't have wanted to say. He concluded his recommendations with hyperbole worthy of Hollywood. 'The scale of the European project,' he said, 'should be assessed in the light of what Europe wants for the future of its culture, its society and its independent survival.'

Cailliau wasn't the only one to feel let down in Boston. François Fluckiger also came away disappointed. 'MIT does not believe in a dual-headed consortium,' he reported, 'and does not wish to share contractually the income with CERN in other form than by possible subcontracting.' But for Fluckiger, all was not lost. He found the discussion straightforward and businesslike and told his colleagues at CERN, 'I think we may make deals with Al Vezza in the future, as long as we talk directly.' Fluckiger had seen how MIT/LCS operated, and he decided that CERN had better learn fast to operate the same way. Fluckiger came back to Europe with the feeling that MIT/LCS did want to establish a collaboration with CERN for the joint development of Web technology, but that they wanted to keep the finances separate. MIT/LCS was working with a different conception of the consortium than CERN had in mind. In their model, funding would be the responsibility of each partner and W3C was no more than MIT/LCS's funding instrument. If Europe wanted to set up its own W3C, that was fine with them. Of course, the MIT World Wide Web Consortium would consider European industry fair game, and with the centre of gravity of the Web in the United States, it would probably look more attractive than anything CERN might set up. MIT/LCS was not negotiating with maliciousness; this was simply the American way of doing business. Although François Fluckiger and Robert Cailliau may have talked up the idea of an independent European consortium, in reality the idea was stillborn and everybody knew it. Robert's dream of Alexandria in Haute Savoie had been limping along and on 25 October a proposal to build

Alexandria at Archamps, just across the border from Geneva, with local government support was penned by a researcher at a nearby laboratory in Annecy. But it was too little, too late. What the Europeans had to do now was manoeuvre themselves into a stronger negotiating position, one where they could put some pressure on MIT/LCS to get the kind of global consortium they wanted. If they didn't, the MIT/LCS consortium would simply become the world standards body for the Web whether Europe liked it or not.

Fluckiger agreed with Cailliau that CERN should register the names World Wide Web, http, and HTML, and soon after CERN's lawyers drew up a copyright statement. Free use of the software on a warranty-free basis was granted on condition that the words 'this product includes computer software created and made available by CERN' appear wherever it was used. CERN removed the latest release of its Web server software from the public domain by making moves to copyright it. This was software that MIT/LCS was relying on, and it put the Americans in an awkward position. Companies were beginning to sign up for the MIT W3C. Marc Andreessen's Mosaic Communications Corporation announced on 25 October that it had become a founding member of the consortium. It was vital for MIT/LCS that everything should go smoothly as the consortium got up to speed. Not being able to deliver software could prove embarrassing.

At the end of October, Robert's boss, Pier Giorgio Innocenti, decided to get involved. He had been following the negotiations with MIT/LCS closely, and on reading Cailliau's and Fluckiger's reports of their meeting in Boston, he decided it was time he dropped a line to Michael Dertouzos and Al Vezza. His letter, dated 28 October, simply pointed out that CERN held the copyright on much of the Web software. Innocenti was a physicist by background and he was used to working with MIT, but in the relatively tranquil waters of pure physics research. He was finding that LCS didn't work in quite the same way. LCS was used to the cut and thrust of the open market, and CERN was not prepared for that. 'It was a time,' says Innocenti, 'in which we had absolutely no idea what patenting and copyrighting meant so we were a bit fishing in the dark.'

MIT/LCS lost no time reacting to Innocenti's letter. Vezza replied by fax on 31 October saying that he believed a misunderstanding had developed over MIT/LCS's actions. He drew Innocenti's attention to the line in the agreement signed between Tim Berners-Lee and Michael Dertouzos back in February that stated that 'consortium membership would be open to any organization willing to execute a participation agreement with MIT'. In other words, Al Vezza was telling CERN that MIT/LCS had been working to its original agenda all along. If CERN believed that anything had changed since February, that was the misunderstanding. Vezza went on to express his worries that CERN's actions over Web software might send out just the kind of message MIT/LCS was hoping to avoid. 'The implication of such action,' he pointed out, 'is that CERN, and by association its partner MIT/LCS, cannot be trusted to act solely for the public good.' It was a letter that said that CERN's message had been received, but that MIT/LCS was not for turning. Vezza was calling Innocenti's bluff.

Knowing CERN a lot better than Vezza, Tim had a pretty good idea of what his old colleagues wanted and it basically boiled down to credit for the work that had been done at CERN. 'I understand that this sort of "strike action" is a plea that CERN feels Europe has been left out,' he told Mike Sendall. 'What can we positively do about it?' He went on to explain that if CERN had felt left out of the design of the W3C contract, that it was not by intention but by misunderstanding, as Vezza had said. CERN had not realized that there was any hurry, and MIT/LCS had taken no comment as meaning no objection, a green light to go ahead. Tim also swiftly dealt with CERN's concern over copyright. 'Would it help if the code was jointly copyrighted between CERN and MIT?' he asked. 'I don't know whether it would make legal sense but Al would be happy to do it. Al does want to make this thing work with CERN, you know!'

Al Vezza had interpreted CERN's move on copyright as the first step on the way to demanding royalties, something that Tim would consider a disaster. Keeping the software free was what he believed had allowed the Web to take off and the best thing that CERN had ever done for the Web. At the beginning of 1992, gopher was the biggest fish on the Internet and the Web was a relative minnow, a curiosity confined to the backwaters of the particle physics community. Then came Viola, and a few more people took notice. Tony Johnson's Midas had some effect, and in 1993, when NCSA released the Mosaic browsers, things really started to take off for the Web. But gopher was still bigger. To Tim, the thing that had really made the difference was not just how good the product was, but also the fact that it was free. When the University of Minnesota decided that Mark McCahill would have to start charging for the gopher server in spring 1993, Tim noticed, 'industry dropped gopher like a hot potato, and I was immediately besieged by questions about CERN's attitude to libwww.' While the Internet was still a tool largely confined to the academic community, the software that got developed was the software that was free. Academics couldn't afford anything else. If history had taken a slightly different course, MIT/LCS might have found itself building the World Wide Gopher Consortium while trying to lure Mark McCahill or Farhad Anklesaria to Boston to be its Director. Instead of three green Ws, a small furry rodent might have been the icon of the information age.

But that is not how it happened, and at the beginning of November 1994, Tim was anxious that the Web didn't suffer gopher's fate. 'I am extremely unhappy about the situation of the MIT–CERN level of trust and understanding,' he told Sendall. He didn't really share Vezza's worries about royalties but there was a niggling doubt. Tim had worked at CERN long enough to know that not everyone there was happy about putting the Web in the public domain and he wanted Sendall's assurance that they were still in the minority. 'Knowing that there have been forces urging CERN to cash in on its successful developments rather than contribute them altruistically to society,' said Tim, 'I wondered whether in my absence this policy had gained the upper hand.' And if that were the case, then Tim made his feelings quite clear: 'If CERN is in fact thinking of asking for royalties or license fees then I will be very disappointed and they had better say now so that MIT can start disentangling themselves.'

Tim's main concern, as ever, was for the Web, and he was in no mood for calling anyone's bluff. 'Both sides are acting as though they would not lose much by taking their marbles and leaving the game,' he said. 'And the truth is, they wouldn't lose much. CERN could get on with physics and MIT could get on with research and the world would lose because they would not have the coordination which the W3C and W3O can give. But that is not what I want and it is not, I think, what anyone wants.'

Meanwhile, MIT/LCS was pushing ahead with the MIT W3C. The same day that he had written to Innocenti, Vezza sent out more letters to potential W3C members, including European companies. These letters explicitly recognized CERN's role, saying, 'The laboratory is collaborating closely with CERN which will provide both a development effort and a center for European activities.' CommerceNet, EIT, NCSA, and OSF, whose names had appeared in the same breath as CERN's in the previous version, had been relegated to a sub-clause.

By now CERN was beginning to feel it had played itself back into the game. After all Tim was right; CERN didn't want the same kind of long-term role in the Web that MIT/LCS was after. Why should it? It was a physics laboratory, not a software development organization. CERN wanted recognition for the fact that the Web had been invented there, and it wanted to tell the world that that was no accident. Defending the kind of basic science that CERN does is always a delicate balance between selling the ideal that curiosity-driven research is a defining feature of civilization and the pragmatic approach of drawing attention to the value of spin-offs. Bob Wilson, the first director of one of CERN's US counterparts, Fermilab, was a master of the former. When asked by Rhode Island Senator Joseph Pastore whether particle accelerators produced anything useful for the security of the United States, he replied, 'It has nothing to do directly with defending our country, except to make it worth defending!' CERN had been pushing that side of the argument for decades. What it needed was a way of beefing up the progress-through-serendipity argument, and the laboratory's management was beginning to realize that the Web was a perfect example.

Pier Giorgio Innocenti may have been taken aback by his first encounter with the MIT/LCS way of doing business, but he was a quick learner. His reply to Vezza on 4 November was written in MIT/LCS's language, and although its tone was conciliatory, it also said that CERN was holding its ground. There was no bluff to be called. Where Vezza had quoted Tim's personal agreement with Dertouzos, Innocenti quoted CERN's official proposal to the European Union. 'In parallel with the WWW organization in Europe hosted by CERN . . . we propose to encourage the formation of a similar organization in the US. These two organizations would work together as an overall WWW organization toward the same goal in a manner consistent with mutual benefit.' He assured Vezza that CERN had 'no intentions whatsoever to take measures which would put the global success of WWW at risk.' And he invited Vezza to a meeting in Europe to clear up whatever misunderstandings had arisen and to shape a collaboration that would take into account the legitimate interests of both MIT/LCS and CERN. Vezza accepted the invitation and assured Innocenti that he was confident that intellectual property issues could be settled to everyone's satisfaction. A meeting was set for 1 December at the European Union's offices in Brussels.

In the lead-up to the meeting, Innocenti was in confident mood. He believed that CERN's agenda was back on course and he told the laboratory's management, 'I assume that we will succeed in re-establishing a balanced partnership with MIT.' Whatever form that partnership took, he believed that CERN's involvement would last for the eighteen months of the EU project, at the end of which CERN would have got the recognition it wanted and would be able to quietly get on with physics.

The EU's position, as faxed to Mike Sendall on 8 November, stressed that the fundamental requirement was for a balanced project with mutual benefit. Meanwhile, Tim Berners-Lee was feeling confident enough that things were back on the rails to start giving interviews, and on 8 November a reporter for O'Reilly's GNN billed him as 'Director of W3O, the new WWW organization based at MIT and CERN.' The interview covered where the Web had come from, where it was going, and how what Tim was now calling the W3O Consortium would ensure that the world would have one Web standard.

The first of December arrived. Robert's half-moon diagram went through another iteration, this time at the hand of Michael Dertouzos and this time with all the cash-flow arrows clearly defined. The MIT W3C would become the International World Wide Web Consortium. Its income would be managed by MIT/LCS but it would have an independent International Coordination Board and an advisory board made up of its members. US government funds would go to MIT/LCS, EU funds to CERN, and there would be a two-way flow of funds across the Atlantic. Tim Berners-Lee hovered 'en cheval' between the two halves, although he would physically be in Boston. It was a formula everyone could live with.

With agreement between MIT/LCS and CERN, the path to a credible World Wide Web Organization looked clear. MIT/LCS had invited the first North American members to an inaugural meeting of the International W3C on 14 December, and when Robert got back to CERN from Brussels, he set about inviting potential European members to an information meeting in Brussels on the 15th. Some European industrialists were invited to both and one in particular happened to be a friend of Robert Cailliau's. When he received invitations to Boston and Brussels on consecutive days, Robert's friend dropped a line to Robert pointing out that 'just theoretically, leaving Boston at 6.15 p.m. allows one to be in Brussels at 9 a.m. the next morning'. He was not the only one to have noticed: Al Vezza planned to be on that plane.

That week in December 1994 proved to be decisive for the future of both the Web and of CERN. Not only were the W3C meetings scheduled for Boston and Brussels on the Wednesday and Thursday, but on the Friday CERN's Council would vote on the laboratory's proposed new accelerator, a vote that would determine whether or not the laboratory had a future. A 'yes' would guarantee CERN a place at the heart of the global particle physics research community until well into the new century. A 'no' would mean that the laboratory might as well start thinking about shutting up shop.

FRAMEWORK FOR W3 EUROPEAN AMERICAN COOPERATION

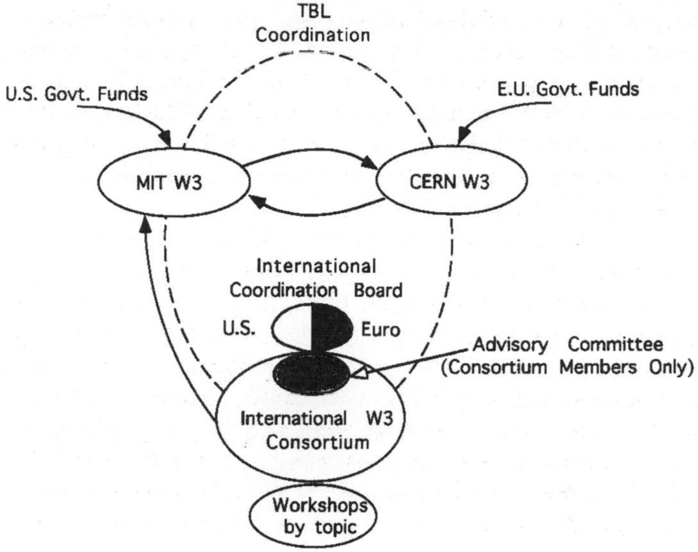

Premise:

Cooperation is timely, and desirable and can result in more than the sum of its parts. Competition for setting the W3 standard exists already and will increase further.

Framework

1. TBL *en cheval*
2. One W3 Standard
3. One Consortium
   - not for profit
   - reflects voice of industry, worldwide
4. Fund flows to match services rendered
5. Tight Cooperation and Trust

Brussels - 12/1/94

Figure 28: On 1 December 1994, Robert Cailliau's half-moon diagram went through another iteration. This time the cash-flows were clearly defined and the International W3 Consortium would feed directly into MIT.

CERN's delegation at the Brussels meeting was made up of Robert Cailliau, François Fluckiger, and Mike Sendall. The meeting was held in a long room filled with a big U-shaped table at 5 avenue de Beaulieu, some way out from the centre of town. George Metakides, Director of the ESPRIT programme, presided over a room filled with European industrialists and representatives of computer science research institutes. Everyone believed that an information revolution was just around the corner, and Metakides was the man charged with making sure that Europe did not get left out. He was convinced that the Web was the way to forward and was ready to back up his conviction with nearly $2 million of ESPRIT funding. One of the people who had most influenced Metakides's thinking was none other Michael Dertouzos.

Metakides and Dertouzos were old friends. Both held dual US and Greek citizenship, and they had met in the early 1970s when Dertouzos was a young professor at MIT and Metakides was working in the maths department there. They had kept in touch, and in 1993 Dertouzos had given the ESPRIT conference banquet speech. He had talked about his dreams of an information marketplace. 'Not many of us understood or believed it at the time,' Metakides admits, but the seed of an idea had been planted. Later on, when he had met Tim and Robert and they had demonstrated the Web to him, the seed had taken root. 'Tim came across as an earnest, dedicated person,' he recalls, 'with a good dose of idealism.' The demonstration impressed Metakides. 'It was the sort of thing that stayed with you,' he says. 'And how shall I put it? The vision began to take shape and it was an exciting one.' It took another six months and another meeting with Michael Dertouzos, however, for Metakides to fully realize that the Web, and the information marketplace it would create, really was the future.

In March 1994, Dertouzos and Metakides were attending the inauguration of a new conference centre in the northern Greek town of Metsovo. In the evenings they would go out to dinner at a local taverna. 'While drinking the local wine and eating delicious Greek sausages,' recalls Dertouzos, 'we brainstormed on a dual American–European strategy that would make the Web a truly international standard that served the two homes we both loved.' Before that meeting, Metakides knew about the Web, but it was Dertouzos who had really opened his eyes to how big it was going to be. 'This was, for me personally,' he explains, 'sort of putting the vision together, and I began to see more clearly what could be.' From that moment on, MIT/LCS was a valuable ingredient in the European Union's strategy for the Web.

The results of their brainstorming were on the point of being realized in that room in Brussels. There were well over sixty people around the table, with Al Vezza being a noticeable absentee. He was still making his way from the airport to the avenue de Beaulieu. He had rushed from the first meeting of the W3C at MIT/LCS to catch his plane to Brussels, but the flight was a little late arriving. The message he had got from the first W3C members in Boston just hours before was that the consortium had better not just be an American affair, it had better be world wide. Vezza was pleased to be able to tell them that he was just on his way to Brussels to ensure that it would be. He arrived to find the meeting already underway.

When George Metakides recognized Vezza, he invited him to introduce himself. Vezza told the room that he had come directly from the first meeting of W3C in Boston where there were about forty signed-up members. He then sat down to listen to CERN's presentation. The CERN people stood up and presented the consortium as they saw it, as an organization consisting of two parts of equal stature collaborating towards a common goal.

That was not what Al Vezza was expecting to hear. He had come to Brussels with a slightly different understanding of what the International World Wide Web Consortium would be. He saw it as a single organization coordinated from MIT/LCS by its 'en cheval' director Tim Berners-Lee, but with a second European headquarters of equal standing to the American one. The difference may seem slight to the casual observer, but to Al Vezza and the CERN people around the table, it didn't seem slight at the time. 'I was furious,' said Vezza years later. 'I felt that I was being ambushed because what they said is, "We can't let these Americans run off with this Web, we invented it here. We're going to keep it in Europe. We're going to start a consortium at CERN."'

When the CERN people heard Vezza's version of the consortium, they reacted in pretty much the same way. Robert leaned over to Mike and said, 'What do we do now, walk out? Tell the audience they're being had?' Mike replied, 'No, you cannot do that.' So they sat through the remaining minutes of the meeting and didn't rock the boat. Metakides thanked everyone for coming and exhorted them to join the Consortium. The overwhelming feeling was that most of them would. As people were leaving, Metakides asked the CERN people if they could now sign all the agreed papers. Sendall said there were issues he would have to take back to CERN for discussion, and the CERN people left.

It was clear that CERN and MIT/LCS still had some bargaining to do if they were going to make their relationship work, but the message was that European industry was prepared to back the new organization. The

World Wide Web Consortium was off the ground, but there would still be one more twist in the story before the consortium would assume its final form. Metakides was well aware of the discussions taking place at CERN and their impact on the laboratory's future. 'The decision on the Web consortium,' he explains, 'would probably be a corollary of this other decision.' Moreover, Metakides had already been primed that INRIA might make a strong European partner for MIT/LCS. 'In early 1994, I told Metakides that W3O would need input from institutes other than just CERN and that he should not forget INRIA,' remembers Robert Cailliau. Metakides took that advice on board, and knowing all too well how long it could take to put a big agreement together, he wanted to be sure that if CERN did have to pull out, INRIA would be ready to pick up the reins. So just as Al Vezza was about to leave the meeting, Metakides invited him into his office. 'I don't believe that they will do it,' Vezza remembers Metakides saying. 'You should think in terms of INRIA. That's all I'll say.' Jean-François Abramatic, INRIA's representative at the meeting, had a similar encounter as the meeting was breaking up. 'In the corridor, Metakides took me to one side for a minute, he explains, 'and he said, "There might be big changes." That's all he told me.'

A new dawn for CERN and the World Wide Web

Meanwhile, during a tense week in Geneva, CERN's Council burnt a lot of midnight oil in hammering out acceptable conditions for the approval of the LHC, culminating in Director General Chris Llewellyn-Smith's finest hour as one after another Council delegates raised their hands to give the project a unanimous seal of approval. But the victory had been hard won. There would be some serious belt-tightening to be done at CERN, and Llewellyn-Smith was condemned to spend the remaining years of his mandate travelling the world to secure extra funding for the LHC so that it could start up on time in 2005. He was successful in doing so, with Canada, India, Israel, Japan, Russia, and the United States all signing up to the project before Llewellyn-Smith left in 1998.

When the partying had died down, a hastily arranged meeting of CERN's management decided that hosting the W3C would be pushing the laboratory's resources, and its luck, too far. There were those at CERN who had felt uncomfortable with the Web all along, especially once it became clear just how big it would be, and to them the LHC was an opportunity for CERN to withdraw honourably. 'At the beginning when we had not realized that this would become a very big operation,' explains Pier Giorgio Innocenti, 'the idea of keeping a foot in the W3 consortium and maybe housing the European part was an idea which was attractive.' When the size of the commitment required became clear, CERN started thinking along the lines of working with INRIA, but then with the LHC's approval, the laboratory decided that its best policy would be to show that it was totally focused on the new project. 'So in the end,' Innocenti continues, 'we decided that we would help the European Commission to pass the flag to INRIA as the European *porte parole* in the consortium.'

George Metakides had clearly foreseen the possibility of CERN pulling out—he had said as much to Vezza and Abramatic at the Brussels meeting—so he wasn't too surprised when Pier Giorgio Innocenti gave him a call to tell him of CERN's decision. 'With the hierarchy of CERN,' he later explained, 'you didn't get the same enthusiasm as with some of the people that were directly involved. And then later events probably explained that; they could probably see what was coming.' Metakides called the head of INRIA, Alain Bensoussan, who in turn called Jean-François Abramatic and gave him the news that would ensure that he didn't enjoy a peaceful Christmas. Abramatic was not entirely surprised either: 'CERN is a Nobel Prize maker and there is no Nobel Prize in computer science,' he later explained. As Vice-Chairman of the W3C, as the new organization would now be called, and most senior member of its European branch, it was his job to make sure that European industry signed up.

W3C

By the mid-1990s, France's national research organization for computer science had become the jewel in the crown of the 'Plan Calcul'. Whereas the country's domestic computer industry was still struggling to make an impact on the global scene, INRIA was respected the world over. From its roots outside Paris, it had grown to have research units from Lorraine to the Côte d'Azur and from Brittany to the Alps.

What had prompted Robert Cailliau to suggest INRIA as a potential partner in the World Wide Web Consortium to George Metakides was the research of a group at INRIA's Grenoble branch. INRIA may not have been the only academic computer science research organization in Europe, but thanks to the direction taken by one of its principal researchers, Vincent Quint, in the early 1980s it was the best placed to pick up the European end of W3C. Because of Quint, INRIA had built up a lot of expertise in the right areas. And despite being a French research organization, INRIA also had sound pan-European credentials as a founder member of the European Research Consortium for Informatics and Mathematics (ERCIM), a network that began with six of Europe's leading national research institutes in applied mathematics and information technology. As a computer science research organization, INRIA also had better credentials than CERN to develop the Web to its full potential. Moreover, since CERN had been working with INRIA as a partner in the European end of the organization, the French institution was already fully up to speed. In short, INRIA was the natural choice for an organization to promote the Web in Europe.

Inroads to INRIA

INRIA's first contact with the Web came in 1993 when CERN held a workshop on SGML. Even if most of the laboratory's physicists preferred $\TeX$, CERN's computer scientists had officially adopted SGML because they liked the way it allowed structure to be built into documents. Led by Eric van Herwijnen, they were playing a significant part in SGML development. The CERN implementation of SGML had already served as the model for Tim Berners-Lee's HTML, and by this time it was becoming a much more sophisticated tool than the simple markup first invented in 1969. Vincent Quint was at the workshop. He had been working on an SGML implementation himself, and since he was based in Grenoble he didn't have far to go, CERN being just a couple of hours away up the A41 autoroute. Quint had been at INRIA's Grenoble laboratories for quite some time, starting his career running the Grenoble node of Louis Pouzin's pioneering Cyclades network, but by the 1990s his interest had moved on from networking to document structure. 'I started off in the lower layers of network architecture,' he explains, 'that's to say the communications protocols. Then afterwards I got interested in the transport layers and climbing like that through the architecture I became interested in the format of the data transported over networks and in particular the format of documents. That's how my research activity has moved from networks to documents.'

As a result of his upward migration through network layers, he had started a research group in the early 1980s to develop structured documentation. Back then, WYSIWYG word processing was at a rudimentary stage and simple markups like Robert Cailliau's 'Report' still ruled the roost. What Quint wanted to do was combine the intuitive ease of use of a WYSIWYG documentation system with the powerful structural capabilities offered by a markup language. The result was a program called Grif that allowed several representations of the same document. One window might show the markup, another what the printed page would look like. Yet another might show just the chapter headings. And no matter what window you happened to be working in, your edits would appear in all of them at once. Grif came along at the end of the 1980s, and by the time of the CERN SGML workshop, it had been spun off by INRIA into a successful commercial product.

Vincent Quint ran into Tim Berners-Lee at that CERN workshop and recognized the similarities between Tim's ideas for the Web and what he had already been doing with Grif. The Web, as originally envisioned by Tim, was like Grif on the Internet, and once Quint knew about the Web he steered his research team off in the Web's direction and started working on a browser/editor they called Tamaya.

When Al Vezza had come to Europe in May 1994, INRIA was working closely with CERN as a partner in the proposed European end of the Web, and INRIA's Paris headquarters was one of his ports of call. Vezza's itinerary took him first to CERN, then to INRIA and Oxford University which were both potential partners for CERN in the European arm of the consortium, and finally to Brussels for meetings with the European Union. But by the time he left CERN, his agenda had changed. He had had meetings with all the laboratory's top brass and there was something about those meetings that worried him. 'And you know,' he explains, 'when I left there I said to myself, "Gee, I can't figure out whether these guys want to do this or not."' Unknown to Vezza, CERN's top brass were already preoccupied with the LHC and the future of particle physics. They may not have said it, but their worries must have shown through. So Vezza left for INRIA to check out the organization's credentials not only as a partner for CERN in the European side of the consortium, but as a potential European host for W3C in its own right.

Al Vezza had got the impression that even if Robert Cailliau's heart was in the Web, CERN's wasn't. He didn't want to be left without a European partner, and so when he got to INRIA he told Jean-François Abramatic, 'CERN has told me that they want to do it, but I don't have a good feeling that they can do it.' He went on to Oxford where he found a thriving computer department, but not one that would be interested in the kind of work the consortium would do. So he returned to Boston with his mind made up. 'When I got back I had a meeting with the director and I said, "Mike, there's no choice here. The only choice is INRIA."'

Jean-François Abramatic, Jeff to his anglophone friends, was in charge of business development at INRIA. When Vincent Quint's Grif was ready to be spun-off, it was Abramatic who set up the company that commercialized it. His company had also been among the first to develop an X-terminal and Abramatic had been at the first meeting of the

X-Consortium, so he was already familiar with MIT/LCS. He spent the day presenting INRIA to Vezza and in the evening he took his guest out to dinner. Vezza had been impressed with what he had seen and heard, and when Abramatic dropped him off at his hotel, Vezza gave him the first hint that INRIA might have a bigger role to play in the World Wide Web Consortium than just being a partner to CERN. 'Just before saying goodbye,' recalls Abramatic, 'he said, "CERN will start but you guys should be ready for takeover."' Abramatic kept that to himself, but later in the year, at the Chicago conference just after MIT had launched the MIT World Wide Web Consortium, he could sense that all was not well in the CERN–MIT marriage. 'I discussed with Robert and François Fluckiger and others,' he recalls, 'and it was obvious that the fit was not perfect.' So he had gone to Brussels on 15 December prepared for anything.

It's official

The transfer of the European end of W3C from CERN to INRIA was officially announced on 12 January 1995, and a meeting was set at CERN for six days later to work out how the transfer would be managed. Tim Berners-Lee might have left CERN already, but most of his followers were still there and so was the CERN server with all of the Web software and information it contained. François Fluckiger outlined two possibilities for smooth transfer of the Web to INRIA. One was based on an eighteen-month transition strategy that Innocenti had envisioned after the 1 December meeting with MIT/LCS. The other foresaw CERN getting out of WebCore, the name that the EU project had acquired, as quickly as possible, with the CERN server being finally switched off as soon as August. The gentle transition would be the ideal scenario but, in the light of the laboratory's budget cuts, it would be dependent on EU funding.

With a workable agreement between a European organization and MIT/LCS settled, Brussels was ready to release its $2 million to get W3C off the ground. Deals were soon struck between all the players. At the end of March 1995, MIT/LCS signed the agreement to set up W3C with INRIA, backdated to 1 October 1994. The European Union's contracts with CERN and INRIA and an agreement between CERN and INRIA completed the formalities. Most of Tim's followers left CERN, some to INRIA to work on the W3C, some to set up their own Web-based companies. One, Arthur Secret, even tried his hand at the restaurant trade before settling into Internet consultancy work back in Geneva. Just one of the original Web team remained at CERN, Robert Cailliau. 'If I had been younger, single, with no kids and cats, I might have left and joined

W3C,' he says. He also had the successful conference series to worry about. And after all, CERN would still need to develop the Web as the tool for physics collaboration that Tim Berners-Lee had envisaged back in 1989. There would be no shortage of work for Cailliau in providing Web support for the physics community for many years to come.

The World Wide Web Consortium was announced to the world on 7 April. Al Vezza gave a presentation in Brussels of the structure of the new organization. Gone were Cailliau's half-moons, replaced by a single full moon in Vezza's slides. The Consortium was presented as a perfectly symmetric structure with Tim Berners-Lee as its director and MIT and INRIA as its hosts. It was precisely the organization that anyone who cared for the Web believed was needed, and now it could set about its business of ensuring that Tim Berners-Lee's original vision of an open collaborative space for everyone could be realized.

Cailliau's half-moons did make one more appearance. When Jean-François Abramatic wrote to European companies in May inviting them to join W3C, the diagram he put on the cover of the accompanying dossier looked a lot like Cailliau's original, with INRIA where CERN had once been. The consortium had managed to become a copy of MIT/LCS's X-Consortium with an international dimension. Pricing was in dollars, $50 000 per year for big companies, $5 000 for small ones, and industrial funding did go to MIT, but what happened to it then was determined by the consortium's members. The contracts sent out to potential members of W3C looked much like those Cailliau, Fluckiger, and Sendall would have liked to have seen at the start, with MIT and INRIA being given equal status in the organization. The road had not always been smooth, but Europe and the USA were working towards a common goal. How different things might have been were it not for that initial misunderstanding between CERN and MIT, if CERN had sent feedback to Vezza before the MIT W3C invitation went out, giving rise to the mistrust that followed. With hindsight, Cailliau puts much of the blame in Europe's camp: things just moved too slowly there. 'There certainly was a need to act fast,' he says, 'and there MIT certainly had the lead. The blame is entirely on Europe for being sluggish. They just did not understand the tsunami that was building up.'

Abramatic worked tirelessly through the year to make sure that enough European companies would join the consortium to give Europe financial and political clout in W3C. The British press, in true jingoistic fashion, had a field day. 'I remember being flamed by the British newspapers,' says Abramatic, 'who were saying that the Yankees have already taken Tim and now the Froggies are taking the consortium.' But not all

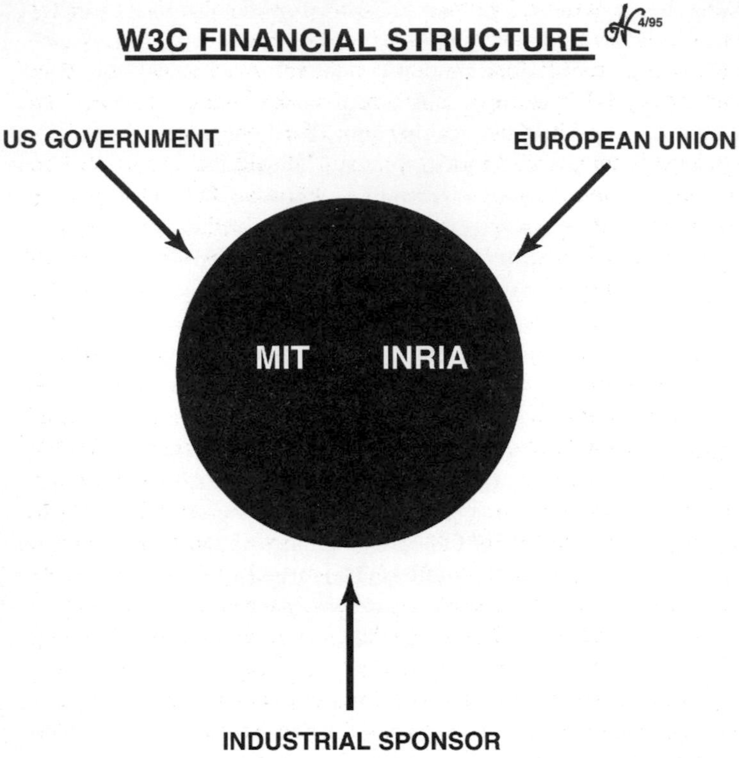

Figure 29: The half-moons merge. In Al Vezza's talk on 7 April 1995, W3C exhibited perfect symmetry.

the British were of that opinion. One at least, Mike Sendall, gave Abramatic the lion's share of the credit for making W3C a global organization. 'INRIA stepped in to hold up the European end,' he said, 'and under the energetic guidance of Abramatic the W3C came to have as many European partners as American ones.' And despite the baying of the British press, they came from all over the continent. By October the consortium had thirty-nine members from Europe to the United States' sixty-four, still a minority but enough to ensure a critical mass and an impressive achievement for someone who had jumped in at the eleventh hour. But the British press were not alone in their criticism of the W3C. The transfer of the Web from CERN also met with a frosty reception from the Spanish daily, *La Vanguardia*. 'The World Wide Web,' it announced on 12 March 1995, 'has passed into the hands of the Massachusetts Institute of Technology in the United States due to lack of economic support from the European Commission.' MIT/LCS's partner INRIA, the article claimed, would be no more than a branch of MIT in Europe, chosen to 'save the honour of France'. *La Vanguardia* saved its most scathing attack for George Metakides. 'This high-level functionary of the Commission,' it said, 'has manifested an unclear position contrary to the interests of Europe.' But *La Vanguardia* hadn't followed the whole story, nor had it bargained for the energy of Jean-François Abramatic. Metakides may well have been working with MIT/LCS, but not because he was anti-European. Both he and MIT/LCS simply wanted to make sure of the right European partner. 'My role was that of honest broker between all parties,' explains Metakides, 'driven by the vision of a global "agora". Had this brokerage failed, the result would have been a W3C with no European pillar.' As for Jean-François Abramatic, the role of second fiddle was not for him. He would settle for nothing less than full and equal partnership, as his energetic recruitment of European companies proved. Abramatic's efforts were rewarded in September 1996 when he took over the W3C chairmanship from Al Vezza. 'Jeff,' says Robert, 'taught me how to look at all sides of a problematic situation, find a positive facet, and then concentrate on that to solve the issues. He was always amazing in getting consensus, damping controversy, motivating individuals. I believe that if the W3C works, it is to a large extent due to his self-effacing but very able stewardship.'

The globalization of W3C was completed in September 1996 when Nobuo Saito, Dean and Professor of Environmental Information at the University of Keio, Japan, became W3C's Associate Chairman and set up an Asian site for the Web hosted at his university.

Thanks to Vincent Quint's group, INRIA already had considerable credibility on the technical front. The successor to Tamaya, called Amaya, is one of W3C's star products. If you want to see what Tim Berners-Lee's vision was all about, Amaya is the best place to find out. It is more than just a browser, including all the powerful structured document-editing capabilities that Quint had worked into Grif. Apart from Tim Berners-Lee's original NeXT browser, Amaya is one of the few Web browsers that lets you publish on the Web as easily as you can read. In 1992, Pei Wei and Tony Johnson had toyed with the idea of turning Viola and Midas into browser/editors, but with the arrival of Mosaic they had never got that far.

Should you choose to try Amaya, you can simply download it from the W3C Web site. The code will be shipped to you from Quint's lab in Grenoble, but you don't need to know that. At the end of the day, just as Tim had foreseen, geography doesn't matter. You are downloading a program from the W3C, and whether that happens to be in Boston, Paris, Keio, or Grenoble is not the point. Through its own Web site, the World Wide Web Consortium is setting an example of what the Web should be, globalization for the good of everyone.

Through INRIA, Europe had got its equal partnership with the United States, but the name W3O had been superseded by W3C. And despite Tim's earlier protestations, government funding did find its way into W3C, and industry didn't seem to mind too much. Seen from the perspective of the Web team at CERN, and from MIT/LCS, the events leading up to the launch of the International W3C in Brussels were not always easy, but perhaps it all boils down to a persistent transatlantic cultural difference. Seen from Boston, speed was of the essence, and setting up the MIT W3C was simple expediency: a way of heading off potential rivals. 'The Europeans would have been happy to have made a committee and set the whole thing up and then they would have taken a few more years to make the standards and follow the standards,' says Tim Berners-Lee. 'But in the US they had products rolling out the door.' He'd seen what had happened that last time the Europeans tried to set a network standard with the OSI protocols and he didn't want that to happen to the Web.

In the end, the protagonists came out as friends. Vezza and Cailliau now work together organizing the Web conferences. 'He was a pain to work with and Al himself admits this, but if you took him away it probably wouldn't have worked,' concedes Cailliau. CERN is an active member of W3C, whose membership had topped 300 by 1999, and in terms of commercial awareness, it is a much wiser organization than it was back at the beginning of 1994. But the laboratory did make one more attempt to attach its name to the Web, not for any financial reason but just to let the world know where it all began. An ultimately unsuccessful attempt to trademark the term World Wide Web and the WWW logo was launched by CERN at the end of 1995. After much legal handwringing, lawyers concluded that by then World Wide Web and WWW were merely descriptive, and therefore not trademarkable. CERN let the case drop, but not before putting on the record that if CERN couldn't have trademarks for that reason, then nor could anyone else, thus making sure that the name remains public property.

Today, CERN never misses an opportunity to remind the world that pure research is what made the Web happen. 'Instead of W.W.W., we should have had C.E.R.N.,' jokes Pier Giorgio Innocenti, 'Common Exchange something or other.' That way the world might have appreciated better the way pure research can contribute to material progress in entirely unforeseen ways.

There is no doubt that something like the Web would have appeared sooner or later; all the ingredients were in place and the time was ripe. But it is no accident that it happened at CERN. The international nature of the laboratory's collaborations and its position at the cutting edge of technology provided the magnet to draw Tim Berners-Lee to Geneva. 'It is hard to imagine that all of this could have happened somewhere other than CERN,' said Mike Sendall. 'Being able to invent the Web was partly a question of being in the right place at the right time,' agrees Tim. 'It was also a question of being in the right environment. A place like CERN where enthusiastic experts congregate from all over the world is the only way to have such an innovative atmosphere. A lab which pushes the boundaries of technology as a matter of course in almost every aspect of its daily work is likely to be the place where you can create a system designed for what, to everyone else, is the future.'

But for Tim it wasn't just the place that mattered, it was the people. 'I had great bosses in Peggie Rimmer and Mike Sendall, and a lot of stimulating colleagues, all prepared to think outside the box,' he explains. 'I think all in all that CERN's existence was critical to the start of the Web. After that, it became a triumph for a distributed grass-roots movement of folks from across the world. The growth of the Web itself was an amazing thing to be involved in. The fact that it worked gives me great hope for the future.'

Epilogue

Just the beginning

This book ends in the mid-1990s, just as the Web and the Internet were becoming household names, but really we are still right at the beginning. At the end of 1994, when the Web was starting to hit the headlines, there were some 10 000 Web servers around the world. By the end of 1999, that number was approaching 10 000 000 and still rising fast. In America and Europe the Internet is already an established part of the communications landscape; think of Mike Sendall's Californian lettuce. And it is no longer necessary to have a degree in computer science to use it. One of Paul Kunz's favourite dinner-table stories is about how he set his mother up with a computer and an Internet connection. 'Now I get e-mail saying, "You never write home!"' he jokes. Even without her own connection, she could easily pop into a Web café to send her e-mails.

But seen from the developed countries of the northern hemisphere, appearances can be deceptive. At the 8th International World Wide Web Conference, held in Toronto in May 1999, Bob Metcalfe calculated that just a few per cent of the world's population have an Internet connection. 'We talk about it as if everybody in the world uses it yet there are only, what's the last figure I've seen, about 146 million people connected to the Internet?' points out Alan Ellis, another delegate at the conference. 'So what are the other five billion people doing that don't know anything about this technology and don't use it? We often get very blinkered, and with something that we talk about as being global we actually should be a bit more inclusive of the rest of the world's population.'

Ellis should know. He is an old hand on the Web conference circuit, having organized the 7th conference in Brisbane and set up a series of 'Ausweb' conferences for the southern hemisphere. Over the coming years, his concerns are likely to be answered as the cost of telecommunications falls and the technology of wireless Internet begins to take off, driving the exponential expansion of Web use that began back in 1991 to every corner of the globe.

And as the Web grows, it will evolve into an ever more useful medium as the tools for managing the ever-increasing reserves of information it contains improve. The Web's biggest problem is a result of its success. There is so much information out there that it is often hard to find what you want. The answer, according to Tim Berners-Lee, is what he calls the semantic Web. The kind of information on the Web today is understandable to humans but not to computers. If Berners-Lee, for example, wanted to buy a yellow car in Massachusetts and his neighbour wanted to sell a primrose automobile in Boston, how would Berners-Lee's search engine know that what he wanted was right on his doorstep? If a current W3C project is successful, some kind of logical schema will tell the search engine that primrose is just a kind of yellow and that automobiles and cars are in fact the same thing.

Another improvement we are likely to see in the coming years will be due to the Web getting back to its roots. The Web we all use today is not the one Tim Berners-Lee first envisaged back in 1989. He foresaw his invention as being a tool for communication in which it would be as easy to author material as to read it. The Web wasn't meant to be the passive medium that it has become for most of us. To others, like Andy van Dam, the roots go much deeper than 1989. He points out that the whole point of hypertext is that it should be as easy to write material and add links as to read and follow. The early hypertext systems, such as Doug Engelbart's NLS and those developed at Brown University in the 1960s, had that feature. Tim Berners-Lee's first browser/editor had it as well. But the Web of today does not. The W3C is addressing these limitations by combining the functionality pioneered by the early hypertext system builders with the pervasiveness and scalability of the Web. A new markup language, called extensible markup language or XML, already provides sophisticated document structure, following the example of NLS. A recent W3C specification spells out how to point your own links or annotations to very precise locations such as single words or phrases in a document, following Brown University's FRESS. And another shows how to keep links outside documents, following the example set by the later Brown University system, Intermedia.

And while today many of us think twice before sending our credit card numbers over the Internet, we will soon come to think nothing of it, using the Web to do our shopping, and perhaps even to read our newspapers, paying by the page. Bob Metcalfe believes that microcharging is just around the corner. He surveyed his readers to find out how much they would be prepared to pay to read his column. The reply came, '0.2 cents', but with half a million readers, he is quite happy about that. As more and more information takes on electronic form, we will need a whole host of virtual librarians to keep track of it all. A start in that direction has already been taken by Brewster Kahle, the author of WAIS, whose next project was called Alexa, for the same reason that Robert Cailliau dubbed his proposal for a European centre of excellence 'Alexandria'. Kahle's idea was to archive the entire Web by copying everything onto huge computers on a regular basis. He was not the only one. In Sweden, former particle physicists Allan Arvidson and Frans Lettenström run the world's first government-sponsored national Web archive. The National Library of Sweden has been archiving everything published in Sweden since the 1600s. 'If you want to see what a shoe advertisement looked like in the 1800s, you can do it. If you want to read a timetable of the horses between one town and another in 1850, well, you can look it up,' explains Lettenström. 'It's good if you write detective stories.' The library contains every issue of every Swedish newspaper right back to the 1600s, but when Web journals started to appear, they were just being lost. Now they archive everything in the .se domain as well as Swedish-registered pages in .org, .com, and .net. More recently, they have started to look at .nu, the domain name corresponding to the tiny Pacific island of Niue. '"Nu" In Swedish means "now",' explains Lettenström, 'so it became very popular among Swedish companies to have a domain name there because you could call it "Buy my product now".' The Swedish project is for the long term. Swedish corporate law prevents anyone, including the archivists, from looking at the archive until seventy years after the death of the people responsible for the information, fodder perhaps for future detective story writers.

The role of academia

Today the Web and the Internet are largely commercial entities, but that is a very recent development. They are built on the back of over two decades of academic research, with the spark that finally lit the fuse coming out of a laboratory specializing in the most esoteric form of research imaginable. There have been many false starts and disappointments as great ideas came before their time and had to wait for technology and society to catch up. Would the commercial companies that dominate the Internet today have had the patience for that? 'I think the general philosophy that you have to rely on industry to tell you what the real needs are is actually a misunderstanding,' says Donald Davies.

'I don't think you can do anything that's fundamentally new without a ten-year timescale.' The hands-off management style is there too, from J. C. R. Licklider at ARPA to Mike Sendall at CERN, simply recognizing talent and giving it free rein. The lesson of the Internet is that serendipity must be allowed a space to breathe. It may have been some time in coming, but the Web has brought a handsome return on the investment in CERN. At today's prices, the annual value of Web based business comes to some three times the total amount of money invested in CERN since the laboratory was founded in the 1950s.

The history of the Internet is a history of ideas and how they are developed. As many of the ideas behind the Internet have come from Europe as the USA, yet it is the USA that has exploited them most successfully. For each of Europe's failures, there is a clear reason. If European countries had fully embraced the CEPT standard, as Hermann Maurer would have liked, perhaps the continent would have its own powerful personal computing industry. If they had not applied a lengthy committee-based approach to designing network protocols, perhaps the Internet would have taken hold earlier, or perhaps we would all be using ISO standards instead of TCP/IP. And if they had not granted telephone companies monopolies that made local calls expensive and led to wonderful information systems being bound to a single country, perhaps the Web would have spread faster. Each reason is different, but if there is a common thread it is that Europe is a collection of collaborating, but bickering, countries whereas the United States is one big entity. What holds in Maryland is also true in California. North Americans don't need to take a vast array of electrical plugs with them as they set off to travel their continent. But it is not all gloom for Europe. Companies like Psion and ARM lead the world in their niches. Europe does have a domestic personal computer industry, albeit one based on American standards. And there is even a counterexample. Mobile telephony started in the United States, but it is European companies that are leading the way.

Tim Berners-Lee's achievement has been recognized by a plethora of awards from bodies as prestigious as the MacArthur Foundation, the IEEE, and the ACM. It has even been suggested that if there were a Nobel Prize for computer science, Tim would have won it. But despite all that, Tim himself says that the Web is just a platform for other things to come. 'Where this will all end up is anyone's guess,' says Internet pioneer Vint Cerf. 'The only way to find out is to get going!'

Timeline

	General	Computers
1935		Vannevar Bush patents differential analyser.
1936		Konrad Zuse begins work on electro-mechanical computing devices.
1944		Colossus operational at Bletchley Park.
1945	Second World War ends.	
1946		ENIAC operational at Princeton.
1947		Transistor invented.
1948		Manchester 'baby' operational.
1949		Manchester Mark 1 operational. EDSAC operational at Cambridge.
1950	US National Science Foundation established.	Pilot ACE operational at NPL.
1951		First Ferranti Mark 1 delivered.
1954	CERN formally comes into existence with 12 member states.	
1955	West Germany joins NATO.	
1956	Suez crisis.	Ken Olsen builds TX-0.
1957	Sputnik launched by USSR.	
1958	Explorer launched by USA ARPA created by Eisenhower.	ACE operational at NPL. First integrated circuits produced.
1959		Timesharing discussed in Paris by Christopher Strachey.

Networks	Hypertext and Documentation	
		1935
		1936
		1944
	Vannevar Bush publishes 'As We May Think' in the *Atlantic Monthly*.	1945
		1946
		1947
		1948
		1949
		1950
		1951
		1954
		1955
		1956
		1957
		1958
Leonard Kleinrock starts working on his thesis about computer communication.		1959

	General	Computers
1961	Berlin wall goes up.	
1962	J.C.R. Licklider creates the Information Processing Techniques Office (IPTO) within ARPA.	Project Mac begins at MIT. Wesley Clark produces the LINC computer. Doug Engelbart publishes Augmenting Human Intelligence, which develops into NLS.
1963	President Kennedy assassinated Licklider's memo to the 'Intergalactic Computer Network'.	
1964	Start of the Vietnam War.	
1965		Ole-Johan Dahl and Kristen Nygaard invent Object Oriented programming.
1966	Bob Taylor becomes director of IPTO.	
1967		
1968	EEC establishes the COST framework for scientific collaboration within Europe.	Doug Engelbart demonstrates NLS at the Fall Joint Computer Conference.
1969	First Moon landing.	
1970		

Networks	Hypertext and Documentation	
		1961
		1962
		1963
Paul Baran publishes a paper on what would come to be called packet switching.		1964
	The term Hypertext is coined by Ted Nelson.	1965
Donald Davies describes his idea of packet switching at the NPL. IPTO funds computer link across the US.		1966
ACM meeting at Gatlinburg brings together network pioneers from UK and US. Donald Davies introduces packet switching to CCITT.	HES hypertext system developed at Brown University.	1967
Network Working Group established. Conversational Computing on the South Bank—Stanley Gill's prophetic presentation on the possible evolution of British networking.	FRESS hypertext system developed at Brown University.	1968
The ARPANET starts up. RFC 1 written by Steve Crocker.	GML developed by Charles Goldfarb, Edward Mosher, and Raymond Lorie.	1969
The NPL Network starts up.		1970

	General	Computers
1971		The first microprocessors are produced.
1972		
1973	Britain joins the Common Market. NORSAR in Norway becomes the first ARPANET site outside the US, closely followed by University College London.	The first microprocessor-based computer, the Micral, is launched in France. The Alto is developed at Xerox PARC.
1974		
1975	End of the Vietnam War.	The Altair 8800 kit computer is released. The Homebrew Computer Club is formed.
1976		Apple Computer is founded by Steve Jobs and Steve Wozniak.
1977		Tandy TRS-80, Commodore PET, and Apple II computers appear.
1978		Acorn computers is founded in the UK.

Networks	Hypertext and Documentation	
Norm Abramson's Alohanet starts up in Hawaii.		1971
Louis Pouzin's Cyclades network is demonstrated in France. The ARPANET is demonstrated in Washington. Ray Tomlinson sends the first e-mail.		1972
Videotex is invented by Sam Fedida at the British Post Office. TCP development begins. PACNET becomes the first packet-broadcasting satellite network. Ceefax and Oracle are launched in the UK. Bob Metcalfe develops Ethernet.		1973
COST project 11, the European Informatics Network links NPL and Cyclades.		1974
The Cambridge Ring is developed. EIN becomes fully operational.		1975
Queen Elizabeth II becomes the first head of state to send an e-mail message. CCITT publishes X.25 standard.		1976
The TITN network becomes operational at CERN. The experimental Internet is demonstrated. The British Post Office launches EPSS.	Robert Cailliau produces Report for use at CERN.	1977
CERNET starts up at CERN. TCP evolves into TCP/IP.		1978

	General	Computers
1979		Alan Kay develops Smalltalk.
1980		PSION founded. Sinclair releases the ZX-80 at under £100 assembled—the world's cheapest computer.
1981		The first IBM-PC is released. Acorn wins contract to produce the BBC Micro.
1982		
1983		ACT launches the Apricot computer.
1984		Macintosh launched.
1985		Sinclair launches the ill-fated C5 electric vehicle.
1986		Steve Jobs founds NeXT. Sinclair sells out to Amstrad.

Networks	Hypertext and Documentation	
Usenet starts up. Joint Network Team established in the UK. Prestel launched in the UK.	Donald Knuth releases $\TeX$.	1979
EIN decommissioned.	The SGML standard is published. Tim Berners-Lee writes 'Enquire' at CERN.	1980
French Télétel project starts, eventually becomes Minitel. STELLA project begins. BITNET starts up. The NSF establishes CSNET. The British Post Office launches PSS.		1981
Hermann Maurer in Graz extends the Videotex concept by building a microprocessor into his Videotex terminals.		1982
The Internet Activities Board is established. ARPANET switches to TCP/IP. TCP/IP available in BSD Unix. Domain Name System invented.		1983
NSF establishes NSFNET. JANET launched using X.25. BITNET acquires a European arm in EARN. CERN starts to evaluate TCP/IP.	CERNDOC produced at CERN.	1984
CERN adopts OSI protocols as official policy with everything else being interim. CERN chooses TCP/IP to network the computers controlling its new LEP accelerator.	Intermedia developed at Brown.	1985
Cleveland Free-Net starts up. NNTP appears.		1986

	General	Computers
1987		
1989	Berlin Wall comes down. Satellite television starts to appear.	
1990		
1991		
1992		
1993		
1994	CERN's LHC project approved.	

Networks	Hypertext and Documentation	
NSFNET and JANET linked. BITNET and CSNET merge. RFC1000.	First Hypertext Conference held at Chapel Hill, North Carolina. Hypercard released by Apple.	1987
With five million Minitel sets, France is the world's most wired country. WAIS. Archie. CERN opens its first external TCP/IP connections.	Tim Berners-Lee writes 'Information Management: A Proposal'.	1989
ARPANET decommissioned.	Microcosm developed at Southampton http://info.cern.ch/ becomes first Web server. HYTELNET.	1990
Commercial use of the Internet permitted. Gopher. JANET starts to run TCP/IP alongside X.25.	San Antonio Hypertext Conference. Line mode browser. Erwise browser. First US server at SLAC. Viola browser.	1991
Internet Society founded.	Midas browser. Lynx.	1992
	First Web developers' meeting in Boston. WISE project. White House Web site established. CERN puts Web software in the public domain. GNN. Viola runs mini application programs. X-Mosaic released. Cello browser for PCs.	1993
SuperJANET launched as a TCP/IP network. Prestel wound up.	Alexandria proposal. Agora. First Web conference held at CERN. Netscape.	1994

General		Computer
1995		
1999		

Networks	Hypertext and Documentation	
World Wide Web carries more data than Minitel for the first time.	W3C founded. Hyper-G handles sound and video. CERN's Web work transferred to INRIA.	1995
	Number of Web servers approaches 10 million.	1999

The Cast (abridged)

A non-exhaustive list of the characters in this book, these short entries should be taken as mnemonic aids and not as complete biographies.

Abramatic, Jean-François French computer scientist, Director of Development at INRIA, chairman of W3C since September 1996.

Abramson, Norm Leader of the team that built the world's first packet-radio network, the ALOHANET, in Hawaii.

Addis, Louise SLAC librarian, ran the SLAC preprint server and founded the SLAC WWW Wizards.

Allen, Paul Co-founder of Microsoft with Bill Gates.

Altaber, Jacques CERN computer scientist responsible for networking for the laboratory's SPS and LEP accelerators.

Andreessen, Marc Developer of the X-Mosaic browser at NCSA with Eric Bina, and co-founder of Netscape with Jim Clark.

Anklesaria, Farhad Main developer of gopher at the University of Minnesota.

Arvidson, Allan Swedish physicist working on the National Library of Sweden's Web archive project.

Atkinson, Bill Inventor of the Apple Hypertext program, HyperCard.

Babbage, Charles Nineteenth-century British mathematician widely regarded as the father of modern computing.

Baran, Paul American computer scientist and inventor of packet switching. The idea was invented independently by the Briton Donald Davies.

Barber, Derek British computer scientist. Headed the data communications research group at the NPL under Donald Davies. Later chaired the European Informatics Network.

Barker, Ben Member of the BBN team put together by Frank Heart to build the ARPANET's Interface Message processors (IMPs).

Bartlett, Keith Member of the data communications research group at the NPL.

Bellovin, Steve Co-inventor with Tom Truscott and Jim Ellis of Usenet news.

Berners-Lee, Mary Lee and Conway British computer scientists who worked on the Ferranti Mark 1 computer. Parents of Tim Berners-Lee, the inventor of the World Wide Web.

Berners-Lee, Tim British computer scientist. Inventor of the World Wide Web and later Director of the World Wide Web Consortium, W3C.

Bertell, Bill Member of the BBN team put together by Frank Heart to build the ARPANET's Interface Message Processors (IMPs).

Bina, Eric Software developer at NCSA. Wrote the X-Mosaic browser with Marc Andreessen.

Bosack, Len Co-founder of the router-manufacturing company Cisco.

Bright, Roy Head of Viewdata International Operations in the late 1970s.

Bruce, Tom Developer of Cello, one of the first Web browsers for PCs at Cornell Law School.

Bush, Vannevar Imagined hypertext in his 1945 article 'As We May Think'. Profoundly influenced Doug Engelbart.

Cailliau, Robert Belgian informatics engineer at CERN. The self-appointed evangelist of the World Wide Web.

Carpenter, Brian CERN computer scientist responsible for system software for the PS control system in the early 1980s, later head of networking at CERN and president of the IAB.

Cerf, Vint American computer scientist often referred to as the father of the Internet for his work on TCP.

Clark, Jim American entrepreneur. Founder of Silicon Graphics and then co-founder of Netscape Communications Corporation with Marc Andreessen.

Clark, Welden American computer scientist and co-author with J. C. R. Licklider of the landmark paper 'On-Line Man-Computer Communication'.

Clark, Wesley American computer scientist, inventor of the concept of a sub-net for the ARPANET. Went on to build the LINC computer.

Connolly, Dan American computer scientist whose early efforts towards standardization of the Web helped to ensure that all documents could be read by all browsers.

Cooper, Bob British computer scientist and founding member of the Joint Network Team that built the UK's JANET and SuperJANET networks.

Cosell, Bernie Member of the BBN team put together by Frank Heart to build the ARPANET's Interface Message processors (IMPs).

Crocker, Steve American computer scientist. Worked on the ARPANET and established the tradition of Requests For Comments (RFQs) when he sent a memo to the Network Working Group in 1969.

Crowther, Will Member of the BBN team put together by Frank Heart to build the ARPANET's Interface Message processors (IMPs). Best known for writing Adventure, the first computer game.

Curry, Christopher Co-founder with Hermann Hauser of Acorn, the British computer company that made the BBC Micro and achieved some success in the early 1980s.

Dahl, Ole-Johan Norwegian computer scientist. Co-inventor with Kristen Nygaard of Object-Oriented Programming.

Daneels, Axel CERN controls engineer. Responsible for applications programming for the CERN PS accelerator in the late 1970s and early 1980s.

Dautry, Raoul French government minister and proponent of creating a European laboratory in the late 1940s and early 1950s.

Davies, Donald British computer scientist and inventor of packet switching. The idea was invented independently by the American Paul Baran.

de Broglie, Louis French Nobel-Prizewinning physicist whose 1949 idea for a pan-European physics laboratory was realised in 1954 when twelve nations signed the convention establishing CERN.

Dertouzos, Michael Greek-American head of the Laboratory for Computer Science at MIT, home of the World Wide Web Consortium.

Deutsch, Peter Co-developer of archie at Canada's McGill University.

Dougherty, Dale Computer book publisher with the firm of O'Reilly. Organized a meeting of Web developers in Boston in 1993 that has come to be known as the 'zeroth' World Wide Web conference.

Ellis, Alan Australian polymath university professor and founder of the Ausweb conferences.

Ellis, Jim Co-inventor with Tom Truscott and Steve Bellovin of Usenet news.

Emtage, Alan Co-developer of archie at Canada's McGill University.

Engelbart, Doug Pioneer of personal computing. Among the first to think of using computers for non-technical purposes like word-processing. Inventor of the mouse.

Favre, Alain French student from the Conservatoire National des Arts et Métiers (CNAM) who worked on an early PC browser at CERN.

Fedida, Sam British engineer who invented Viewdata at the Post Office Research Station in Martlesham Heath.

Filo, David Stanford University graduate student, co-founder of Yahoo! with Jerry Yang.

Fluckiger, François CERN computer scientist who assumed responsibility for the Web at CERN when Tim Berners-Lee left for MIT.

Frystyk Nielsen, Henrik Danish student who joined the Web team at CERN in 1994.

Fu, Ping Scientific visualization expert. Worked on the morphing for Terminator 2. Hired Marc Andreessen at NCSA to work on a browser.

Fuchs, Ira Vice-Chancellor for University Systems at the City University of New York in the early 1980s. Founder of BITNET.

Gassée, Jean-Louis French computer scientist. Head of research and development at Apple in the early 1980s.

Gates, Bill Co-founder of Microsoft with Paul Allen.

Geisman, Jim Member of the BBN team put together by Frank Heart to build the ARPANET's Interface Message Processors (IMPs).

Gerard, Mike CERN computer scientist who worked on the laboratory's packet-switching network, CERNET, in the late 1970s.

Gill, Stanley Professor of Automatic Data Processing at Imperial College, London. Founder of the Real Time Club and outspoken champion of Donald Davies's packet-switching ideas.

Goldfarb, Charles Co-author of SGML, a highly successful markup language for producing structured documentation.

Groff, Jean-François French computer scientist who went to CERN as an alternative to military service and worked with Tim Berners-Lee. The first Web consultant.

Grundner, Tom Cleveland, Ohio-based assistant professor of medicine whose community health bulletin board gave rise to the free-net concept.

Hall, Wendy Hypertext developer and professor at Southampton University, founder of Microcosm.

Hardin, Joseph American sociologist who was head of NCSA's software development group at the time the Mosaic browsers were written.

Hauser, Hermann Co-founder with Christopher Curry of Acorn, the British computer company that made the BBC Micro and achieved some success in the early 1980s.

Heart, Frank Head of the BBN team that won the contract to build the Interface Message Processors (IMPs) for the ARPANET.

Heelan, Bill Co-developer of archie at Canada's McGill University.

Hughes, Kevin Author of an important early Web site about dinosaurs at Honolulu Community College. Historian of the World Wide Web.

Hullot, Jean-Marie French computer scientist whose interface builder became the heart of NeXTStep, the operating system that made the NeXT computer so appealing to Tim Berners-Lee as a development platform for the World Wide Web.

Innocenti, Pier Giorgio Italian boss of Robert Cailliau at CERN. Player in the negotiations leading to the establishment of W3C.

Jobs, Steve Co-founder of Apple Computer, founder of NeXT.

Johnson, Tony British physicist working at SLAC who wrote the Midas browser for the World Wide Web.

Joy, Bill Berkeley graduate student who set up the Berkeley Software Distribution (BSD) in 1977. Co-founder of Sun Microsystems.

Kahle, Brewster Founder of the WAIS project who went on to establish Alexa, a company to archive the World Wide Web.

Kahn, Bob MIT mathematician and ARPANET pioneer. Kahn was one of Frank Heart's team at BBN and later organized a landmark demonstration of the ARPANET in Washington, D.C., in 1972.

Kappe, Frank One of Herman Maurer's graduate students who was involved with the development of Hyper-G and Hyperwave at Graz.

Kay, Alan Computer pioneer from Utah who coined the term 'object-oriented' and, while working at Xerox PARC, produced the Graphical User Interface (GUI) that inspired the Macintosh.

Kelly, Brian Computer scientist from Leeds who offered Robert Cailliau a demo of the World Wide Web.

Kernighan, Brian Co-author with Dennis Ritchie of the C programming language.

Kilby, Jack Built the first integrated circuit for Texas Instruments in 1958.

Kirstein, Peter British network pioneer at University College London who introduced the ARPANET to Britain and championed the use of TCP/IP protocols.

Kjærnsrød, Steinar Norwegian computer scientist and member of the team that put the 1994 Lillehammer winter Olympics on the World Wide Web.

Kleinrock, Leonard Computer networking pioneer who was the first to think about how computers might communicate with each other. Kleinrock's UCLA computer science department became the first node on the ARPANET.

Knuth, Donald Stanford-based author of the $\TeX$ text processing language popular with physicists because of its powerful ability to produce mathematical equations.

Kuiper, Berend Head of the CERN team put together in the 1970s to bring the control system of the laboratory's PS accelerator up to date.

Kunz, Paul SLAC physicist who took the Web to America.

Le Lann, Gérard Member of Louis Pouzin's Cyclades team who ensured that the pure datagram approach pioneered in Cyclades made its way into the Internet protocols.

Leffler, Sam Colleague of Bill Joy's at Berkeley who oversaw the release of 4.2BSD Unix, a Unix implementation with TCP/IP built in.

Lemmke, Ari Finnish computer scientist whose students at the Helsinki University of Technology produced Erwise, one of the first Web browsers for Unix.

Lettenström, Frans Swedish physicist working on the National Library of Sweden's Web archive project.

Levy, Steve BBN vice-president who set up Telenet to capitalize on the ARPANET technology.

Licklider, J. C. R. American computing pioneer who became the first director of ARPA's Information Processing Techniques Office (IPTO) and provided the inspiration for the ARPANET.

Lie, Håkon Norwegian computer scientist who came to CERN in 1994 and later joined the fledgling W3C.

Luotonen, Ari Finnish programming wizard who came to CERN in 1993 and worked on some of the more advanced features of the Web.

Maurer, Hermann Viewdata researcher who had the idea of networked personal computing in the early 1980s, going on to develop the Hyper-G hypertext system.

McCahill, Mark Leader of the team that developed gopher at the University of Minnesota.

McElroy, Neil US Secretary of Defense under Eisenhower who was previously a president of Proctor and Gamble. His idea of establishing a long-range research agency led to the foundation of ARPA.

Metakides, George Greek director of the European Union's ESPRIT programme. Represented Brussels in the negotiations leading to the establishment of W3C.

Metcalfe, Bob Inventor of Ethernet and co-author of the TCP protocol for internetworking.

Meyrowitz, Norman Co-founder of the Institute for Research in Information and Scholarship (IRIS) at Brown University.

Mittelhauser, Jon Member of the NCSA Mosaic team who wrote the PC version of Mosaic with Chris Wilson. Later did the same job at Netscape.

Mockapetris, Paul Inventor of the Internet's Domain Name System (DNS).

Montulli, Lou Developer of the Lynx browser at the University of Kansas. Went on to invent the notorious 'blink' tag and cookies, and to point a camera at the fish tank in Netscape's offices.

Moore, Gordon Intel co-founder who invented Moore's law about the growth of computer power.

Müller, Kurt One of the Swiss delegates on Derek Barber's European Informatics Network team.

Nash, Dennis Founder of the company D. G Nash Limited where Tim Berners-Lee worked before coming to CERN.

Nelson, Bruce Carnegie-Mellon graduate student who wrote a thesis on the idea of Remote Procedure Calls (RPCs).

Nelson, Ted Self-proclaimed computer visionary. Inventor of the Xanadu system, coiner of the term 'Hypertext' in 1965, and collaborator on one of the first hypertext systems with Andy van Dam at Brown University.

Neuman, Clifford University of Washington graduate student who developed Prospero, a way of making the Internet look like a single computer.

Nyberg, Kim Member of the 'otherwise' team at the Helsinki University of Technology that developed 'erwise', one of the first Web browsers for Unix.

Nygaard, Kristen Norwegian computer scientist. Co-inventor with Ole-Johan Dahl of object-oriented programming.

Olsen, Ken MIT computer scientist who built the TX-0, the world's first transistorized computer. Later founded Digital Equipment Corporation (DEC).

Ornstein, Severo Member of the BBN team put together by Frank Heart to build the ARPANET's Interface Message Processors (IMPs).

Partridge, Craig Developer of the Domain Name System (DNS) with Paul Mockapetris and Jon Postel.

Pellow, Nicola British mathematics student who wrote the line mode browser for the Web whilst on a work placement at CERN.

Pollermann, Bernd CERN computer scientist whose XFIND system provided a source of ready-made information for the fledgling World Wide Web.

Poole, John Founder of Image Computer Systems Limited, where Tim Berners-Lee was a director.

Postel, Jon Unofficial archivist of the Internet, co-developer of the Domain Name System (DNS), and later administrator of that system.

Pouzin, Louis French computer scientist and father of the world's first pure datagram computer network, Cyclades.

Quint, Vincent French computer scientist responsible for the team that authored Grif, Tamaya, and the Amaya Web browser/editor.

Raggett, Dave Bristol-based employee of Hewlett Packard and leader of the HTML standardization effort.

Rantanen, Teemu Member of the 'otherwise' team at the Helsinki University of Technology that developed 'erwise', one of the first Web browsers for Unix.

Raskin, Jeff Founder of the Macintosh project at Apple.

Reynolds, Joyce Co-author with Jon Postel of RFC1000 and later co-editor of the RFC series with Postel.

Rimmer, Peggie CERN physicist turned computer scientist. Tim Berners-Lee's boss at CERN when he returned there in 1984.

Rising, Hawley Member of the BBN team put together by Frank Heart to build the ARPANET's Interface Message processors (IMPs).

Ritchie, Dennis Co-author with Brian Kernighan of the C programming language.

Roberts, Larry MIT computer scientist hired by Bob Taylor at ARPA to lead the ARPANET project.

Scantlebury, Roger British computer scientist who worked on the NPL network. It was Scantlebury who presented the NPL project at Gatlinburg in 1967.

Scott, Peter University of Saskatchewan developer who wrote HYTELNET, an early hypertext system for the Internet.

Secret, Arthur French computer scientist and the Web's virtual librarian. Secret also wrote Agora, a system for getting Web pages by e-mail.

Segal, Ben CERN computer scientist who introduced the Internet to the laboratory.

Sendall, Mike CERN physicist turned computer scientist, Sendall ran the laboratory's on-line computing group in 1989 when Tim Berners-Lee brought him a proposal for a distributed information system.

Serre, Christian Tim Berners-Lee's immediate boss at CERN in 1980.

Shapiro, Elmer Early designer of the ARPANET's IMP network and unwitting founder of the Network Working Group.

Shipp, William S. Co-founder of the Institute for Research in Information and Scholarship (IRIS) at Brown University.

Sinclair, Clive British inventor, he built Britain's cheapest personal computers in the 1980s.

Smarr, Larry Founder of the National Center for Supercomputing Applications at the University of Illinois.

Stallman, Richard Founder of the Free Software Foundation which aims to keep the cooperative spirit of software development alive by developing viable alternatives to commercial software.

Stetner, Heidi Berkeley graduate student whose dog 'Biff' gave its name to the Unix command for notifying of incoming e-mail.

Sugar, Alan British entrepreneur and chairman of Amstrad, a company that marketed personal computers in the UK.

Suominen, Kati Member of the 'otherwise' team at the Helsinki University of Technology that developed 'erwise', one of the first Web browsers for Unix.

Sutherland, Ivan Computer graphics pioneer who was the second Director of ARPA's Information Processing Techniques Office (IPTO).

Sydänmaanlakka, Kari Member of the 'otherwise' team at the Helsinki University of Technology that developed 'erwise', one of the first Web browsers for Unix.

Taylor, Bob Third Director of ARPA's Information Processing Techniques Office (IPTO). Taylor founded the ARPANET project and hired Larry Roberts to run it. Later moved to Xerox PARC.

Thach, Truett Los Angeles-based employee of BBN who met IMP Number One off the plane.

Théry, Gérard Head of the French Direction Générale des Télécommunications, founder of the project that led to Minitel.

Thompson, Dave Software developer who introduced the World Wide Web to NCSA.

Thrope, Marty Member of the BBN team put together by Frank Heart to build the ARPANET's Interface Message Processors (IMPs).

Tomlinson, Ray BBN employee and inventor of e-mail.

Torvalds, Linus Helsinki University student who wrote the Linux operating system.

Totic, Aleks Member of the NCSA Mosaic team who wrote the Macintosh version of Mosaic. Later did the same job at Netscape.

Truscott, Tom Co-inventor with Jim Ellis and Steve Bellovin of Usenet news.

Turing, Alan British computer pioneer who worked on code breaking during the Second World War. Later moved onto the National Physical Laboratory to run the ACE project.

van Dam, Andy Hypertext pioneer. Worked with Ted Nelson at Brown on HES, an early hypertext system, and continued with FRESS.

van Herwijnen, Eric CERN SGML expert and co-author of the laboratory's CERNDOC documentation system.

Vezza, Al Associate director of MIT's laboratory for computer science. Vezza handled the MIT end of negotiations leading up to the establishment of W3C.

von Neumann, John Hungarian mathematician who invented the concept of the stored program computer.

Walden, Dave Member of the BBN team put together by Frank Heart to build the ARPANET's Interface Message Processors (IMPs).

Wei, Pei Berkeley geography student who developed the Viola system in his spare time.

Wenninger, Horst CERN Director involved in the negotiations leading up to the establishment of W3C.

White, Bebo One of the SLAC WWW Wizards.

Wiegandt, Dietrich CERN computer scientist whose tinkering with UUCP e-mail and network news led to CERN being a European leader in these fields.

Wiener, Norbert American pioneer of the field of cybernetics.

Wilkes, Maurice Cambridge computer pioneer who built the world's first practical stored program computer, the EDSAC.

Wilkinson, Peter Member of the data communications research group at the NPL.

Wilson, Chris Member of the NCSA Mosaic team who wrote the PC version of Mosaic with Jon Mittelhauser.

Wingfield, Mike UCLA graduate student who built the hardware interface between IMP Number One and the university's Sigma 7 computer.

Wirth, Niklaus Swiss computer scientist and programming language expert. Inventor of the Pascal language.

Womersley, John Reginald Founder of the Mathematics Division at the UK National Physical Laboratory.

Wozniak, Steve Hardware designer. Founded Apple Computer along with Steve Jobs.

Yang, Jerry Stanford University graduate student, co-founder of Yahoo! with David Filo.

Yankelovich, Nicole Hypertext developer at Brown. Worked on Intermedia.

Zimmermann, Hubert Member of Louis Pouzin's Cyclades team. Later president of the CCITT's network architecture working group.

Zuse, Konrad German computer pioneer. Built the first operational programmable calculator.

Bibliography and Notes on Sources

General

Appropriately enough, much of the research for this book was conducted through the Web. Whether by providing important primary sources or by pointing the way to them, the Web demonstrated itself to be an extremely useful tool. Some of the information it revealed, however, proved to be of dubious quality and every effort has been made to cross-check anecdotal accounts with primary sources or with the people involved. Here as elsewhere, the Web is a two-edged sword, as succinctly expressed by Nathan Torkington, erstwhile keeper of the World Wide Web FAQ (Frequently Asked Questions). Our printed copy of the page from 14 June 1993 states, 'In all cases, regard this document as out of date. Definitive information should be on the Web, and static versions such as this should be considered unreliable at best.' In other words, the Web, unlike paper, provides us with the opportunity to keep information up to date all the time. It also removes the barriers to publication that make some traditional media more reliable sources.

We have split the bibliography and notes by chapter. Resources that were used in several chapters appear only under the chapter where they were first used. Those that were of general utility throughout the book are listed here.

Printed material

Aboba, B. *The Online User's Encyclopedia*. Reading, Mass.: Addison Wesley, 1993.

Berners-Lee, T. *Weaving the Web*. New York: HarperCollins, 1999.

Hafner, K., and Lyon, M. *Where Wizards Stay Up Late: The Origins of the Internet*. New York: Simon & Schuster, 1996.

Hahn, H. *The Internet Complete Reference*. Berkeley: Osborne McGraw-Hill, 1996.

Hameri, A.-P., and Nordberg, M. 'From Experience: Linking Available Resources and Technologies to Create a Solution for Document Sharing—The Early Years of the WWW.' *Journal of Product Innovation Management,* 15 (1998): 332–334.

Malamud, C. *Exploring the Internet.* Englewood Cliffs, N.J.: Prentice Hall, 1992.

The CERN Mini and Micro Computer Newsletters from 1983 to 1991, the CERN Online Newsletter from 1992 to 1994, and the CERN Computing Newsletter from 1989 to 1995 were useful for verifying the comings and goings of people at CERN.

Encyclopedia Britannica, 15th ed. Encyclopedia Brittanica Inc.: Chicago, 1994 (and online).

The Oxford Encyclopedia of World History. Oxford: Oxford University Press, 1998.

Who's Who 1998. London: A. & C. Black, 1998.

Useful Web pages

There is a lot of Internet history at the Internet Society's Web site. Robert Zakon's 'Hobbes' Internet timeline', which can be found at

http://info.isoc.org/guest/zakon/Internet/History/HIT.html,

has been found by the authors to be the most accurate of its kind available on the Net and it has been a valuable resource throughout.

The World Wide Web Consortium Web pages contain a lot of historical information. It can be assessed through the W3C home page at

http://www.w3.org/

Kevin Hughes maintains a Web history site at

http://www.webhistory.org

The www-talk archives, which can be found on the W3C pages and on Kevin Hughes's pages, provide an interesting record of who was doing what and when.

Chapter 1

Personal interviews conducted by the authors with Donald Davies and Louis Pouzin provided the framework for chapter 1. Interviews with Vint Cerf, Wes Clark, Steve Crocker, Will Crowther, Frank Heart, Bob Kahn, Leonard Kleinrock, J. C. R. Licklider, Larry Roberts, Jack Ruina, and Bob Taylor from the oral history collection of the Charles Babbage Institute helped to fill in the details. The transcripts from Leonard

Kleinrock's 1989 'Act One' conference also came from the Charles Babbage Institute. Ray Tomlinson provided the account of the first ever e-mail, appropriately enough by e-mail. Leonard Kleinrock kindly answered many questions about the early days of packet switching. Thanks are also due to Vint Cerf for answering questions and for permission to quote from his 'Requiem for the ARPANET'. The section on the ALOHANET was developed through e-mail correspondence with Norm Abramson. Jan Walker at DARPA answered many questions and dug out the relevant aspects from the Barber Associates report. Bob Metcalfe gave us an interview at the 8th International World Wide Web conference which was useful for understanding the origins of Ethernet, and also useful for writing chapter 7.

Printed material

Abbate, J. 'A Tale of Two Networks: Early Data Communications Experiments in England and America.' Paper presented to the History of Computing and Information Processing Conference, University of Pennsylvania, 17 May 1996.

Abramson, N. 'Development of the ALOHANET.' *IEEE Transactions on Information Theory*, vol. IT-31 no. 2, March 1985.

Abramson, N., and Kuo, F. F., eds. *Computer Communication Networks*. Englewood Cliffs, N.J.: Prentice Hall, 1973

Baran, P. 'On Distributed Communications Networks.' *IEEE Transactions on Communications Systems*, vol. CS-12 (March 1964): 1–9.

Campbell-Kelly, M. 'Data Communications at the National Physical Laboratory (1965–1975).' *Annals of the History of Computing*, 9, no. 3/4 (1988): 221–247.

Cerf, V. G., et al. 'A Brief History of the Internet.' Preprint cs. NI/9901011, 23 January 1999.

Corbató, F. J., and Vyssotsky, V. A. 'Introduction and Overview of the Multics System.' Paper presented to the AFIPS Fall Joint Computer Conference, 1965.

Crocker, S. 'RFC 10: Documentation Conventions', 29 July 1969.

Davies, D. W. 'Proposal for a Digital Communication Network.' NPL, June 1996.

—— 'Historical Note on the Early Development of Packet Switching.' Unpublished.

Davies D. W., et al. 'A Digital Communication Network for Computers giving Rapid Response at Remote Terminals.' Paper presented to the ACM Symposium on Operating System Principles, Gatlinburg, Tenn., 1967.

Dettmer, R. 'Almost an Accident.' *IEE Review*, 44, no. 4 (July 1998): 169.

Eisenhower, D. D. 'Annual Message to the Congress on the State of the Union', January 1958.

Kantor, B., and Lapsley, P. 'RFC 977: Network News Transfer Protocol', February 1986.

Kuo, F. F., and Binder, R. D. 'Computer Communications by Radio and Satellite: The ALOHA System.' *Proceedings of the NATO Advanced Study Institute on Computer Communication Networks, Sussex, UK, September 1973*, 113–128. Leiden: Noordhoff, 1975.

Licklider, J. C. R. 'Memorandum for Members and Affiliates of the Intergalactic Computer Network.' ARPA, 23 April 1963.

Licklider, J. C. R., and Clark, W. E. 'On-Line Man-Computer Communication.' Paper presented to the AFIPS Spring Joint Computer Conference, 1962.

McKusick, M. K. 'A Berkeley Odyssey: Ten Years of BSD History.' *UNIX Reviews*, 3, no. 1 (January 1985): 30-42.

Melcalfe, R. 'RFC 602: The Stockings were Hung by the Chimney with Care', December 1973.

Mockapetris, P. 'RFC 882: Domain Names—Concepts and Facilities', November 1983.

Pouzin, L. 'Presentation and Major Design Aspects of the Cyclades Computer Network.' *Proceedings of the NATO Advanced Study Institute on Computer Communication Networks, Sussex, UK, September 1973*, 415–434. Leiden: Noordhoff, 1975.

R. J. Barber Associates Inc. *The Advanced Research Projects Agency 1958–1974*. Washington, D.C., December 1975.

Reynolds, J., and Postel, J. 'RFC 1000: The Request for Comments Reference Guide', August 1987.

Roberts, L. G. 'Multiple Computer Networks and Intercomputer Communication.' Paper presented to the ACM Symposium on Operating System Principles, Gatlinburg, Tenn., 1967.

Salus, P. H. 'Origins.' *Matrix News*, 4, no. 7 (July 1994): 3.

—— 'Early Networking in Europe.' *Matrix News*, 5, no. 3 (March 1995): 1–2.

—— 'The Vogue of History.' *Matrix News*, 6, no. 7 (July 1996).

Scantlebury, R. A. 'Report on Visit of R. A. Scantlebury to the 1967 A.C.M. Symposium U.S.A.' Unpublished, 1967.

Scantlebury, R. A., and Wilkinson, P. T. 'The National Physical Laboratory Data Communication Network.' NPL Report Com 85, December 1976.

Strachey, C. 'Timesharing in Large Fast Computers.' *Information Processing*. Paris: UNESCO, June 1959.

Pouzin, L., ed. *The Cyclades Computer Network*. Amsterdam: North-Holland, 1982.

White, B. 'The World Wide Web and High-Energy Physics.' *Physics Today*, 51, no. 11 (November 1998): 30.

Yates, D. M. *Turing's Legacy: A History of Computing at the National Physical Laboratory 1945–1995*. London: Science Museum, 1997.

Useful Web Pages

Vint Cerf has a lot of interesting information on his Web pages:

http://www.wcom.com/about_the_company/cerfs_up/

For Multics see

http://www.lilli.com/history.html

For Internet jargon:

http://www.wins.uva.nl/~mes/jargon

Larry Roberts has some recollections on his Web pages:

http://www.ziplink.net/~lroberts

Chapter 2

Personal interviews and conversations with Derek Barber, Brian Carpenter, Bob Cooper, Donald Davies, Mike Gerard, Daniel Karrenberg, Peter Kirstein, Louis Pouzin, Ben Segal, and Dietrich Wiegandt form the basis of chapter 2. Jacques Altaber provided information about the SPS and LEP networks. The authors enjoyed many instructive conversations with Mike Sendall about the rise of networking in the European physics community. Buckingham Palace provided the transcript of the Queen's first e-mail. Historical information about CERN came from the laboratory's annual reports.

Printed material

'Agreement on the Establishment of a European Informatics Network.' Miscellaneous No. 14. London: HMSO, 1972.

Barber, D. L. A. 'Cost–Benefit.' *NPL News*, December 1971.

—— 'Costic Comments.' *NPL News*, December 1973.

—— 'The Cost Project 11: The European Informatics Network.' In *Proceedings of the NATO Advanced Study Institute on Computer Communication Networks, Sussex, UK, September 1973*, 409–414. Leiden: Noordhoff, 1975.

Barber, D. L. A., et al. 'An Implementation of the X.25 Interface in a Datagram Network.' *Computer Networks*, 2 (1978): 340–345.

Carpenter, B. E., et al. 'Two Years of Real Progress in European HEP Networking: A CERN Perspective.' *Computer Physics Communications*, 45 (1987): 83–92.

Cooper, R. 'The Joint Network Team 1979–1994.' Unpublished, March 1994.

Condon, C., ed. *NetMonth: An Independent Guide to BITNET*, no. 37 (October 1998).

COST. 'Presentation of the European Informatics Network.' Publicity leaflet, Spring 1978.

ECFA Working Group on Data Processing Standards Subgroup 5 (Links and Neworks). 'ECFA/86/99 Status Report and Recommendations', February 1986.

Fuchs, I. H. 'BITNET Makes "Splash".' *EDUNET News* (Winter 1981): 7–8.

—— 'BITNET: Because It's Time.' *Perspectives in Computing*, 3, no. 1 (March 1983): 16–27.

Gerard, J. M., ed. 'CERNET: A High Speed Packet Switching Network.' CERN Yellow Report 81/12, 22 December 1981.

—— 'Local Area Networks for Microcomputers.' CERN DD Report DD/87/20, October 1987.

Howlett, J. *Report of the National Committee on Computer Networks*. London: Department of Industry, 1978.

Jennings, D. M., et al. 'Computer Networking for Scientists.' *Science*, 231 (28 February 1986): 943–950.

Joint Network Team. 'SuperJanet, the Meeting of Minds.' Promotional information pack.

Kirstein, P. 'Early Experiences with the ARPANET and INTERNET in the UK.' Unpublished, 28 July 1998.

Larmouth, J. *Understanding OSI*. London: International Thomson Computer Press, 1996.

Padlipsky, M. A. 'RFC 871: A Perspective on the ARPANET Reference Model', September 1982.

Piney, C. 'Bridges Open the Way to Metanetworking.' CERN DD Report DD/87/2, January 1987.

'Queen Unveils RSRE.' *Malvern Gazette*, 1 April 1976.

Rimmer, E. M. 'ECFA Working Group on Data Processing Standards.' *ECFA Working Group on Data Processing Standards Newsletter*, no. 1 (June 1981).

Segal, B. 'A Short History of Internet Protocols at CERN.' Unpublished (April 1995). (See useful Web pages below.)

Tannenbaum, A. S. *Computer Networks*, 2nd ed. Englewood Cliffs, N.J.: Prentice Hall, 1988

Useful Web pages

For the history of the Royal Radar Establishment see
http://www.dra.hmg.gb/

For the introduction of Internet protocols at CERN, see Ben Segal's account at
http://wwwinfo.cern.ch/pdp/ns/ben/MyHome.html

For NORSAR, see
http://www.norsar.no/

For RIPE, see
http://www.ripe.net/

For GTE's acquisition of BBN, see
http://www.gte.com/

Video material

'SuperJANET: The Enabler.' The JNT Association, April 1996.

Chapter 3

Farhad Anklesaria, Mark McCahill, Alan Emtage, Doug Engelbart, Wendy Hall, Brewster Kahle, Frank Kappe, Ted Nelson, and Andy van Dam all gave interviews for this chapter. Further interviews conducted by Judy Adams and Henry Lowood with Doug Engelbart and held in the Stanford University Library were also used. The Prospero section is the result of correspondence with Clifford Neuman. Paul Kahn provided much information about hypertext at Brown University, and put the authors in touch with Nicole Yankelovich, who provided even more.

Printed material

Anklesaria, F., et al. 'RFC 1436: The Internet Gopher Protocol (A Distributed Document Search and Retrieval Protocol)', March 1993.

Barnes, S. B. 'Douglas Carl Engelbart: Developing the Underlying Concepts for Contemporary Computing.' *IEEE Annals of the History of Computing*, 19, no 3 (1997), 16–26.

Bardini, T. 'Bridging the Gulfs: From Hypertext to Cyberspace [1].' *Journal of Computer Mediated Communication*, 3, no. 2 (September 1997).

Bourcier, N. 'Et André inventa le PC.' *Le Monde*, 17 February 1999.

Bright, R. 'Telecommuting by Viewdata.' *Proceedings of the First International Telecommunication Exposition, Atlanta, Ga., 9–15 October 1977.*, 595–599.

Bush, V. 'As We May Think.' *Atlantic Monthly,* July 1945.

—— 'Proposals for Improving the Patent System.' Washington, D.C.: United States Government Printing Office, 1956.

Campbell-Kelly, M., and Aspray, W. *Computer: A History of the Information Machine.* New York: Basic Books, 1996.

Cook, J. 'Lights out for Last Linc.' *MIT RLE Currents,* 6, no. 1 (Fall 1992).

Cour des Comptes, Paris. Rapport au President de la République: 'Le Minitel', *Journal Officiel,* 1989.

Elliot-Green, R., ed. *Videotex: Key to the Information Revolution.* Proceedings of Videotex '82, New York, 28–30 June 1992. Northwood Hills, Middlesex, UK: Online Publications Ltd, 1982.

Engelbart, D. C. 'Augmenting Human Intellect: A Conceptual Framework.' SRI Summary Report AFOSR-3223, 1962.

Erskine, G. A. 'The History of the Computer.' CERN DD Report DD/76/16, October 1976.

Evans, C. *The Mighty Micro.* London: Victor Gollancz, 1979

Fedida, S., and Malik, R. *The Viewdata Revolution.* London: Associated Business Press, 1979.

Friedrich, O. 'Machine of the Year: The Computer Moves In.' *Time Magazine,* 3 January 1983.

'The Genius behind HyperCard: Bill Atkinson.' *Quick Connect,* November 1987.

Goff, L. '1972: Xerox Parc and the Alto.' *Computerworld,* 8 July 1999.

Grossman, W. M., ed. *Remembering the Future: Interviews from Personal Computer World.* London: Springer-Verlag, 1997.

Hooper, R. 'Advances in the United Kingdom.' In R. Elliott-Green, ed., *Videotex: Key to the Information Revolution.* Proceedings of Videotex '82, New York, 28–30 June 1992. Northwood Hills, Middlesex, UK: Online Publications Ltd, 1982.

Kahle, B., and Medlar, A. 'An Information System for Corporate Users: Wide Area Information Servers.' *Online,* 15 (5 September 1991): 56–60.

Landow, G. P. *Hypertext 2.0.* Baltimore, Md.: Johns Hopkins University Press, 1997.

Levy, S. *Insanely Great.* London: Penguin, 1995.

—— *Hackers: Heroes of the Compuer Revolution.* Garden City, N.Y: Anchor Press/Doubleday, 1984.

Maurer, H. A. 'Will MUPID revolutionize Austria's Videotex?' In R. Elliott-Green, ed., *Videotex: Key to the Information Revolution.* Proceedings of Videotex '82, New York, 28–30 June 1992. Northwood Hills, Middlesex, UK: Online Publications Ltd, 1982.

—— *Hyper-G now Hyperwave: The Next Generation Web Solution.* Addison-Harlow, Middlesex, UK: Wesley, 1996.

Maurer, H. A., and Sebestyen, I. 'On Some Unusual Applications of Videotex.' In R. Elliott-Green, ed., *Videotex: Key to the Information Revolution.* Proceedings of Videotex '82, New York, 28–30 June 1992. Northwood Hills, Middlesex, UK: Online Publications Ltd, 1982.

McIntyre, C. 'Broadcast Teletext: Who Says It Isn't Interactive?' In R. Elliott-Green, ed., *Videotex: Key to the Information Revolution.* Proceedings of Videotex '82, New York, 28–30 June 1992. Northwood Hills, Middlesex, UK: Online Publications Ltd, 1982.

Nelson, T. H. *Literary Machines 90.1.* Sausalito, Calif.: Mindful Press, 1990.

—— 'The Crafting of Media [1970].' From the catalog of the 'Software' art show, The Jewish Museum, New York, 1970.

—— 'A New Home for the Mind?' *Datamation Magazine,* March 1982.

Neuman, B. C. 'Prospero: A Tool for Organizing Internet Resources.' *Electronic Networking: Research, Applications, and Policy,* 2 (Spring 1992): 30–37.

Saletan, W. 'Searching for Xanadu.' *Swarthmore College Bulletin,* December 1998.

St. Pierre, M., et al. 'RFC 1625: WAIS over Z39.50—1988', June 1994.

Smith, D. K., and Alexander, R. C. *Fumbling the Future: How Xerox Invented, Then Ignored, the First Personal Computer.* New York: toExcel, 1999.

Rheingold, H. *Tools for Thought.* New York: Simon & Schuster, 1985. New edition published Cambridge, Mass.: MIT Press, 2000.

van Dam, A. 'Hypertext '87 Keynote Address.' *Communications of the ACM,* 31, no. 7 (1988): 887–895.

Wolf, G. 'The Curse of Xanadu.' *Wired,* June 1995. (Replies to this article appeared in *Wired,* September 1995.)

Useful Web pages

For Vannevar Bush and early hypertext, Brown University's 'Memex and Beyond' Web site, see

http://www.cs.brown.edu/memex/

For Steve Wozniak's role in the Apple story, including an interview conducted by Manish Srivastava, see Wozniak's Web pages at

http://www.woz.org/

For computer history, see Ken Polsson's History of Microcomputers at

http://www.islandnet.com/~kpolsson/comphist.html

For the history of Apricot computers, see this Apricot user's page at

http://www.geocities.com/SiliconValley/4462/apricot_history.html

The ARM Web site is at
http://www.arm.com/
For the LINC, see
http://www.newmedianews.com/tech_hist/linc.html
For Videotex, the 'History of Electronic Publishing' by W. Johnstone and D. Carlson is useful at
http://iml.jou.ufl.edu/carlson/NewMedia/ehist/ehistory.htm
For Minitel, E. Sutherland, 'Minitel, the Resistable Rise of French Videotex', is good at
http://www.sutherla.dircon.co.uk/minitel/
(This is based on an article originally published in the *International Journal for Information Resource Management*, 1, no. 4: 4–14).
For Doug Engelbart, see his Web pages at
http://www.bootstrap.org/
Ted Nelson's pages are at
http://www.sfc.keio.ac.jp/~ted/
For hypertext at Brown University, see
http://landow.stg.brown.edu/HTatBrown/BrownHT.html

Video material

Engelbart, D. C. 'The Augmented Knowledge Workshop', ACM Conference on the History of Personal Workstations, Palo Alto, California, 9–10 January 1985. Copies available from the Bootstrap Institute.

Engelbart, D. C. 'A Research Center for Augmenting Human Intellect', Fall Joint Computer Conference, San Francisco, California, 1968. Copies available from the Bootstrap Institute.

Chapter 4

Chapter 4 is based on personal interviews with Tim Berners-Lee, Axel Daneels, Berend Kuiper, and Christian Serre. George Shering gave us useful information about the history of Nodal. John Poole and John Moffat gave us permission to quote from references they had written for Tim Berners-Lee. Derek Pennell helped us with the Emanuel part of the story. Christian Serre provided examples of Tim's work whilst in CERN's PS division.

Printed material

Bates, D., et al. 'Report User's Guide for the writing of Documents', CERN PS Note CERN/PS/CCI/Note 77-24, 26 September 1977.

Berners-Lee, T. 'Enquire: An Interactive Project Management Tool.' Online help file, unpublished.

—— 'Problems with the Interface between Equipment Modules and Application Programs in the PS Control Systems.' CERN PS Note CERN/PS/CO/Note 80-36, 20 November 1980.

Cailliau, R. 'The Programming Language P+.' *Journal A*, 24 (1983): 184–6.

Cailliau, R., et. al. 'Early Experience with the Programming Language P+.' Unpublished.

Holloway, M. 'Moulding the Web.' *Scientific American*, December 1997, pp. 21–22.

Knuth, D. E. *TEX: A System for Technical Tex.* Providence, R.I.: American Mathematical Society, 1979.

Ritchie, D. M. 'The Development of the C Language.' Paper presented at the ACM Second History of Programming Languages Conference, Cambridge, Mass., 1993.

Wright, R. 'The Man Who Invented the Web.' *Time Magazine*, 19 May 1997, pp. 46–49.

Useful Web pages

Emanuel School has a Web site at
http://www.emanuel.org.uk/

Manchester University keeps useful information about the Manchester 'baby', and the Manchester and Ferranti Mark I computers at
http://www.computer50.org/

The International SGML Users' group has Web pages at
http://www.isgmlug.org/

For biographical information on John von Neumann, see
http://www-history.mcs.st-andrews.ac.uk/history/Mathematicians/Von_Neumann.html

Chapter 5

Tim Berners-Lee, Jean-Marie Hullot, Nicola Pellow, Bernd Pollermann, Peggie Rimmer, and Eric van Herwijnen all gave interviews for this chapter. In addition, the interviews conducted by Markus Nordberg and Ari Pekka Hameri with Robert Cailliau and Ben Segal were useful.

Printed material

Adye, T., et al. 'Online Communications in the Delphi Experiment.' *Computer Physics Communications*, 57 (1989): 466–471.

Berners-Lee, T. 'Requirement for a Dynamic Module Loader within Readout Systems.' CERN internal memorandum to Mike Sendall, 4 February 1985.

—— 'Tim's Reflections on Mike's RPC Note.' Unpublished, 19 August 1985.

—— 'Experience with Remote Procedure Call in Data Acquisition and Control.' *IEEE Transactions on Nuclear Science* (August 1987): 1050–1053.

—— 'Programming Distributed Systems: Remote Procedure Call.' In C. Eck and C. Perkman, eds., *VMEbus in Research.* Amsterdam: Elsevier, 1988.

—— 'Information Management: A Proposal.' Unpublished, March 1989.

—— 'US Trip 1989/90: Fermilab and Hypertext.' Trip Report, unpublished, January 1990.

—— 'Information Management: A Proposal.' Unpublished, May 1990.

—— 'Electronic Publishing and Visions of Hypertext.' *Physics World,* 5, no. 6 (June 1992): 14–16.

Berners-Lee, T., and Cailliau, R. 'WorldWideWeb: Proposal for a Hypertext Project.' Unpublished memo, 12 November 1990.

Berners-Lee, T., and Rimmer, E. M. 'An Intelligent Approach to Complex System Architectures.' CERN DD Report DD/85/24, October 1985.

Berners-Lee, T., et al. 'The VALET-Plus: A VMEbus Based Microcomputer for Physics Applications.' *IEEE Transactions on Nuclear Science,* n.s. 34, no. 4 (August 1987): 835–839.

Berners-Lee, T., et al. 'World-Wide Web: The Information Universe.' *Electronic Networking: Research, Applications and Policy,* 1, no. 2 (Spring 1992): 74–82.

Berners-Lee, T., et al. 'The World-Wide Web.' *Computer Networks and ISDN Systems,* 25 (1992): 454–459.

Blair, G., Gallagher, J., Hutchison, D., and Shepherd, D., eds. *Object-Oriented Languages, Systems and Applications.* London: Pitman, 1991.

Dahl, O.-J., and Nygaard, K. 'SIMULA: An ALGOL Based Simulation Language.' *Communications of the ACM,* 9, no 9 (September 1966): 671–678.

Nelson, B. J. 'Remote Procedure Call.' Ph.D. diss., Carnegie-Mellon University, CMU-CS-81-119, 1981.

Rimmer, E. M. 'CERN's approach to FASTBUS software.' CERN DD Report, DD/83/13, May 1983.

Sendall, D. M. 'Real Programmers Don't Use Remote Procedure Calls . . . (But Maybe They Should).' Unpublished, 16 August 1985.

—— 'Tim—Reflections^3.' Unpublished memo to Tim Berners-Lee, 26 August 1985.

Useful Web pages

For Alan Kay and Smalltalk see
http://www.smalltalk.org/

Chapter 6

Louise Addis, Tim Berners-Lee, Dan Connolly, Jean-François Groff, Tony Johnson, Brian Kelly, Paul Kunz, Lou Montulli, Pei Wei, and Bebo White gave us interviews that were used in this chapter. Correspondence with Ari Lemmke helped to tell the Erwise story.

Printed material

Berners-Lee, T. 'Minutes of C5 Friday 17 May 1991.' Unpublished presentation to CERN management.

—— 'WorldWideWeb: Executive Summary.' Message posted to alt.hypertext news group announcing the World Wide Web, 6 August 1991.

Berners-Lee, T., and Cailliau, R. 'World-Wide Web.' *In Proceedings of the 10th International Conference on Computing in High Energy Physics (CHEP '92), Annecy-le-Vieux, September 1992.* Geneva: CERN, 1992.

Berners-Lee, T., and Pellow, N. 'Generic Network Hypertext Browser.' E-mail announcing beta release of the line mode browser, 8 April 1991.

Berners-Lee, T., et al. 'W3 Status Report: 1 year.' Unpublished CERN memo, October 1991.

Berners-Lee, T., et al. 'World-Wide Web: An Information Infrastructure for High Energy Physics.' In D. Perret-Gallix, ed., *Proceedings of the 2nd International Workshop on Software Engineering, Artificial Intelligence and Expert Systems in High Energy and Nuclear Physics (AIHEP), La Londe-les-Maures, 13–18 January 1992.* Singapore: World Scientific, 1992.

Berners-Lee, T., et al. 'World Wide Web or: How to Access CERN Information.' CERN information leaflet, 19 February 1992.

Berners-Lee, T., et al. 'The World-Wide Web.' *Communications of the ACM,* 37, no. 8 (August 1994).

Cailliau, R. 'WorldWideWeb Status and Plans.' Unpublished CERN memo, 6 November 1991.

—— 'Resource Request for WWW.' Unpublished CERN internal memo, Summer 1992.

Deken, J. M. 'First in the Web, but Where Are the Pieces?' Presentation at the Society of American Archivists, 1997 Annual Meeting, Chicago, 28 August 1997.

Hardman, L. 'Hypertext '91 Trip Report.' Unpublished CWI Trip Report, February 1992.

Sendall, D. M. 'The World-Wide Web Past Present and Future, and its Application to Medicine.' Invited paper at the Second International Symposium on Hadrontherapy, CERN, 11–13 September 1996.

Sendall, D. M., et al. 'STING: Software Technology Interest Group.' CERN information leaflet, March 1993.

Useful Web pages

For GNU and the Free Software Foundation see

http://www.gnu.org

For the CELLO browser see

http://www.law.cornell.edu/cello/cellotop.html

Pei Wei maintains information about Viola at

http://www.viola.org/

Louise Addis keeps a 'Brief and Biased History of Preprint and Database Activities at the SLAC Library' at

http://www.slac.stanford.edu/~addis/history.html

Transparancies from a talk given by Paul Kunz entitled 'Bringing the World Wide Web to America' can be found at

http://www.slac.stanford.edu/~mcdunn/earlyweb/EarlyWeb.html

The University of Kansas Academic Computing Services have historical information about Lynx at

http://www.cc.ukans.edu/~grobe/early-lynx.html

Chapter 7

Tim Berners-Lee, Mick Draper, Ping Fu, Joseph Hardin, Kevin Hughes, Steinar Kjærnsrød, Håkon Lie, Bob Metcalfe, Arthur Secret, and Dave Thompson all gave us interviews that were used in this chapter. We have Chris Neuss to thank for the 'marca mode' anecdote. The Canadian Broadcasting Corporation's 'Ideas' programme on the future of cyberspace, first broadcast on 10 December 1997 and presented by Lister Sinclair, contained useful interview material with, among others, Tim Berners-Lee, Brewster Kahle, and Jon Mittelhauser. Tim Berners-Lee's World Wide Web newsletters were a useful reference. Tony Johnson provided us with his entire e-mail correspondence with Marc Andreessen during the latter half of November 1992, and Dave Thompson provided a chronology of the Mosaic story. Bebo White gave us correspondence and information relating to the 'Client Fest' at SLAC. Nathan Torkington's www-faq provided an interesting snapshot of the Web as it was in summer 1993.

Printed material

Andreessen, M. 'NCSA Mosaic Technical Summary.' NCSA, 20 February 1993.

Andreessen, M., and Bina, E. 'NCSA Mosaic: A Global Hypermedia System.' *Internet Research*, 4, no. 1 (Spring 1994): 7–17.

Berger, E. 'High Energy Physics—Birthplace of the Web.' *FermiNews*, 19, no. 16 (16 August 1996): 1.

Deutschman, A. 'Imposter Boy.' *GQ Magazine*, January 1997.

Hoogland, W., and Weber, H. 'Statement Concerning CERN W3 Software Release into Public Domain.' CERN, 30 April 1993.

Johnson, T. 'Spinning the World Wide Web.' *SLAC Beamline Magazine*, 24, no.3 (Fall 1994): 2–9.

O'Reilly and Associates. 'O'Reilly and Associates Launches Free, Internet-based Information Center: Global Network Navigator (GNN).' Press Release, 1 October 1993.

Reid, R. H. *Architects of the Web*, New York: John Wiley & Sons, 1997.

'The Web Maestro: An Interview with Tim Berners-Lee.' *Technology Review Magazine*, July 1996.

Useful Web pages

The Norwegian Olympic Web site is preserved for posterity at **http://www.norsktele.museum.no/ol94**

Chapter 8

Jean-François Abramatic, Tim Berners-Lee, Pier Giorgio Innocenti, George Metakides, Vincent Quint, Al Vezza, and Horst Wenninger all gave interviews that were used in this chapter. Vincent Quint gave us a breathtaking demonstration of what the Web could be with Amaya. Mike Sendall provided copious correspondence and documentation relating to the establishment of W3C, and to the relationships between CERN and MIT, CERN and INRIA, and CERN and the European Union. Much of Mike's archive is unpublished, consisting of correspondence and internal memoranda, and it has not been itemized below. It provided, however, the framework for this chapter. Michael Dertouzos answered questions about himself and MIT/LCS's role by e-mail.

Printed material

Abramatic, J. F. 'Le consortium international World Wide Web.' Unpublished note, 24 October 1995.

Abramatic, J. F., and Vezza, A. 'MIT and INRIA Will Jointly Host the International World-Wide Web Consortium.' INRIA press statement, 7 April 1995.

Berners-Lee, T. 'World-Wide Web Decision Point for CERN.' Unpublished CERN internal memorandum, October 1993.

Berners-Lee, T., Cailliau, R., and Sendall, M. 'Proposal to the Commission of the European Communities for a World-Wide Web Coordinating Organization.' CERN document DG/DI/HW-cmd (94-22), 6 June 1994.

Berners-Lee, T., and Dertouzos, M. 'MIT/LCS W3 Draft Agreement.' Unpublished, 24 February 1994.

Berners-Lee, T., and Hardin, J. 'CERN/NCSA Collaboration: Memo of Understanding.' Draft, 14 February 1993.

Cailliau, R. 'Alexandria: Proposal for a European Centre for Networked Information Systems.' Unpublished, December 1993.

Cailliau, R., ed. *Selected Papers of the First World Wide Web Conference.* In *Computer Networks and ISDN Systems,* Special Issue, vol. 27, no. 2 (November 1994).

Cailliau, R., et al. 'CERN and INRIA Join Forces in World Wide Web Core Development.' Text for joint statement on transfer of Web activity from CERN to INRIA, Spring 1995, *ERCIM News,* 21 (April 1995).

CERN Media Service. 'First International Conference on the World-Wide Web.' Press release, 25 May 1994.

—— 'CERN Celebrates 40th Anniversary.' Press release, 8 September 1994.

Dertouzos, M. *What Will Be.* New York: HarperCollins, 1997.

European Research Consortium for Informatics and Mathematics. 'ERCIM: At the Service of Information Technology in Europe.' Publicity document, n.d.

Fluckiger, F. 'From World-Wide Web to Information Superhighway.' Paper presented at JENC6 Conference, Tel Aviv, 15–18 May 1995.

Leutwyler, K. 'What Will Really Be.' *Scientific American,* July 1997.

MIT/LCS. 'Draft Proposal to E.U.' Unpublished, February 1994.

—— 'MIT World Wide Web Consortium Participation Agreement.' October 1994.

MIT/LCS and INRIA. 'International World Wide Web Consortium Participation Agreement.' May 1995 (backdated to October 1994).

MIT News Office. 'International Initiative Announced at MIT for Universal Framework for Information Web.' Press release, 7 July 1994.

Mosaic Communications. 'Mosaic Communications becomes Founding Member of W3 Consortium for Internet.' Press release, 25 October1994.
Reales, L. 'Europa cede a EE.UU. el protagonismo en el desarrollo de las autopistas de la información.' *La Vanguardia*, 12 March 1995.
Fernández Hermana, L. Á. 'Europa entrega a EEUU las claves del futuro de Internet.' *Periódio de Catalunya*, 12 March 1995.
Scheifler, R. 'X Consortium, Inc.' Presentation of the X Consortium, n.d.
Sendall, D. M. 'WWW: Background to the Current Situation.' Unpublished note, October 1994.
Vezza, A. 'International World Wide Web: Evolving to Information Infrastructure.' Presentation in Brussels, 7 April 1995.
World Wide Web Consortium. 'W3C: Leading the Web to its Full Potential.' Publicity document, 1999.

Useful Web pages

INRIA's Web pages are at
http://www.inria.fr/
MIT/LCS has a Web site at
http://www.lcs.mit.edu/
CERN's Web site is at
http://www.cern.ch/

Video material

CERN video recording of Tim Berners-Lee's talk at the first World Wide Web conference, CERN, May 1994.

Epilogue

We have used interviews with Alan Ellis and Frans Lettenstrøm in the Epilogue. A good account of the important role played by the academic world through much of the history of computers and networks is Brad Myers's paper:

Myers, B. A. 'A Brief History of Human Computer Interaction Technology.' *ACM Interactions*, 5, no. 2 (March 1998): 44–54.

List of Acronyms

AA	Antiproton Accumulator
ACE	Automatic Calculating Engine
ACM	Association for Computing Machinery
ACPL	A Computer Programming Language
ACT	Applied Computer Techniques
AFOSR	Air Force Office for Scientific Research
AIHEP	international workshop on software engineering, Artifical Intelligence and expert systems for High Energy and nuclear Physics
Amstrad	Alan Michael Sugar TRADing
ANSI	American National Standards Institute
API	Application Program Interface
ARM	Advanced RISC Machines
ARPA	Advanced Research Projects Agency
ARPANET	ARPA NETwork
AT&T	American Telephone and Telegraph
BBC	British Broadcasting Corporation
BBN	Bolt, Beranek, and Newman
BCPL	B Computer Programming Language
BITNET	Because It's There NETwork or Because It's Time NETwork
BSD	Berkeley Software Distribution
CAMAC	Computer Automated Measurement And Control
CCITT	Comité Consultatif International de Téléphonie et de Télégraphie
CEA	Commisariat à l'Énergie Atomique
CEPT	Conférence Européenne des administrations des Postes et des Télécommunications
CERN	Conseil Européen pour la Recherche Nucléaire (European Organization for Nuclear Research)

CERNET	CERN NETwork
CHEP	Computing in High-Energy Physics (conference)
CII	Compagnie Internationale pour l'Informatique
CNAM	Conservatoire National des Arts et Métiers
COST	COopération européenne dans le domaine de la recherche Scientifique et Technique
CPU	Central Processing Unit
CRT	Cathode Ray Tube
CSNET	Computer Science NETwork
CUNY	City University of New York
CWIS	Campus Wide Information System
DAQ	Data AQuisition
DARPA	Defense Advanced Research Projects Agency
DEC	Digital Equipment Corporation
DECNET	Digital Equipment Corporation NETwork
DELPHI	Detector with Lepton, Photon and Hadron Identification (LEP Experiment)
DESY	Deutsches Elektronen-SYnchrotron
DGT	Direction Générale des Télécommunications
DNS	Domain Name System
DoI	Department of Industry
DTD	Document Type Definition
EARN	European Academic Research Network
EASInet	European Academic Supercomputing Initiative network
EBT	Electronic Book Technologies
ECFA	European Committee for Future Accelerators
ECP	Electronics and Computing for Physics
ECU	European Currency Unit
EDSAC	Electronic Delay Storage Automatic Calculator
EDVAC	Electronic Discrete Variable Automatic Computer
EEC	European Economic Community
EIN	European Informatics Network
EIT	Enterprise Integration Technologies
EMC	European Muon Collaboration
ENIAC	Electronic Numerical Integrator And Computer
EPSS	Experimental Packet-Switched Service
ERCIM	European Research Consortium for Informatics and Mathematics
ESPRIT	European Strategic Programme for Research and Development in Information Technology
ETH	Eidgenössische Technische Hochschule (Zurich)

EU	European Union
FJCC	Fall Joint Computer Conference
FNAL	Fermi National Accelerator Laboratory
FORTRAN	FORmula TRANslator
FRESS	File Retrieval and Editing System
FTP	File Transfer Protocol
FUNET	Finnish University NETwork
GML	Goldfarb Mosher Lorie or Generalized Markup Language
GNN	Global Network Navigator
GNU	Gnu's Not Unix
GTE	General TElephone
GUI	Graphical User Interface
HEPNET	High-Energy Physics NETwork
HES	Hypertext Editing System
HP	Hewlett-Packard
HTML	HyperText Markup Language
HTTP	HyperText Transfer Protocol
HUT	Helsinki University of Technology
IAB	Internet Activities Board
IBA	Independent Broadcasting Authority
IBM	International Business Machines
IC	Integrated Circuit
ICCC	International Conference on Computer Communication
IDA	Interactive Data Analysis
IEEE	Institute of Electronic and Electrical Engineers
IETF	Internet Engineering Task Force
IFIP	Iternational Federation for Information Processing
IMHO	In My Humble Opinion
IMP	Interface Message Processor
INRIA	Institut National pour la Recherche en Informatique et en Automatique
IP	Internet Protocol
IPTO	Information Processing Techniques Office
IRC	Internet Relay Chat
IRIA	Institut pour la Recherche en Informatique et en Automatique
IRIS	Institute for Research in Information and Scholarship
IRTF	Internet Research Task Force
ISO	International Standards Organization
ISOC	Internet SOCiety
ISP	Internet Service Provider

ITU	International Telecommunications Union
IW3C2	International World Wide Web Conference Committee
JANET	Joint Academic NETwork
JENC	Joint European Networking Conference
JNT	Joint Network Team
KUTGW	Keep Up The Good Work
LAN	Local Area Network
LCS	Laboratory for Computer Science (MIT)
LEP	Large Electron Positron collider
LHC	Large Hadron Collider
libwww	Library for World Wide Web code
LINC	Laboratory INstrument Computer
Lybido	LYnx BInary Distribution Outlet
MAC	Man And Computer or Multiple Access Computer
MCC	Mosaic Communications Corporation (later Netscape)
MIDAS	Motif Interactive Data Analysis Shell
MIT	Massachusetts Institute of Technology
MITS	Micro Instrumentation Telemetry Systems
MoD	Ministry of Defence
MUPID	Mehrzweck Universell Programmierbarer Intelligenter Decoder
N-PL	Nord Programming Language
NASA	National Aeronautics and Space Administration
NATO	North Atlantic Treaty Organization
NCC	Network Coordination Centre
NCP	Network Control Protocol
NCSA	National Center for Supercomputing Applications
NII	National Information Infrastructure
NLS	oN Line System
NNTP	Network News Transfer Protocol
NPL	National Physical Laboratory
NSF	National Science Foundation
NSFNET	National Science Foundation NETwork
NWG	Network Working Group
OMNET	OMega NETwork
OOPS	Object Oriented Programming System
OPAL	Omni Purpose Apparatus at LEP (LEP experiment)
Oracle	Optical Reception of Announcements by Coded Line Electronics
OSI	Open Systems Interconnection
OWL	Office Workstations Limited

PARC	Palo Alto Research Center
PC	Personal Computer
PET	Personal Electronic Transactor
PS	Proton Synchrotron
PSD	Program Structure Diagram
PSS	Packet-Switched Service
PTT	Post Telephone and Telegraph
RAND	Research ANd Development corporation
RARE	Réseaux Académiques pour la Recherche Européenne
RFC	Request For Comments
RIPE	Réseaux IP Européens
RISC	Reduced Instruction Set Computing
RPC	Remote Procedure Call
RSCS	Remote Spooling Communications Subsystem
SGML	Standard Generalized Markup Language
SJCC	Spring Joint Computer Conference
SLAC	Stanford Linear Accelerator Center
SPIRES	Standard Public Information REtrieval System
SPS	Super Proton Synchrotron
SRC	Science Research Council
SRI	Stanford Research Insitute
STING	Software Technology INterest Group
SUN	Stanford University Network
T3V	Télétel Vélizy, Versailles, Val de Bièvre
TCP	Transfer Control Protocol
TCP/IP	Transfer Control Protocol/Internet Protocol
TGV	Train à Grande Vitesse
TIP	Terminal IMP
TITN	Traitement de l'Information et Techniques Nouvelles
TX-0 (2)	Transistorized eXperimental computer 0 (2)
UCL	University College London
UCLA	University of California at Los Angeles
UDI	Universal Document Identifier
URL	Uniform Resource Locator
UUCP	Unix to Unix CoPy
VAT	Value Added Tax
VDU	Visual Display Unit
VERONICA	Very Easy Rodent Oriented Net-wide Index to Computerized Archives
VIOLA	Visually Interactive Object-oriented Language and Application

VMS	Virtual Machine System
W3C	WWW Consortium
W3O	WWW Organization
WAIS	Wide Area Information Servers
WAN	Wide Area Network
WISE	World-wide Information system for Support of R&D Efforts
WWW	World Wide Web
WYSIWYG	What You See Is What You Get
XML	eXtensible Markup Language
XNS	Xerox Network System

Index